The Portland Black Panthers

Lucas N. N. Burke

and

Judson L. Jeffries

V Ethel Willis White Books

THE PORTLAND BLACK PANTHERS

Empowering Albina

and

Remaking a City

University of Washington Press | Seattle and London

This book is published with the assistance of a grant
from the V Ethel Willis White Endowed Fund,
established through the generosity of Deehan Wyman,
Virginia Wyman, and the Wyman Youth Trust.

University of Washington Press
www.washington.edu/uwpress

Library of Congress Cataloging-in-Publication Data
Names: Burke, Lucas N. N. author. | Jeffries, J. L. (Judson L.), 1965–
    author.
Title: The Portland Black Panthers : empowering Albina and
    remaking a city / Lucas N. N. Burke and Judson L. Jeffries.
Other titles: Empowering Albina and remaking a city
    p.   cm.
Description: 1st edition. | Seattle : University of Washington Press,
    [2016] | Includes bibliographical references and index.
Identifiers: LCCN 2015034530 | ISBN 9780295995168 (hardcover : alk.
    paper)
Subjects: LCSH: Black Panther Party. Portland Branch—History. |
    African Americans—Oregon—Portland—History—20th century. |
    African Americans—Oregon—Portland—Social conditions—20th
    century. | Portland (Or.)—Race relations—History. | Portland
    (Or.)—Politics and government—History—20th century. | African
    Americans—Political activity—Oregon—Portland. | African
    Americans—Oregon—Portland—Biography.
Classification: LCC E185.615 .B865 2016 | DDC 322.4/20979549—dc23
LC record available at http://lccn.loc.gov/2015034530

Contents

Illustrations follow pages 46 and 180

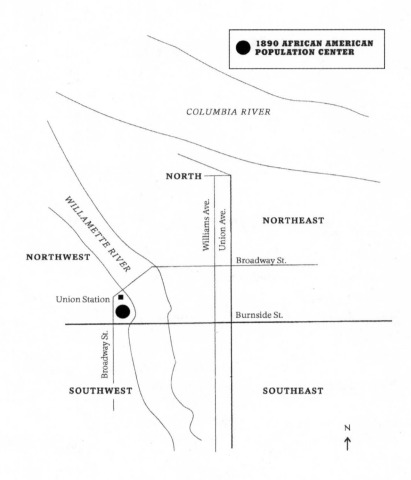

1890 AFRICAN AMERICAN
POPULATION CENTER

COLUMBIA RIVER

WILLAMETTE RIVER

NORTH

NORTHEAST

Williams Ave.

Union Ave.

NORTHWEST

Broadway St.

Union Station

Burnside St.

Broadway St.

SOUTHWEST

SOUTHEAST

N

African American Population Centers in
Portland, Oregon, 1890. Adapted from
*Cornerstones of Community: Buildings
of Portland's African American History*
(Portland: Bosco-Milligan Foundation,
1995).

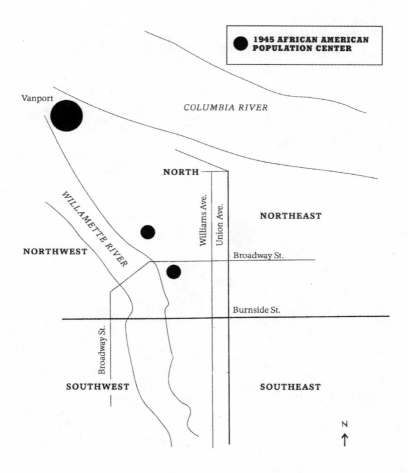

African American Population Centers in Portland, Oregon, 1945. Adapted from *Cornerstones of Community: Buildings of Portland's African American History* (Portland: Bosco-Milligan Foundation, 1995).

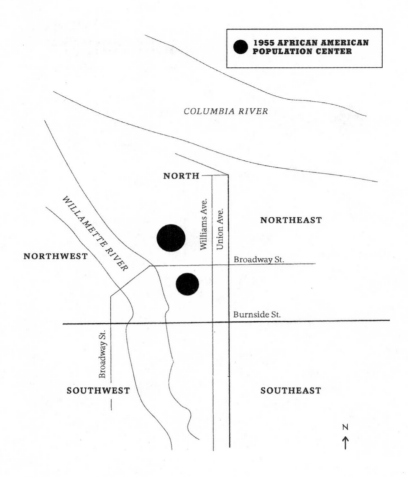

African American Population Centers
in Portland, Oregon, 1955. Adapted from
*Cornerstones of Community: Buildings
of Portland's African American History*
(Portland: Bosco-Milligan Foundation,
1995).

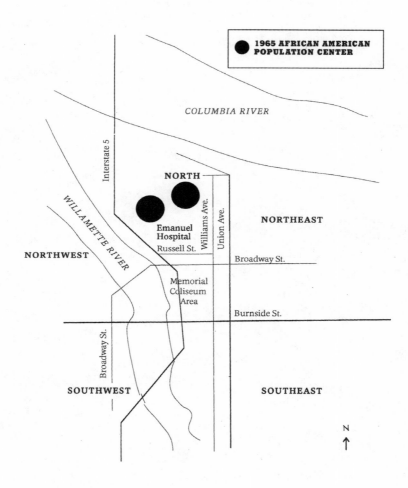

African American Population Centers
in Portland, Oregon, 1965. Adapted from
*Cornerstones of Community: Buildings
of Portland's African American History*
(Portland: Bosco-Milligan Foundation,
1995).

The Portland Black Panthers

INTRODUCTION

Venturing into Uncharted Waters

No Black Power movement organization has garnered more scholarly interest than the Black Panther Party (BPP). The reasons for this preoccupation are not hard to pinpoint. The Panthers' exploits are legendary. From descending upon the California statehouse to protest a bill intended to render the group's police patrols impotent[1] to their Hollywood-like standoffs with law enforcement officers that some viewed as suicidal, the Black Panther Party has written a chapter in the annals of American radicalism that ranks with the African Blood Brotherhood and the Industrial Workers of the World ("Wobblies") "for grit and élan."[2] Ask any student of 1960s history to name a half a dozen Panthers, and among those he or she will undoubtedly rattle off are Eldridge Cleaver, Huey P. Newton, Bobby Seale, Kathleen Cleaver, Fred Hampton, and Elaine Brown. Ask that same person to name some members of other Black Power organizations and observe as he or she struggles to recite half that many. Still, while academics and laypersons alike are more familiar with the BPP than with any other Black Power movement organization, until recently little attention has been given to the various branches and chapters outside of Northern California. Indeed, it is likely that few are aware that 630 miles north of Oakland, California, a branch of the Black Panther Party was alive and bustling in Portland, Oregon.

Portland, the county seat of Multnomah County, is the largest city in Oregon and lies at the northern end of the fertile Willamette Valley. It is known for its mild climate and breathtaking scenery in addition to its proximity to both the Pacific Ocean and the Cascade Range. The mountains of the Coast Range rise twenty miles west of the city. Approximately fifty miles to the east stands the picturesque snow-capped Mount Hood. As an inland port city, Portland is a major commercial distribution and shipping center for the Pacific Northwest. A large number of its residents are employed in industries such as textiles, food and timber processing, paper production, chemicals, and aluminum product manufacturing. Portland is not readily associated with civil rights or Black Power. Even among many of the Panthers with whom we have interacted over the years, the Portland branch of the BPP remains a relatively unknown entity. Few are familiar with the dedicated cadre of Panthers that includes Kent and Sandra Ford, Linda Thornton, Percy Hampton, Joyce Radford, and Oscar Johnson, to name a few.

Since the Portland branch of the BPP folded thirty-five years ago, the city has been the subject of numerous books, journal articles, master's theses, and dissertations; yet, in many of them, the Portland branch of the BPP has barely garnered a mention. In recent decades, "the City of Roses" has been the subject of numerous studies of city planning and urban history by scholars from an array of fields, and has given Portland a unique personality and image. Due to the commitment of its citizens and of the city and state government to neighborhood engagement in politics, statewide environmental preservation, and slow-growth urbanism, both residents and academics of this newly hip, postmodern "Portlandia" have crafted a proud and self-laudatory image of the city as a national model for urban revitalization and sustainability. However, like many other utopian promises in the annals of the American West, this mythic urban ecotopia of the Pacific Northwest has a more complex historical reality. Behind the façade of go-green bicycling, coffee-sipping, and white middle-class urbanites is a bitterly tragic and ironic history of the political, social, economic, and spatial exclusion of Portland's black community.[3] Moreover, although Portland is frequently held up as a model of regional and urban planning, particularly for transportation, citizen involvement and activism, environmental protection, and land use policies, scholars have largely neglected the historical role of Portland's relatively small yet centralized black community in the city's northeast Albina district. As a result, in the popular ahistorical imagination of today's Portlanders, the roots of the city's modern urban reinvention began in the early 1970s with the emergence of widespread neighborhood activism, a new generation of state and city political leadership, and the role the city played in the national freeway revolts.[4]

Unfortunately, this narrative ignores the longer historical development of the city's new urbanism. Specifically, it ignores the nearly century-long struggle of the black community in the city's northeast Albina district to gain representation in Portland's undemocratic and exclusionary political structure. And it is perhaps the greatest tragedy of this urban reinvention that the very communities that deserve credit for the rise of neighborhood activism and political reform ultimately benefitted the least from this new political order. With the exception of Karen Gibson and her 2007 article "Bleeding Albina," scholars who have focused on the history of African Americans and the struggle for racial equality in Portland have only tacitly acknowledged the important connection between urban planning policies in Albina and their effects on the black community and on localized civil rights efforts. Those who have recognized this connection, however, have still failed to explain the relationship's effect on the development and the trajectory of radical protest movements during the 1960s and 1970s. This book begins to address that oversight through a history of the local branch of the Black Panther Party, which began as a branch of the National Committee to Combat Fascism (an organizing bureau of the BPP).[5]

In framing the historical context of the Black Panther Party in Portland, this book works within the conceptual framework of the Long Civil Rights Movement, also referred to as the "long movement," popularized by twentieth-century African American historians, sociologists, and political scientists in recent decades. Within this longer historical struggle, the Portland branch of the BPP played an important yet historically marginalized role. The emergence of the Panthers marked an important turning point in the city's approach to urban planning and development and in the long freedom struggle of Albina's black residents. After decades of systematic exclusion from the political arena, spatial confinements and relocations to environmentally toxic parts of the city, and urban renewal projects that destroyed black homes and businesses, African Americans in northeast Portland fought back in a variety of ways. Excluded from access to traditional levers of power to determine the future of their own neighborhoods, these men and women developed an array of innovative and creative approaches to find a voice within city politics and urban planning processes. These alternative forms of political protest and control over the production of social space ranged from pushing for greater input and collaboration with urban planners, on one end of the spectrum, to openly opposing city government and demanding complete control of Albina, on the other. The Portland Panthers represented the latter end of that continuum. Although their antithetical vision of complete community control and socioeconomic uplift was never actualized, the Panthers were essential to putting pressure on the city's power brokers with the expressed purpose of dismantling Portland's undemocratic, insular power structure.[6]

In unpacking this urban dialectic between city-directed and neighborhood-led planning approaches, this history of the Portland branch of the BPP takes a longer approach to understanding the organization's historical significance. Beginning with Progressive Era political reforms and the increasing growth of Portland's black population since 1900, the Panthers drew on a long history of civil rights, urban planning, and political struggles. Our approach, which further expands the geographic and chronological boundaries of the struggle for civil rights beyond the South and the narrow postwar timeframe of the 1950s and 1960s, is designed to urge more scholars to understand and appreciate both the localized nature of the black freedom struggle and the diverse yet continuous nature of the movement. While there are potential shortcomings to this approach, including blurring the generational, ideological, and regional differences among activists and organizations, framing the history of the Portland Panthers within this larger context is essential if one is to understand the rise and decline of the Black Panther Party in this Pacific Northwest city. To view the growth of the Portland Panthers in the late 1960s and early 1970s in isolation, or even only within the context of the postwar Civil Rights Movement, diminishes the group's importance and obscures the underlying reasons for its existence. Furthermore, such a narrow perspective relegates the emergence of the Portland branch of the BPP to a nationally simplified expression of 1960s radicalism instead of the outgrowth of decades of socioeconomic and political civil rights struggles in this city.[7]

By adopting this broader chronological and geographical approach, this work also contributes to an expanding field of literature on civil rights in the urban West and Pacific Northwest, and to a growing body of studies on local branches and chapters of the Black Panther Party. Although in recent decades scholars have produced numerous case studies on western US cities, generally ranging from Los Angeles and Phoenix in the Southwest to Seattle in the Pacific Northwest, Portland remains a major West Coast urban center that scholars have not yet fully vetted. This study seeks to fill in that gap in the historiography of the Long Civil Rights Movement in western cities by examining one of the largest West Coast cities with comparatively the smallest black population. On a related note, it is important to remember that West Coast cities such as Portland, Seattle, Los Angeles, San Francisco, and Oakland have tended to be highly multiethnic and multiracial given their history in relation to the United States' western expansion and their geographic proximity to Mexico, Latin America, and the Pacific Rim. This diversity became even more pronounced in the period following the Hart-Cellar Immigration and Nationality Act of 1965, which significantly altered the region's demographics during the temporal focus of this work. Consequently, in studying this period, recent historians and political scientists have increasingly tried to develop more racially and ethnically complex, inclusive, and dynamic approaches to their work. Indeed, any study that presents race relations solely within a black-white dichotomous framework is inherently incomplete. However, as Stuart McElderry noted in his 1998 dissertation on the Civil Rights Movement in Portland between 1945 and 1966, throughout the postwar era and well into the late twentieth century, Portland remained unmistakably divided—demographically, rhetorically, and, as we suggest, spatially—along a black-white color line. To ignore such a divide ignores the entire way in which blacks and whites in Portland viewed racial dynamics at the time. As a result, this book uses the black-white dichotomy to present a more focused perspective at the expense of a broader and more inclusive approach. Nevertheless, we encourage readers and other scholars to make further comparisons with other racial and ethnic groups in and around Portland within the same time frame to create a more detailed and holistic understanding of the period.[8]

Again, in addition to its contribution to the history of the Long Civil Rights Movement, this study also builds on an already rapidly growing and diverse array of localized case studies on the Black Panther Party that have emerged in the past fifteen years. Scholars of the late twentieth century have had a tendency to view the Black Panther Party through a very narrow lens. They have, for the most part, chosen to focus predominately on the organization's headquarters in Oakland and on sensational events involving the party, such as the elaborate plots on the part of the FBI to sabotage the Panthers' work, skirmishes with the police, and some of the Panthers' riveting and sometimes inflammatory declarations about the forces that opposed them and conspired to keep poor people consigned to an inferior place in

America and abroad. This historically negligent approach has unwittingly contributed to a body of work that has long portrayed the Panthers as gun-brandishing anarchists and unapologetic race-mongers. While the party's image has in fact been forged largely by the histrionics that unfolded in the Bay Area, what many fail to understand is that those goings-on are not representative of the organization generally. To reap the benefits of a more complete portrait of the party, one must interrogate Panther history in national locales. Consequently, it is imperative that scholars expand the arduous task of excavating, documenting, and publishing the history of previously unexamined Panther branches.

To date, only New Haven, Connecticut; Milwaukee, Wisconsin; New Orleans, Louisiana; Chicago, Illinois; and Philadelphia, Pennsylvania, have been the subjects of book-length manuscripts concerning the Black Panther Party. J. F. Rice's *Up on Madison, Down on 75th Street: A History of the Illinois Black Panther Party*, published more than thirty years ago, was the first such effort. Rice's work was timely; that same year, $1.85 million was awarded to plaintiffs in a civil suit brought by the survivors of Peoria Panther leader Mark Clark and Fred Hampton, deputy chairman of the Illinois state chapter of the BPP, who were murdered in a predawn raid on December 4, 1969, by law enforcement officers in Chicago. Nearly twenty years passed before another case study of a Black Panther branch was published, but since then work in this area seems to have picked up, as three impressive works on local BPP branches have appeared in the last seven years. Still, many scholars have chosen to focus their attention on Panther activity in the Bay Area. If other branches and chapters are discussed along the way, they are done so in brief, oftentimes in a disjointed manner, with little connection to the overall history of the organization.[9]

Still, over the past several years, a fresh wave of academics, some of whom were barely school age and others who were not yet born during the Panthers' heyday, have uncovered and explored the histories of some of the BPP's reported forty or so branches and chapters. While these studies have revealed a previously unappreciated diverse yet unified coalition of semiautonomous units, several important branches have gone unexamined. Most notable among these underexplored branches is the Portland branch of the BPP. There are a few exceptions, however. In Matt Nelson and Bill Nygren's *Radicals in the Rose City: Portland's Revolutionaries, 1960–1975*, an entire chapter is devoted to the Portland branch of the BPP. Similarly, Jules Boykoff and Martha Gies produced an article on media portrayals of the Portland

Panthers, and Gies also wrote a short magazine article on the Portland Panthers' dental and medical clinics. Finally, the Portland Panthers are also the subject of a chapter in Polina Olsen's book *Portland in the 1960s: Stories from the Counterculture*, although, at seven pages, Olsen's discussion of the Panthers is significantly less substantive than that of Nelson and Nygren. Taken together, and shortcomings notwithstanding, these works offer a starting point for understanding the Portland Panthers' history, but the larger social and political history remains untouched and unexamined despite the significant role the organization played in northeast Portland for more than a decade. This book fills that void. At the same time, this volume makes no claim to being the definitive work on the Portland branch of the Black Panther Party. It is however, the first in-depth examination of this understudied but important branch of the Black Panther Party.[10]

In the following pages, readers will find that, in spite of the branch's relatively short life span, the Panthers' presence and work has had a far-reaching impact on the city of Portland generally and on the residents of Albina in particular. According to Ron Herndon, a student leader and graduate of Reed College in the late 1960s and longtime activist in the city of Portland, "The Black Panther Party was the only black organization at that time that residents could count on to speak up against injustice and actually do something about what was going on." Within these pages, special care has been taken to foreground the voices of former Portland Panthers who, until now, had been content to live in anonymity as far as the larger American public is concerned. Readers will find that some voices are featured more prominently than others. The reasons for this include accessibility, willingness to share information, position held within the branch, and duties for which the individual was responsible. Also featured, with varying degrees of prominence, are the stories, voices, and ephemera of student activists, volunteers, and others who were convinced that a society in which racial, class, and gender inequality was not only allowed to flourish but was propagated by Portland's city fathers was one that merited confrontation and, in some instances, dismantling.[11]

Finally, this study expands on those works that frame the history of the Civil Rights and Black Power Movements within the history of urban space and planning. By linking modernist urban planning and urban space with the history of civil rights, Black Power, and other political and social struggles, scholars can develop a more meaningful understanding of the history of place and nation. Building on the works of noted French philosophers and social theorists since the 1970s, specifically Michel Foucault and Henri Lefebvre, urban civil rights and Black Power scholars now emphasize the importance of the social production of urban spaces and how spatialized power relationships emerge between institutions and the people they intend to govern. Most notably, in his 2003 book *American Babylon: Race and the Struggle for Postwar Oakland*, Robert Self astutely points out, "Civil rights, black power, and . . . [other] political movements did not call for rights in abstract terms and ill-defined places. They called for very specific things in relation to very specific places. Space is not the whole story, but it would be a strange and incoherent one without it." From this perspective, an intricate and nuanced history of the Portland Black Panther Party requires both the larger historical context of Portland's localized black freedom struggle and the history of the physical and socially produced spatial urban environment of Portland's black community in Albina.[12]

By situating this study within these broader historiographical arenas—the Long Civil Rights and Black Power Movements, the history of the Black Panther Party, and the history of urban planning and metropolitan space in the West and Pacific Northwest—a larger story of political exclusion, spatial conflict, and social and political experimentation within the city of Portland emerges. The emergence and decline of the Portland branch of the Black Panther Party, this book contends, marks an important turning point in the civil rights struggle for Albina's black residents and for the city's approach to urban planning and development. Barred from traditional political routes for determining the future of their own neighborhoods and communities, African Americans had to engage in a wide range of political experimentation to find a voice within city politics and urban planning. The Panthers were instrumental in putting pressure on the city government to respond to more moderate voices within the African American community, such as the Model Cities Citizen Planning Board, to create the kind of government envisioned by the country's founders.

In telling this story, we have tapped into a bevy of rich sources, including a diverse set of more than seventy interview subjects. Some of the subjects were interviewed several times. All told, 120 interviews were conducted over several years. The breadth and scope of our interviewees is unprecedented for a book on the BPP, but necessary if one is to chronicle the history of a branch of the Black Panther Party through the widest possible lens. These robust interviews include longtime Portland residents of varying stations and student activists at area colleges and universities who were members of such groups as the Black Student Union, Students for a Democratic Society, and the Portland Revolutionary Youth movement. We also tracked down news reporters from the *Oregonian* and from student run newspapers, grassroots activists and other agents of change, former members of the Portland branch of the BPP, volunteer doctors and dentists at the Panthers' health and dental clinics, individuals who participated in the Panthers' breakfast program, and retired members of the Portland Police Bureau. Longtime residents helped us understand the inner workings of Portland and the challenges the city and its residents faced as far back as the Progressive Era and World War II through the Vietnam War period. Student activists gave us insight into the type of campus radicalism that had transpired at institutions such as the prestigious Reed College, Portland State College (later University), and Lewis and Clark College, to name a few. Talking to reporters enabled us to gain insight into the manner in which the Panthers were covered and why. By tapping into grassroots activists and other agents of change we had the benefit of both a street-level and mid-level view to understanding the issues they were attempting to address and resolve. Conversations with volunteers, especially volunteer physicians at the Panthers' clinics, offered us a firsthand account of the clinics' activities and helped us visualize a typical workday. We were fortunate in that we were also able to locate individuals who enjoyed the free breakfast program provided by the Panthers. These conversations allowed us to convey, in bold relief, the effect that this sorely needed initiative had on some families in northeast Portland.

Also, the second author, via his contacts with the law enforcement community and his intimate knowledge of police work, was able to identify several retired Portland police officers whose careers spanned the years that the Panthers were in existence. Officers ranged from patrolman to vice squad to detective to deputy chief to police chief, including the country's first woman to serve as chief of a major American police department. Most of the officers began their careers before the emergence of the National Committee to Combat Fascism and retired years after the Panthers' apex. This kind of longevity proved immensely helpful, as we were able to explore a range of topics that greatly enhanced our ability to contextualize the Black Panther Party in the city of Portland, the anti–Vietnam War movement, as well as blacks and the racism they faced in this Pacific Northwest city.

Likewise, we spoke to members of the Portland branch of the BPP who provided us with a detailed account of one of the most productive, however little known, branches of the Black Panther Party. Some former Panthers were easier to locate than others, and some were less eager to participate than others. Some of the stories shared with us were shared in confidence and are therefore not detailed in this volume, but many are featured prominently in the text. While many people are captivated by the cloak-and-dagger activities that undoubtedly played out around the Panthers, readers will find none of that here. To include material about the Panthers' clandestine or underground activities, be they in Portland or elsewhere, would be imprudent in this Orwellian era of heightened security. Equally important, the rapport that we have developed with former Panthers over many years is the primary reason we have had unlimited access to the branch's principal founder and to other members of the leadership cadre. Some of our subjects were consulted on numerous occasions over the course of days, weeks, months, and, in some cases, years. Without this level of cooperation, this book would be inadequate in a number of ways. We have also interspersed relevant quotes throughout the book for the purposes of helping the reader visualize both the characters and the goings-on in Portland.

We understand that the use of oral testimonies can present some challenges, as an account could be skewed in one direction or another, politically motivated, or unwittingly prone to nostalgia. The use of newspaper articles can also be problematic, due to reporters' or editors' political leanings. Although journalists strive for objectivity and impartiality, they do not always hit their mark. Still, while using this wide array of resources, every measure was taken to ensure the authenticity of historical accounts and details and to corroborate the recollections and remembrances that were conveyed to us. These challenges notwithstanding, oral testimonies can provide rich insights into the lives of activists, especially those who, for a variety of reasons, shied away from the spotlight's glare and are therefore not widely known, either among the general public or to students of 1960s history and politics. As Bruce C. Berg wrote in his book *Qualitative Research Methods for the Social Sciences*, documenting stories accomplishes a key research goal, which is to "assure that the real-life experiences and memories of people cannot be so easily omitted, edited, shredded, or swept away." Collecting stories is a constant paleontological endeavor. The oral histories contained in this book help us bring to life the voices and experiences of those who made history. Additionally, incorporating these various oral testimonies into this scholarly endeavor allowed us as authors to illuminate our arguments in a much more relatable way than we ever could using impersonal and staid theory or by simply relying on historical documents or the words of famous national leaders from outside the city and state. In the end, the value of this oral history is that it allows readers to grapple with the magnitude of important, and sometimes life-affecting, events through the eyes and voices of real people.[13]

In addition to this diverse collection of interviews, we were fortunate to be able to access an invaluable treasure trove of documents and manuscripts that helped ground us in the politics of Portland over several decades. We drew on Model Cities and city urban planning records from city and state archives, regional newspaper coverage of politics (both mainstream and alternative), and urban planning policies. Additionally, we combed through the important yet frequently overlooked Portland Police Bureau records housed at the City of Portland Archives and Records Center. Given the Portland Police Bureau's colorful history before, during, and after World War II, we were fairly confident that a close examination of said records would bear fruit. For example, in 1948, the City Club Committee on Law Enforcement in Portland and Multnomah County found "Portland and its environs to be wide open with syndicated vice, gambling, prostitution, bootlegging and others forms of organized crime flourishing under police protection, often on a pay-off basis." Twenty years later, the same committee found through interviews with residents and local attorneys (both black and white) that some officers policed blacks more harshly than whites. When one attorney was asked about this, he submitted that "there is sufficient evidence to believe that the Portland Police Department indulges in stop and frisk practices in Albina. They seem to feel they have the right to stop and frisk someone because his skin is black and he is in the black part of town." Other comments gleaned from the City Club's study suggest that some police officers demonstrated an antipathy for blacks that they did not seem to manifest for whites. After meticulously going through the police bureau records on the BPP, we found nothing that undermined that assertion.[14]

The surveillance files kept on the Portland branch of the BPP by the Portland Police Bureau are available to the public only because officer Winfield Falk confiscated the documents, taking them home rather than shredding them as required by a state law passed in 1981 that made it illegal for police officers to spy on residents or groups not involved in criminal activity. Unwilling to part with a project that had consumed a good portion of his career, Falk removed the documents and stored them in his garage for safekeeping. In the ensuing years, he continued to add to the files. The documents surfaced many years after Falk died in 1987. The files sat in a dilapidated barn for more than a decade before they were discovered by an op-portunistic columnist with the *Portland Tribune*. From 1965 until the early 1980s, files were kept not only on student activists and militants but also on hundreds of seemingly ordinary citizens who were monitored simply for signing petitions, attending meetings, writing letters to representatives, and joining organizations. These manila folders offer a unique glimpse into the secret activities of the Portland Police Bureau.[15]

Other archives that proved helpful were the Oregon Historical Society, the Lewis and Clark College Special Collections and Archives, the Oregon Health and Science University Historical Collections and Archives, and the University of Oregon Special Collections and University Archive. Such a broad array of source materials reflects an equally broad, and at times con-flicting, collection of perspectives on the Portland Panthers and their legacy. This vast swath of resources was crucial in helping the authors cross-refer-ence stories, events, activities, names, and dates for the purpose of recording history as accurately as humanly possible. Despite these safeguards, how-ever, there are sure to be faux pas due to source inaccuracies and the fallibil-ity of human memory in recalling events that transpired more than forty years ago, not to mention the errors that sometime occur in the course of a research project that stretches over a period of years. For that, we offer our mea culpa in advance.

The Portland Black Panthers: Empowering Albina and Remaking a City differs from other books on the BPP not just because of the immense trea-sures into which we tapped, but also because of the manner in which the Portland branch is historicized and the ways in which its members navi-gated the multidimensional political terrain in a city in which the Panthers purported primary support base was less than 6 percent of the total popula-tion. Given that relatively low percentage, we know of no other branch of the Black Panther Party (save the short-lived branch in Eugene, Oregon, or per-haps in Des Moines, Iowa) that operated in a milieu in which the prospects of establishing and sustaining a branch seemed more unlikely. As was the case with other Panther branches, the odds were not in favor of the Panthers succeeding in pressuring those in power to foster a government that would ensure that its residents received their fair share of the city's opportunities and resources, regardless of race or station. With the deck stacked against them from the outset, the Portland Panthers nevertheless chose to tackle such issues as poverty, police use of extralegal force, inadequate health care, disfranchisement, and miseducation. In doing so, they engaged in an uncompromising political tug-of-war with those responsible for creating and sustaining said conditions.

In the Panthers' attempts to empower the city's dispossessed, they undoubtedly made mistakes. Our intention, however, is not to praise, denigrate, pass judgment, or critique strategic moves by members of the Portland branch made almost fifty years ago, under circumstances very different than today. It is our hope that current and future activists will find in this history lessons that might inform them how best to pursue change in their communities. We further hope that our work inspires others to probe deeply into the goings-on in other branches of the BPP, and to continue to think of new, unconventional, and exciting ways to best contextualize the party and to disentangle the complex and nuanced history that is this black radical organization. Of the scholarly works published in the last ten years, Jakobi Williams's *From the Bullet to the Ballot*, Alondra Nelson's *Body and Soul*, Omari L. Dyson's *Transformative Pedagogy and the Black Panther Party*, Andrew Witt's *The Black Panthers in the Midwest*, Curtis Austin's *Up Against the Wall*, and Chris Davenport's *Media Bias, Perspective, and State Repression* represent the best in that tradition. Only by doing such work can we gain greater insight into questions such as, Why did the Black Panther Party sprout up in some cities and not in others? Why did some individuals choose to put their lives in peril and join the BPP rather than a different organization (with less associated risk)? And why do scholars, two generations removed from the organization's heyday, seemingly find the Black Panther Party so captivating that they are willing to devote years of their lives to researching and writing book-length manuscripts on a subject whose actual life span lasted less than twenty years?

To answer those questions, the chronologic and narrative arc of this book consists of five chapters. Chapter 1, "Making and Remaking Albina," examines the growth of Portland's African American community in the city's northeast Albina district and its struggle for racial equality from the early 1900s to the mid-1960s. In addition, the chapter outlines the ways in which Portland's city government and urban planners excluded African Americans from political participation in the early 1900s, conceptually spatialized and constructed Albina as a black urban ghetto after World War II, and developed urban renewal projects that destroyed the center of the black community during the 1950s and 1960s.

The next two chapters detail the origins, development, inner workings, and effects of the Portland Black Panther Party and their community survival programs. Chapter 2, "Claiming Albina in the Era of Model Cities and the National Committee to Combat Fascism," and chapter 3, "Serving Albina and Becoming Panthers under the Watchful Eye of the Portland Police Bureau," reveal the various tactics that the black community used to fight back against the city's vision of the future of Albina in the late 1960s. In these chapters, we argue that the National Committee to Combat Fascism, which evolved into the Portland Black Panther Party in 1970, emerged as a new form of black political experimentation and as one adversative response to the Portland Development Commission's (PDC) top-down Model Cities plan to revitalize the Albina district. On the one hand, the PDC envisioned a reconstruction of Albina rooted in capitalizing on the location and commercial potential of the land, regardless of their plan's effect on the black community's homes and businesses. On the other, the Portland Black Panthers' vision emphasized giving communities complete control over their neighborhoods and promoting community survival programs aimed at socioeconomic uplift rather than physical urban renewal. These diametrically opposed conceptions of the future of Albina necessitated a middle path, or political compromise, to ensure peace, tranquility, and stability in northeast Portland.

Chapter 4, "The Emanuel Hospital Expansion, the James Family Saga, and Portland's Dream of a New Urbanism," explores the rise of citizen activism and neighborhood control of the Model Cities program, as well as the political repression of Cheryl James that traumatized a family and a community. While the PDC lost control of the Model Cities program to local citizen boards and planning committees, its continuation with the Emanuel Hospital renovation and expansion project still leveled a large portion of the black community's homes and businesses. Moreover, combined with the concentrated efforts of local police and the FBI, the PDC's hospital project undercut the Panthers' effectiveness, resulting in the branch's closure in the early 1980s. In the end, however, the PDC's continued dominance in urban planning, much like the Panthers' branch in Portland, was relatively short-lived.

Finally, chapter 5, "Winning the War?" explores the spread of citizen participation and neighborhood activism throughout Portland in the 1970s, the election of Mayor Neil Goldschmidt and his attempts to reorganize the city's power structure and urban planning apparatus, and the emergence of African American political leadership in Portland and in the state of Oregon. In the end, the leadership of Mayor Goldschmidt, along with moderate activist voices within Albina's black community, stripped the PDC of its power and helped bring a small component of the Portland Panthers' antithetical vision of community control and socioeconomic uplift into mainstream politics by the mid-to-late 1970s. However, more than one hundred years of social, political, economic, and spatial discrimination and exclusion left an indelible legacy of poverty that both the black community in Albina and the city government could not easily eradicate in the course of a single decade of community-led planning and development.

To begin this historical narrative with the decline of the postwar Civil Rights Movement and the rise of the Portland Black Panther Party in the early 1970s would not be sufficient to contextualize the organization's historical roots or purpose. To tell this story properly, to appreciate the deeply rooted nature of the political, spatial, and socioeconomic exclusions of African Americans in Portland, and to understand exactly what the Portland Panthers fought for, we must begin at least two generations before the emergence of the local branch. Only by beginning with the dawn of the Long Civil Rights Movement in Portland during the early 1900s can we begin to understand the complex factors that led to the rise and decline of the Portland branch of the Black Panther Party.

CHAPTER 1

Making and Remaking Albina

The Long Civil Rights Movement in Portland

For two days in the summer of 1967, young African Americans, most of them in their teens and twenties, revolted in and around the area of Irving Park in northeast Portland. Defying attempts by police as well as local black ministers and community leaders to quell the disorder, Portland's black youth attacked, vandalized, and looted local businesses and threw rocks and bottles at white passersby. This upheaval was part of a nationwide rebellion that, according to the Civil Disorder Data Clearinghouse, manifested in 233 uprisings, thirty-four hundred persons injured, and eighty-three killed. Unlike many of those revolts during the long hot summer of 1967, the Portland disorders resulted in no deaths, though one man was shot and more than fifty African Americans were arrested over two days. Like their contemporaries in Newark, Detroit, Los Angeles, Seattle, Chicago, New York, and other cities, the youth of this generation had grown up in the cradle of the modern American urban crisis. Many of these young black Portlanders were just infants and young children during the Vanport City flood of May 1948, which washed away black homes, and they grew up witnessing firsthand the destruction of black neighborhoods to make way for highways, sports arenas, and hospital renovations. At each turn, white politicians and business leaders in Portland ignored the plight of African Americans and willingly destroyed poorer neighborhoods in the name of progress and urban renewal.[1]

Throughout the twentieth century, and especially in the years following World War II, African Americans gradually achieved legislative victories in their long struggle for civil rights in Oregon. Despite these breakthroughs, Portland—like many other major US metropolitan areas—experienced the worst race revolts in the history of the city during the late 1960s. As city officials and African American community leaders searched for inventive ways to curb the disturbances, many of Portland's citizens were left to wonder why these revolts were happening. Historians of the struggle for civil rights in Portland have been similarly unsuccessful in constructing a fully explanatory narrative of the roots of this rise in radicalism, violence, and discontent. While a wide variety of secondary historical literature exists on civil rights in Oregon, historiography on the subject is fragmented and misleading. To remedy that, this chapter synthesizes research by urban and civil rights historians, examining works on early twentieth-century, World War II, and postwar civil rights efforts as well as literature on urban development and renewal to present a thumbnail sketch of the Long Civil Rights Movement in Portland. Placing the black freedom struggle in this larger historical narrative, the major turn in civil rights during the late 1960s becomes less surprising. Moreover, this approach further emphasizes the problem of presenting the black freedom struggle in the West and Pacific Northwest—and in the broader United States in general—in the traditional and limited postwar narrative. Ultimately, this perspective suggests that the turn toward Black Power and radicalism was not a deterioration of the mythologized postwar Civil Rights Movement; instead, such sentiments were the culmination of a century of racial discrimination, political neglect, spatial isolation, and the unresolved socioeconomic problems that these policies produced.

Between 1900 and the late 1960s, blacks in Portland managed to achieve only the most basic civil rights victories, including the repeal of voting bans and exclusionary language in the state constitution, and the passage of bills providing for public accommodations, fair employment practices, and open housing. However, a century of discrimination, neglect, and community destruction in the name of urban development and renewal had undermined the socioeconomic foundation of Portland's African American community. Portland's inherently undemocratic political system, which was ironically grounded in the Progressive Era values of rooting out political corruption and increasing efficiency in government to make it more responsive to the needs of the people, ultimately ignored the needs of African Americans and created an urban ghetto in the Albina district through the government's unwillingness to pass substantive civil rights legislation and its misguided and destructive postwar urban renewal efforts.[2] From the early years of the twentieth century through the 1960s, Portland's African American community developed slowly in comparison to those other major West Coast cities such as Seattle, Oakland, and Los Angeles. Nevertheless, this relatively small black population in Albina gave birth to one of the longest and most arduous struggles for civil rights in the urban West.

As early as the 1850s, small numbers of African Americans had begun to settle in Portland despite a constitutional exclusion clause banning blacks and many other minorities, particularly Chinese, from residing in the state. That 1837 law not only prohibited blacks from becoming residents, it also prevented them from owning property or securing contracts of any kind. Furthermore, those few who did reside in Portland were often subject to violent extralegal treatment. At the turn of the century, the lynching of a black man named Alonzo Tucker, for example, made quite an impression on blacks who were newly arrived in Portland. Reportedly, Tucker had been accused of raping a white woman and then escaping from jail as lawmen attempted to move him to another facility. He was caught by a white mob, shot, and hung from a bridge. No charges were brought against any member of the mob. The *Oregon Journal* referred to Tucker as a "nigger" and declared him to be a "wild beast" worthy of death. Commenting on his attackers, the correspondent reported curiously that the mob was "quiet and orderly." Given this racial climate, it is no wonder that prior to 1900 blacks composed less than one-quarter of 1 percent of the city's population. Most frequently employed by railroads, members of Portland's black community in this early period lived primarily downtown near Union Station. Two major waves of the Great Migration during the twentieth century, however, dramatically altered the size and spatial geography of Portland's black population. As the black community grew and changed in demographic in the years after the Civil War and in the first four decades of the twentieth century, so too did a vigorous, although protracted and often unsuccessful, Civil Rights Movement consisting of blacks and white progressive political allies.[3]

The restructuring of Portland's city government at the beginning of the twentieth century reshaped the trajectory of Portland politics for subsequent decades and effectively eliminated, perhaps unintentionally, the potential for African American participation in the city's political processes. With the adoption of a new city charter in 1903 and major reforms to that charter in 1913, Portland entered a period of substantial growth and urban development—and rampant political corruption. Based on progressive ideals and a widespread belief that the mayor needed more authority to improve the social environment of the city, the charter granted Portland's mayor more power than previous mayors had possessed. It eliminated the independently elected city boards and replaced them with a civic commission and an executive board whose members the mayor had the power to appoint and remove. As a result, the mayor exercised a previously unprecedented level of control over many of the city's municipal services. Moreover, while the charter stipulated that residents of the city's various wards could elect ten of the fifteen city council members, the other five members were selected through at-large elections. Taken together, these changes diminished local power and representation in favor of greater centralization and efficiency.[4]

By the early 1910s, increasing corruption in the new political system, especially under the leadership of Mayor Joseph Simon, led Portlanders to revise the city's charter in 1913. The charter was revised following a scathing report on corruption in Portland's city government published by the New York Bureau of Municipal Research in April 1913. In an effort to eliminate corruption and inefficiency, the city placed new limitations on the power of the mayor, reduced the size of the city council, and replaced the ward-based system of city council representation with an entirely at-large system in which all council members were selected by a citywide popular vote. Although a coalition of political progressives intended for this new system of city governance to reduce competition between neighborhood interests, the new political structure also resulted in the elimination of the voice of minority neighborhoods and communities. According to urban historian Carl Abbott, this change in Portland city politics "undermined the indigenous democratic socialism and put government firmly in the hand of the middle class." Despite underlying concerns with the new system, Portlanders defeated two measures to repeal and abolish it in 1917. Without district- or ward-based representation, the new structure of Portland politics removed the city's small yet gradually growing black population from the political process and forced them to rely on the support of white progressive leaders in the city government and state legislature to advance civil rights efforts throughout much of the twentieth century.[5]

Because of the nature of Portland politics, African Americans had little success in reforming civil rights issues in the first decades of the twentieth century. According to Elizabeth McLagan, a scholar of African American history in Portland, "Oregon, progressive in many ways, resisted the necessary legislation which would correct historical inequalities in the treatment of blacks and other minorities. In the absence of a significant black population before 1940 that could [affect] legislation, it remained a West Coast ecological paradise with a peculiar resistance to change." In addition to not repealing outdated constitutional restrictions on black settlements that were nullified after the Civil War, the Oregon State Supreme Court established a legal basis for segregation in Oregon movie theaters in the 1906 case of *Taylor v. Cohn*, which quickly carried over to restaurants and other private businesses.[6]

In addition, the Ku Klux Klan (KKK), which had experienced a revival across the United States after 1915, triggered by the hugely popular movie *The Birth of a Nation* (a film that received the endorsement of President Woodrow Wilson), arrived in Portland in 1921. As Klan membership soared to the millions nationally, 35,000 card-carrying members were in Oregon, where there were at least that many sympathizers. Finding the "Rose City" to be fertile recruiting ground, the KKK formed a large chapter in Portland and held initiation ceremonies on Mount Scott, where large burning crosses could be seen from miles away, making for a terrifying climate not only for the city's black population but for Catholics and Jews as well. The KKK soon spread throughout Oregon, quickly becoming one of the largest social and political organizations in the state. Klan parades were a common sight in Portland. In 1922, KKK-supported candidates won seats on the Multnomah County Commission and twelve of the county's thirteen seats in the state legislature. Moreover, unlike California and Washington, which passed laws barring KKK members from wearing hoods or engaging in intimidating behaviors, Oregon allowed the Klan to operate without interference. For example, the Klan assisted a ballot measure that required all children within the state to attend public schools, shutting down the parochial schools run by the Catholic Church. The bill was later ruled unconstitutional by the US Supreme Court in 1925. Still, the KKK became a powerful voice in Oregon electoral politics and served as a major obstacle to the passage of civil rights legislation until the organization's decline in the mid-1920s as a result of internal conflict and political corruption. In his book *Sundown Towns*, James Loewen echoes Elizabeth McLagan's remarks when he submits that the KKK dominated state politics in Oregon for a time during the 1920s. The most prominent example of this dominance was demonstrated in 1923, when the voters of Oregon unseated Ben Olcott, the KKK's most outspoken critic, and elected KKK member Walter Pierce as governor.[7]

Nevertheless, African Americans were not passive victims of segregation and discrimination; they actively pursued civil rights legislation despite their numbers and lack of representation. Through organizations like the short-lived New Port Republican Club, early black Oregonians worked with white progressive allies in the state government to pass new legislation improving access to public accommodations and removing discriminatory language from the state constitution, including outdated exclusion clauses and bans on voting and interracial marriage. However, although the legislature eventually passed amendments to the state constitution regarding exclusion and voting bans, by 1915 the public had on numerous occasions narrowly defeated each measure when brought to a popular vote for ratification. As a result, prior to 1920 and the presence of a sizable black population, the Oregon legislature failed to enact even the most basic civil rights legislation.[8]

The migration of African Americans from the rural South to major urban centers in the North and the West during the early decades of the twentieth century, commonly known as the Great Migration, dramatically altered the population and the demographics of Portland's black community and laid the foundation for social, economic, and political changes. In the first phase of migration between 1900 and 1920, the geographical center of the black community shifted from the area surrounding the Union Station to the Albina district on the northeastern bank of the Willamette River. Portland's African American population grew slowly in comparison to the populations of other major West Coast cities. During that twenty-year period, the African American population in Portland doubled from 775 to 1,556, yet black communities remained the smallest of the three largest minority communities, behind the Chinese and Japanese. Even so, the African American community became the fastest-growing nonwhite community in the city, while the Chinese population declined rapidly from 7,841 to 1,846, and the Japanese population, which transitioned increasingly from wage-labor jobs in the city to business ownership and rural farming, grew from 1,189 to 1,715 during the same period. Still, compared with other West Coast cities, the increase in Portland's African American population was relatively small. Los Angeles and Oakland experienced a particularly rapid rise in the black population. The number of African Americans in Oakland increased from 1,026 to 5,489 over the two decades, while Los Angeles' black population exploded from 2,131 to 15,579. Seattle's black population also grew at a much faster rate than Portland's, expanding from 405 in 1900 to 2,894 by 1920. San Francisco, the only major West Coast city in which black population growth was comparable to that of Portland, saw a rise from 1,654 to 2,414 African Americans, a relatively mild increase compared with the dramatic black population growth across the bay in Oakland.[9]

Despite the relatively slow growth of Portland's black community, the sudden increase of the African American population resulted in distinct changes in the community's social, cultural, spatial, and economic demographics. Prior to the Great Migration, Portland's black population was largely male, and most of the jobs were in the menial service sector, including cooks, waiters, janitors, servants, chauffeurs, and—most importantly—railroad porters. According to census data from 1910, roughly 70 percent of all employed black males worked one of these service jobs, with 29.5 percent of the population working as porters in particular. The relatively small population of black women tended to have no occupation, and the few who did worked as domestic servants, cooks, or waitresses. As a result, the majority of Portland's blacks resided in the northern part of downtown, west of the Willamette River, near Union Station and the hotels and restaurants where they worked.[10]

Given the black community's relatively small population compared with Asian communities in the early decades of the twentieth century, historian William Toll notes that a "general though subdued anti-Asian xenophobia" at that time allowed for a gradual proletarianization of Portland blacks in service jobs without mass resistance from white Portlanders. By 1920, as the population of African Americans grew, blacks increasingly found jobs as laborers, skilled trade workers, and even business owners and managers, and the percentage of African Americans working as porters dropped to 17.5. Likewise, the number of black women without an occupation fell below 50 percent for the first time in the census record as more women moved to the city and found work as domestic servants and hairdressers and at various small business jobs within the black community. Regardless of these employment opportunities and the growth of black businesses such as W. D. Allen's Golden West Hotel, located at 707 NW Everett, near downtown, which opened in 1906 and became a major hub for the black community, Toll notes, "blacks nevertheless found themselves shunted into traditional

service jobs on the fringe of the urban working class. . . . Portland's employers were not willing to admit blacks to higher paying jobs . . . and blacks
lacked the numbers and power to start banks of their own or to challenge
discrimination through the political system." Major advances in employment opportunities for Portland's African Americans did not occur until the
latter half of the twentieth century.[11]

The slow decline of the black community's strict dependence on railroad work and the gradual increase in wage-labor jobs also resulted in distinct resettlement patterns and increased spatial segregation among African Americans and whites in Portland. While blacks had initially tended
to settle in the northern part of downtown, many, particularly those with
families, could afford to relocate across the Willamette River to houses in the
Albina district. However, the congregation of blacks in the Albina district
was primarily the result of white popular preference for segregated communities, discriminatory real estate practices, and restrictive covenants,
rather than an intentional decision by African Americans to establish a
black community in northeast Portland. By 1920, 63 percent of blacks living in Albina were married couples, more than half of whom had children.
In contrast, the "old" black neighborhood of northern downtown remained
overwhelmingly single and male, with occasional relatives and boarders residing among the men. Similarly, in 1920, about 53 percent of black Albina
residents owned their own homes, while an overwhelming 95 percent of
blacks in the downtown neighborhood were renters. As a result, as Albina's
African American population grew over the course of the twentieth century,
the social and cultural heart of the black community, including churches
and other social organizations, began to move east of the river.[12]

Demographic and economic growth as well as changes in settlement
patterns translated into the development of new social institutions among
Portland's blacks in Albina, including black newspapers, civil rights organizations, and churches. Newspapers, perhaps more than any other early
institution, sought to improve literacy and education among the black population in order to agitate for civil rights and encourage self-determination.
Until the 1930s, newspapers such as *New Age* (est. 1896), the *Advocate* (1903),
and the *Portland Times* (1918) continually emphasized civil rights agitation
and activism within the black community. Following the closure of *New Age*
in 1907, the *Advocate*, which was founded by E. D. Cannady and his remark-
ably influential and politically active wife, Beatrice Morrow Cannady, became the leading black newspaper and advocate for civil rights in Portland.

Beatrice, who, beginning in 1912, served as the paper's assistant editor ultimately went on to become the first black female attorney in Oregon, helped
found the Portland branch of the National Association for the Advancement
of Colored People (NAACP), and launched an unsuccessful bid for state
representative from Multnomah County in early 1932. This final endeavor
made her the first black woman to run for office in the state of Oregon.[13]

While newspapers provided an early foundation for the Long Civil
Rights Movement in Portland, social and political organizations such as
the NAACP, local churches, and the Oregon Association of Colored Wom-
en's Clubs translated calls for civil rights into action. In 1914, a coalition of
blacks and whites in Portland that included the Cannadys, Dr. J. N. Merri-
man, and J. S. Bell established a branch of the NAACP in Portland, making it the oldest continuously chartered branch of the organization west of
the Mississippi River. Relying on the assistance of Portland's northeastern
black churches, including the First African Methodist Episcopal (AME)
Zion Church, the Bethel African Methodist Episcopal Church, the First
African Baptist Church, and the Mt. Olivet Baptist Church, the NAACP
quickly became the lead organizer in Oregon's civil rights struggle. While
the organization's focus on legislation and court cases achieved little success in the 1910s, its presence was instrumental in civil rights advancements in Oregon during the 1920s and after World War II. Similarly, other
organizations—such as the Oregon Association of Colored Women's Clubs,
founded in 1917 following the merger of several women's civil rights, Christian temperance, and other progressive groups—worked to improve social
conditions among Portland's blacks. In particular, the Oregon Association
of Colored Women's Clubs sought to improve women's education and the
social, economic, and moral welfare of the community, and to develop
black leadership and secure civil rights. Together, these organizations
formed the backbone of a rapidly emerging, socially active Civil Rights
Movement in Portland.[14]

The growth of Portland's black population in Albina, the establishment
of black newspapers, and the opening of the Portland branch of the NAACP
and other organizations during the 1920s led to the first major breakthroughs in civil rights legislation in the state of Oregon. In 1925, Republican William F. Woodward of Multnomah County proposed a bill to repeal
the exclusion clause in the state constitution, which finally passed the state
legislature and won statewide ratification in 1926 by a margin of 62.5 to 37.5
percent. Likewise, in 1927, Salem Representative John Geisy proposed, and

the legislature passed, an amendment to repeal the voting ban, which the public ratified later that year by a similar margin of 62.4 to 37.6 percent. However, these measures lacked substance, since neither constitutional clause had been enforced in more than two decades. Other civil rights measures were less successful. The removal of the ban on interracial marriage continued to meet fierce opposition from state representatives, who voted down the repeal in 1893 and 1917. "Clearly," Elizabeth McLagan notes, "it was acceptable to modify the state constitution in order to affirm rights guaranteed by the federal Constitution, but the legislators of Oregon were not ready to grant additional rights to minorities, including the right to marry whom they pleased." Ultimately, the intermarriage ban remained law until 1951. Similarly, although the Afro-American League of Portland, led by McCants Stewart, Portland's first black attorney, originally presented a public accommodations bill to Oregon lawmakers in 1919, the legislature did not approve such legislation until 1953. California and Washington, on the other hand, passed similar public accommodations laws in 1905 and 1909, respectively.[15]

With the collapse of the stock market in 1929 and the onset of the Great Depression by the early 1930s, economic opportunities for and the growth of the black community in Portland stagnated. Without capital, many black-owned businesses failed during the early 1930s. One such business was the Golden West Hotel, which had not only served as home to some of the railroad's black workers but had also played host to numerous black luminaries of the period—such as A. Philip Randolph, founder and president of the Brotherhood of Sleeping Car Porters, and Illinois congressman Oscar De-Priest—and was for the home of many black businesses, large and small. Unemployed blacks struggled to find service jobs, as business owners preferred giving work to unemployed whites. This employment discrimination, in turn, threatened the growth of Portland's small yet gradually emerging middle class. Moreover, after the Golden West Hotel closed in 1931 and the *Advocate* folded in 1933, most of Portland's major black businesses and all of the black newspapers were out of business, striking yet another blow to the civil rights struggle. As a result, Portland's African American community grew very little, and by 1940 the population remained around 2,000. However, with the outbreak of war in the Pacific in 1941, this lost decade of political and socioeconomic civil rights advancements became little more than a prelude to the largest historical expansion of Portland's African American population and the strongest push for civil rights in the city in the twentieth century.[16]

Although the Albina district had become home to the majority of Portland's black social and political institutions, the area was also home to many other populations, mostly poorer whites. However, beginning with a major influx of African Americans into the city during World War II, Albina rapidly transitioned from a multiracial community with an African American presence to a neighborhood that whites perceived as an urban ghetto. By 1950, Portland's black population had swelled from roughly 2,000 to nearly 10,000, almost half of which lived in Albina. No longer were Native Americans, the Japanese, or the Chinese the largest minority groups in the city. Due to this rapid influx of blacks, the NAACP worked to abolish the practice that had blocked recently arrived blacks from obtaining work cards that would allow them to be promoted. That same year, white Portlanders responded by voting down a civil rights ordinance that was presented and approved by the city council. The measure would have guaranteed all races equal use of all public facilities and services. Undaunted, the following year the local NAACP chapter sponsored a Fair Employment Practice Law while at the same time quietly but systematically working to dismantle segregation in public places. By 1960, the population of African Americans would stand at roughly 15,637, with 73 percent of those individuals residing in Albina. During this twenty-year period, Portlanders—mostly whites who were uncomfortable with the sudden and rapid growth of the city's black population and the prospect of integration—increasingly reconceived Albina as a black neighborhood. This new conception of Albina, in turn, created a self-fulfilling prophecy of economic and racial inequality and triggered a new phase in the civil rights struggle.[17]

The second phase of the Great Migration occurred during World War II and strained social tensions in Portland. The bombing of Pearl Harbor and the United States' entry into the war dramatically increased the presence of wartime industries in Portland and along the Willamette and Columbia Rivers. On January 10, 1941, the US Maritime Commission approved the development of the Oregon Shipbuilding Company, to be operated by a consortium of Todd Shipyards Corporation and famed industrialist Henry J. Kaiser. In September of that same year, the Oregon Shipbuilding Company produced the first of 330 Liberty ships and 120 Victory ships. In the city's busy shipyards Kaiser's construction empire built more than one thousand oceangoing vessels worth $2.4 billion in US Maritime Commission contracts. Following the passage of the Lend-Lease Act of 1941, Portland also became a key supplier of ships to the Soviet Union. Initially Kaiser founded the Oregon Shipbuilding Company to supply ships to the British, but the United States' entry into the war led to a rapid expansion in facilities and production. By March 1941 Kaiser had bought out the Todd interests and created two more yards. The Kaiser Company–Portland used the site of the city's old airport at Swan Island for the construction of T2 tankers. The Kaiser Company–Vancouver, situated on the northern bank of the Columbia River, built thirty LSTs (landing ship tanks), fifty cargo ships, and fifty escort carriers. The Oregon Shipbuilding Corporation was fast becoming the country's largest producer of Liberty ships.[18]

Since Portland was unable to provide a large enough workforce to fuel Kaiser's ship industry, the industrialist was forced to run "help wanted" ads in several of the nation's largest newspapers, and workers from across the country poured into Portland as early as 1942 on seventeen-car trains called "magic carpet specials" and the "Kaiser karavan." Approximately twenty-five hundred workers were recruited by Kaiser from New York City, three hundred of which were black. The Kaiser shipyards alone hired more than ninety thousand workers during the war.[19] Portland's ship-building industry lured many people from across the country, especially from the South, where black southerners who, after years of working for low wages, were now optimistic that in Portland they could find a good job at a much higher wage while working in significantly better conditions. As late as the start of the 1940s, some ten million people in the South—or one of every three who lived there—had cash incomes of less than $250 a year. Because of these new-found job opportunities in the North, in the 1940s two million more blacks left the South than moved to it. Theoretically, securing a better job meant finding better housing than in the South. During the 1940s, for a huge sector of the southern population, housing could be fairly described as primitive, devoid of the basic comforts and conveniences that mainstream Americans considered standard. This meant no electricity, no telephone, and no indoor plumbing. For many, the North was seen as an earthly paradise. The famed writer Richard Wright poetically recalled, "I was leaving the South to fling myself into the unknown . . . I was taking part of the South to transplant in alien soil, to see if it could drink of new and cool rains, bend in strange winds, respond to the warmth of other suns, and perhaps, to bloom."[20]

Prior to 1940 the net black migration to Oregon had never been greater than 1.0 percent, but by 1950, it reached 6.9 percent. Although Kaiser promised good-paying jobs, local unions scoffed at the thought of working alongside nonwhites. Most "help wanted" ads specified "white only." It was only after President Franklin D. Roosevelt issued Executive Order 8802, which forbade discrimination in federal hiring, job-training programs, and the defense industries, in June 1941, that jobs opened up to blacks. It should be noted, however, that Roosevelt's mandate followed increasing pressure from blacks who had formed the Committee on Participation of Negroes in the National Defense Program in May 1940. Joined by representatives of the NAACP, the National Urban League, and others, black leaders met with Roosevelt and later responded to the federal government's intransigence with a wave of protest, culminating in a January call by A. Philip Randolph for ten thousand blacks to march on Washington demanding jobs and integration of the military. The idea caught on in black communities across the country. March committees were established in several major northern cities. By the time the organizers had agreed on an early July date for the march, they were expecting upward of one hundred thousand marchers. Officials in Washington tried to get the march cancelled. On June 24, one week before the march was to take place, the committee agreed to call it off in exchange for an executive order banning discrimination in the defense industries. The executive order also empowered the Fair Employment Practices Commission to investigate discrimination against black employees and to take the necessary action if racially exclusionary practices were found to exist.[21]

Blacks were now permitted to work in union-controlled shops and pay union dues but were denied union benefits. Still, for the first time in Portland's history, African Americans found themselves with the opportunity to work in large numbers as industrial laborers rather than as service workers. Because a major migration occurred after the 1940 census and a large number of African American workers left the city before the 1950 census, it is difficult to ascertain how many blacks migrated to Portland over the decade. Many scholars nonetheless estimate that between twenty thousand and twenty-five thousand blacks travelled to Portland for employment in wartime industries, and their numbers constituted roughly 25 percent of the total number of new workers.[22]

The first significant obstacles that African American migrants encountered after arriving in Portland was a shortage of housing. There were conflicts over how much housing whites wanted to make available to black migrants. Initially, many blacks continued to move into the Albina district, where Japanese Americans had vacated housing following their deportation and internment in 1942. But such housing was quickly filled, and local whites grew increasingly vocal in their opposition to allowing large numbers of blacks to settle in the city. By September 1942, the *Oregonian* reported, "Several thousand Negroes have moved into Portland, taxing the housing facilities of the Albina district, center of the city's colored population. . . . Previous population of the eastside Negro colony ranged from 1,500 to 2,000 . . . but in recent months it has increased to about 5,000." Initially, the Housing Authority of Portland (HAP), which had been created in 1941, proposed constructing forty-nine hundred apartment units and a dormitory in Albina. Many of Portland's whites, however, who had long been ambivalent about the relatively small presence of blacks in the city, spoke out forcefully against the permanent integration of new African American migrants and opposed the proposed housing projects in Albina. In particular, white civic leaders and neighborhood organizations relied on racial stereotypes to prevent the construction of new housing projects by suggesting that African Americans were primarily responsible for increasing crime rates in US cities. A group of five hundred white Albina residents presented a plan for housing black workers. "If it is necessary to bring in large numbers of Negro workers, locate them on the edge of the city," urged the president of the Central East Portland Community Club. "It would be much better for all concerned," he continued, "If they are allowed to fan out through the city, it soon will be necessary to station a policeman on every corner." Even J. E. Bennett, a former city commissioner, publicly stated that the city should "actively discourage" large numbers of black workers from migrating into the city. Portland was unprepared for such a massive influx of people.[23]

Following HAP's failure to build new housing within Portland by late 1942, Kaiser and HAP worked quickly, quietly, and without the consent of the city council or the planning commission to establish a temporary wartime city. The largest and perhaps most historically significant of these housing projects was a complex called Vanport City, more commonly known as Vanport (a hybridization of Vancouver and Portland), and was nestled between the Columbia River on the north and the industrially polluted Columbia Slough on the south. The slough, a small waterway between Portland and its northern industrial district, had for decades been the dumping ground for waste from slaughterhouses and manufacturers, making it the most polluted stream in the state by midcentury. Regardless of the health hazards, residents flocked to Vanport. By June 1943, Vanport, which already had six thousand housing units, had 25,088 residents, of which 2,156 (or roughly 8.6 percent) were black. In June of the next year, the

African American population of Vanport had increased to 3,818 and represented 14 percent of the total population. Moreover, by the time of Vanport's last census in May 1945, the number of blacks there totaled 6,317 and constituted more than 20 percent of residents. At the end of the war, nearly three times as many African Americans lived in Vanport as had lived in the entire city of Portland just five years earlier. Based on population data collected from Vanport, most of the city's black population migrated from states on the western fringe of the South, including Texas, Arkansas, Oklahoma, Missouri, and Louisiana, and from larger northern, Midwestern, and western cities in states such as Illinois, California, and New York. As a result, by the end of the war, the black population in Portland and in the state of Oregon was much different in size and demographics than it had been in the 1920s and 1930s.[24]

Although HAP regularly (although unofficially) practiced segregation in their assignment of Vanport homes and other temporary housing projects, these new communities provided some blacks with employment opportunities that had been unheard of prior to 1940. For example, before 1945, there were no black teachers in Portland schools; by 1945, however, the Vanport school system employed seven African American teachers, two of whom, Leota E. Stone and Robert G. Ford, went on to become the first black teachers in Portland. Similarly, Vanport hired two black sheriffs, Bill Travis and Matt Dishman, both of whom later became Multnomah County sheriffs. In addition, several African Americans owned and operated small businesses, most of which catered predominately to Vanport's black community. While these types of jobs were rare, such opportunities undoubtedly represented a breakthrough in the lives of many African Americans, who for the first time found jobs outside of the service sector. As these opportunities were opening up to blacks, the Oregon House of Representatives passed Joint Memorial No. 9, which called on President Roosevelt to prevent the return of Japanese Americans "for the duration of the present war with Japan." The basis on which the lawmakers argued their case was "considerable antagonism to such return" to Oregon. They also claimed that the internees would be "safer and cause less civilian disturbance in the relocation centers." Whether the legislators were motivated by racism or a sense of compassion for the well-being of Japanese Americans is difficult to discern. What is clear, however, is that the removal of Japanese Americans from Portland undoubtedly benefitted blacks in some measure, as it made for one less group with whom they had to compete for jobs and housing.[25]

Despite the new social and economic opportunities that wartime industries seemed to provide, African Americans in and around Portland faced
another civil rights struggle over their ability to gain access to local unions.
The Boilermakers Union, which dominated the shipbuilding industry, limited its membership to whites and refused to allow African Americans to
join. In response, in late 1942, a group of African Americans workers, most
of whom had been recruited to come to Portland to work for Kaiser because
of their previous experience in New York shipbuilding industries, formed
the Shipyard Negro Organization for Victory. Outraged over unfulfilled
promises of equal rights and fair treatment, the organization threatened to
go on strike and issued a public statement that received widespread media
attention: "We, the Negro people employed by the Kaiser Company, maintain that under false pretense we were brought from east to west to work for
defense, and we demand, with due process of law, the following rights: (1) to
work at our trades on equal rights with whites; (2) to go to vocational school
or take vocational training on equal rights with whites." In response, the federal government launched an inquiry into the Boilermakers Union and the
Kaiser Company's practices, and demanded substantial reforms. Ultimately,
the Boilermakers created a secondary union for black members that collected dues but lacked the benefits and job security afforded to white union
members. Consequently, by the end of the war in 1945, African Americans
were struggling to both keep their jobs as industrial workers and find permanent housing.[26]

As the war ended, African Americans found themselves in a precarious
and fragile social position. The lack of job security and the evaporation of
wartime jobs compelled many blacks to return to service work, but the overall growth of Portland's population in the 1940s offered blacks greater access to these jobs than they had had during the 1920s and 1930s. Likewise,
housing projects such as Vanport, which were never meant to be more than
temporary wartime housing, persisted well after the end of the war due to
the continuing housing shortage in Portland. Although roughly half of the
African Americans who had migrated to Vanport and Portland left after the
war for opportunities in booming postwar industries in such cities as Seattle
and Los Angeles, a large percentage of blacks stayed in their temporary Vanport homes while searching for housing in Portland.[27]

However, at approximately 4:17 p.m. on Memorial Day, May 30, 1948, one
of the dikes holding back the Columbia River along the western edge of Vanport broke, and in less than an hour a flood wiped out the entire city. More-

over, the flood sealed off the only canal providing fresh river water to the Columbia Slough, setting the stage for decades of continued and increasingly concentrated industrial sewage in the water. Toxic brew rapidly encroached on the far north and northeastern neighborhoods of the Albina district that lie along the slough's southern bank. Anita Palmer, a retired state health department employee and longtime Portland resident, has painful memories of the flood. "The flood was devastating," she recalled, "the black community in Vanport was close-knit ... there was a community center there called the Oasis that I used to frequent as a young person. . . . I used to take tap dance lessons and gymnastics there. Paul Robeson even visited once. . . . that flood really had a negative impact on a lot of people's lives . . . it destroyed everything there."[28]

After the dike broke, residents could be seen wading through waters that ranged from an inch to waist-deep with suitcases, pillowcases, and paper bags in hand filled with whatever they had had time to pack. Photos of the flood show black men in suits, others traipsing through muddy waters in wingtip spectator shoes and Sanforized gabardine slacks, with still others wading through waist-high water in an effort to reach higher ground. Even in all the chaos, some men still had the presence of mind to retrieve their fedoras, which sat atop their heads. On the shoulders, backs, and hips of many were children they were carrying to safety. Vanport residents fled to evacuation buses on Denver Avenue that ushered them to local schools for shelter. When they arrived, the Red Cross worked feverishly to reunite them with their families. Since segregation was the order of the day, finding a place to house the displaced residents made a difficult situation all the more trying. A decision was made to house the refugees in war-surplus temporary houses on Guilds Lake. Within two weeks, war-surplus trailers, courtesy of the US government, were provided to supplement the temporary housing. Others took refuge in pool halls, lodges, taverns, and rooming houses. After weeks of living under these conditions, some residents traveled to the state capital to register their grievances. Signs on cars read, "We Want Permanent Homes Not Kennels on Wheels" and "Vanport Dead Cry Out for Justice." The Guilds Lake temporary housing was subsequently dismantled and shut down without any attempt to resettle the flood victims.

Estimates concerning the exact number of African Americans residing in Vanport at the time of the flood are somewhat unclear due to the suddenness of the event, but most historians agree that it displaced roughly seventeen thousand people. At the time, blacks made up more than one-third of

Vanport's population, making it the largest percentage of blacks among the city's inhabitants at any point leading up to the disaster. This sudden displacement, combined with housing restrictions, forced them to crowd into Albina's neighborhoods, where the community's black churches and social organizations struggled to provide jobs and housing for the sudden influx of refugees.[29]

In response to the mounting housing crisis in Portland, a coalition of white and black Portlanders consisting of Dr. DeNorval Unthank, Father Thomas J. Tobin of the Catholic Archdioceses, Bishop Benjamin Dunlap Dagwell of the Episcopal Diocese, and David Robinson of the Jewish B'Nai Brith—a group similar to the progressive coalition that had helped found the NAACP decades earlier—founded a branch of the Urban League in Portland in 1945. The creation of the Urban League was timely. That same year, the *Journal of Social Work* dubbed Portland the "worst Northern City in Racial Relations." While scholars have noted that the original purpose of the Portland Urban League was to find ways for blacks to emigrate from the city, black leadership within the organization redirected their efforts toward finding ways to integrate blacks into the city. Specifically, Chicago-born Edwin C. "Bill" Berry, the Portland Urban League's first executive director, worked to open new job and housing opportunities to Portland blacks for more than a decade until his departure in 1956. Indeed, by 1956, the three-thousand-member Portland Urban League had become quite the power broker. Other leaders and groups within the African American community campaigned to increase public support for settling and integrating new African American migrants in Portland. In particular, black leaders believed that housing limitations and the increasing ghettoization of Albina were the primary obstacles to African American social and economic success.[30]

In a 1945 report by the Portland City Club, which had been the city's leading nonprofit civic improvement organization for nearly three decades, Dr. DeNorval Unthank warned that there would be negative consequences if the city did not address the housing issue. As one of Portland's most prominent black physicians and civil rights advocates, and as cofounder of the Portland Urban League, Dr. Unthank stated, "For the safety factor in Portland, we should avoid a definitely segregated area which in the long run would prove a bad thing for the city." Unfortunately, the migration to Albina following the flood of Vanport in 1948, and white spatialized conceptions of that neighborhood as black, combined to make it a postwar urban ghetto by the late 1940s. The Housing Act of 1949 authorized the construction of 810,000 new units of low-cost housing over a four-year period. According to the 1950 census, half of Portland's black population resided within the two census tracts of Albina. However, in this supposedly black neighborhood, whites still outnumbered nonwhites by a ratio of two to one.[31]

By 1950, Albina had transformed into a neighborhood that the broader white community conceptualized spatially as a black urban ghetto, a transformation that—like those of many other cities in the United States—was not inevitable. In the conclusion to her 1978 report for Portland State University concerning African Americans in Portland during and after the war, researcher Diane Pancoast placed the onus for the creation of the black ghetto on Portland's white population. "Whites," she contended, "considered Albina to be a black neighborhood much earlier than blacks did." Moreover, she suggested, "it seems clear that whites rather than blacks created Albina and the blacks have suffered as a result while whites have profited.... The recent development of black pride, whatever its merits, has tended to obscure, to some extent, the origins of our ghettos, at least to whites who are looking for an escape from responsibility." As a result, regardless of the successes of half a century of civil rights struggles, Portland's African American community found itself facing devastating socioeconomic conditions that were just as bad if not worse than they had been in the past.[32]

Despite the problems caused by the ghettoization of Albina, Portland's African American population had reached such a critical mass that community leaders believed that they could launch an effective assault on the underpinnings of racism and prejudice at the core of Portland's social, political, and economic climate. With organizations such as the NAACP and the Urban League, blacks felt that they had the tools to improve their social and economic standing in the city, regardless of their lack of representation within the political process. Unfortunately, over the course of the next two decades, city government and urban planners attempted to rebuild the Albina district through costly and destructive urban renewal efforts rather than address the underlying social causes of the economic and racial inequalities that created the ghetto. Once again, African Americans met these misguided policies with resistance. Ultimately, the resulting postwar Civil Rights Movement marked the most important turning point in the century-long struggle. That movement's successes and failures laid the foundation for the next phase of the black freedom struggle and shaped the course of Portland's history for the remainder of the twentieth century.

Between the early 1950s and the mid-1960s, Portland, along with the rest of the nation, entered a period of rapid civil rights reforms that some scholars classically refer to as the singular "Civil Rights Movement." By 1960, the black population of Portland exceeded fifteen thousand and comprised 4 percent of the city's permanent population. Henry Stevenson, a military veteran who moved to Portland from Washington, DC, in November 1960, described the city this way: "Living in Portland at that time was almost like living in Alabama . . . black folk had it rough in Portland. . . . The system, especially the police had a whole lot of feet on black peoples' necks . . . it was nothing for a cop to just shoot a brother . . . now this wasn't an everyday occurrence, but when it did happen, there was no consequences . . . the cops weren't afraid of being reprimanded in any way." It is possible that Stevenson's depiction of black life in Portland is exaggerated, especially in its comparison to Bull Connor's Alabama, but the marginalized position of African Americans in the Rose City is well documented. Consequently, by 1960, for the first time in the city's history civil rights became a prominent issue in political discourse. According to historian Stuart McElderry, whose dissertation constitutes the most detailed analysis of this postwar moment in Portland's civil rights, the movement's success in the areas of public accommodations, employment, housing, and public education rested on the formation of a strong and effective coalition of black organizations, specifically the NAACP and the Urban League, and white progressives. But, as McElderry notes, by 1965, the ideological grounds of racial liberalism on which this coalition had formed began to fall apart. While McElderry correctly attributes a distinct shift in racial ideology to be part of the basis for the coalition's collapse, his analysis neglects to identify one of the most fundamental reasons for the shift: urban renewal and redevelopment. African Americans' frustration with destructive urban planning policies within the Albina district including demolishing hundreds of African American homes and businesses to make way for events centers, highways, and other large public works projects bred resentment toward public officials and shifted the trajectory of the classical period of postwar civil rights toward the Black Power era by the late 1960s. Consequently, the city's negligent assault on the physical and spatial constructs of the African American community in Albina eventually undermined the legislative successes of the postwar coalition and culminated in the abrupt and violent end to the postwar Civil Rights Movement in the summer of 1967.[33]

Early in 1950, the Portland City Council had passed a public accommodations ordinance making discrimination based on race, religion, or national origin illegal in all public places and temporarily overturning the state's ruling in *Taylor v. Cohn* more than forty years earlier. Following a petition campaign to place the ordinance on the ballot, the public resoundingly repealed the measure that November. Nevertheless, on April 13, 1953, under the leadership of NAACP president Otto Rutherford and Representative Mark Hatfield of Salem, and a coalition of other civil rights organizations that included the Urban League, the Portland League of Women Voters, and local churches, the House of Representatives passed and the Senate approved the Public Accommodations Bill by a margin of 46 to 11, the first major legislative breakthrough for civil rights since the 1920s. Despite efforts by groups such as the Civil Freedom Committee, a conservative organization led by Rev. Elbert D. Riddick that opposed the bill and sought to delay its enactment until the passage of a public referendum in 1954, Representative Hatfield was successful in garnering support for the bill and defeating opposition movements through a closely coordinated public campaign with the NAACP. The opposing efforts of the Civil Freedom Committee ultimately failed to collect the 23,375 valid signatures required. At any rate, the Public Accommodations Bill outlawed discrimination in restaurants, courtrooms, parks, hotels, theaters, and the like. The bill also gave those discriminated against the right to sue for up to $500. Although public discrimination continued in parts of the city for decades after the bill's passage, blacks in Portland now had a solid political and legal defense against discrimination, and a strong, albeit temporary, political coalition for advancing civil rights legislation. Edgar Williams, a lifelong member and eventual leader of the Portland NAACP, had been pushing for a civil rights bill since he first arrived in Oregon in 1919. Since that time, such a bill had been introduced at seventeen different legislative sessions. When the house vote was announced in 1953, tears of joy streamed down Williams's face.[34]

Following the passage of the Public Accommodations Bill, organizations such as the NAACP and the Urban League turned their attention to three major civil rights issues that continued to plague Portland's African American population: housing, employment, and education. The most pressing issue of the postwar Civil Rights Movement was resolving the housing crisis. According to a 1960 census, 15.6 million of the 58 million occupied dwellings in the United States were substandard. This represented 27 percent of the nation's total housing. Of these 15.6 million, some 3 million were shacks, hovels, and tenements. Another 8.3 million were "deteriorat-ing," and 4.3 million were structurally sound but lacking some or all of the essential plumbing needs. It should be noted that these figures do not in-clude "sound" housing that was terribly overcrowded. Civil rights groups, given their numbers and mounting successes, believed that they finally had the political support to challenge both the codified and unwritten though well-known practices of spatial discrimination that had been in place since African Americans first began arriving in Oregon in the mid-1800s. In par-ticular, the NAACP and the Urban League targeted discriminatory real es-tate practices such as redlining, which sought to confine African American home buyers to specific neighborhoods. Until the early 1950s, the Portland Realty Board had publicly maintained that the presence of African Ameri-cans in a neighborhood depreciated property values, an idea that some in-creasingly saw as nothing more than a self-fulfilling prophecy. Eventually, in 1957, the Oregon legislature passed the Fair Housing Law, which allowed many blacks to relocate to formerly all-white neighborhoods outside the Al-bina district. But the effects of the Fair Housing Law, like those of the Public Accommodations Bill, were not always immediate, and many white neigh-borhoods resisted the relocation of black families into their communities with threats and destruction of property. In addition, with the gradual open-ing up of the suburbs to Portland's black middle class, many African Ameri-cans left behind an increasingly impoverished black inner-city population that lacked the social or economic resources to improve their community.[35]

Employment was another central concern of the postwar Civil Rights Movement. Although service jobs were plentiful in Portland after the war, blacks continued to struggle to open up new avenues for skilled nonservice employment outside of the growing business center of the black commu-nity along N. Williams Avenue. Moreover, unlike in Los Angeles and Seattle, where new aircraft industries continued to produce jobs well after the end of the war, Portland's loss of shipbuilding contracts and lack of postwar in-dustries limited new job opportunities for African American workers who had migrated to the city in the 1940s. Nevertheless, civil rights organiza-tions, most prominently the Urban League, worked tirelessly to break down the color line in housing and employment after the war. Both the Urban League and the NAACP backed a fair employment practices bill that was introduced in the Oregon legislature in 1947 but was quickly defeated. The state legislature eventually passed the Fair Employment Practices Act in 1949, only after the Urban League launched a statewide campaign to drum up support, working in concert with the *Oregonian*; Senator Richard Neuberger, who would be elected to the House in 1950; Neuberger's wife, Maureen; and Mark Hatfield, a political science professor at Willamette University, who would also be elected to the state legislature in 1950. The bill passed and made discrimination in job hiring illegal. However, because the measure was not as strong as its proponents had envisioned, it did not greatly improve employment prospects for blacks. Instead of creating an agency to monitor discrimination, the Fair Employment Practices Law channeled all complaints through the state labor commissioner's office. Still, some saw the law a major victory. Indeed, by December 1949, the Urban League had placed three hundred blacks in jobs, forty of which were new positions. Less than five years later, nearly one thousand blacks had jobs in commerce, industry, and city, state, and federal departments and agencies.[36]

Portland's Urban League, under the leadership of Edwin "Bill" Berry, William Boone, and E. Shelton "Shelly" Hill, made employment its highest priority during the 1950s. Indeed blacks' foray into industries that were once closed to them can be attributed to the Urban League's advocacy. During these men's tenure, blacks were hired on as school teachers, school principals, bus drivers, bank officers, and police officers. In 1946, Charles Duke became the city's first black police officer. Some of the more notable success stories included Mark A. Smith, the first African American deputy commissioner for the Oregon Bureau of Labor; William Carr, a member of the Portland Fire Department; Dr. William Couch, a faculty member at Reed College; William Hilliard, a writer for the *Oregonian*; and several noncustodial employees of Sears and Montgomery Ward. Speaking of the Urban League and its successes, journalist and political activist Julia Ruuttila noted, "The Urban League had more guts than the NAACP in those days.[37]

By the early 1960s, however, the NAACP and the Urban League had developed an increasingly confrontational approach toward the gradualism and tokenism of employment integration, and adopted the practices of public protest and picketing, activities that contradicted the widely held perception that black interest groups limited themselves to such tactics as litigation and lobbying. In November 1961, for instance, under the tenure of Executive Director Hill, the Urban League invited Dr. Martin Luther King, Jr., to speak at its Equal Opportunity Day program at the Portland's civic auditorium. The program's theme, "Eliminating the Barriers to Equal Opportunity," drew more than thirty-five hundred attendees. King's appearance in Portland was part of a West Coast speaking tour. He spoke eloquently and passionately of the successful Freedom Rides, the bus boycott in Montgomery, Alabama, and the lunch counter sit-ins.

The Freedom Rides, launched in the spring of 1961, put the race question on America's front burner in a way that it had not been since the early to mid-1950s. The "Negro problem" was no longer an in-house matter discussed in hush tones among American citizens but had become a matter of international interest. When the United States showed stiff opposition to China's being allowed to join the United Nations (UN), the Russians took the opportunity to rub the race question, which had hovered over the head of every American since 1619, in Americans' faces. Ambassador Adlai Stevenson had vehemently opposed the admission of the supposedly ruthless Chinese Communist state to the UN in part because of China's treatment of its own citizens. Upon hearing this, Ambassador Valerian Zorin of the Soviet Union quickly responded that if the manner in which citizens of a country are treated is a basis for membership in the UN, then the United States should be voted out of because of its treatment of blacks.[38]

By the fall of 1961, more than seventy thousand students throughout the South, both black and white, had taken part in sit-ins, and approximately thirty-six hundred had been arrested. In Portland, Dr. Martin Luther King, Jr., encouraged freedom-loving citizens to use creative nonviolent protest to bring about full integration in their city. What's more, King called on President John F. Kennedy to issue an executive order to end discrimination and segregation, just as Abraham Lincoln had done to end slavery. Despite King's reputation among many blacks as the apostle of peace, some whites viewed him as an outside agitator. "My publisher M. J. Frey at the *Oregonian*, thought King was a communist and didn't think we should cover the Urban League event, but we did," said reporter Bill Hilliard. Throughout his life, King was constantly mislabeled as a communist despite his anticommunist stance. His rejection of communism stemmed from his religious belief that divine laws set all standards of justice. A Marxist society, King maintained, is based on "no divine government, no absolute moral order." As a result, "almost anything—force, violence, murder, lying—is a justifiable means to the 'millennial' end." Nevertheless, the perception that King was a communist, and most certainly a troublemaker, only increased. However, King's visit to Portland left a big imprint, as over the next year the Portland NAACP launched boycotts of Fred Meyer and Sears Roebuck stores for refusing to hire black sales clerks, and of the International Longshore and Warehouse Union for discriminating against African American dockworkers. Such confrontations with businesses and institutions that were popular among sympathetic whites marked the first major signs of erosion within the black-white postwar Civil Rights Movement's coalition. Ultimately, while civil rights groups were quick to emphasize their successes in breaking through discriminatory hiring practices, the changes had not come quickly enough to improve the economic livelihoods of members of the black community in Albina.[39]

The third concentrated effort of the postwar Civil Rights Movement centered on public education and the integration of Portland schools. Unlike in southern states, where segregation was the result of directly legal (de jure) segregation, the division between whites and people of color in Portland schools was the result of preexisting spatial settlement patterns, or de facto segregation, which was the product of legalized housing inequalities. The Supreme Court's 1954 landmark ruling in *Brown v. Board of Education* therefore had little effect on the composition of Portland's school system. For example, even as late as the 1964–65 school year, four elementary schools in northeastern Portland—Boise Elementary, Eliot Elementary, Humboldt Elementary, and Highland Elementary—all had more than 85 percent black enrollment. As a result, challenging segregation in Portland required breaking down spatial arrangements rather than legal blockades. Having made progress with housing by the early 1960s, the NAACP began pressuring the city council to address school segregation. After the emergence of strong public opposition to citywide busing proposals aimed at desegregating schools, the city instead developed a small "pilot relocation assistance project" in 1964 that gave financial assistance to twenty-five African American families to relocate and switch schools. However, a special commission appointed by the city council ultimately decided on a policy whereby the city would close schools within the African American community in northeast Portland and evenly redistribute black students among neighboring school districts. In addition, schools that had previously been nearly all white sought to hire more African American teachers as black student enrollment increased. Although this approach was well-intentioned and successful in some ways, by the late 1960s, many black families in Albina increasingly came to resent it and began to push for new methods that would not, as many perceived it, divide and weaken their own social and cultural community.[40]

While housing, employment, and education comprised the three main areas of focus for studies of the postwar Civil Rights Movement, students of civil rights in Portland have neglected the importance of a fourth overarching element of the movement: urban renewal and redevelopment. Like many cities in the United States during the 1950s and 1960s, Portland began to adopt urban planning policies that focused on tearing down older, supposedly unsalvageable, neighborhoods to improve urban infrastructure and downtown attractions. Moreover, the city planning commission had little or no interest in the voices or opinions of local citizens or neighborhood organizations concerning the construction of their policies. As a result, the city's efforts to remake and thereby revitalize the Albina district through demolition, rezoning, and the construction of new buildings in many ways limited the overall success of all three of the postwar Civil Rights Movement's goals. These policies forced members of the black community to relocate once again while helping create a new generation of resentment and disillusionment within the movement. In particular, the construction of the Memorial Coliseum and Interstate 5 (I-5), the city's proposed "Central Albina Plan," and the Emanuel Hospital renovations all had devastating effects on the black community of northeast Portland.[41]

The first phase of urban redevelopment in Albina in the late 1950s moved quickly and focused primarily on the construction of the Memorial Coliseum and I-5, both of which the city carved out of the highly concentrated black neighborhoods of Albina. After receiving public support in November 1956 for building a war memorial events center and sports venue, Portland's planning commission chose for the building's location the east bank of the Willamette River, across from downtown. The clearance of that area, which contained the densest concentration of African Americans in the Albina district, involved demolishing 476 homes, the majority of which were nonwhite residences. The project effectively wiped out large portions of the African American community south of Broadway Street and involved the destruction or relocation of many of the area's most important landmarks and institutions, including the medical office of Dr. DeNorval Unthank, the Bethel AME Church, and many other black-owned shops and businesses. Similarly, even before the completion of the Memorial Coliseum in 1960, Portland's planning commission approved and began additional redevelopment projects in the Albina district, including the construction of I-5. Like the construction of the Memorial Coliseum, the expansion of Highway 99 into I-5 required the demolition and relocation of 125 homes and businesses, including (once again) the recently opened new medical offices of Dr. Unthank. The Black Oregon Fraternal Association (also known as "Frat Hall"), and the ever-popular McClendon's Rhythm Room, both of which were on Williams Avenue, also fell victim to I-5 construction. In both instances, the displaced black population, which received no assistance from the city government, was forced to relocate to already overcrowded neighborhoods or to go further northeast to the area around Irving Park, where white flight and new housing opportunities gradually expanded the boundaries of the "black neighborhood" east of Williams Avenue.[42]

By the early 1960s, urban renewal and redevelopment projects in Albina had had devastating social and economic results, but no project appeared more threatening to African Americans than the city's Central Albina study of 1962. In 1958, an approved amendment to the city charter created the Portland Development Commission (PDC), under the leadership of Mayor Terry Schrunk (1957–73). The amendment gave the new commission almost limitless power "promote industrial expansion and location and acquire such property, real or personal . . . inside or outside the city, as the Commission . . . may find appropriate or convenient in accordance with comprehensive zoning and development plans." In November 1962, the PDC published its Central Albina study, a report that defined an urban renewal plan for a 3.4-square mile area in Central Albina known as the Eliot neighborhood. Ultimately, the area, which contained 12,844 African Americans and roughly 80 percent of the city's total black population, was designated as a region in "an advanced stage of urban blight" that could not be revitalized. In particular, the report concluded, "urban renewal, largely clearance, appears to be the only solution to, not only blight that presently exists in central Albina, but also to avoid the spread of that blight to other surrounding areas." Moreover, the report further emphasized the usefulness of the neighborhood's location for city infrastructure and noted that it was "unusually well suited to transportation, distribution, and service industries."[43]

If the Central Albina Plan had been fully implemented, at least one-third of the entire city's black population would have had to relocate. However, following widespread public resistance spearheaded by NAACP president Mayfield K. Webb and the Albina Neighborhood Improvement Committee (ANIC), whose council was comprised of local black religious leaders, professionals, and neighborhood residents, the PDC backed away from some but not all of its proposed renewal plans in Albina. One year prior to the Central Albina study, the PDC had set aside a small thirty-five-block area just north of Fremont for the ANIC-directed Albina Neighborhood Improvement Project (ANIP). In doing so, the PDC had approved its first redevelopment project in the area that focused on revitalization rather than demolition. Over the course of twelve years, the ANIP successfully rebuilt dilapidated homes, repaired streets, established a tree-planting program, and created a five-acre park named after Dr. DeNorval Unthank.[44]

During the early to mid-1960s, both the Albina Neighborhood Council and its community council (previously known as the community welfare council) surveyed agencies with the express purpose of crafting a proposal seeking funding from the Office of Economic Opportunity (OEO). In October 1964, Albina was selected to receive federal funds from President Lyndon B. Johnson's War on Poverty program. These funds went to founding the Albina Citizen's War on Poverty Committee, which led to the creation of a local Head Start program and the Low Income Family Emergency Center. However, despite these early successes and petitions by more than one thousand Albina residents to expand the project in 1967, the local leaders of the ANIC were unsuccessful in their attempts to push the boundaries of the ANIP south of Fremont Avenue. The PDC's rejection of these efforts resulted in the continuation of the Central Albina Plan and in further clearances and displacements. As a result, by the mid- to late 1960s, large portions of Portland's black population had been driven from the lower southeast portion of the Albina district to the north side of Fremont and east toward Irving Park.[45]

After two decades of frustrating and often devastating relocation and urban renewal projects, the city of Portland's decision to expand Emanuel Hospital in the mid-1960s marked a turning point in the minds of many African Americans living in northeast Portland. To expand its facilities to meet the increasing needs of Portland's growing population, under the Central Albina Plan, the city and the PDC granted the hospital, located on the western edge of N. Williams Avenue, ten blocks surrounding the complex. The hospital then proceeded to demolish another 188 businesses and residences, forcing people to relocate. Repeating the usual pattern, the majority of these shops and homes belonged to African American residents. Among the displaced were the Blessed Martin Day Nursery, a daycare center dating back to World War II; Scotty's Barbeque; and the home of Ina Warren, who later formed the Emanuel Displaced Persons Association. To make matters worse, federal budget cuts eventually forced an abrupt end to the hospital's expansion and temporarily left the land vacant. For many African Americans living in Albina, especially younger individuals who had grown up in the crucible of Vanport, Memorial Coliseum, I-5, and the Central Albina Plan, the Emanuel Hospital renovations marked the last straw in a long chain of civil rights and urban renewal abuses. By the end of the 1960s, over just two decades, the hospital expansion ultimately displaced more than half of the population of the Albina district's Eliot neighborhood.[46]

Despite the passage of state legislation, the federal Civil Rights Act of 1964, and the Voting Rights Act of 1965, the history of the Long Civil Rights Movement in Portland was far from over. By 1967, African Americans had made important, although sometimes minimal, improvements in their long struggle for civil rights. Still, even after the Great Migration of the early twentieth century, the rapid influx of African Americans into Portland during World War II, and the postwar Civil Rights Movement, blacks in Portland lacked district representation in city politics and were forced to rely on a fragile and often ineffective coalition of black civil rights advocates and white progressives to enact reforms. By the end of the postwar era, African Americans had achieved their greatest legislative victories, but concrete solutions to visible socioeconomic problems in Albina remained elusive. The passage of the Public Accommodations Bill, the Fair Housing Law, and the Fair Employment Practices Act, as well as attempts to reform the segregation in public education that had resulted from settlement patterns, met with mixed results. Furthermore, urban renewal policies, the flight of wealthier blacks from the Albina district to the suburbs and other parts of Portland, and the integration of blacks into Portland schools through the dissolution of black majority schools in Albina combined to limit the perceived successes of the postwar Civil Rights Movement. Indeed, by the summer of 1967, the struggle for civil rights and black empowerment in Portland and in other major cities across the United States would take a disturbingly chaotic turn. With this new phase of black activism and radicalism came a search for new solutions to the old problems of urban neglect and social indifference. The face of this new generation of young leaders and radical activists would ultimately help reimagine and redefine Portland politics and urban development, and the modern social and political landscape in the United States.

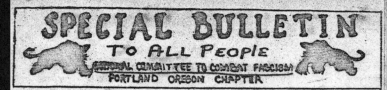

SPECIAL BULLETIN
TO ALL People
NATIONAL COMMITTEE TO COMBAT FASCISM
PORTLAND OREGON CHAPTER

MASS RALLY
Sunday Jan. 11th 3:00

Portland Educational Center
Union & Russell

To ALL the B.S.U.S & People of the Black Community

FREE PANTHER

PURPOSE:

To Educate The people on The RACIST oppres-sion of Black youth At Roosevelt High School.

To Support, To de-FEND KENT FORD From RACIST INJUSTICE

N.C.C.F.

Although the Portland branch of the NCCF did not receive official Black Panther status until the summer of 1970, it frequently used Black Panther imagery in its leaflets and postings. This bulletin calling for a "Mass Rally" in January 1970, found in police surveillance records, heavily uses the Black Panther logo while downplaying "National Committee to Combat Fascism" and "N.C.C.F" in smaller print. Courtesy of City of Portland Archives, Oregon, A2004-005.

On February 14, 1970, the Portland Black Panthers marched with students from the Portland State University campus through the Southwest Park blocks to the US courthouse downtown in support of a "community control" ballot initiative. Prominently out in front is Sandra Ford carrying a sign reading, "FREE THE PANTHERS." On the right is Percy Hampton, wearing a black jacket and dark glasses. To his left are Patty Hampton (in a quilted coat) and Linda Thornton (with her hands in her pockets). Courtesy of City of Portland Archives, A2004-005.2960.

Sandra Ford leading the procession
toward the courthouse. Courtesy of City of
Portland Archives, A2004-005.2957.

Portland Panthers and their supporters concluded the march by gathering on the steps of the courthouse, where group leaders addressed the crowd. Courtesy of City of Portland Archives, A2004-005.2958.

Standing at the microphone between
Kent Ford (*left*) and Percy Hampton (*right*),
Freddy Whitlow addresses the crowd
gathered on the steps of the courthouse.
Courtesy of City of Portland Archives,
A2004-005.2959.

This photo capturing one of the Panther's crowded free breakfasts for local schoolchildren was taken for a multipart series of articles by Rick Goodfellow on the Portland Panthers' community survival programs in the *Pioneer Log*, Lewis and Clark College's student-run newspaper. *Pioneer Log*, March 6, 1970. Courtesy of Watzek Library Special Collections and Archives, Lewis and Clark College, Portland, Oregon.

Also taken as part of the *Pioneer Log*'s multipart series on the Panthers' efforts in north and northeast Portland, this photo shows a bustling evening at the Fred Hampton People's Free Health Clinic. *Pioneer Log*, March 10, 1970. Courtesy of Watzek Library Special Collections and Archives, Lewis and Clark College, Portland, Oregon.

Dr. Clarence O. Pruitt, pictured here at his desk, was the first black graduate of the University of Oregon Dental School and a critical source of support for the Malcolm X People's Dental Clinic. Courtesy of Oregon Health and Science University Historical Collections and Archives Digital Commons, Portland.

White liberals and leftists in Portland, such as Jon Moscow (left) and Dr. Gerry Morrell (right), provided valuable support for the Portland Panthers' community survival programs, especially the health and dental clinics. Images courtesy of Jon Moscow and Gerry Morrell.

CHAPTER 2

Claiming Albina in the Era of Model Cities and the National Committee to Combat Fascism

Within the larger contexts of Portland's history of urban planning and the post–civil rights era, two seemingly unrelated occurrences in October 1966 set in motion a series of events that converged on the city, radically redefined the local political power structure and urban planning policies, and altered the trajectory of the black community's long struggle for civil rights. One event took place in the halls of Congress in Washington, DC, the other on the streets of Oakland, California. On October 20, the US Senate narrowly passed the Demonstration Cities and Metropolitan Development Act. Championed by President Lyndon B. Johnson and his Democratic allies in Congress, the act provided federal grants through the Department of Housing and Urban Development (HUD) to assist cities with comprehensive and locally planned urban redevelopment and infrastructure improvement projects.[1]

Days earlier, in Oakland, Huey P. Newton and Bobby Seale founded the Black Panther Party for Self-Defense (BPP). As self-professed revolutionaries, Newton and Seale understood that all revolutions need an ideology to guide it. Consequently, the two not only studied closely revolutions and decolonization movements across the globe but also immersed themselves in the works and deeds of such radical figures as Frantz Fanon, Carlos Marighella, Ernesto "Che" Guevara, Mao Tse-tung, Mikhail Bakunin, Robert F. Williams, and, of course, Malcolm X. They also studied Raúl Sendic's Tupamaros National Liberation Movement. At a time when Dr. Martin Luther King, Jr.'s method of nonviolence was, for some, the preferred response to violent whites, Malcolm X encouraged blacks to form rifle clubs if government agents were unwilling or incapable of protecting them from white mobs. King took the opposite approach. In the mid 1950s, when King's Montgomery home was bombed, he reportedly implored a group of black residents who had assembled on his lawn armed with guns, clubs, and knives not to retaliate. Said King,

> If you have weapons, take them home.... If you do not have them, please do not seek to get them. We cannot solve this problem through retaliatory violence.... We must love our white brothers, no matter what they do to us. We must make them know that we love them. Jesus still cries out in words that echo across centuries: "Love your enemies; bless them that curse you; pray for them that despitefully use you." This is what we must live by. We must meet hate with love.

As Reinhold Niebuhr, who is considered one of America's greatest Protestant theologians, pointed out in *Moral Man and Immoral Society*, there are advantages to using nonviolent methods, but they must be pragmatically considered in light of the circumstances. Robert F. Williams, the former head of the Monroe chapter of the NAACP and a veteran of multiple branches of the US Armed Forces (including the US Marine Corps), did just that, training members of his chapter and others in marksmanship and the art of self-defense. His 1962 book, *Negroes with Guns*, which influenced Newton greatly, chronicles those exploits. From Malcolm X's and Williams's standpoints, the most reliable defendants of black people's liberty were blacks themselves. Inspired by these models, Newton and Seale emphasized armed self-defense and a revitalization of black inner-city communities that included building and governing its own institutions. In their manifesto, titled the "Ten-Point Platform and Program," the Panthers demanded the right to self-determination and community control; an end to police brutality and black economic exploitation by whites; exemption from military service in Vietnam; the immediate release of all blacks from federal, state, county, and city prisons; and improved employment, housing, and education opportunities.[2]

   Although the founding of the BPP and the passage of the Demonstration Cities and Metropolitan Development Act occurred three thousand miles apart and seemed, at best, only tangentially related, their interconnectedness became apparent by 1969. Under the act, the stewardship of Mayor Terry Schrunk, a fiscal and social conservative and former sheriff, and Portland Development Commission (PDC) chairman Ira Keller, the city developed its Model Cities program. Approached by the PDC as another urban renewal project, this new program once again targeted the Albina district. While the leaders of the Model Cities program made a more concerted effort than city government had in the past to engage Portland's African American community, the PDC initially offered blacks nothing more than token representation in minor planning positions and public forums. As a result, Portland's black community became openly hostile toward the proposed program and viewed it as another instance of the city's destructive urban renewal policies in the region. As African Americans experimented with new and diverse methods of resisting city government and the PDC's redevelopment plans, the PDC lost control of the program. In this increasingly radical atmosphere, the Portland branch of the National Committee to Combat Fascism (NCCF, an affiliate of the BPP) emerged following the "United Front Against Fascism" conference in Oakland in July of 1969 as one of several forms of political experimentation in a city that had effectively stifled the black community's political voice.[3]

The Model Cities program, as originally envisioned by the PDC, and the Portland NCCF represented two radical and polarized visions of space in northeast Portland. To the city government and the PDC leadership, Albina was a potentially valuable neighborhood plagued by urban blight, lacking the ability to cure itself, and in need of city planners' redevelopment projects to reach its full potential. To NCCF members, Albina was their community, their land, and they were poised to defend it, no matter the consequences.

When the citizens of Portland elected Mayor Schrunk to the first of four four-year terms in 1956, they did so based on campaign promises that Schrunk would govern as a self-described "moderate progressive" with a policy platform of citywide urban renewal. Defeating one-term incumbent mayor Fred Peterson in both a nine-candidate primary and a run-off election later that fall, Schrunk came into office with a strong mandate to consolidate Portland's previously disparate urban planning agencies. In a sweeping overhaul of the system in early 1958, Schrunk replaced the frequently conservative and ineffective leadership of the Housing Authority of Portland (HAP), the planning commission, and the planning bureau with political allies such as John Kenward, former executive secretary of Downtown Portland, and longtime urban planner Lloyd Keefe. He then gained permission from the state legislature to place each of these semiautonomous agencies under the authority of a single new entity that had almost total control over all urban renewal and redevelopment policies—the Portland Development Commission. After securing public approval for the PDC by a narrow margin of 52 to 48 percent in the summer of 1958, Schrunk quickly appointed Keller, a powerful business executive who originally hailed from Chicago, as the chair. Throughout the late 1950s, Mayor Schrunk and Chairman Keller oversaw several major urban renewal projects, including the construction of the Memorial Coliseum in the Albina district and the South Auditorium renewal project south of downtown.[4]

During the conservative, business-minded Schrunk's tenure as mayor from 1957 to 1973, the PDC embraced policies that favored the clearance of "blighted" neighborhoods throughout the city, but especially in the predominately black Albina district. Guided by the city's 1958 Comprehensive Development Plan and, later, by the 1966 Community Renewal Program, the PDC operated under the assumption that the decline of inner-city neighborhoods was inevitable and that city planners offered the best vision for revitalizing these areas. Consequently, PDC Chairman Keller took a top-down approach to urban renewal that neglected to engage the people of the very neighborhoods and communities he and others sought to change. But the Model Cities program, initiated by the PDC in late 1966 and early 1967, changed everything. Though initially proposed as a way to receive federal funds to continue the city's redevelopment of northeast Portland, a backlash against the program by the African American community in Albina between 1967 and 1970 derailed this strategy. Through a combination of radical resistance and an effort to wrestle some control of urban planning away from the PDC through the creation of the Citizens' Planning Board, Portland's black community helped force a distinct shift in postwar urban planning that set the stage for significant social and political changes in the 1970s.[5]

The passage of the Demonstration Cities and Metropolitan Development Act in October 1966 ushered in yet another phase of redevelopment in northeast Portland. Congress designed the act commonly known as the Demonstration Cities Act to support "locally prepared programs for rebuilding or restoring entire sections and neighborhoods of slums and blighted areas by the concentrated and coordinated use of all available Federal aids together with local, private, and governmental resources." The act consisted of federal assistance in two stages. In the first stage, (HUD) would provide assistance in the development of demonstration plans during the first half of 1967. Then, in the second stage after July 1, HUD would offer $400 million in federal funds to selected programs and another $500 million the following year. The act also stipulated several specific standards that any city applying for funding had to meet. In particular, it stated that "programs must be designed to ... renew entire slum neighborhoods by combined use of physical and social development programs, ... make marked progress in reducing social and educational disadvantages, ill health, underemployment and forced idleness, and contribute toward a well-balanced city." In other words, the Demonstration Cities Act required cities to address the social—not just the physical—problems of urban decay.[6]

In late November 1966, only a month after the passage of the Demonstration Cities Act, the PDC drafted its "Report and Recommendations on Demonstration Cities Program for the City of Portland." The report, which highlighted most of northeast Portland as the region of the city in the most advanced stages of blight, proposed a project that would establish "a model community for urban living" by "upgrad[ing] badly run-down sections in declining areas . . . as part of creating an overall model neighborhood" in Albina. "Without a doubt," the PDC's proposal claimed, "the area extending north from Memorial Coliseum and Lloyd Center to the City limits . . . fulfills [the Demonstration Cities Act conditions] and many more criteria." This area included the Eliot, Boise-Humboldt, Irvington, King-Vernon-Sabin, and Woodlawn neighborhoods of the Albina district, which stretched east to west from I-5 to NE 22nd Avenue, and north to south from Broadway Street to Columbia Boulevard. After fine-tuning its proposal, the city of Portland submitted its official planning grant application to HUD in late April 1967. Over the next few months, the city of Portland and the PDC promoted this new urban planning project, which they increasingly described as "Model Cities." Shortly thereafter, the *Oregonian* newspaper began publishing a series of articles touting the projects commercial benefits for northeast Portland. Following a short review process, Portland's Model Cities program was among several projects that the federal government began to consider for funds. However, as the city and the PDC began to move forward with urban development plans and the selection of a head for the Model Cities program, the project met with stiff resistance from Albina's African American community. Sensing the possibility of a backlash, HUD's regional office in San Francisco responded to Portland's proposal in early July 1967 with concerns about the city's potentially haphazard and precarious implementation of its urban renewal project. Specifically, HUD questioned the PDC's administrative ability to carry out the program, the ill-defined neighborhood area, and the lack of citizen input or participation in the planning process. HUD officials were most concerned about citizen participation, noting, "Although Portland has established a coordinating, planning, and policy-making body, there is no explanation of how the neighborhoods will have any influence over its decisions. . . . Portland's citizen participation proposal is mostly at the level of informing residents rather than involving them." In short, HUD had finally challenged the city of Portland's and the PDC's decade-long approach to urban renewal and redevelopment.[7]

Drawing on lessons from recent uprisings in cities across the United States, HUD's response to the proposed Model Cities plan was prescient. Two years after the devastating Watts revolt in Los Angeles in August 1965, large violent clashes broke out in June 1967 between African Americans and police in several US cities, including Atlanta, Boston, and Cincinnati. The following month, New York City, Birmingham, Chicago, Detroit, Newark, and many other cities erupted in violence in what has come to be known as the long hot summer of 1967. Despite these warning signs, however, Portland careened toward a similar fate.

After decades of social and political neglect and devastating redevelopment projects, the simmering tensions between the Portland city government and Albina exploded in Irving Park on the evening of July 30, 1967. The day began with a large, nonviolent "Sunday in the Park" rally focused on building community unity and voicing opposition to racist employment, housing, and urban renewal practices. During the week leading up to the demonstration, rumors had circulated throughout the black community that Eldridge Cleaver, author of the best-selling book *Soul on Ice* and one of the leading spokespersons for the Black Panther Party in Oakland, would make an appearance. However, as the day progressed, the rally in the park turned violent. Blacks began throwing rocks and bottles at white passersby, and a few individuals began attacking and vandalizing businesses. According to the *Oregonian*, within a matter of hours, "Roving bands of Negroes, most of them teen-agers, surged through the streets." Portland police arrived shortly thereafter to restore order. In an attempt to regain control as night fell, the mayor imposed a curfew and dispatched four hundred police officers, along with sheriff's deputies, to seal off a thirty-block area around Irving Park. That night, more than twenty fire alarms were reported in the area as revelers looted and firebombed several buildings and businesses. Police arrested nineteen persons whom they suspected of having thrown rocks and bottles. Despite the pervasive vandalism that typically occurs during such disorder, surprisingly little looting took place. And despite cries of "Whitey go home!" police officers in helmets riding four and five to a patrol car kept things under control.[8]

By morning, a calm had fallen over northeast Portland, but more than two hundred African Americans continued to occupy Irving Park and the surrounding areas. The next night, things turned ugly again. Targeting the machinery of urban renewal and city government, unknown culprits set fire to fuel trucks and firebombed the Morris Yard northwest of the park, which housed city equipment. While firefighters raced to contain the massive blaze, Mayor Schrunk ordered police to move past the barricades that they had assembled the previous day around Irving Park, clear the park, and arrest anyone they suspected of being a rabble-rouser. In the aftermath of two nights of vandalism, fires, and confrontations with law enforcement, the *Oregonian* reported that police had shot one man and arrested almost one hundred people, the overwhelming majority of which were black. More than a quarter of those the police arrested were juveniles. As the sun rose the next morning through the smoke-filled air, over looted shops with broken windows, burned-out buildings, and the glass-strewn streets of northeast Portland, people awoke to the realization that the city had just experienced its worst and most destructive disorder to date. All told, ninety-eight people had been arrested, and damages totaled $50,000.[9]

Preferring to portray the upheaval as an abnormal occurrence or a fluke, city leadership and the local media framed the incident as the product of "outside agitators" and emphasized local blacks' firm opposition to violence and Black Power ideologies. The *Oregonian* confidently reported that "Negroes in the Albina area have failed to buy the Black Power revolution theory," citing unsupported rumors that blacks from outside of the state, who had come to Portland with the intent to cause a disturbance, were responsible for the chaos. The Rev. John H. Jackson, pastor of Mt. Olivet Baptist Church, was one of several black notables who promulgated this theory. Rev. Jackson urged parents to keep their children away from the rally and said he was "positive" the disturbances were caused by outside persons. Al Rivers, another longtime Portland resident, averred, "Portland's the best town a Negro can live in on the West Coast. . . . The city could stop this thing in a minute by simply driving these outside trouble makers out of town." Portland police, however, were never able to corroborate the outside agitator rumors. Similarly, Republican governor Tom McCall and Mayor Schrunk were at a loss to explain the violent outburst in Albina, suggesting a possible, but unlikely, connection between the disorders and the failed passage of a school levy in a local election. Ultimately, both the media and elected officials refused to recognize the underlying persistent social problems that had caused the upheaval.[10]

When a delegation of area youth sought to gain an audience with Mayor Schrunk to share their concerns and air their grievances, they were rebuffed. Items on the delegation's wish list had included three hundred jobs, a new and improved school curricula, and a less-invasive police presence in the park and in various sections of Albina. To the dismay of those in attendance, Mayor Schrunk responded by saying that he would not withdraw police from Albina "under the present circumstances," and that he was not in a position to provide jobs or influence school curricula. Many felt that the forty-five-minute meeting with Schrunk was a waste of time. After the meeting, *Oregonian* reporters tracked down several members of the delegation at their headquarters, the "Operation Contact" center on 3928 N. Williams Avenue, and solicited their reactions regarding the meeting. Said Beverly Williams, "The three hundred jobs we asked for aren't any big deal . . . manual labor . . . certainly we are qualified to do manual labor." Unemployment among black males in Portland was especially high. A study by the Oregon State Department of Employment revealed that 8.2 percent of nonwhite males were generally unemployed, compared with 3.7 percent of white males. The disparity was even greater among men between the ages of twenty-four and thirty-five, where 16.6 percent of nonwhite men were unemployed, compared to 6.8 percent of whites. What's more, of 4,188 city employees, only 136 were black. And of the 136, all but 24 were employed in jobs that paid between $194 and $551 per month. Later in the same interview, Williams lamented, "School history books make Negroes look like flunkies. . . . We'd like to see courses that would offer Negroes a better understanding of their heritage." Twenty-year-old Oliver O'Ferrell complained that "the police cause tension by hanging around Irving Park on Sunday afternoons. . . . I think they provoke many of the incidents that happen." O'Ferrell summed up area youths' frustration with the meeting when he understandably quipped, "The mayor said he could not get the curriculum improved, but he said he can get a community college for Albina. I don't understand that."[11]

The *Oregonian*, in shorter articles, also tacitly acknowledged the neglected socioeconomic problems in Albina and noted the growing anger
among African American teenagers in response to these conditions, but
they buried those articles deep within the newspaper and hesitated to suggest that the uprisings were the direct product of such issues. On the morning after the second day of upheaval, a story that got the main headline on
the front page of the *Oregonian*, page sixteen contained a small article on
E. Shelton Hill and the Portland Urban League's call to create more job opportunities for black youth in Albina that was largely ignored. Likewise,
statements by black teens in Albina in the days following the disorder expressing concern that the city's older black leadership "won't listen to what
we have to say and have lost all contact with people on the street" were relegated to page fifteen and ignored as well. Ultimately, despite the persistent
social concerns of young African Americans in northeast Portland, the city
for the most part simply swept problems of racism and urban renewal under the rug. Turning a blind eye to race prejudice and economic inequality
were matters on which Dr. King spent a fair amount of time expounding in
the weeks leading up to his death.[12] King wrote in *Look* magazine, "White
America has allowed itself to be indifferent to race prejudice and economic
denial. It has treated them as superficial blemishes, but now awakes to the
horrifying reality of a potentially fatal disease. The urban outbreaks are a
'fire bell in the light': clamorously warning that the seams of our entire social order are weakening under strains of neglect."[13]

In the wake of the national upheavals of 1967, with the most violent in-
surrections occurring in Detroit and Newark, the federal government established the Report of the National Advisory Commission on Civil Disorders
(known as the Kerner Commission) to study the country's racial problems.
After much deliberation and analysis, members of the Kerner Commission
issued a report recommending that cities end racial isolation, especially in
education. But the economic marginalization, social alienation, and institu-
tional racism identified by the Kerner Report as the causes of the 1967 disorders continued unabated in Portland and contributed to the frustration
felt by many of the city's African Americans. As the summer of 1967 turned
to autumn, black leadership within the Portland community kept up pressure on the PDC to incorporate the black community's voice in the Model
Cities planning process. During public meetings held by the PDC throughout Albina in late 1967, hundreds of neighborhood residents turned out to
call, often heatedly, for the need for citizen participation at all levels of the

planning process. In particular, African Americans demanded a black director of the program, offering E. Shelton Hill of the Urban League and Tom Vickers of the NAACP as possible candidates. However, to the surprise and dismay of many, the PDC once again ignored the black community's voice and instead selected Rev. Paul Schulze, a white Albina minster and head of the Church-Community Action Program (C-CAP). Prior to his appointment as director of the Model Cities program, Schulze had been director of community services for the Portland Interfaith Council of Churches, where he helped congregations establish programs to counter racism and to meet the needs of poverty-stricken residents. The Lutheran pastor was believed to be an experienced bridge builder, having well served congregations in Washington, Oregon, and California.[14]

In the days following the appointment of Schulze, black residents hit the streets with newsletters and flyers attacking the Model Cities program and the PDC. One widely circulated newsletter, "The Spirithouse Rap," called upon the residents of Albina and Portland "to recognize that the Model Cities Program is one of those rare historic moments where the problems confronting a people comes [sic] into sharp focus.... The MCP, unless it is halted NOW—will follow other Urban Renewal (Negro Removal) programs in this city ... like the Memorial Coliseum, where black people were forced out to build a 'palace' for them (whites) and an Emanuel Hospital addition for them (Emanuel Hospital is a place for black people to die, not to be cured)." Likening the Model Cities program to previous urban renewal projects of the postwar era, the newsletter's authors viewed the selection of a white program director as another instance of discrimination or indifference. The newsletter encouraged black residents to support local black-owned businesses and to protest at upcoming public Model Cities meetings. Similarly, an anonymous flyer posted around the Portland State College (PSC) campus called the PDC "a small group of self-selected volunteers from the rich friends of City Hall" and described PDC chairman Ira Keller as a millionaire "outsider" from Chicago. Moreover, the flyer claimed, "Students, workers and community people must join together, fight back and win honest POWER TO THE PEOPLE." In light of this sudden and intense backlash against Model Cities and the PDC, Portland's political leadership found itself in the middle of a quickly escalating conflict in Albina.[15]

The city held two public meetings in response to Schulze's appointment. At the first meeting, Schulze's appointment was approved by those in attendance. The second meeting, however, proved more eventful; as attendees demanded a recall by signing a statement demanding that all permanent appointments for positions of planning and coordination be rescinded until a duly elected citizen's board representing the Albina target area approve such appointments and plans. Mayor Schrunk responded by denying the recall while at the same time conceding that he would consider more grassroots participation. The appointment stood. The next order of business was to establish a governing body—the Citizens Planning Board (CPB). As a compromise between the mayor and community residents, the planning board was given the power to veto decisions made by the mayor and the city council, but was not afforded the power to initiate decisions of any kind.

Despite many blacks' disapproval of the choice of Schulze and intense vitriol directed toward the PDC and Model Cities, Schulze focused the majority of his efforts on making Model Cities work for all of Albina's residents by bringing the black community's voice into the discussion through the creation of the CPB. At a public meeting with Albina residents on January 4, 1968, Schulze attempted to assuage concerns by constructing a temporary handpicked advisory committee consisting of local black leadership and involved citizens that included individuals such as Tom Vickers, the chairman of the Urban League Education Committee, and grassroots activists like Tom Wilson, a former member of the Albina Citizen's War on Poverty Committee. In addition, Schulze pledged that in March of that same year each neighborhood would have the opportunity to elect local representatives to the board, which would replace the original committee and would assist the director in the creation of Model Cities programs and policies. On March 2, 1968, nearly 1,800 out of the nearly 30,000 total residents of Albina turned out to elect two representatives from each of the eight neighborhoods to the sixteen-person board. Nine of the sixteen were African American. Mayor Schrunk then appointed six whites and five African Americans. All told, the board consisted of five unemployed women (two of whom were African American), an African American contractor, a white roofer, two white bankers, two African American entrepreneurs, two African American social workers, an African American deputy sheriff, a white attorney, a white printer, four clergy (two of whom were African American), three primary school teachers (two of whom were African American), a white secondary school administrator in a suburb of Portland, an African American housing director, an African American job placement counselor, and a white assistant commissioner of the Oregon Bureau of Labor. When Kent Ford, the eventual leader of Portland's Black Panthers, was asked why neither he nor any member of his cadre attempted to position themselves for an appointment on the board, he responded, "The powers that be weren't going to allow any of us to get on that board . . . anyway, Tom Wilson, who was an ally of ours, was already on it, so we had that base covered, as much as you could have it covered."[16]

On Wednesday, April 4, the work of the PDC and the Model Cities program was placed on hold when Dr. Martin Luther King, Jr., was assassinated in Memphis, Tennessee, amid his efforts to support striking sanitation workers. In their award-winning book *Ghetto Revolts*, Joe Feagin and Harlan Hahn note that in the month after King was murdered, no less than 202 disorders occurred in 172 cities, resulting in 27,000 arrests, 3,500 persons injured, and 43 killed. Some whites understood the frustration felt by blacks, who for years had put up with being socially, politically, and economically marginalized but now had to deal with having their leaders snatched from them. Two days after Dr. King's murder, Eldridge Cleaver wrote an essay titled "Requiem for Nonviolence" in which he said that the murder of King marked the "final repudiation by white America of any hope of reconciliation" with blacks. Not everyone could appreciate the circumstances that, left to simmer over time, eventually boiled over with King's murder.[17]

Fortunately for Portland and its residents, the city escaped unscathed, despite the prognostications of a Northwestern University professor who conducted a quantitative study of eighty-five cities and found that of those, Portland was twenty-first on the riot list. Of the fourteen cities west of the Rocky Mountains, Portland was rated third most likely to experience upheaval. Still, the impact of King's murder on the residents of Portland was not inconsiderable. One of the most visible signs of restlessness occurred at Jefferson High School. Despite having a student body of 2,000 students, 38 percent of which were African American, the school had only one black teacher and one black counselor. On Friday, April 6, classes at Jefferson High School were cancelled, mainly because students refused to go to class, choosing instead to roam the halls. That morning, fires were set in the school's laboratories, and there were a few skirmishes between students. School officials responded by cancelling school for the first two days of the following week. When classes resumed, Mayor Schrunk beefed up security by sending in extra police officers. Racial tensions continued to simmer throughout the remainder of the school year, and, as a result, the Portland Public School District considered permanently closing the school.[18]

Portland's black leaders responded to the news of King's death by issuing a renewed commitment to unity in their fight for racial equality. This was evident in a statement offered by Dennis Payne, president of the Black Student Union at Portland Community College. Speaking for the Black United Front, a newly created consortium of twenty-one black organizations, Payne said, in part, "Last night Martin Luther King, the black Moses, was assassinated. We must work for the . . . freedoms, the rights and the justice that our black brother, Martin Luther King died for." Jimmy "Bang Bang" Walker, editor of the *Clarion Defender*, a black-owned newspaper, warned against retaliatory violence and, in Kinglike fashion, urged the African American community to "forgive the white race for the unjust things they have done to us in the past and work to fulfill Dr. King's wishes by gaining our just place in society." Many in the African American community were eager to demonstrate their commitment to King's philosophy of nonviolence, and several marches took place over the next several days. On Saturday, April 6, a racially mixed gathering of approximately 500 people participated in a memorial march through downtown Portland. Students at the local colleges and universities held a "silent march" through the city to honor King. A group of 125 students from Portland State College, Portland Community College, Reed College, the University of Portland, and other neighboring schools marched on Tuesday, April 9. Meanwhile, memorial services took place in numerous churches throughout the city. Portland's public schools and all Catholic schools were closed, as were many businesses throughout Albina. The largest memorial service occurred on Sunday, April 7, at the Vancouver Avenue First Baptist Church. More than 1,000 residents were in attendance, including a number of well-known dignitaries. Governor Tom McCall was one of them.[19]

As the shock of King's assassination began to dissipate, PDC and Model Cities work resumed. Throughout the summer of 1968, the CPB sent out weekly mailers across Albina to announce public working committees on topics ranging from housing and physical planning to health, environment, education, and public safety. On the one-year anniversary of the 1967 uprising, the CPB held a Model Cities rally in Irving Park to encourage citizen participation in the construction of education and neighborhood development plans. As the residents of Albina increasingly found a voice in the CPB and its working committees, Schulze happily reported to the *Oregonian* that the Model Cities program was finally engaging with Portland's black community and creating a new generation of black leadership within the city's government and urban apparatus.[20]

Although, prior to King's death, some African Americans had warmed to the idea of Schulze as director of Model Cities, the call for a black director grew louder from those who had opposed the appointment in the first place, and so, despite his increasing favorability among some blacks, Schulze announced his resignation as director in October. In a departing interview with the *Oregonian*, he reaffirmed the program's growing successes and his continued optimistic vision for the future. In the interview, Schulze maintained that no one had asked him to resign, and added, "I had the technical skills to do what has been done up to now. I don't feel I have the technical skills to put the thing together from here on out." Schulze also expressed confidence that Mayor Schrunk would appoint an African American as the next director of Model Cities and noted, "Never again will key appointments be made without sufficient community advice. Important bridges have been built between the 'power structure' and the community, and I take pride in having been a part of that process."[21] The preoccupation with Model Cities' having a black director is indicative of the mood of black America at that time. On a local level, there was little black representation in Portland at any level of government at that time. There was a dearth of black political representation not only in the city but also across the state. For example, there were no black members of the Oregon State Legislature, either in the thirty-member house or the sixty-member senate.

Meanwhile, the end of 1968 saw ominous changes in Portland and the rest of the nation. The United States was deeply divided, as evidenced by Richard Nixon's narrow margin of victory in the presidential election. Drawing on racially coded "law and order" rhetoric, Nixon won by the slimmest margin since 1912, edging out Hubert Humphrey 43.4 percent to 42.7 percent in the popular vote, but winning the Electoral College (including Oregon's six electoral votes) 301 to 191. Also telling was the 13.5 percent of the vote captured by the American Independent Party candidate and former Alabama governor George Wallace, who appealed to white resentment and fears of unrestrained civil rights activists and antiwar demonstrators. Feeding on the white backlash to black urban outbursts, the antiblack demagogue secured nearly as many votes in the North as he did in the South in what was then the best showing of a third-party candidate since 1924. "On November 5," Wallace had predicted, "they're going to find out there are a lot of rednecks in this country." The Wallace campaign raised more money than anyone had expected—more than $9 million during the 1967–68 campaign cycle, mostly from small private donors. Although Nixon was not the self-identified and avowed racist that Wallace was, his overall campaign message was no less polarizing. Spiro Agnew, Nixon's running mate, chided Democrats for being "soft on inflation, soft on Communism, and soft on law and order." Nixon warned that crime would double within a year if the "soft on criminals" Democrats retained the presidency. He was convinced that the Warren court favored "the criminal forces over the peace forces," and he pledged to appoint "strict constructionist" judges who understood that their charge was to interpret the law, not make the law.[22]

Back in Portland, following Schulze's resignation as the Model Cities director, the program entered a period of uncertainty and instability as the PDC struggled to maintain funding and find a permanent director. On December 1, Kenneth Gervais, assistant director of the Urban Studies Center at Portland State College, became the program's temporary head and immediately drafted a comprehensive plan. Shortly thereafter, the program entered a period of crisis. When submitted to the city council on December 16, 1968, the "Comprehensive City Demonstration Plan" drafted by the Model Cities' CPB and the residents of northeast Portland shocked and outraged conservative members of the council. The report specifically outlined the history of racial discrimination in Albina and targeted agencies like the PDC for their destructive approach to urban renewal in the 1950s and 1960s. Commissioner Francis Ivancie, who served Mayor Schrunk on the planning commission, was particularly appalled with the proposal and edited the document to remove any reference to Albina as a "ghetto." "Portland was a racist city," Gervais said of the council's reaction, "but the thing that made Portland unique was that we were in total denial that there was any racism here." Moreover, with the election of President Nixon, the city of Portland only had until January 20, 1969, to submit its final program proposal and gain federal approval before running out of funding under the Johnson administration. Consequently, the city council and the PDC found themselves pressed for time in resolving their differences with the Model Cities' CPB and the PSC's Urban Studies Center. Moreover, due to bureaucratic disagreements about the report's data between city council members and CPB allies at the Urban Studies Center, Keller delayed the vote on the proposal, and the city council announced that it could not meet the deadline before the end of January.[23]

In the midst of the proposal and funding crisis, a rift developed between Keller and Professor Lyndon Musolf, head of the Urban Studies Center and Gervais's boss, after Keller accused Musolf and Gervais of "promoting dissidence and regional, local and racial jealousies" in the city to undermine the power of the PDC. Keller even went so far as to make a public demand for PSC president Gregory Wolfe to review Musolf's and Gervais's performances and the necessity of their positions. Ultimately, despite delays and concerns that the Nixon administration might discontinue the project's funding, HUD approved the Model Cities program proposal in February 1969. Still, the PDC and PSC had begun a two-year struggle to share control of the Model Cities. As a result, despite the continued existence of the CPB, which the PDC now viewed as a threat to their control over planning in northeast Portland, the voices of Albina once again became lost, as the district lacked a local representative to head the program.

The PDC's inability to steer the Model Cities program through a difficult transition or to engage with Albina's black population on a meaningful level heated frustrations to yet another boiling point during the summer of 1969. In the early hours of June 14, violence once again erupted throughout Albina after Portland police arrested large numbers of black teenagers. What began as a few large groups of black youth congregating in isolated areas throughout northeast Portland quickly escalated as police attempted to disperse the groups. In an *Oregonian* article, George Davis, night manager at Lidio's (a popular drive-in restaurant on Union Avenue and Shaver Street) is quoted saying that he saw police beat youngsters with their clubs. He went on to state that he was strictly neutral: "I stay out of all this trouble." Capt. William Taylor, commander of the north precinct, denied Davis's charge, claiming that "if there was any brutality practiced, it was against our officers.... I'm sure there were some blows struck by our officers—but they were in self-defense." Exactly what caused things to get out of hand is unclear, but as police abrasively commanded loiterers to go home, blacks began attacking predominately white-owned businesses in the neighborhood, and within a few hours, fires and clashes with police spread rapidly throughout the area.[24]

For five days, scattered pockets of violence and fire engulfed parts of northeast Portland as police struggled to put down insurrectionists. Caught in the cross fire was Jimmy "Bang Bang" Walker, who was beaten by police officers after he failed to disperse when ordered to do so. During the melee, police officers confiscated his camera and smashed it on the ground. Walker claimed that he was on assignment. Police officers accused Walker of having provoked them by yelling obscenities in their direction. Walker's injuries were serious enough that he had to be hospitalized for several days.

He criticized the police for their handling of the situation and for their mistreatment of him. Not long after the incident, much to the chagrin of some residents, huge billboards in support of the Portland Police Bureau appeared throughout the north and northeast sections of the city. The billboards featured a photo of Walker with the words: "We should support the men in blue, because they will always protect you." At one point Portland police withdrew their heavy-handed presence from the neighborhood to see if tempers would cool. As the police backed down, calm slowly returned to the Albina district, with its smoldering and wrecked shops and homes. However, just as tensions appeared to be easing, black resistance to the PDC and Model Cities took an unexpected turn with the seemingly innocuous arrest of one man during the upheaval.[25]

On the muggy evening of Friday, June 13, 1969, shorty before the city became enveloped in disorder, twenty-six-year-old Kent Ford, Tommy Mills, and Percy Hampton were driving south down Union Avenue when a confrontation between police officers and a group of African American youth caught their attention. Curious, Ford stopped his car, walked over to see what was happening, and noticed one of the boys sitting in the back of the police cruiser while the police confronted the others. From what he could gather, the young men had been throwing dice in the Lidio's parking lot. In the heat of the moment, Ford made a bold decision. He flung open the back door of the squad car and told the boy to run home to his mother. "He couldn't have been more than ten years old," said Ford. As the boy bolted, two officers whirled around and attempted to apprehend Ford, at which point a fistfight broke out. By that time, half a dozen police officers had surrounded Ford. After several minutes of struggle, six officers maced Ford, placed him in handcuffs, and threw him into the backseat of the cruiser. The cruiser headed south on Union Avenue, and moments later pulled into the McDonald's parking lot, where officers got out of their vehicle and started conversing. By then there were anywhere from fifteen to twenty officers on the scene. One of them spotted Ford chewing something and yelled out, "He's swallowing something!" The same officer then yanked open the door and another officer dragged Ford out by his feet, causing him to hit his head on the asphalt. One officer then stuck his finger in Ford's mouth to ascertain what he was chewing. Ford bit down on the officer's finger, causing him to jump up and down and yelp, "He's got my finger! He's got my finger!" Ford then quickly consumed the marijuana that he had had in his possession, knowing that it would only have given the police another criminal count with which to charge him. Outraged by his defiance, the officers proceeded to beat Ford as he lay on the ground. The officers then hauled Ford, bloodied and subdued, to the police station downtown, where they charged him with "rioting" and attempt to "incite a riot."[26]

Dave Dawson, co-owner of the House of Sounds record store, originally bailed Ford out on Saturday morning, June 14. Over the course of the next twenty-four hours, Dawson and Ford plotted their next move. They decided to contact Vern Summers, the assistant human relations director for the city of Portland. Ford recalls,

> We figured he could help us . . . so we went to Vern's house on Sunday morn-
> ing and knocked on his door and asked to speak to him. . . . He graciously
> invited us in, and we sat down in the living room. We told him what hap-
> pened. . . . I showed him my bruises, how the police tore my shirt and leather
> jacket, and ripped my pants. My face was all red from the mace they used on
> me. Summers blurted out, "They must have thought you were a Black Pan-
> ther or something," to which I responded, "Whether I am a Black Panther or
> not they had no right to do me like this." . . . Summers listened and then said,
> "I'll look into it." . . . A week went by without a response, then two weeks, no
> response, then we contacted him again a month later, no response. By then
> we realized that Summers wasn't going to do anything to help.

"Looking back on the whole situation, my biggest mistake of all," said Ford jokingly, "was letting go of that cop's finger. . . . When I let go, they all pounced on me." Rance Spruill, director of the C-CAP, said, "I remember the incident. . . . I happened to be walking through the neighborhood, and I saw Kent standing in the parking lot of McDonald's with handcuffs on. Then two officers, one on each side, picked him up off the ground and tossed him in the back seat of the police car and drove off."[27]

Upon arrest, Ford was hit with the charge of "riot" but was later acquitted in Multnomah County Circuit Court in February 1970. Testimony during the one-day trial benefitted Ford and his lawyer. The point on which US District Court judge Alfred T. Goodwin focused was whether handcuffs were placed on Ford before leaving the scene of arrest or in transit. After listening to the testimony of someone whom he believed to be a disinterested bystander, Judge Goodwin ruled that "Mr. Ford was handcuffed at the time he was dragged out of the car." In light of this finding, the judge submitted that there was then "no valid excuse for applying force and violence to him after he was under control. . . . I find that officers Ronald Hegge and Lt. Lawrence Brown violated the plaintiff's rights and that he is entitled to some damages." While Judge Goodwin recognized that Ford's injuries were minor, he nevertheless awarded him $1,000 in damages for "indignities" suffered. He added another $5,000 punitive damages "because it is time the community realizes that the police are not free to inflict punishment."[28]

Weeks earlier, on January 25, 1970, Ford and his supporters held a mock trial foreshadowing his acquittal. The "People's Court," as it was called, was held at the Albina Arts Center at 14 NE Killingsworth Street, and it garnered the attention of the alternative press, the *Willamette Bridge*, which printed a notice for the mock trial in its January 16–22 issue. According to a police intelligence report, there were "approximately 150 people in attendance, 1/3rd black and 2/3rds white." R. L. Anderson, another local activist who was known for having a flair for the dramatic, arrived draped in a long, flowing robe and served as the judge and master of ceremonies. Nick Chaivoe, Ford's attorney of record, did not participate, choosing instead to sit among the audience and observe the proceedings. During the ninety-minute affair, several attendees proffered verbal testimony of abrasive encounters with police officers, while others submitted depositions of varying kinds. Among the individuals who testified were Percy Hampton and John Duehart, both of whom had been right in the thick of it that fateful June evening. It was proposed that "a petition should be circulated demanding the removal of certain police officers, including officers Traversi, McNabb, Stan Harmon, Clyde Harmon, Cox, and Kanzler" from the Albina area. Kent Ford remembers being struck by "the seriousness with which people took this exercise . . . the people who attended this were not treating it lightly." Based on the prosecutor's lack of evidence, the evening culminated in Ford's acquittal. After the verdict was read, attendees partook of a delicious meal of barbeque chicken and potato salad prepared by a local culinary wizard by the name of Robert "Bob" Frost.[29]

While the June 13 arrest was one of many to which Ford would be subjected in the years to come, it is not inconceivable that this particular arrest was in part the result of an overzealous police bureau that was hell-bent on ensuring order in anticipation of the First Lady's impending visit on June 16. Over the course of the two–day visit, Pat Nixon and her daughter, Julie Eisenhower, toured various parts of Portland, one of which was Albina, to get a sense of the volunteer efforts in which people were involved. It is possible that the police sweep in the part of town where Ford was arrested was part of a plan by the city fathers to put the best possible face on their fair city in anticipation of their distinguished guests. It should be noted, however, that Ford was not unknown to the police prior to the night of June 13, 1969. Two years earlier, two Portland police officers who were investigating a break-in in a building in which Ford lived felt compelled, after meeting him, to draft a report on him titled "Possible Subversive Subject." Ford remembers that day well:

> I had an apartment at 23 NE San Rafael back then, and there was a break-in. One of my upstairs neighbors called the police after we realized that someone had forced open a basement window. The officers knocked on the door. I answered it, and after a minute or so of conversation I invited them in. Once they were in the apartment their demeanor changed. Back then I had a lot of books and photos of various figures posted on my walls. I had framed photos of Malcolm X and Dr. King on the wall. There was also a picture of a bombing in Vietnam on the wall over my desk with a caption that read "Will this ever end?" I told them that I was missing $1,000, but they seemed more interested in the materials I had laying around than in investigating the burglary. We had a conversation that lasted no more than five minutes.... I never did see them write anything down ... then they left, no "we'll be in touch," no nothing.

In the report, the officers noted "two large poster size pictures of Ho Chi Minh, Presidence [sic] of Viet Nam, and the other of Mao, the Premier of Community China" and "numerous pamphlets and literature, which appeared to be concerning Black Power, and this sort of thing." The officers also pointed out that Ford had many books scattered about his apartment, "one of which was titled 'White Man Beware.'" This report suggests that the officers believed Ford to be someone on whom a close eye should be kept.[30]

Kent Ford was born in Maringouin, Louisiana, in 1943, the oldest of four children. When Ford was an infant, the family moved to Detroit and stayed there until he was seven years old. While there, Ford's father, previously a Pullman porter, went to work at the Kaiser-Frazer automotive plant. Several years later, Ford's parents split up. Ford and his siblings went with their mother back to Iberville Parish in Louisiana, where Ford had been born. His father remained in Detroit. In the mid-1950s, Ford's mother remarried and moved her children to California, finally putting down stakes in South Richmond, where Ford's stepfather, an Army veteran, found work at the Mare Island Naval Shipyard in Vallejo, California. After spending his freshman year at El Cerrito High School, Ford transferred, along with his younger sister, to Harry Ells High School. In high school, Ford picked up a job selling candy door-to-door, a job he kept from 1958 to 1961. "There were twenty-four boxes of candy in a case . . . Donna Lee mints, Butterfingers, Baby Ruths, stuff like that," Ford recalls. "I could sell a case of candy in about an hour and a half. I'd start at 4:00 p.m. and get off at 7:00 p.m. . . . I met all kinds of people." With an income of forty to fifty dollars a week, Ford was earning more than some adults. Much of the money Ford earned went toward clothing and other items for his siblings, and after helping out with bills as well, he had little left for himself. Consequently, by the time Ford graduated in 1961 he had not saved much.[31]

Weeks after graduating from high school, Ford received a ticket for driving fifteen miles over the speed limit and spent three days in jail. He had just turned eighteen. Following this incident, he chose to leave the Bay Area and moved to Portland in search of better job opportunities. After being in Portland for three months, Ford moved back to South Richmond. Two months later, believing that Seattle was a good market for selling candy, Ford moved to the state of Washington. Over the next eighteen months Ford canvassed the city with a crew consisting of a dozen teenagers, selling candy door-to-door. In the summer of 1962, Ford left Seattle and headed to Arizona, but no sooner had he rented an apartment than he was on the go again. Ford said, "I left Arizona for two reasons . . . first, racism in Arizona was too much. . . . Whites in Phoenix and Scottsdale made whites in the South look like school kids, especially whites in North Phoenix." Phoenix's African American population numbered just 25,119 in 1960 and comprised a mere 3.8 percent of the metropolitan area. The overwhelming majority of blacks, moreover, were concentrated in racially homogenous neighborhoods south of downtown, away from the more affluent white neighborhoods. The second reason Ford left, he said, was that "I would start selling candy in the morning, but because it was so hot, by the afternoon the remaining candy would melt in the boxes . . . it was just too hot there."[32]

Ford returned to Seattle, which proved to be a lucrative market for a door-to-door salesman. "I pulled in about five hundred dollars a week; that was good money back then. . . . This time I stayed in Seattle for about a year," said Ford. "Everything was going well until word circulated that this Kent Ford guy was raking in good money, then all of a sudden people started coming out of the woodwork and setting up their own free market enterprises and that saturated the market," he recalled.[33] Rather than compete with this new crop of entrepreneurs, Ford returned to Portland. In many ways, the pastures were no greener in Portland than they were in the Bay Area—or anywhere else for that matter. In Portland, blacks were subjugated not only economically but politically and socially, and the police played a key role in black people's plight.

Over the next few years, Ford would continue in his enterprising ways by selling candy door-to-door. His fortunes turned when he was hired on full time as a computer operator for a Safeway distribution center in Clackamas, a suburb of Portland. A computer data processing course at a local business school prepared Ford for the position. "I worked for Safeway from 1966 to 1968," said Ford. "I worked the graveyard shift. When I got off, I went home, took a nap, ate, and got ready to go sell candy." Ford continued selling candy because it supplemented his income, but he enjoyed his position as a computer operator. Still, Ford had greater aspirations. He wanted something bigger and better—he just didn't know what.

> Initially I had hopes of going to college. Reverend Booker T. Anderson, head pastor at Easter Hill Methodist Church, the church I attended in California as a youth, had graduated from the University of the Pacific [in Stockton, California], and he wanted me to go there as well. He also thought I should take up the ministry. He would take me, along with several other guys, to conferences and football games at the University of the Pacific.... I ended up being offered an academic scholarship, but didn't accept it because I had to find work to support the family.... Since I was the oldest child, it was sort of expected that I would help support the family.[34]

In the ensuing years, Ford made several trips to the Bay Area to visit his mother, who by then had moved to Emeryville, yet he had not come across the Black Panther Party. "I had heard bits and pieces about this new group called the Black Panther Party, but that's about it," said Ford. It was not until a caseworker for the state of Oregon brought Ford's attention to an article in the *New York Times Magazine* about the Panthers' 1967 protest in Sacramento that he began to put all the pieces together. "I saw the photo of the Panthers standing on the steps of the capital and I was astonished," said Ford. "Two of the guys in the photo were guys I went to high school with. Also, I still had friends and relatives back in the Bay Area.... When I spoke to them, I learned that after the protest, the party was the talk of the town...."

When I went back to my apartment, I couldn't get the party out of my mind . . . it was all I could think about." The image of black men and women in black leather jackets, carrying guns in defense of black people's right to arm themselves, prompted Ford to think long and hard about the movement and about his role in it.[35]

The previous year Ford had met two men who claimed to be members of the Student Nonviolent Coordinating Committee (SNCC) and had participated in civil rights work in the South. Ford started hanging around them, thinking that he might perhaps join them if they were doing something for the people.

> After interacting with them a half dozen times at something called the Black
> Impact Meetings,[36] . . . a gathering of supposed change agents who convened
> at a warehouse down on Williams Avenue, . . . I realized that they weren't
> for me. . . . They would try to get people in the power structure to meet with
> them. . . . One of the people who came to the meetings was Shag Thomas, an
> African American and well-known professional wrestler. Of the folk who
> came to the meetings the only one who was serious was Shag. . . . When he
> took a stance he stood by it. I didn't see this from the others; all they wanted
> to do was sit around and philosophize all day; they were all talk and no
> action, so I knew they weren't for me, so I quit hanging with them.[37]

The more Ford learned of the Black Panther Party, the more he began to think that he might have found what he was looking for. Ford shared his preoccupation with Tommy Mills, an Army veteran who had done two tours in Vietnam. Awarded the Silver Star for gallantry as a tank gunner, as well as the Air Medal with three oak leaf clusters, Mills was a decorated veteran who had been in Vietnam when the Viet Cong attacked the Pleiku airbase on February 6, 1965, an attack that left eight Americans dead and 128 wounded, and prompted the United States to launch Operation Flaming Dart against North Vietnam in retaliation. Mills's discharge from the army could not have been timelier. By the time he met Ford, the number of American troops sent to Vietnam had surged from two hundred thousand in 1966 to nearly five hundred thousand in 1967. By 1967, there were 3,384,000 men and women in the US military. Of that number, approximately 10 percent, or 303,000, were black. Given the rate at which black males were being drafted into the military, finding willing and able bodies for Ford's plan to open a branch of the BPP would not be easy.

Ford met Mills in 1966 at the Theme Tavern, an establishment on Union Avenue owned by a black beatnik, where one could find socially conscious blacks debating the issues of the day. According to Ford, "Tommy liked to go there to play chess. . . . He and I hit it off immediately. . . . When we'd run into one another, we'd talk about the current situation in Portland where black folks were concerned." Ford and Mills became fast friends, hanging out more frequently and going to the Reed College bookstore, the Sportsman Barber Shop, and the House of Sounds, where they listened to recordings of Malcolm X speeches. "The owners of the House of Sounds and the Sportsman Barber Shop were sympathetic to the party's cause," said Percy Hampton. Ford admitted that Mills was not all that politically inclined at first. "Mills was more concerned with making a living after returning from overseas. . . . In fact, when I met him, he was working at S & H Green Stamps over on 42nd and Sandy Boulevard." As a result, Ford said, "I didn't bombard him with a lot of political talk at the beginning, because I wanted to feel him out and that took some time. . . . Then, around 1967, Tommy and I began engaging in political work, such as raising bail money for people who we believed the police were unjustifiably singling out."[38]

In 1968, Ford and Mills started holding community meetings at Martin Luther King Elementary School; they offered political education (PE) classes there as well, an idea they appropriated from the Black Panther Party in Oakland. The classes were scheduled on Wednesday and Sunday evenings, usually starting around 7:00 and lasting until everyone had had enough. Over time the classes evolved. Although members were required to attend and the classes were open to the public, attendance varied from week to week. Sandra Ford, an early member of the group and eventual wife of Kent Ford, remembers that the classes "were always sparsely attended." Kent Ford, on the other hand, recalls the classes being "well attended during the early years, but by the mid 1970s attendance started to suffer." Sometimes people would come from as far away as Salem, Oregon, to attend the classes. Each week's topic of discussion depended on what was going on at the time, both locally and nationally. Said Sandra Ford, "Subjects varied from local concerns to world concerns, history of various revolutionary movements around the world, and historical figures." A constant throughout was the use of some of the more popular books within left-wing circles. Among the most frequently used texts and documents were *The Autobiography of Malcolm X*, Frantz Fanon's *The Wretched of the Earth*, and Mao Tse-tung's *Red Book*. These were considered must-reads within the Black Panther Party. During one session, one attendee and eventual Portland Panther, Tom Venters, became so visibly moved by the reading of "The Foolish Old Man Who Removed the Mountains" from the *Selected Works* of Mao Tse-tung that he was nearly brought to tears. The fable tells of an old man who lived in Northern China. His house faced south, and beyond his door, in all of their grandeur, stood two great peaks, Taihang and Wangwu, obstructing the path ahead. The foolish old man called his sons, and with nothing but a hoe and great determination they began to dig up the two mountains. A wise old man saw them and said derisively, "How silly of you to do this! It is quite impossible for you few to dig up these two huge mountains." To which the foolish old man replied, "When I die, my sons will carry on; when they die, there will be my grandsons, and then their sons and grandsons, and so on to infinity. High as they are, the mountains cannot grow any higher, and with every bit we dig, they will be that much lower."[39]

The group also had an affinity for Fidel Castro, whose "History Will Absolve Me" speech resonated with Ford and the others. After all, Castro and Che Guevara were two of the few radicals who had successfully carried out a revolution in the Western Hemisphere. More often than not, the PE classes were conducted by Kent Ford, Percy Hampton, or Oscar Johnson, another early leader within the group. When the men were pulled away for some unforeseen reason, Sandra Ford or other consistent members like Linda Thornton might be pressed into duty. "Whenever I taught PE classes, the discussion revolved around the differences between Eastern and Western cultures" said Sandra Ford. While this may be true, one of the branch's rank-and-file members remembers well what Sandra Ford taught. Yvonne Joe, who joined the group when she was in her early twenties, recalls that the prevailing theme during the classes that Kent Ford taught was "the importance of standing up for what you believe in and defending yourself when necessary.... When Sandra was in charge, she talked a lot about how women should carry themselves in public and private . . . how to dress . . . how to be a wife. I learned so much about life from her that I passed on to my kids and grandkids." Unlike in some other party branches and chapters, the PE classes in Portland were conducted in a rather relaxed atmosphere. There was no anxiety or intimidation associated with attending the classes, as there was in other Panther branches and chapters throughout the country. "We didn't get off into dialectical materialism like they were doing in Oakland . . . that stuff was just too deep for the clientele we were dealing with," said Kent Ford.[40]

At the Portland classes, there was no pressure to know all the answers, and no use of the Socratic method—being an active participant in the discussions was voluntary. "There were times when some audience members chose to listen and not read or discuss the material.... That was okay with us ... we just wanted to keep people informed and to help raise their consciousness," said Ford. "We believed as Fidel Castro said, 'The weapon of today is not guns but consciousness.'" To keep discussions fresh and lively, instructors might deviate from the standard texts and pore over the Black Panther Party's "Ten-Point Platform and Program," read from Huey Newton's "Executive Mandate No. 1," or discuss issues that were close to home, such as Emanuel Hospital's encroachment on the black community or police brutality in northeast Portland. Although politics lay at the center of the PE classes, the sessions were not limited to sharing information. Instead, much of the discourse could be characterized as a search for moral knowledge, a sort of political philosophizing. In other words, the classes were intended not so much to get people to understand how people and governments behave but rather how they themselves ought to behave. If a student of politics studies reality in an attempt to explain its functioning, the political philosopher goes a step further by studying ideas and trying to discover which have the greatest moral validity. Indeed, psychologist Naim Akbar asserts that inadequate amounts of the proper kinds of knowledge can be injurious to the mind's development. Learning how to think for oneself, therefore, is paramount. As a result, reading was strongly encouraged in the classes as a means of increasing one's knowledge base and developing one's analytical and critical thinking skills. Aaron Dixon, founder of the Seattle chapter of the BPP, remembers when he first approached founding member Bobby Seale about starting a chapter. Seale gave him a list of twenty-five books and told him that all members were required to read two hours a day.[41]

Like the Italian Marxist Antonio Gramsci, the Portland Panthers were trying to create a community of working-class intellectuals who actively participated in matters that affected their lives. Gramsci believed in the innate capacity of all men and women to understand the world and their place in it with an eye toward changing it. In *Selections from the Prison Notebooks*, Gramsci contended that revolutionaries had to be critical and was clear that "the starting point of critical elaboration is the consciousness of what one really is." Those who led PE classes in Portland were the kind of informal educators he had envisioned: people who worked tirelessly in their communities and were fully invested in their neighborhoods. Of the two types of intellectuals about which Gramsci wrote—the traditional and the organic intellectual—the Portland cadre most resembled the organic intellectual, or those thinkers and instructors who grow organically alongside the ruling class. However, they were produced by the educational system designed to help the ruling class maintain its hegemony. While members of the Portland cadre may have undoubtedly started out as such organic intellectuals, over time, in the tradition of the early twentieth-century African American scholar Carter G. Woodson, they reeducated themselves and in turn sought, in the words of the Nation of Islam's Elijah Muhammad, to go about the business of completely reprogramming the thinking processes of the American black. For Gramsci, intellectuals were more than simply scholars or teachers in the traditional sense, they were ordinary men and women who developed and sustained relationships with local residents, who came to see such intellectuals as stalwarts actively involved in their personal and professional growth. Gramsci maintained, "The relationships between these informal educators must always be active and creative, just as the relation of the worker to his tools is active and creative." Like Gramsci, the Portland Panthers envisioned the growth of a community of organic intellectuals, culled from the working-class residents of Albina, who would dedicate themselves to creating the kind of counterhegemony needed to dismantle the city's entrenched political, social, and economic order.[42]

While the Portland cadre may have believed that everyone had the potential to be an intellectual or an agent of change, Kent Ford was quick to note that "the speed at which people learn or grasp things intellectually varies.... It takes some longer than others.... Some are more willing than others.... You have to put in the work.... There's a lot of self-introspection that has to take place." He went on, "A lot of the people we were dealing with had a very limited vocabulary, so we wanted to help them expand their vocabulary." Ford's position is reminiscent of something Stokely Carmichael once said about black Americans: "Every Negro is a *potential* black man." But only those willing to be challenged intellectually and to engage in the laborious work of self-reflection and the rigors of soul searching on a consistent basis over a long period of time will graduate to a higher level of consciousness. Only those who are committed to this type of hard work and who understand the importance of recognizing on whose shoulders they stand are apt to make the necessary transformation from "Negro" to "Black man" or from mere "being" to "intellectual."[43]

It should be noted that for some people, the Panthers' PE classes were an adult version of Reading Is Fundamental (RIF), the 1966 program that nurtured in kids a love of reading and learning. Kent Ford acknowledges that not everyone who attended the classes could read.

> There were a few community people who were semi-illiterate. It was especially important that we not only encouraged them to read but in some cases teach them how to read. At the end of the day, however, we could do all the teaching we wanted, but ultimately the person had to put in the work. They couldn't wait until we held PE classes thinking they could learn how to read by just coming to our PE classes.... Even after they learned how to read they had to continue to work on their own if they had any hopes of becoming a serious thinker.

"Obviously," Ford said, "we could aid in helping a person develop and raise their level of social consciousness, but at the end of the day some of the work had to be done by the individual person in solitude."[44] In addition to facilitating personal and professional development, the PE classes were a great way to stimulate interest in what the Portland cadre was trying to create. Unfortunately, they also elicited the interest of the Portland Police Bureau. Ford received the lion's share of that attention.

Once Ford moved to Portland permanently, he kept a relatively clean police record, but starting in the spring of 1968, he was harassed, arrested, or cited by the police on numerous occasions for jaywalking and for minor and not so minor traffic violations, including driving without a "license plate light" and possession of an unnamed illegal substance. It may be coincidental that Ford's troubles with the police in Portland coincided with his increased political activity. The police were a constant thorn in the side of blacks and those on the Left. In 1968, the City Club of Portland issued a paper titled "Report on Law Enforcement in the City of Portland" that reiterated what many black Portlanders had been saying for years: that the police department was there to keep them in their place, not to protect and serve their interests. In the Albina neighborhood in particular, the harassment and social control of residents were a higher priority for the police bureau than the citizenry's well-being. At that time, blacks comprised more than 60 percent of the district but only 1 percent of the police force. The City Club's findings were in no sense revelatory. Indeed, during the early 1960s,

45 percent of all Portland arrestees were black, yet blacks made up less than 5 percent of the city's total population.[45]

Ford and Mills increasingly attended political gatherings and met with radical groups such as Students for a Democratic Society. But a visit from members of the Seattle chapter of the Black Panther Party at Portland State College had as great an effect on Ford's political trajectory as anything up to that point. Ford recalls the sequence of events:

> Aaron Dixon, head of the Seattle chapter of the Black Panther Party, was invited to speak at Portland State College in the spring of 1968. His brother Elmer was with him. I was hanging out at a house with some Portland State students, some of whom claimed to be followers of Elijah Muhammad. They were planning to form a black student union. I informed them that Aaron Dixon of the Black Panther Party was speaking at the university and I asked if anyone wanted to go hear him speak. The Muslim brothers chafed at the suggestion, but I went anyway. That was my first time hearing a Panther speak.... I liked what Dixon had to say. Later on, a reception was held for Dixon at the house of two black women school teachers who also happened to be twins.... I'll never forget them. It was there that I met Aaron, who encouraged me to start selling the Panther newspaper. Next thing you know, Seattle started sending us the newspaper. Not long after, we opened a NCCF office. At the time, the party stopped accepting new members.
> They had a moratorium in place, I believe, so party officials urged aspiring Panthers to open up NCCF offices instead.[46]

Ford's chronology seems a bit off, as the moratorium to which he refers actually began in January 1969. At that time, the BPP's central committee moved aggressively to tighten discipline by ridding the party of counterrevolutionaries, informants, and renegades. On January 12, 1969, Bobby Seale issued a statement, "We aren't taking in any new members for the next three to six months.... We are turning inward to tighten security, [to] get rid of agents and provocateurs, and to promote political education among those who have joined the Panthers, but still don't understand what we're all about."[47]

Regardless, Dixon's visit to Portland confirmed for Ford what he had really wanted to do all along: start a Black Panther branch in Portland. "I knew we had to step up after Dr. King and Bobby Hutton were killed in April," said Ford. That summer, following John Carlos's and Tommie Smith's iconic protest at the Mexico City Olympics, where their clenched fists atop the medal podium thrust Black Power into the living rooms of more than six hundred million viewers, Ford and Mills secured a facility from which to organize. They moved into a two-story house on the southeast corner of Cook Street and Union Avenue that was occupied by an antiwar outfit called The Resistance. In exchange for having access to the entire first floor, The Resistance asked only that Ford and Mills split the cost of the electric bill. "It was a big, old, but beautiful wood-frame house with a huge living room and a large front porch. . . . It had hardwood floors. . . . I liked it, but you couldn't see it from the street; it wasn't the best location," recalled Raymond Joe, one of the group's early recruits.[48]

Over the next few months, Ford and Mills decorated the office with artifacts and posters of famous Panthers, such as Huey P. Newton and other Black Power movement luminaries. The two men used the space to hold meetings, leaflet the community about issues pertaining to black Portlanders, and, most importantly, launch the Portland branch of the Black Panther Party not realizing that to start a branch of the BPP one had to obtain permission from national headquarters in Oakland. It did not take long before Ford and Mills were receiving visitors at the Cook Street locale. People stopped by wanting to find out who was plastering posters of Panthers and other black militant images in the windows of this first-floor set-up. One of those who came by was young Percy Hampton. Remembering their early interactions, Ford recalls, "Percy had an air of humility about himself. . . . He was also ambitious, but his ambition was channeled in the right direction. . . . He wanted to do something for the people and he was smart. . . . After that first visit Percy just kept coming back wanting to get involved. . . . Tommy and I embraced him right away." In the days and weeks that followed, others stopped by and ultimately joined the NCCF, including Tommy Hayden and Sandra Britt. At about the same time, Hampton recalls how he was "jumped on by the police . . . and Kent and Tommy came by my mother's house looking for me. They wanted to find out what had happened, recommend a few attorneys that I should call . . . they also wanted to recruit me to be in the Black Panther Party."[49]

Asked to elaborate on the abrasive encounter he had with members of the Portland Police Bureau, Hampton recalled that one evening, sometime between six and seven, "I was walking to a neighborhood convenience store called Maxey, which was located on Williams and Going, when out of nowhere a police car pulled directly into my path, cutting me off. . . . One officer blurted out, 'Boy where are you going?' I replied, 'First off, I'm not your boy, and second, I'm going to the store,' at which point the officer muttered something about me having a smart mouth ... things escalated from there." For Hampton's defiance, he was convicted of disorderly conduct, resisting arrest, and assaulting a police officer and was sentenced to ninety days in jail and two years' probation. Hampton recalled,

> I wasn't even six months past my eighteenth birthday before this stuff happened. Plus I was all set to go to Portland State in the fall. . . . I had already been accepted, but after I got thrown in jail, I wasn't sure I was going to be able to go to school. Unexpectedly, two weeks into my sentence, I was released, but of course I still had a record that would stay with me for seven years until it was expunged. That whole situation reinforced for me my decision to do what I was planning to do anyway, and that was to become a member of the Black Panther Party.[50]

A few months after that incident, the group's early membership began to grow quickly, and Ford and Mills decided to move the operation to a more suitable, spacious, and centrally located building at 3619 NE Union Avenue. Not long after transitioning to Union Avenue, Oscar Johnson signed up, at the urging of his cousin Tommy Mills. According to Johnson, "The Union Avenue spot was a storefront, visible from the street and accessible. . . . We had two loud speakers out front. . . . We were always playing records of Malcolm's speeches or something like that. . . . The building also had several offices upstairs. . . . It was a nice building." The six-foot-four Johnson was a key addition to the cadre. Although he lacked Mills's combat experience, Ford knew that as a marine Johnson had acquired training that would be of tremendous benefit to the group. Describing Johnson's commitment to the cause, Ford noted that "if Oscar said he was going to do something, he did it. He was also the kind of guy who didn't buckle under pressure ... he wasn't scared. . . . Oscar wasn't going to be intimated by anyone or anything." Johnson exemplified the Marine Corps values of honor, courage, and commitment. Even though Ford was not yet an official member of the Black Panther Party, he and a small band of "brothers and sisters" still engaged in the kind of tireless grunt work typical of many Panthers across the country. Said Rita Clinton, another cousin of Tommy Mills, "I was surprised when I found out that Tommy was involved with the Panthers. . . . Growing up, he was sort of a mama's boy ... always tugging on his mother's apron strings." Within a short period, the group grew to thirty or forty members. As a result, Ford's growing role as a radical leader within the black community and his ability to mobilize people had earned him a reputation within the Portland Police Bureau as someone to keep an eye on, culminating in his arrest during the chaotic evenings of mid-June 1969.[51]

In late June, following his release from his thirteen-day stay at Rocky Butte Jail on $80,000 bail (paid through large donations by local anti–Vietnam War activists and radical leftists), Ford emerged from the city police station to face a small crowd of black and white supporters. Standing on the steps of the station, Ford made a concise statement. "If they keep coming in with these fascist tactics," he proclaimed, "we're going to defend ourselves." Ford's pronouncement invoked a deep tradition of self-defense dating back to David Walker's *Appeal, in Four Articles* 140 years earlier, in which he wrote, "They want us for their slaves and think nothing of murdering us . . . [therefore,] it is no more harm for you to kill a man who is trying to kill you, than it is for you to take a drink of water when thirsty."[52] Ford's proclamation may have seemed extreme to some, but it mirrored the goings-on in some quarters of the city.

By 1969, the city was fast shedding its image as (in the words of Michael Wells, founder of the *Willamette Bridge*) a "sleepy overgrown lumber town."[53] In October 1960, the eccentric sociologist C. Wright Mills had written a prophetic essay in which he called attention to a new kind of radicalism, which he dubbed the "New Left." Different from the "old Left," which had become cautious and trade unionist, the New Left, Mills pointed out, had found a vibrant and intellectually fresh home among a new breed of students and their more politically engaged professors. No doubt Mills included himself in this grouping. Indeed, the 1960s began with a sense among many young people that they were on the threshold of a bright new era. This sentiment even permeated the music industry, and no artist at the time understood this better than thirty-six-year-old Max Roach, arguably the most influential drummer of his generation. Roach's politically charged 1960 album *We Insist! Freedom Now Suite*, featuring Abbey Lincoln, Coleman Hawkins, and Olatunji, and with its heart-pounding melodies and haunting message, captured the civil rights struggle's anguish and aspirations. The album's black-and-white cover pictured three black male artists at a lunch counter, behind which stood a white male attendant in a waiter's outfit.

In Portland, the decade began with Reed College students and others picketing the Kress and Woolworth's department stores in support of the famous February 1, 1960, Greensboro sit-in at which four freshman from historically black North Carolina A&T College (later University) defiantly sat down at a Woolworth's lunch counter and refused to move until they were served. Featured prominently in the demonstrators' discussions, of course, were the writings and example set by both Dr. Martin Luther King, Jr., and Gandhi, the leader of India's struggle for independence from British rule. The students decided that a protest that integrated the teachings of nonviolence was the best way to proceed. The major principles of a nonviolent strategy were (1) that it was not a method for cowards or for the faint of heart; (2) that it seeks to win the friendship and understanding of its opponent; (3) that the attack is aimed at the forces of evil rather than at the evildoer; (4) that the nonviolent resister be willing to turn himself or herself into the target of violence but never inflict it; (5) that it is better to love than to hate one's oppressor; and (6) that the universe is on the side of justice and that the nonviolent ideologue have faith in the future. Over the course of a few days, students entered the Woolworth's and asked to be served, only to be turned away or ignored altogether. When told to move, they refused. When the manager closed down the counter, they opened their textbooks and began to study. And when the local radio station interrupted its regularly scheduled programming to deliver the news, scores of other students poured into town and joined the demonstration. By the end of the week, students from Bennett, a nearby black women's college, joined in. So did members of the North Carolina A&T football team, after a group of white Confederate-flag-waving street toughs showed up to make life difficult for the protesters. When asked by the locals, "Who do you think you are?" the student-athletes replied, "We the Union Army."[54]

The Greensboro sit-in was a watershed event in the Civil Rights Movement inasmuch as it set the stage for the avalanche of protest activity that would define the decade. By April 1960, lunch counter sit-ins had sprouted up in fifty-four different southern cities as well as in Ohio, Illinois, and Nevada. Joseph McNeil, who had participated in the Greensboro sit-in and is now a retired US Air Force general, put the sit-ins in perspective: "There was a lot of anger back then about how we [blacks] were being treated . . . and that anger needed an escape value . . . that escape value turned out to be the sit-ins that everyone witnessed." By the end of the academic school year in 1960, young people, both black and white, had sat in libraries, visited all-white beaches and swimming pools, and slept in the lobbies of highfalutin hotels. Not long afterward, lunch counters and other facilities throughout the South began serving blacks even though it was against custom or the law to do so. By October 1961, the matter had reached the US Supreme Court, which ruled in favor of the sit-ins. A new brand of "Negro" was emerging. Blacks were no longer timid or worried about getting into trouble. At times, their courage was nothing short of alarming.[55]

Several months earlier, on January 20, 1961, a fresh-faced John F. Kennedy had taken the presidential oath of office and promised to lead the country toward a "new frontier"—one in which Americans would unite to achieve what had once seemed improbable: equal rights for African Americans, the alleviation of widespread and abject poverty at home and abroad, the peaceful neutralization of perceived communist threats, and the manned exploration of space. When, at the emotional high point of his inaugural address, Kennedy made his famous declaration, "Let the word go forth from this time and place, to friend and foe alike, that the torch has been passed to a new generation of Americans. . . . My fellow Americans: ask not what your country can do for you but what you can do for your country. . . . My fellow citizens of the world: ask not what America will do for you, but what together we can do for the freedom of man," much of the country was swept up by his unabashed enthusiasm. Many youngsters were eager to answer this call. In the ensuing years, some signed up for the Peace Corps, while others interpreted Kennedy's message differently, choosing instead to form or join groups whose primary goal was to pressure America to live up to the promises espoused by the country's founders and to Kennedy's "new frontier."

Three years after Kennedy's inauguration, Students for a Democratic Society (SDS), the premier white leftist organization of the period, sprouted up on the Reed College campus in Portland and among a younger generation of politicized Portlanders. Matt Nelson and Bill Nygren write that a year later, in 1965, fifteen hundred Portlanders staged a protest march in response to the beating death of Rev. James Reeb, a Unitarian minister from Boston who had answered Dr. King's call for a peace march in Selma—a follow-up to Bloody Sunday, in which six hundred marchers were trampled by police officers on horseback and clubbed by state troopers as they attempted to cross the Edmund Pettus Bridge. In Portland, protesters marched 2.8 miles across the Broadway Bridge to the US courthouse at Broadway and Main. Marchers held signs that read "Alabama Has Been a National Emergency for 100 Years," "Rescue Selma," and "Remember Those Killed for Freedom."[56]

Around the same time, violence in Southeast Asia was escalating and the US Armed Forces initiated a ground war in Vietnam. To no one's surprise, the draft was hugely unpopular at this time, resulting in the proliferation of various white left-wing, Maoist, militant, and draft-resistance groups. This coterie of dissidents was by no means monolithic in their ideology, tactics, or objectives, but stood as one in their collective opposition to the war and to the oppression of people of color, both at home and abroad. It should be noted that the glue holding the young Portland Left together, especially after the collapse of the SDS, was the underground press—first the *Willamette Bridge*, and later the *Scribe*, which started up in 1972. Michael Kazin, a history professor at Georgetown University (and son of the famed writer Alfred Kazin), was so taken with Portland's underground press that, after being suspended from Harvard, he moved there for the opportunity to write for the *Willamette Bridge*. "I had read the *Willamette Bridge* and I liked what the paper stood for . . . , so I hitchhiked from Detroit to Portland in the summer of 1970 to go work for the paper," said Kazin. Absent Portland's alternative press, the New Left could not have circulated its news, ideas, trends, opinions, and strategies without having them strained through a mainstream filter. Indeed, the failure of the country's sleek magazines and news dailies to cover the youth rebellion adequately helped fuel the creation of a subterranean press. And when a clump of alternative newspapers banded together to form the Underground Press Syndicate (UPS) in the mid-1960s, the genre proliferated. UPS facilitated the free exchange of news items and ideas among underground newspapers, producing a broad range of left-leaning, counterculture-oriented publications.[57]

By 1966, the national anti–Vietnam War movement was in full bloom. During the previous summer, Dr. King had given his first public speech on the war at a Virginia statewide meeting of Southern Christian Leadership Conference (SCLC) affiliates in Petersburg, Virginia, in July. In the speech he said, "I am certainly as concerned about seeing the defeat of communism as anyone else, . . . but we won't defeat communism by guns or bombs or gasses. We shall do it by making democracy work." He called for an immediate end to US military involvement in Southeast Asia and a "negotiated settlement even with the Viet Cong." Portland was replete with protesters as nearly 400,000 men were inducted into the military nationwide. In June, the *New York Times* printed an ad signed by 6,400 academics calling for an end to the war, and veterans and noteworthy politicians began to question President Johnson's handling of the war. Even some of the president's allies in the Senate broke ranks, including majority leader Mike Mansfield and Foreign Relations Committee chairman J. William Fulbright. George Mc-Govern, Eugene McCarthy, and Robert F. Kennedy eventually followed suit. Surprisingly, even Senator Stuart Symington of Missouri, once a proponent of giving the military what it asked for, became an outspoken and effective critic of the war and of military spending. Critics of the war effort could also be found in the business community, which argued that the war was driving the economy into the ground. Groups such as Business Executives Move for Vietnam Peace and the Fund for New Priorities were two such organizations. Given the interconnectedness of politics and war, it was only a matter of time before party loyalty would be pushed aside by business elites in favor of economic considerations. Despite open opposition from these important and influential sectors of the country, President Johnson publicly remained steadfast in his decision to continue with the war.[58]

On September 27, 1966, war protesters in Portland, including many students, demonstrated both inside and outside the Sheraton Motor Inn. Inside the hotel, Vice President Hubert Humphrey, in an address to one thousand supporters, stated that he believed the nation was right in pursuing the painful but necessary war in Vietnam. Holly Hart, then a student at Reed College, recalls the events of that day:

> Many of the kids and adults who demonstrated in front of the Sheraton wore black to represent the war dead. They laid down so that guests would have to walk over them to enter the hotel. Inside the hotel I yelled out, "Mr. Hubert Humphrey, the war dead indict you for collaborating in their murders. We are the aggressors in Vietnam." Then I poured temper red all over myself and fell to the floor. The Secret Service came and picked me up.... I wasn't arrested. Instead I was rushed to the hospital. I played possum. When I arrived, the emergency room staff were worried... they thought I was unconscious... they couldn't get me to come to. At some point I overheard a resident say they were going to transport me to Holliday Park, which was a mental institution. At that point I decided to put an end to the charade.

The protest was one of the first major anti–Vietnam War demonstrations in the Pacific Northwest, and it was covered by all three major news networks. As was the case with many antiwar demonstrations, some accused police officers of using extralegal force when confronting protesters, one of whom was journalist and labor activist Julia Ruuttila. A Harris Poll taken the following year, in 1967, showed that more than 40 percent of the American people favored withdrawing from Vietnam. Around this same time, Dr. King emerged as the leading spokesperson of the US peace movement, addressing rallies and proposing concrete details for US disengagement from Vietnam. As part of a nationwide "Stop the Draft" week effort that year, eighteen-year-old Reed student Clayton Axelrod was arrested and roughed up while protesting along with two hundred demonstrators at the Oregon Selective Service headquarters in northeast Portland. Tuli Kupferberg and Robert Bashlow's 1966 book *1001 Ways to Beat the Draft* was a popular pop-culture read among war protesters and draft dodgers in Portland. For those who wished to dodge the draft but were unwilling to take the extreme step of fleeing to Canada, Kupferberg suggested such off-beat tactics as "marry your sister," "ask what's in it for you," "become the publisher of the Little Mao Tse-tung Library," and "grope J. Edgar Hoover."[59]

Jim Houser, a native Ohioan who joined a group called the Society for New Action Politics (SNAP) upon moving to Portland in 1967, remembers that the antiwar demonstrations "in Portland were some of the largest on the West Coast."[60] Meanwhile, students at Reed College, following the model set by their brethren at San Francisco State College (later University), formed a black student union of their own, and by 1969 students at Portland State University had done likewise. Naturally, with the founding of black student unions came the push for Black studies programs and departments. Fed up with studying a world history that had been whitewashed of any contributions by people of color, black students in particular endeavored to create a curriculum that more accurately reflected their geographic, social, and cultural heritage. If taking over campus buildings and boycotting classes were the only ways students could get administrators to take seriously their demands for a Black studies program, so be it.

On December 11, 1968, after Reed administrators failed to respond favorably to the Black Student Union's demand for a Black studies program, the union took over the top floor of Eliot Hall, including the president's office, and called for a general boycott of classes. Linda Howard, a junior from Virginia, remembers standing in the cold morning air while waiting to greet President Victor Rosenblum. She said, "Good morning, President Rosenblum... your office has been converted to other purposes by the Black Student Union. You are invited to a meeting at noon today in the chapel, where all of the details will be made clear to you." By afternoon, pickets and demonstrators, mainly white students, were circulating around campus, disrupting classes. Faculty and administrators scrambled to plot their response. In the ensuing days, meetings and negotiations among faculty, students, and administrators were chronicled by the media. On December 18, students surrendered Eliot Hall after a resolution to create a Black studies program passed by the slim margin of 55 to 53. Three months later, the program hired William McClendon as its first director.[61]

Although radical black student efforts forever altered the educational landscape of higher education by bringing into being a curriculum that was more inclusive and representative of the mosaic that is America, at least one prominent academic and theoretician viewed black student dissidence as an unfortunate development of the Vietnam War era. Said Hannah Arendt, "Negro students, the majority of them admitted without academic qualification . . . organized themselves as an interest group . . . their intent was to lower academic standards." Arendt's analysis, if one can call it that, was both shallow and curious. The interest group to which Arendt was referring was, of course, the Black Student Union. Given Arendt's unwillingness to recognize the merits of black student unions, and that their mission was not to lower academic standards but to make universities acknowledge black history as a subject worthy of study, one cannot help but wonder if her position was on some level racially motivated or if it was the result of a generational divide. Indeed, Arendt's observations were in lock-step with those who believed that the 1960s had given rise to a "crisis of democracy" or an "excess of democracy," in which historically passive and marginalized segments of American society began to press for their demands. Clearly the college students Arendt wrote about in the 1970s were more politically rambunctious than those of her era. The founding of Students for a Democratic Society, and the Free Speech movement, and "modern" student sit-ins offered a glimpse into the future. No longer willing to tolerate the longstanding "business as usual" approach, students and nonstudents alike were increasingly asserting themselves in unprecedented ways. Journalist and academic Samuel F. Yette submits that the black togetherness of the 1960s—the newfound blackness—produced a new visibility and a tighter grip on the issues affecting black lives.[62]

While much of the antiestablishment resistance was carried out by protesters who happened to be members of a collective or an organization, there were plenty of lone acts of defiance. For example, the June 1969 commencement ceremony at the University of Oregon was interrupted by Ray

Eaglin, a nontraditional student and graduating senior who had at one time played football for the university. After the invocation, the twenty-seven-year-old African American climbed onto the stage and asked the school's acting president, Dr. Charles Johnson, for five minutes. He was greeted with a chorus of boos and shouts of "No! We don't want to hear him!" To the surprise and dismay of some, Eaglin's request was granted. Eaglin's opening salvo set the tone: "You people are all under arrest for supporting a murderous war from afar." Whether Eaglin was directing his comments toward the dignitaries in attendance or indicting the entire graduating class of 1969 and their guests is not entirely clear, but the theater was not lost on those in attendance. Eaglin then proceeded to lament the state of the country, citing "greed and gluttony on Wall Street . . . the war in Vietnam and poverty in African American neighborhoods in Portland." As one might imagine, the president was sharply criticized for giving Eaglin a platform. Days later, early in the morning of Tuesday, June 17, Johnson asked his wife to drive him to work. After agreeing to do so, his wife went up upstairs to freshen up. Moments later, when Mrs. Johnson reappeared, she found that her husband had taken off without her. Shortly thereafter, at approximately 8:00 a.m., Dr. Johnson's small foreign car collided head-on with a Crawford logging truck on the McKenzie River Highway near Leaburg, Oregon. Johnson died instantly. The truck driver was uninjured.[63]

By late summer 1969, the Portland cadre, which by now was considered a branch of the NCCF, had made a name for itself. In fact, its members had become so well known that residents outside the leftist community had begun to look to them when problems arose, as was the case when racial strife reared its ugly head at Roosevelt High School in north Portland. At the beginning of the 1969–70 school year, black students reportedly could not walk the halls without being harassed by both white students and some members of the faculty, despite the existence of a Committee on Race and Education that had been established in 1964. The stated purpose of the committee was "to improve conditions which have special bearing on the status, well-being, and achievement of children of minority races." David Morris, who was a freshman at the time, remembers, "It was unsafe for us to go to school. . . . Whites would throw bottles and rocks at us. . . . These white boys were different than the typical white boy, they weren't scared of brothers the way many whites were, plus there were just maybe fifty black students out of five hundred students . . . we were severely outnumbered." Word of the harassment reached Oscar Johnson through a friend who was employed at the high school. Johnson relayed the story to Kent Ford, who contacted an administrator to find out what was going on. Ford remembers,

> Apparently the staff was unable to address the students' concerns, so the black students contacted us. First thing I did was call the school ... I believe I spoke to the vice principal. I asked him what was being done to address the matter, and his response was "We're looking into it." I knew what that meant, so I asked if we could meet to discuss the problem. I was surprised when he said that he wouldn't meet with members of the Black Panther Party, that he was, however, willing to meet with more moderate representatives in the area ... so I said, okay, fine, and hung up. Imagine someone saying something like that. We gave the school a week to remedy the problem. A week went by, and still no change. After the comrades and I talked about it, Sandra, who graduated from Roosevelt, called some of the parents there and they agreed to let us go out there and walk the kids home from school. I remember it like it was yesterday ... it was me, Sandra, Oscar, Percy, Tommy Mills, Tommy Hayden, Tom Venters, and Linda Thornton, I think. Members of SDS and the Peace and Freedom Party joined us as well as some neighborhood residents. One Monday morning, we arrived at the steps of the school right before school ended. We instructed the students to line up in two rows ... we then flanked them on each side and walked them home. The students may have been scared, but they were very disciplined, I'll give them that.

Although everything went according to plan, there were some tense moments. On more than one occasion as students were being escorted home, a white mob consisting of students and neighbors, some of whom were adults, formed at nearby Columbia Park. Fortunately for all involved, at the same time, a team of police officers on motorcycles arrived, deterring any thoughts of violence. "Once the Panthers got involved, my fear went away. ... Kent sent in soldiers to protect us. ... The first day they arrived, they were wearing army fatigues and marching on each side of us ... they had us shouting slogans and everything. ... I'll never forget that experience," said Morris.[64]

According to Sandra Ford, around that same time, a contingent of students and their parents traveled to the state capital, Salem, where they expressed their frustration before members of the state legislature about not being able to start a black student union. Initially school officials were opposed to the idea altogether. However, officials at Roosevelt High School eventually came around to the idea, but were opposed to the name Black Student Union; instead they preferred Negro Student Union. The students and their parents felt they had no other choice but to appeal to the state's lawmakers. Meanwhile, every day for a week the students were provided with their own private security force as they walked from home to school and back. Still, according to some students, little was done to shield them during the school day from the racial epithets hurled their way or from physical violence. Consequently, a meeting of community residents was held on a Sunday at the Portland State University education extension center on Union and Russell. At the meeting, it was decided that the parents would keep their children at home until the administration sufficiently addressed black students' concerns. "A vote took place, and it was unanimous . . . there wasn't even much debate about it, basically everyone agreed that this had to be done," said Ford. The next day, students stayed home. The boycott lasted two weeks. In the meantime, Ford recalled, "we set up a school at the extension center so that the kids wouldn't fall too behind in their school work." When asked how the group was able to secure the university's extension center for the purposes of educating the youth, Ford recalled the sequence of events:

> I went to Harold Williams, who headed the extension center. . . . He was hesitant at first, but I convinced him it was for a good cause. He said only the president of the university could authorize this move. The next day I was at a local record store, and in walked Harold . . . he said we had to go see President Wolfe right now . . . , so I got into Harold's car and we drove over to see the president. Once there, he asked us a few questions, one of which was "How long will the boycott last?" to which I responded, "I don't know." Wolfe mulled it over for a moment and then gave us the go-ahead.

Local businessman Paul Knauls, owner of a restaurant called Geneva's, offered to provide the kids with lunch for as long as the boycott lasted. Every day, the kids were treated to a buffet-style meal. Two weeks into the boycott, the newly hired superintendent of Portland's public schools, Dr. Robert Blanchard, called the students' parents and invited them and their children to a retreat at Camp Menucha in Corbett, Oregon, at no expense for the purpose of addressing their concerns in hopes that the students would return to school. At the retreat, the students and their families were afforded the opportunity to air their grievances. Parents' primary concern was the safety and well-being of their children—that they not be subjected to verbal or physical harassment by students or staff members. Additionally, the students believed they had the right to establish a black student union, something to which some school officials and white students had initially objected. The retreat proved successful, and both the parents and the students were satisfied with the outcome. Needless to say, news of the victory reverberated throughout north Portland.[65]

Few were surprised by the developments at Roosevelt High School. A staff report by the United States Commission on Civil Rights revealed that Portland School District No. 1, to which Roosevelt High School belonged, included 95 elementary schools, 14 high schools, and 16 special education schools. The total student enrollment for the 1968–69 academic year was 77,445, of which only 6,304 were African American. Other groups included 468 Native Americans, 986 Asian Americans, 708 Latinos, and whites, who made up 68,979 of the student population. Of the faculty, 104 instructors were African American; 2, Native American; 37, Asian American; 6, Latino; and 3,666, white. Given the striking racial imbalances, one can understand why racial hostilities may have boiled over.

The decision to boycott Roosevelt High School was part of a larger effort by Portland's black community to confront injustice head-on. Case in point, in August 1969, some Portland residents decided to confront the long-standing problem—this time by pursuing a litigious course of action. Twenty-two-year-old Robert Probasco, along with thirteen other complainants, filed a class-action lawsuit in US District Court on behalf of more than twenty-thousand black residents against Mayor Terry Schrunk, the city council, the police chief, and thirty-eight Portland police officers. The suit petitioned the court to put a stop to the systematic harassment of black residents by the Portland Police Bureau. Police harassment, the complainants claimed, resulted in black Portlanders living in "an atmosphere of fear and persecution" that had a "chilling effect upon the exercise of their federally protected rights." A 1968 report compiled by the City Club found widespread distrust among blacks where the police were concerned. Many believed that members of the Portland bureau policed black residents more harshly than white residents.[66]

As classes resumed in the fall, and the anti–Vietnam War movement consumed much of the country, the campuses of Portland State University and Reed College were bustling with resistance efforts and teeming with ideas for unconventional protest tactics. According to one student activist, "By the time school started in 1969, the city of Portland was really a hornet's nest of activity." While few would mistake Portland for Berkeley, there was a strong radical presence there, and a burgeoning counterculture. According to Penny Harrington, a police officer who later served as the city's police chief (becoming the first woman to head a major American police department), "Kids were flocking to Portland from everywhere in the country . . . some of them taking up residence in Lair Hill Park . . . where they would indulge in drugs like LSD and marijuana. . . . If for whatever reason they couldn't or didn't want go to San Francisco or Berkeley they came to Portland."[67]

By late summer of 1970, the NCCF not only continued to grow but received official charter membership from national headquarters, giving birth to the Portland branch of the Black Panther Party. "With all that was happening around the country, I knew that we had to kick it up a notch . . . the struggle that is. . . . Mark and Fred had gotten killed in Chicago, Nixon had gotten elected president . . . we had to do more," Kent Ford said. Nixon's election had not raised the hopes of America's youth, as Kennedy's had. In fact, on inauguration day in January 1969, of the ten thousand citizens lining the streets of Washington, DC, roughly a tenth were protesters, who pelted Nixon's limousine with beer cans, rocks, and balloons filled with red ink, while shouting antiwar epithets such as "Four more years of death!"[68]

The Portland Panthers' initial leadership cadre was structured like that of central headquarters. Whereas some heads of Panther branches and chapters preferred the title "deputy minister of defense" or "defense captain," Ford simply took on the title of "captain." According to Ford's comrades, "Kent being in charge made sense. . . . He was all business, very studious . . . he thought things through, and he was very disciplined. . . . He would also listen to you . . . he would hear you out, but in the end he assumed full responsibility for whatever happened," said Oscar Johnson. Although Tommy Mills was deputy minister of defense, he was second in command; Floyd Cruse acted as deputy minister of information, Oscar Johnson served as assistant deputy minister of information, Tom Venters as deputy minister of education, Raymond Joe as deputy chief of staff, Vernell Carter as deputy minister of culture, and Percy Hampton as distribution manager of the Black Panther newspaper. As veterans of the US Armed Forces, Mills (army) and Johnson (marine corps) were key in carrying out tasks related to weapons training, counterinsurgency, and propaganda. "Mills was the go-to guy when it came to securing our facilities and protecting the rank and file," said Ford. When asked how responsibilities and titles were assigned, Ford recalled,

> We had many meetings about this over a period of a few months.... We first
> started having all-night meetings at Tommy Mills' place.... Tom Venters
> took notes.... Tommy's apartment was an ideal meeting place, because it
> was not easy to access for someone not familiar with the setup, if you know
> what I mean ... any unwanted visitors arriving for the first time would have
> a difficult time gaining entry.... Anyway, I had observed these guys for
> many months, in some cases years, so I knew who would be good at what....
> Tommy and Oscar were veterans with knowledge of firearms, so I knew they
> would be good at certain tasks involving weapons and security, so I assigned
> them accordingly. Floyd liked to talk; he was very talkative.... Venters was
> a natural-born street organizer; Joe was good at solving problems at the
> street level; Oscar was a no-nonsense person, and when it was time to get
> down, Oscar was ready; Percy was a self-starter, you didn't have to tell him
> much, he was a go-getter; and Carter could really draw, he was a heck of a
> good artist, so knowing all this allowed me to put comrades in a position
> that would best help the party. In sum, there were times I just assigned
> individuals certain responsibilities, other times titles and responsibilities
> were assigned based on ability and mutual agreement.

Conversations with Ford's comrades suggest that they trusted his judgment, and that he knew best which tasks should be assigned to whom. Their faith in him was perhaps due to his style of servant leadership. In servant leadership, the leader advocates service to others as his or her primary purpose. If people feel that their leader is genuinely interested in serving others, they will be prepared not just to follow him or her but to dedicate themselves to the common cause. Such was the case with Kent Ford.[69]

Other key members of the cadre were Linda Thornton, Sandra Ford, and Joyce Radford. Thornton coordinated the free breakfast program, while Sandra Ford and Radford oversaw the health clinics. Inasmuch as the position existed, Radford served as officer of the day. Although the coordinators of both the breakfast program and the health clinics were not officers in the traditional sense, Ford maintains that "the comrades who held those positions were equal in stature to those of us whose titles may have sounded more impressive to people on the outside looking in ... everyone had an equal say regardless of position or rank." Still, from the outside looking in, the absence of women among the leadership cadre suggests male chauvinism. In retrospect, Ford acknowledges that Thornton, Sandra, and Radford should have been made part of the branch's leadership. "All three of them were very capable people. Joyce was damn smart and one of the party's finest workers . . . she a was down-to-earth person who knew her way around Portland's black communities. . . . Linda was a quiet person, smart, good with kids, always prompt and very professional about her work. . . . Sandra was highly intelligent . . . she had worked at First National Bank, so she had excellent verbal and writing skills, and she was very efficient. With her manner and training, she was the perfect person to be the face of the health and dental clinics."[70]

Even though he maintains that the women were on par with their male counterparts in terms of their contribution and influence within the party, a reflective Ford readily admits that

> a leadership cadre that consisted of men only may not have been the best idea, and I should have realized that then, but my thinking was . . . we need to put a protective curtain around them, because they ran our programs. . . . If we lost any of them to arrest or imprisonment, that would have hurt us dearly. By keeping them out of the limelight . . . by not assigning any of them a title, like deputy minister of this or that, I thought I was making it difficult for the government to target them, but, again, maybe I should have rethought that.

Ford's reassessment of this matter suggests a certain level of introspection that hopefully other former Black Panther leaders have experienced over the years. As bell hooks writes in *Outlaw Culture*, "The ability to acknowledge blind spots can emerge only as we expand our concern about politics of domination and our capacity to care about the oppression and exploitation of others." She further opines that "acknowledging the truth of our reality, both individual and collective, is a necessary stage for personal and political growth." Still, the absence of women in official leadership posts in Portland was somewhat atypical. In many other branches and chapters of the BPP, women at least held the position of communications secretary, a post that did not exist within the Portland branch of the BPP.[71]

Despite having titles and areas for which they were responsible, the members had no strict chain of command, as was the case in some other party branches throughout the country. For example, in the event that Kent Ford was arrested and taken off the street, Tommy Mills, as second in command, was expected to step up and take charge. After Mills, however, the hierarchy was less clear. If Mills became unavailable, it is likely that the responsibility of leading the branch would have fallen on the shoulders of either Hampton or Johnson. In any case, it is evident that a strict hierarchical order was something that the comrades in Portland did not see fit to install.

As with nearly every Panther office in the country, the contributions made by Panther women were immeasurable. According to Oscar Johnson, "Basically, the women did everything the men did, sometimes better . . . they manned the office, sold newspapers, solicited funds, and ran all of our breakfast programs and health clinics." Hampton's praise is even stronger: "They helped organize marches and rallies. . . . Without them, we would not have been able to man our clinics . . . we would have been lost. . . . They were indispensable, especially Linda, Joyce, and Sandra . . . we could always count on them." When asked to comment on the women in the Portland branch, Sandra Ford thoughtfully offered, "The sisters were brave, smart, and hardworking." Assessments of Sandra Ford by others were no less glowing. Patty Hampton (now Carter), a fellow Panther member and sister of Percy Hampton, recalls that "Sandra was a powerful, young, intelligent woman . . . she was our Kathleen Cleaver." Frances Storrs, a dermatologist who volunteered at the health clinic, described Sandra as "brilliant, a wonderful person who had the organizational skills to make things happen." But despite Kent Ford's acknowledgment of the invaluable contributions made by the Portland women and the long tradition of black female activism upheld by his female comrades, the absence of women in the leadership only gives currency to Frances Beal's observation about some black men of that period. Writing in 1970, Beal opined that the black male "sees the System for what it really is, for the most part, but where he rejects its values and mores on many issues, when it comes to women, he seems to take his guidelines from the pages of the *Ladies' Home Journal*."[72]

The women in the Portland branch brought three perspectives to their community activism that made them good fits for the aspiring Panther branch. First, their consciousness was shaped by their experiences in American society in general, particularly in the work force. With one or two exceptions, all of the women activists worked in some capacity, whether part time or full time. Second, they observed black mens' suffering and experienced its effects in their own lives. And third, and perhaps most important, they were motivated by the racial oppression in the lives of their children. Several of the women were mothers as well as members of the NCCF in Portland. Sandra Ford, for example, was a divorced mother of two when she joined the cadre. Joyce Radford, the first woman to join the group, was also a mother, as were some of the rank-and-file members. In her essay *Women in the Black Liberation Movement*, Beal suggested that "it is idle dreaming to think of black women simply caring for their homes and children like the middle-class white model. Most black women have to work to help house, feed, and clothe their families. Black women make up a substantial percentage of the black work force and this is true for the poorest black family as well as the . . . 'middle-class' family." The experiences that the Portland women picked up as mothers (and many as working moms), such as coordinating schedules, managing personalities, multitasking, nurturing, and navigating conflict resolution, were skills on which they drew heavily as members of the Portland NCCF and later as members of the Portland branch of the BPP.[73]

Over the years, many male Panthers in various parts of the country have acknowledged the pivotal role played by Panther women. Moreover, the importance of Black Panther women in what many consider the Black Power movement's most preeminent organization is well documented, albeit only recently. No one has highlighted the importance of fully incorporating women into the struggle for Black liberation than Frantz Fanon, who maintained, "[We] must guard against the danger of perpetuating the feudal tradition which holds sacred the superiority of the masculine element over the feminine." Fanon's words are poignant, but for many Panther men this was more easily said than done, no matter how good one's intentions. "I assure you," said Kent Ford, "the woman question was not something that was a problem for us. The women did everything everyone did . . . they even took target practices right alongside the men."[74]

Working alongside the leadership was a core of dedicated rank-and-file Panthers that included Patty Carter, Jeffrey Lynn Washington Fikes, Fern Parker, Willie James Brown, R. V. Poston, Tommy Hayden, Darlene Fisher, Melina Jones, Shayla Brown (pseudonym), Charles Moore, Claude Hawkins, Linda Miller, and Freddy Whitlow. Sandra Ford characterized the rank-and-file cadre as "a smart, high-energy, resourceful, tough, street-smart group of young men and women." Among those who stand out in Ford's mind are Fisher and Parker. Said Ford, "Fern was tough, brave, outspoken, and stubborn, but she was dedicated and a hard worker." About Fisher, Ford said, "She was amazing . . . a brave soul, really, really smart . . . outgoing, but had a temper. . . . Darlene was a hard worker too." Ford's descriptions mirror those of cadres in West Coast locales such as Seattle, Sacramento, Los Angeles, and the Bay Area.[75]

With the exception of Kent Ford, Floyd Cruse, Tom Venters, and perhaps a few others, the leadership cadre and the rank-and-file were largely native Portlanders, many of whom had graduated from Thomas Jefferson High School in north Portland. As was the case with some other Panther branches or aspiring Panther branches, the principal organizer of the Portland cadre, Kent Ford, was not raised in Portland. In this regard, Portland was atypical. An examination of Panther and NCCFs branches throughout the country reveals that many of them were founded by men and women who grew up in that particular city.[76]

Conversations with former Portland Panthers and their allies suggest that the men and women worked well alongside one another. This is not to say that issues did not arise along the way—they did—but misogynistic and chauvinistic behavior displayed by men in some other branches and chapters did not play out in any discernible way in Portland. For example, one Panther from the Seattle chapter shared that during one of his visits to the organization's central headquarters in California in 1969, one high-ranking Panther made lewd comments to his wife, who had accompanied him on the trip. The offending Panther talked of how he intended to bed her and what he desired to do with her. Another Panther admits that there were a few Panthers who used their status as Panther warriors as a way of getting close to women, Panther or otherwise. Still others had no qualms about impregnating one or two women under the subterfuge of providing soldiers for the revolution or replenishing the black race, which some believed to be the victim of a genocidal plot on the part of the US government. This dubious position was not novel; University of Chicago pathologist Dr. Julian Lewis took a similar stance in the mid-1940s when he curiously argued that the survival of the black race in the United States was dependent upon "a high birth rate." In his opinion, blacks who condoned birth control were advocating "race suicide." There were some Panthers who thought similarly.[77]

When asked about the gender dynamics in Portland, Sandra Ford maintained, "We didn't have the kind of problems that the women in Oakland and elsewhere encountered." When Percy Hampton was informed that in Elaine Brown's book *A Taste of Power: A Black Woman's Story*, Brown, who served as chairman of the BPP from 1974 until 1977, had written, "Women in the Black Panther Party were expected to clean up after 'their' men, to have sex with them on demand, and to never question their authority or the decisions they made," Hampton responded, "That didn't happen in Portland.... Even if brothers here had tried the stuff that went down in Oakland, the sisters in Portland weren't going to have that. . . . We had sisters in the party who would scrap with a dude. . . . I remember one time a sister had to be pulled off of a brother because of something he did. . . . No! Sisters in Portland wouldn't tolerate the kind of stuff that we heard about in Oakland!" A number of factors account for the low level of sexism in the Portland branch, but in the main it can be attributed to the type of young people that formed the branch.[78]

The Portland cadre was a close-knit group despite being of relatively diverse backgrounds. "We supported one another, we helped one another with stuff outside of the party . . . we were like family," said Sandra Ford. "I agree with Sandra," said Raymond Joe. "We looked out for one another, we didn't always agree with one another . . . at times we argued, but we were always there for each other regardless." Similarly, Kent Ford said, "'Til this day, many of us still keep in touch with one another."[79]

Like other branches around the country, the Portland group varied in socioeconomic makeup. An examination of the backgrounds of those who held leadership positions, either formally or informally, for example, reveals that nearly all were high school graduates, and a few were first-generation college students. Several attended college either before joining the NCCF or being members of the branch, but none graduated during those years. All joined the aspiring Panther branch while in their late teens or early twenties, with the exception of Kent Ford, Tom Venters, Tommy Mills, Oscar Johnson, and Floyd Cruse (four of whom served in the armed forces before becoming members), and Joyce Radford, Linda Thornton, and Sandra Ford, who were in their mid- to late twenties. Mills, Johnson, and Cruse were all in their late twenties at the time the Portland branch was formed. Venters, a married veteran of the US Air Force, was the oldest of them all at thirty-two years of age.[80]

Most were raised in two-parent households at some point in their lives. Some of the parents were part of the Great Migration of blacks who fled the South in search of better job opportunities and to escape the sweltering climate of racial injustice. For example, Percy Hampton's father hailed from Arkansas and initially worked in the Kaiser shipyards, while Sandra Ford's mom was raised in Louisiana. The households in which these former activists grew up ranged from low-income to middle-class. Willie James Brown, one of the cadre's rank-and-file members, was reared under extremely trying circumstances, for a time bouncing from one foster home to another. Raymond Joe, whose biological father died when he was five years old, remembers that his stepfather, an Arkansas native could not read or write, signed his name with an X. Joe's mother and stepfather divorced after two years of marriage, leaving Joe without the strong father figure that characterized Hampton's and Mills's upbringings; these two men were raised in stable households. A product of the public school system, Mills came from a loving two-parent household; his mother worked at the Pendleton Woolen Mills, and his father retired after a long career with Amtrak. After working in the shipyards, Percy Hampton's father worked in construction for many years, while his mother worked at Kaiser Permanente as a social worker. Said Hampton, "My parents owned rental property. . . . My father always bought a Cadillac . . . , and for a time my siblings and I attended Blessed Sacrament, a private Catholic school, before transitioning to Benson and Jefferson High Schools later on." Owning a Cadillac had symbolic significance. According to the famed African-American author Julius Lester,

> In the black community, a Cadillac is a symbol of resistance, because its proud owner is refusing to be what society wants him to be. His Cadillac is a weapon in his fight to convince himself that he is as much of a man as any white man. Conversely, a white man need not own a Cadillac to be considered a man, a human being. His worth as a human being is established in the whiteness of his skin. A black man has to fight for his dignity . . . a Cadillac is part of that battery.[81]

As was the case with other parents whose children joined the Black Panther Party, it seems that the majority of the parents whose sons and daughters became involved with the Portland branch of the BPP were supportive, while others were less enthusiastic about their children's decision. "Both my parents were very good about me joining the party," said Raymond Joe. "They believed that something needed to be done." Percy Hampton's parents were divided on the matter. "My dad didn't like me joining the party. . . . My mom was more of an activist type . . . she would say everyone has to make his or her mark on life." "She was more tolerant," Hampton said. A few of the parents even volunteered to help out when needed. The father of one Panther joined the picket line in which his daughter was participating, and one mother would regularly come by the health clinic and make coffee and assist the receptionist "with signing patients in."[82]

One prevailing theme among the members, even before signing up with the NCCF, was a burning desire to uplift marginalized peoples, namely African Americans. Sandra Ford's commitment to racial equality was evident: she had been a member of the NAACP youth group before joining the NCCF. "There was a lot going on in America at the time in terms of civil rights," said Oscar Johnson, former lance corporal and infantryman. "I thought I should be doing something to help my own people, but after being in the Marine Corps, I wasn't interested in doing sit-ins . . . no sir, I wasn't going to do any anybody's sit-in." Percy Hampton said, "I wanted to get into something to help black people, so I started going to the [Nation of Islam] mosque. . . . I went there about a half dozen times, but stopped, because I didn't agree with their philosophy . . . their views on whites was something I could not accept."[83]

Hampton's feelings about the Nation of Islam (NOI) were apparently shared by many blacks in Portland. From the time the NOI first arrived in Portland in the early 1960s, its reception among blacks was, at best, luke-warm. Blacks in Portland did not take to the NOI as did blacks in other West Coast cities, such as Los Angeles, Phoenix, and Seattle. Clarence "Charles CX" Debiew and his wife, both advocates of the Black Muslim movement who had moved to Portland in the years after World War II, attempted to establish a temple on Williams Avenue in July 1961. Promoting the notion that all whites were devils, Portlanders both blacks and white accused the NOI of black supremacy. E. Shelton Hill of the Urban League was quoted in the *Oregonian* as saying, "Any group, black or white, that advocates ra-cial hatred is a detriment to the well-being of the community."[84] When the Debiews failed to garner sufficient interest, they moved on. Several years later, in 1968, a second attempt was made, with greater success. The political climate made it easier to attract members this time around. The NOI also purchased a building on Seventh and Fremont that was converted into a mosque (formerly called a "temple") for worship. By the late 1970s, with the purchase of a bakery, a fish market, and a school, it appeared as though the NOI might establish a foothold in the City of Roses. Still, like Hampton, to many blacks in Portland, the Nation of Islam's strict code of conduct, dietary restrictions, and unconventional racial philosophy was too much to bear.

Between October 1966 and the early months of 1970, much changed in Portland. Bookended by two disorders in the summers of 1967 and 1969, Portland—from the streets, schools, and businesses of Albina to the offices of urban planners and politicians—found itself in the midst of a growing civil war for space and place. Out of this moment of transformation and un-certainty, a common commitment to help strengthen their community led this diverse group of young African American men and women, led by Kent Ford, Tommy Mills, and others, to coalesce into the Portland NCCF. As the NCCF laid their claim on Albina, they did so with a purposefully optimistic and grassroots vision of what their community ought to look like and of how they might better serve it—not with the reactionary or violent zealotry that was popularly caricatured. By pursuing that positive vision of community survival and socioeconomic uplift, these early members of Portland's NCCF quickly earned their status as official Black Panthers by the summer of 1970.

CHAPTER 3

Serving Albina and Becoming Panthers under the Watchful Eye of the Portland Police Bureau

ortland's National Committee to Combat Fascism (NCCF) co-alesced in direct response to issues facing Albina's residents, and within the framework of the Black Panthers' national "Ten-Point Platform and Program." The soon-to-be Portland Panthers established neighborhood programs, such as medical clinics and a free children's breakfast program, and mounted a radical and unyielding confrontational resistance to police brutality. However, due to an odd set of circumstances, the Portland cadre operated with a distinct level of autonomy. Even before they had sought approval to open an NCCF office, Kent Ford had erroneously declared both himself and his comrades to be Black Panthers. Since they were not officially an office of the NCCF or a branch of the BPP, they did not come under the supervision of the Panthers' headquarters, hence there was no one to whom the Portland cadre was compelled to answer. Moreover, following the arrest and imprisonment of Huey Newton in 1967, leadership within the national headquarters was in a state of flux as it grappled with creating a coherent national vision for the organization. During this period, NCCF branches, chapters, and offices around the country continued to work with the Black Panther Party's (BPP) national headquarters, but they often focused on local issues rather than the national platform. As a result, while the objectives of the Portland cadre and Black Panthers were similar to those of the national organization, the tactics used to carry out these goals were local and were shaped by the city's unique socioeconomic demographics. In particular, the Portland cadre's localized vision for urban planning started with community control in Albina and the improvement of socioeconomic conditions within black neighborhoods.[1]

Despite the Panthers' reputation as a violent and separatist organization, the group's primary objective in Portland was the establishment of community survival programs that met the needs of the city's indigent and neglected populations, regardless of race. To this end, the NCCF's first significant achievements between 1969 and 1970 centered on the formation of a free health clinic, a dental clinic, and a breakfast program for children akin to those community survival programs found in Oakland and other cities. These programs carved out spaces of sanctuary for poor blacks in an unjust social and economic system by providing necessities and breaking the cycle of poverty. During a visit with Panther leadership in Oakland in July 1969 at the Conference for a United Front Against Fascism, Bay Area Panthers were impressed with the desire of Kent Ford and his fellow Portlanders to expand the party in a city where the racial demographics did not, on the surface, appear to favor the sustainability of a Panther branch.

It should be noted that by that time, Ford had already forged a reputation as a serious grassroots activist. Even though he was not yet an official member of the Black Panther Party, he was accorded the respect of a Panther. Consequently, he was highly sought-after, not only because people perceived him to be a Panther but because of his ability to talk passionately and frankly about the hot-button issues of the day and his willingness to intervene in matters involving racial and class injustice. Ford's popularity seemed to rise concurrently with that of the Black Panther Party nationally, most notably gaining attention during the nationwide movement to free Huey Newton from prison in the late 1960s. The "Free Huey" campaign kept the party in the spotlight while its supporters hailed it as the vanguard of the people's revolution. The support of notable individuals such as Jean Genet, the famous French novelist and playwright, also helped boost the Panthers and their local leaders' popularity. Arriving in the United States under questionable circumstances in March 1970, Genet embarked on a three-month tour of college campuses on the West and East Coasts, proselytizing on behalf of the Black Panther Party. Having written two plays that dealt with French colonialism in Africa, *The Blacks* (1959) and *The Screens* (1966), Genet empathized with the oppressed. In fact, Genet so identified with the black race that he recognized himself "only in the oppressed of the colored races, the oppressed who revolted against the whites. I am a black whose skin happens to be white, but I am definitely a black." On a March 20 tour stop in Los Angeles, Genet exclaimed, "It is fashionable to accuse the Black Panther Party of violence ... but white Americans have been violent to blacks for over two hundred years. How do you expect the Panthers to react?" He ended the speech by proclaiming that America had reached the eve of her downfall: an insurrection led by the Panthers would spark her collapse, and Genet urged affluent young Americans to join this people's revolution. This kind of national notoriety undoubtedly benefitted local Panther branches.[2]

Toward the end of Genet's visit to America, and days after the tragic shootings at Kent State University in the spring of 1970, Gary Waller, a sociology graduate student at Portland State University, put together a panel of activists for a public event on campus. One of these panelists was Kent Ford, who talked extensively about the state of America and the Black Panther Party's "Ten Point Program and Platform." Around that same time, Paul Knauls, the owner of Paul's Paradise, a local nightclub, asked Ford to intervene in a matter involving his white patrons. It seems that blacks who hung out at Slaughter's pool hall on North Russell Street had assaulted and mugged several of his white customers. According to Ford,

> Some knuckleheads would lay in wait in an alley ... at the end of the night [and] as the white customers were making their way back to their cars a bunch of black guys would jump out and mug them for their money, jewelry ... anything of value that they could sell. Knauls asked me to look into the matter, so I rounded up a few guys and we went to the pool hall to a meeting that Knauls had already arranged. When we arrived, Knauls introduced me, then I took over. I stressed to the guys the importance of refraining from that kind of criminal behavior, because it would only bring heat on everybody. "I know a lot of you can't find work, but this ain't the way to go about it," I said. Plus, I explained that since our clinic was close by, some of our people would eventually get caught in the crossfire, so to speak. I closed out my comments by saying if anything happens to any of these doctors or nurses, the police are going to come down on you and everybody else.[3]

The type of crime described above was characteristic of the street robberies and burglaries that occurred in Portland during the late 1960s and early 1970s. According to a Gallup Poll, one in every three people living in a densely populated metropolitan area had been mugged or robbed or had suffered some sort of property loss. Again, Ford's efforts to improve the health and welfare of the black community in Albina ultimately earned him Huey Newton's respect, resulting in the Portland branch being granted official charter status after Newton's release from prison in the summer of 1970. By that time, Ford had developed a reputation as someone who could get things done. Newton may have sensed this upon meeting Ford. When Ford met Newton, the only thing on Ford's mind was getting Newton to realize that he and his comrades were worthy of the "Panther" moniker. After a short conversation, Newton saw that gaining full status as a branch of the Black Panther Party was important to Ford. Ford recounts the sequence of events:

> Huey had just gotten out of jail in August 1970. . . . I was in Oakland at the time. One Saturday afternoon I, along with several other comrades, were at the Peralta street office lifting weights; Huey was there. We all took turns spotting one another. . . . After we finished lifting and putting away the weights, Huey comes over and introduces himself, like I don't know who he is . . . then I say, "My name is Kent Ford and I'm from Portland, Oregon." A short exchange took place . . . and Huey asked, "You guys have any buildings?" I say, "Yeah, we have three buildings." Something then said to me that this was a golden opportunity to bring up something that the comrades and I had been talking about for a while. So . . . I said, "Hey, Huey, the comrades in Portland aren't enthusiastic about this NCCF stuff . . . we want to be full-fledged Panthers. Huey just stood there listening, never said a word. Moments later, we all went inside, and Huey started in on one of his long intellectual diatribes about politics and the system. We formed a semicircle around him and just listened. Ten days later, I'm back in Portland. By that time, I receive a letter from the central committee, and it's signed by Huey authorizing us as an official branch of the Black Panther Party.

Ford's zeal for securing full Panther status was understandable; after all, the Portland cadre had already established several community programs, and they were known throughout the city for their work in Albina.[4]

The first officially sanctioned Panther branch in Oregon, however, was in the college town of Eugene. From Ford's point of view, "Eugene's demographics made the prospects of building and sustaining an effective branch extremely unlikely . . . but if Eugene could get a branch," said Ford, "we should be able to as well." Located ninety miles south of Portland, Eugene is the home of the University of Oregon, which is the area's largest employer; the city was even whiter than Portland and considerably smaller. Furthermore, the town's black population was inconsiderable. The Eugene branch of the BPP, founded on the University of Oregon campus by brothers Howard and Tommy Anderson, relied on the university's student body for support. The branch's support by the larger Eugene community was tenuous. Chuck Armsbury, a leader and founder of the Patriot Party in Eugene and Portland and a doctoral candidate in sociology at the University of Oregon at that time, commented, "Local blacks in Eugene weren't accustomed to hearing Black Power rhetoric, so Panthers were a tough sell." Despite these challenges, however, the Eugene Panthers were able to put together a breakfast program and a liberation school, but the branch was short-lived and closed its doors in 1970 after a series of run-ins with the police. Initially the Eugene branch had reported to central headquarters in California, but then a decision was made to have the Seattle chapter oversee it. "It just made more sense for us to oversee the branch . . . it was more practical, but doing so turned out to be a hassle. . . . There was always something going on there . . . we kept having to go down there to straighten stuff out. . . . Eventually we just shut the branch down," said Aaron Dixon, captain of the Seattle chapter.[5]

Even before the Portland cadre was permitted to call itself a NCCF branch, Ford and his comrades had established several programs for which the Black Panther Party was nationally known. Bobby Seale introduced the "Serve the People" programs in the fall of 1968, ordering all branches and chapters to establish free breakfast programs and the like. Several months later, in March 1969, Seale identified four initiatives around which the BPP would organize: the free breakfast program, the petition campaign for community control of police, the establishment of free health clinics, and the black liberation schools. The "Serve the People" programs were renamed "community survival" programs in 1971: "Survival pending revolution—not something to replace revolution or challenge the power relations demanding radical action, but an activity that strengthens us for the coming fight, a lifeboat or raft leading us safely to shore."[6] In his book *Survival Pending Revolution*, Paul Alkebulan, professor of history at historically black Virginia State University and a former Black Panther, has an interesting take on the community survival programs. Alkebulan writes that, while the community programs addressed real needs, objectively speaking, "they were more important to the existence of the party as an organization than they were to the survival of the black community. Survival programs were originally instituted not only to serve the people but also to improve the party's image in the black community." If this is true, then the strategy proved immensely helpful not only to the organizers in Portland but to other budding and aspiring Panthers around the country who might have incurred their fair share of skepticism from local residents whose knowledge of the BPP came largely from media reports or hearsay out of the Bay Area. Without the "Serve the People" programs, earning the trust and respect of the community would have been no small feat.[7]

Panther critics who viewed such programs as reformist and questioned the Panthers' revolutionary fervor were answered by the Panthers' minister of defense, Huey Newton himself, when he opined, "Reforms are all right. Reforms are good as long as they don't put up an obstacle to your final revolutionary goal." In keeping with this position, Ford and other early members of the Portland NCCF, including Tommy Mills, Sandra Ford, Percy and Patty Hampton, Floyd Cruse, Oscar Johnson, and Linda Thornton, initiated a free clothing giveaway for their first formal community initiative in Portland. The circumstances under which this initiative was launched can only be described as fortuitous. Ford recalls how the program materialized: "The parents of an NCCF member owned a secondhand store on Union Avenue and Beach. After many years, the parents decided they wanted to get out of that business, so the mother contacted the party and offered to donate all the merchandise. We gladly accepted her offer; we also took over the lease for the building. I think the rent was no more than one hundred dollars a month, maybe less. When we acquired both the building and the clothes, we had a ready-made free clothing giveaway program." The clothing giveaway was short-lived, however. According to Sandra Ford, "I don't think it lasted more than a year.... We didn't know anything about the secondhand clothing business... we didn't have the connections in that industry to bring in the volume that the previous owner did. Every once in a while someone would donate something, but this didn't happen with any regularity... once we gave away the clothes, we weren't able to replenish the shelves.... When we gave away everything, the free clothing giveaway came to an end."[8]

Between 1969 and 1970, the Portland NCCF created three additional important community survival programs. One of the needs that the Panthers addressed was the lack of nourishment for children. The first Free Breakfast for Children program was created in 1969 at St. Augustine's Episcopal Church in Oakland. Huey P. Newton believed that everyone had a right to eat, and to eat as much as they liked. Rights are a special kind of freedom, however, because they must be accorded to all persons equally. If some people are allowed access to food and others are not, then food is a privilege and not a right. In theory, the chief characteristic of a right in a democracy is its equalitarian basis. Indeed, having access to food is a part of being a citizen, particularly in America, the richest nation on earth. For a democracy to function properly, Aristotle maintained, "measures should be taken which will give [all people] lasting prosperity." "The proceeds of the public revenues should be accumulated and distributed among its poor," he further emphasized, to enable them to "purchase a little farm, or, at any rate, make a beginning in trade or husbandry," along with other means, such as "common meals" with costs defrayed by "public land."[9]

The Panthers took seriously the belief that denying children access to food was an act of endangerment. If children are unable to eat, they will die, and since children in America are largely prohibited from working, they are dependent upon adults to provide for them. Adults who are unwilling or unable to provide children with food are (deliberately or unwittingly) guilty of child endangerment. Yet it hardly needs to be said that some people, because of a lack of resources, are unable to buy food. Despite the equalitarian character of the right to eat, there will always be some people who have the availability and purchasing power to buy food more frequently than others. When a child's family, friends, or loved ones are unable or unwilling to provide food for them, it becomes incumbent upon the government to step in and offer sustenance. John Locke, one of the most important thinkers on government and liberty, insisted that people are sovereign and that a government has a moral obligation to serve and protect the lives of its citizens. Using Locke's and Aristotle's logic as a point of departure, it is paramount to ensure that children, the most vulnerable citizens, have enough to eat. Until activists such as the Panthers made an issue out of school kids who left home in the mornings on an empty stomach, providing school-age children with a healthy breakfast was a responsibility with which the United States government did not concern itself. Simply put, by not providing the most vulnerable segment of society with food, life's most basic necessity, the government was committing an egregious act of violence against the most defenseless sector of the American populace.

Even though they were not yet card-carrying members of the Black Panther Party, NCCF members in Portland worked diligently in the fall of 1969 to establish a free breakfast program for school kids. "The government had money to fight a war thousands and thousands of miles away . . . and send astronauts to the moon," Kent Ford said, "but ensuring that kids received a well-balanced meal before heading off to school was not a priority . . . so the Panthers made it a priority." In 1967, the US government spent a mere $600,000 on breakfast programs nationwide. But as more and more Panther branches started their own free breakfast programs, government-sponsored breakfast initiatives proliferated. By 1972, government-sponsored breakfast programs were feeding more than a million children of the approximately five million who qualified for such aid.[10]

Doing the work of a Panther without being acknowledged as a Panther frustrated some of the Portland members. Their community survival initiatives, among other things, were indicative of the NCCF's burning desire and commitment to be recognized as full-fledged Panthers. Becoming an official Panther came with a tremendous amount of responsibility, but to some it was not significantly different from what they had become accustomed to doing as members of the NCCF. Oscar Johnson remembers how he structured his days around Panther activities: "My work as a Panther was not all that different than what I was doing as a member of the NCCF. I worked nights, so I was the driver. I'd finish my shift and pick up kids who needed a ride to breakfast. Go home and sleep. We solicited cash and food from neighborhood businesses in the afternoon and attended political education classes at night. It felt good. . . . We were doing something. We had the respect of the community." Drawing on a small but diverse group of young working-class and student activists, these African American men and women used a variety of networks and connections to build a robust breakfast program. The Portland NCCF made the announcement that it was going to start a free breakfast program at a community meeting. "From the outset, people were receptive to the program," said Black Panther Patty (Hampton) Carter. Believing the program to be a worthwhile endeavor, Rev. Samuel L. Johnson, head pastor of the Highland United Church of Christ, offered his church as the venue for the program. The church, located at 4635 NE Ninth Ave, was ideal, as it was spacious, met building and health code inspections, and was in close proximity to Martin Luther King Elementary School, which was located at 4906 NE Sixth Avenue. One week into the 1969–70 school year, NCCF members distributed leaflets (outlining the schedule, goals, and objective of the free breakfast program) to various community groups and passed them out to kids as they walked to and from school. Ford remembered that "people were so supportive of the program.... Rev. Johnson didn't charge us a dime ... neither did the Wonderbread company that gave us fifty loaves of bread each week, no questions asked ... then there was this one nice lady who (within a month of starting the breakfast program) came in one day with seventy-five cartons of eggs. When I attempted to pay her for her trouble, she turned me down flat saying, 'You guys are doing good work.'"[11]

By early 1970, the NCCF cadre was serving between 75 and 125 children each weekday morning. Panther supporters who had experience working in child care and child development programs helped prepare the menus, which varied depending on the contributions of area businesses and supermarkets. Percy Hampton noted that to have a breakfast program, "We all had to get the approval of the health department ... we all had to get food handlers' cards in order to serve food." The program ran from Monday through Friday. Service was interrupted on holidays, when school was cancelled due to inclement weather, and during the summer months. The kids ate well, including "sweet rolls from Wonder Bread, ground beef from McDonald's, milk from Standard Dairy, produce from Cornos," said Ford. One of the program's best cooks was a middle-aged volunteer name Robert "Bob" Frost. A former Navy man and reportedly a native of Ohio, Frost claimed to have been a professional chef. Said Ford, "Frost was an old-school southern style cook who could whip up anything at the drop of a hat and it would be delicious." Sandra Ford's praise of Frost was equaling glowing: "He could cook out of this world." While Frost is remembered for his superior culinary skills, the majority of the cooks were women. "The men mainly kept order, passed out the utensils ... stuff like that," said Ford.[12]

Rick Goodfellow, a writer for the *Pioneer Log* (Lewis and Clark College's student newspaper), wrote a four-part series on what he described as the Portland Panthers (although they were actually an office of the NCCF at the time), chronicling in great detail his visit to the breakfast program. According to Goodfellow,

> We had expected some idealist whose blurred dogma interfered with
> their work. What we saw were four people just working. There were no
> propaganda posters on the wall, no black berets on the men's heads, and,
> at least at that moment, no talk of party ideology. Of course, we soon came

to an obvious conclusion—if anybody wanted to feed a bunch of kids every morning, they had to get up and work. There was no time for politics. By 7:30 a.m. all of the preparations had been completed except for actually cooking the food. When the first little girl walked in, the cooking began. In another ten minutes, another nine children had arrived, filling one of the four tables. The breakfast workers kept a close eye on the kids and prepared food at the same pace in which the children arrived. No one was served anything but hot, freshly cooked sausage, eggs, hotcakes, syrup, and hot chocolate. The food smelled good, and we did not see a single child who did not eat everything that was on his plate.

Reflecting back some forty years, Goodfellow freely admits, "Writing those articles was not an easy thing to do, as the Panthers were not at all what I had expected."[13]

The Panthers also received praise from *Oregonian* reporter Bill Keller, who wrote in a news article, "The breakfasts are more orderly than meals in most cafeterias. Even a soft drink machine in the church annex is taped up each morning so that children won't spend their lunch money." Some former participants of the breakfast program have vivid memories of that time. Ollie Robertson, who was a regular at the free breakfast program, remembers, "Every time I see Mr. Ford to this day I thank him for doing that breakfast program." When asked what she remembered about the free breakfast program, Kim Green, who is now in her midfifties, said, "I remember being happy whenever I went there." Nathaniel Cross, another Martin Luther King Elementary School graduate, exclaimed, "I loved going to the breakfast program. I went there for about two years straight. I remember Mr. Ford used to talk to us about staying in school, doing the right thing, and getting our lives together. I looked forward to seeing the Panthers. They always had something positive to say." For Albina residents, the breakfast program was not only a blessing, it was also an important element in breaking the cycle of poverty and a dependency on government. Brochures distributed by the NCCF pointed to the circular logic of poverty: "They TELL US, you're hungry because you're poor . . . . You're poor because you haven't got the best jobs. . . . You can't get the best jobs because you're uneducated, and you're uneducated because you didn't learn in school because you weren't interested. And every time the teacher mentioned 5 apples or 6 bananas, your stomach growled. How can a person learn about remainders and quotients when his mind is concentrating on a very real and concrete problem?"[14]

From the perspective of NCCF members and many blacks in Albina, children whose parents could not afford basic foodstuffs were stuck in a vicious cycle of poverty. Linda Thornton, who spent much of her time working in the breakfast program, said, "This program was much needed . . . a lot of the kids at the breakfast program were from broken homes. . . they were going to school hungry." Poverty was one of the greatest obstacles facing the African American community, and it stood in the way of any hope of meaningful social or economic progress. Therefore, addressing poverty was an essential step toward other neighborhood improvements. According to Portland Panther Vernell Carter, "The breakfast program showed the city what we [black people] could do it on our own." As the need for a wide range of services became clearer to members of the NCCF, additional programs were created that benefitted thousands of Portlanders throughout the 1970s. Still, of all the programs offered by the NCCF, the breakfast program is the one that residents seem to remember most fondly. Darryl Thomas, now fifty-seven, remembers vividly the Panthers' free breakfast program:

> I was attending Martin Luther King Jr. Elementary School at the time and a bunch of us from school would walk over to the Highland United Church of Christ and eat breakfast. This was in 1969. The Panthers fed us well. We would have pancakes or waffles, juice and milk. Eggs mixed with sausage was a staple. The Panthers also served potatoes. The Panthers had a saying: . . . if a kid is hungry, he isn't thinking about learning, he's thinking about his stomach growling. The Panthers fed everyone a hearty breakfast.

Like Thomas, Teddy Sanders also had fond memories of the breakfast program. He said,

> I ate at the breakfast program religiously . . . all of my friends did too. We would knock on each other's door and holler "Let's go get some breakfast!" More kids ate at the Black Panther breakfast program than at the school. We had to pay to eat breakfast at my school. Not only that, but the breakfast served at the school wasn't very healthy. They served some type of yellow cornmeal-looking mush with one little carton of milk . . . I will never forget that. The school's breakfast didn't compare to what the Panthers gave us. The Panthers program wasn't a good program, it was an excellent program.[15]

Dolores Bowman, who was in charge of the breakfast program at Martin Luther King Elementary School, admitted that the public schools' program could not compete with the Panthers' in quality of hot food, but said that her program served an average of 100 to 150 children a day. In early March 1970, a photographer for a local publication dropped in on the elementary school breakfast program, and while he did not find the children eating the type of mush described by Teddy Sanders, what he did witness was a breakfast that consisted of toast with some sort of syrup and butter coating, along with milk and juice. "We fed them real food," Joyce Radford (now Williams) noted of the Panthers' breakfasts, "unlike what they were getting from the school." When asked why more children attended the school's breakfast program despite the fact that the Panthers' breakfast was more appealing, Bowman speculated that the answer probably lay with parental reaction to some of the films and literature associated with the Panthers' breakfast program. "But," she said, "if it was just a matter of the kind of food served, I'd eat with the Panthers." Although the program was a hit in the community, Ford noted that "it only lasted for four years." In November 1971, Bill D. White, principal of Martin Luther King Elementary School, said in an interview by *Oregonian* reporter Bill Keller, "The Panthers express something that many of the people here feel ... they may express it more strongly, but if you took a vote on the street, the Panthers would get a good majority of support, mostly because of programs like the free breakfast and the clinics."[16]

In addition to the free breakfast program, another of the Portland NCCF's important endeavors was the establishment of a health clinic. In the spring of 1970, Bobby Seale ordered that all BPP chapters and branches set up free and accessible healthcare facilities. Although neither Seale nor Newton referenced the Haight-Ashbury free medical clinic as their inspiration, the similarities between the two are unmistakable. Founded by Dr. David Smith in June 1967, the Haight-Ashbury clinic was designed to cater to the needs of the thousands of young people, regardless of race, who flocked to the city during the Summer of Love. The discrepancy between the quality of health care given to blacks and whites was well known, as was blacks' limited access to health care facilities, hospitals, clinics, and the like. Historically, when blacks took ill, they were relegated to all-black wards or turned away from white hospitals—even in cases of an emergency. In 1963, the Supreme Court ruled in *Simkins v. Moses Cone Hospital* that the "separate but equal" doctrine was unconstitutional in the health field. Despite this edict, in the following years, many blacks were still being turned away from white hospitals, placed in segregated wings, or treated poorly by the physicians who begrudgingly gave them treatment. The aspiring Panthers recognized that the medical needs of blacks were more acute, complicated, and neglected than those of other Americans, yet despite this greater need for care, blacks were less likely than others to get it. Dr. Martin Luther King, Jr., put it best when he said, "Injustice in health is the most shocking and most inhuman." The aspiring Panthers hoped to fulfill this need with a health clinic. In early 1969, they began assembling a health clinic in a small building on the northeast corner of North Vancouver and Russell Street.[17]

In June 1969, Don Hamerquist, a white former member of the local Communist Party who had organized the fundraising for Ford's bail, approached the Portland NCCF captain with the name of an individual who could help: Jon Moscow. A graduate of Reed College and a writer and ad manager for the Willamette Bridge during the late 1960s, Moscow, along with Robert Spindel, now a doctor in New York City, cofounded the Health Research Action Project (Health RAP) in the spring of 1969. Health RAP specialized in research on the Portland health care system and in bringing to people's attention the ways in which hospitals and the health care system were complicit in the oppression of poor people. As health care activists, Moscow and Spindel were keenly aware of the shortage of community clinics. Health RAP and the NCCF ultimately entered into an alliance that proved to be invaluable in many ways, especially to the aspiring Panthers, and launched the Fred Hampton People's Free Health Clinic. By early 1970, Moscow, who, like Hamerquist, was white, located an old doctor's office at 109 N. Russell Street for the Panthers' clinic and filed the necessary permit paperwork to operate and solicit funds, although no solicitation permit was ever granted. Once the Panthers had the building, Jon Moscow, Kent Ford, and Sandra Ford began looking for doctors who were willing to volunteer. They found, somewhat to their surprise, a number of white doctors, particularly those associated with the Oregon Health and Science University (OHSU) in Portland, who were willing to volunteer and to help fund the clinic. As a result, the Panthers were able to open their health clinic in 1970, which they decided to name after Fred Hampton, the twenty-one-year-old deputy chairman of the Illinois state chapter of the BPP whom police had shot and killed while he slept in his bed during a raid a few months earlier on December 4, 1969. Yvonne Joe, who served as a receptionist for the clinic at one point, said, "We were a life saver for a lot of people. . . . All kinds of people walked through the doors— blacks, whites, even Latinos . . . but not everyone who came in for treatment was poor." Sandra Ford recalls about recruiting physicians, "We got a lot more no's than we did yes's, but we persevered." Volunteer physicians to whom we have spoken remember how dedicated Sandra was to making the health clinic a success. She spent countless hours checking schedules, cleaning up, making sure the volunteers were where they were supposed to be, checking in patients, and assisting the male doctors with female patients.[18]

One of the clinic's first volunteers was George Barton, a neurosurgeon and 1957 graduate of the University of Oregon Medical School. Barton received an unexpected call one day from Sandra Ford, who asked him to volunteer at the clinic. When he asked how she had gotten his name, she responded that she had consulted a directory of physicians, and since his surname began with the letter B, he was one of the first on the list. Barton turned out to be a good fit. He said, "I was glad that Sandra contacted me, because I missed out on the Civil Rights Movement.... My family and I were in Africa at the time ... I always felt bad about that." Barton had worked in Tunisia while serving in the Peace Corps from 1966 to 1968. After that, he had volunteered with Outside In, a neighborhood clinic founded in 1968 in Portland's west side as a response to the city's purported drug epidemic. Recalling his experience at Outside In, Barton said, "The clinic was supposedly founded to care for the indigent, but the folk there seemed to be more concerned with treating rich kids and hippies ... after a while I got sick of that and left." Barton's experience at the Fred Hampton clinic, however, was in keeping with his larger concerns and interests. "The Panthers' clinic was more my style." said Barton, "I think I volunteered there one day a week for two years.... I used to ride my bicycle over to the clinic." Frances Storrs, a dermatologist and the first woman faculty member to get tenure at the University of Oregon Medical School, volunteered at the clinic for three years. "I had always worked in free clinics, so working at the Panthers' clinic was not new for me. Although the clinic was in a rough part of town, I never had any problems ... I met wonderful people."[19]

One of the clinic's more famous volunteer physicians was Lendon Smith, a pediatrician and television personality known as "The Children's Doctor." Smith reportedly volunteered at the clinic for five years. One Saturday a month Smith conducted a well-baby clinic. Ford and others understood that a baby's survival in the first month of life is contingent upon the mother's health and the adequacy of her medical care. Babies that survive the first month but die before the end of first year tend to do so as a result of being exposed to unfavorable or harsh environmental factors, and to infectious diseases, the flu, congested lungs, and the like, for which medical science has cures. A well-baby clinic was a welcome addition to the Fred Hampton People's Free Health Clinic. Smith boasted impressive credentials. He was the author of nearly a dozen books, including *Improving Your Child's Behavior Chemistry*, *Dr. Smith's Diet Plan for Teenagers*, and *Feed Your Body Right*. And long before it was in vogue, Smith preached that nutrition plays a major role in behavior and that nutritional strategies are helpful in preventing a wide variety of diseases and conditions. Throughout the 1970s, Smith's ideas were widely promoted on his own syndicated TV show and via hundreds of guest appearances on such programs as *The Tonight Show with Johnny Carson* and *The Phil Donahue Show*. Vicki Nakashima, a clinic volunteer and community agent for John Adams High School who took her son to the clinic, notes, "Dr. Smith was a remarkable individual. He had such commitment to the residents of north and northeast Portland."[20]

Throughout the late 1960s and the 1970s, the clinic, housed in a nondescript but suitable storefront with a large glass plate window that read "Fred Hampton's People's Free Health Clinic" in black stencil, became an integral part of Albina's black community. It was particularly appreciated by those who needed medical treatment but lacked health insurance or those who may have been insured but dreaded the hassle of being peppered with question after question, filling out mountains of paperwork, or simply having to endure a long wait to see a physician. Said a white production planner whose work was suffering due to severe back pain, "At the county hospital they told me it would be thirty days before I could get somebody to look at my back . . . here I don't have to wait." Some patients faced the possibility of being turned away from a hospital due to a lack of insurance. "A lot of people in Portland couldn't afford health care," said Black Panther Raymond Joe. Dr. Barton remembers, "We didn't turn anyone away, regardless of their financial situation . . . it didn't matter if they didn't have health insurance, we still treated them." In addition to being uninsured, some patients were without transportation. On many occasions, the Panthers provided rides to patients who did not live within walking distance. When they themselves were unable to give patients a lift to and from the clinic, the Panthers relied on the benevolence of the Rose City Cab Company, a black-owned establishment with whom they had an arrangement. Naturally, however, there were times when the Panthers were unable to provide transportation due to a lack of manpower or last-minute notices, or because of the hectic schedules that many of them maintained. Kent Ford laid out his daily routine:

Even though the clinic did not open until seven in the evening, I would get
there somewhere between 9:00 and 10:00 a.m. to get everything ready for
that night. I would straighten up, mop the floors, take and return phone
calls ... stuff like that. I would also call the volunteers to make sure everyone
was on the same page with regard to that day's schedule. I would finish
up what I needed to do by 3:00 p.m. and hit the streets ... trying to sell as
many newspapers as I could. Thirty minutes before the clinic was scheduled
to close for the night, I would pop back in to make sure everything went
smoothly and to see all of our volunteers off safely.[21]

In 1972 Newton and Elaine Brown revised the BPP's "Ten-Point Platform and Program" and called for "completely free healthcare for all black
and oppressed people." The Portland branch had as comprehensive a
health clinic as any branch or chapter within the Black Panther Party. Not
only was it centrally located, but the volunteer physicians were some of the
most lauded in their fields of specialty. The clinic operated with more than
twenty volunteer physicians from across Portland—all of whom, with the
exception of pathologist Dr. Bill Davis (brother of actor Ossie Davis), were
white—and a team of volunteer nurses and medical students. At the time,
Davis was the laboratory director at Emanuel Hospital. Said Sandra Ford,
"Each evening, the clinic required a staff of eight people: two doctors, two
nurses, two clerical aids, and two lab technicians." Paul Hull, a cardiologist
who volunteered at the clinic once a week, said, "I saw between twenty-five
and thirty-five patients per night ... most of them had colds, flus, bladder
infections, sprains, and bruises, ... the usual stuff." The clinic, open every
weeknight from 7:00 to 10:00 p.m., served roughly twenty-five to fifty patients and helped anyone who sought medical assistance, regardless of skin
color. Although, as Hull pointed out, many of those who walked through
the clinic's front door were afflicted with minor illnesses, there were
among the clientele a fair number of drug addicts and prostitutes, many
of whom sought treatment for sexually transmitted diseases. According to
Kent Ford, "The clinic was popular among that group, because they knew
they could come in and get treated without having to be put through any
changes." It did not take long before word about the clinic spread throughout the city. Said one student reporter who toured the Panthers' clinic for
a four-part series, "The facilities were clean and functional. The medicine
storage areas could never be mistaken for a pharmacy, but the range of
drugs on hand was surprisingly varied." When the clinic closed at 10:00

p.m., Panthers escorted doctors and other volunteers to their cars past bustling taverns and other after-hours joints.[22]

Over the years the clinic became one of Albina's most talked-about grassroots community efforts and even attracted some notable visitors. One evening in the early 1970s, longtime Oregon politician Wayne Morse stopped by the health clinic while stumping on the campaign trail for the US Senate and marveled at what he saw. Morse is perhaps best remembered for being one of only two senators who voted against the Gulf of Tonkin Resolution years earlier, which had authorized the escalation of the Vietnam War following what remain historically suspicious and controversial skirmishes between North Vietnamese and American forces. Kent Ford remembers Morse's visit, recalling, "Morse and his chauffeur arrived soon after we opened up for the evening. . . . We gave him and his chauffeur a tour of the clinic, and they couldn't stop raving about it. . . . The more I downplayed it, the more they praised us. I remember Morse's chauffeur saying, 'You guys are really to be commended for the way you all went after those doctors.'" Morse was not the only curious notable to visit the clinic, but he was the only elected official or former elected official to do so. Within two years, the clinic would be the subject of more than one featured news story in the city's mainstream newspapers and alternative press.[23]

The Fred Hampton People's Free Health Clinic, like many other Panther health clinics across the United States, also worked to raise awareness of specific environmental and hereditary medical conditions affecting African Americans, notably high blood pressure and sickle cell anemia, an illness that disproportionately affects blacks. "Most people didn't know anything about sickle cell anemia until we started testing people for it," said Raymond Joe. A sickle cell anemia committee, which consisted of laypersons, healthcare professionals, clergy, and professional basketball player Stan McKenzie, a swingman for the Portland Trailblazers, oversaw the testing of local residents. Davis arranged for the clinic to have both Sickledex and electrophoresis testing capabilities. There may be some truth to Joe's statement, but it should be noted that black professionals in the areas of science, medicine, and public policy had begun making a national issue of sickle cell anemia as early as 1969. The October 1970 issue of the *Journal of the American Medical Association* (*JAMA*) had spotlighted sickle cell anemia, bringing national attention to the disease. In an article titled "Health Care Priority and Sickle Cell Anemia," Robert B. Scott brought to light glaring disparities in funding for research on genetic diseases. Moreover, one of the party's consultants was a Detroit-based physician by the name of Dr. Charles Whitten, a graduate of Meharry Medical College and a leader in sickle cell anemia research. Whitten's credentials included being the principal founder of the Sickle Cell Detection and Information Center in 1971. He created color-coded "Whitten dice" to educate couples about the genetic risks of having children with sickle cell disease. Additionally, Whitten helped develop the National Association for Sickle Cell Anemia Disease. By the spring of 1972, President Richard Nixon signed the National Sickle Cell Anemia Control Act. Given the national discussion surrounding this affliction and the media coverage that so often accompanies such matters, it is improbable that most people were unaware of the disease. It is likely, however, that few people were as knowledgeable about the condition as those who administered testing. At the time, the disease affected one black birth in five hundred but had received little attention from the white medical and scientific community.[24]

Testing kids for lead poisoning was also high on the Panthers' list of priorities. In the first half of the twentieth century, lead paint was used extensively throughout the United States and was not banned for residential use until the late 1970s. Portland, an old seaport town, was comprised of a lot of old housing stock. In the United States, over 40 percent of homes built between 1940 and 1959, and more than 65 percent of homes built prior to 1940 contained hazards due to lead paint. In Portland specifically, 60 percent of the population within the city limits in 1970 lived in housing built before World War II. Also, in 1970, experts estimated that the annual incidence of symptomatic and asymptomatic lead poisoning in the United States was as high as 250,000 cases. The lead from the paint sloughed off, forming household dust, and was both inhaled and ingested by small children, who are prone to putting small items in their mouths. Issues such as this propelled the Panthers to establish an outreach component to their health clinic. For example, the Panthers would go door to door distributing pamphlets about breast cancer, oftentimes striking up a conversation with the woman of the house in an effort to encourage her to get a breast exam. This effort was in response to reports that deaths among black women from breast cancer had soared during the 1960s. Throughout the 1950s, white women had accounted for the vast majority of breast cancer deaths; the death rate for black women at that time was 22 percent lower than for white women. However, during the 1960s that trend reversed itself. In general, only 63 out of 100 women who were diagnosed with breast cancer in the 1960s were still living after five years, compared to more than 80 out of 100 women today.[25]

Reaching out to petition school administrators to set up health awareness and testing programs was something the Panthers did regularly. Other times, the Panthers would go into the schools, such as Woodlawn Elementary School, Highland Elementary School, and Harriet Tubman Middle School in north Portland, to administer lead poisoning tests to kids. As part of the branch's community outreach, the Panthers used community barbecues and live music to attract hundreds of people who lacked proper health care. "We had barbecue chicken and potato salad," Ford remembers. "All you had to do was get a sickle cell test, get a plate, sit down, and enjoy the music." As in the typical clinic, when more serious ailments called for further treatment, patients were referred to the Oregon Health and Science University. When appropriate, referrals were made to private specialists. "We have specialty referrals to private offices on a free basis in surgery, internal medicine, dermatology, hematology, neurology, pediatrics and cancer therapy," wrote Jon Moscow in a 1970 issue of the *Willamette Bridge*.[26]

The same year that the health clinic got underway, the Panthers, again with the help of Jon Moscow and his connections at OHSU and the Portland medical community, came up with the novel and revolutionary idea to establish a dental clinic. Several Panther branches and chapters had their own health clinics, but none had a dental clinic. Initially, the clinic was located at 2337 N. Williams Avenue. The clinic, according to Ford, "was equipped with a waiting room, a reception area, and one operatory." As with the health clinic, the Portland BPP named the dental clinic after another fallen freedom fighter, calling it the Malcolm X People's Dental Clinic. Naming the clinic in honor of Malcolm X was befitting, given the reverence blacks had for him and what Malcolm represented to a generation of African Americans. No one wrote more poignantly about Malcolm X's influence than literary critic Addison Gayle, who penned,

> Malcolm represented something important to me. To say merely that he was a man is not to explain his enormous influence upon those who, like myself, have lost faith in an American dream of egalitarian democracy. He was the first acknowledged prophet of our era to preach the moral decadence of Western civilization, to bring to the conscience of black people the truth concerning that culture in which we seem bent on immersing ourselves, and to force us to question the idols which we had accepted without question from those who were said to be wiser than we, our leaders.[27]

Despite the powerful person after whom the clinic was named, Sandra Ford remembers the clinic's early struggles, noting, "Of all our programs, the dental clinic was the most difficult to get off the ground.... We had to find volunteer dentists who were willing to be associated with us.... We also had to obtain supplies and equipment.... There was a lot of special equipment we had to secure, which wasn't easy to do ... but we did it." Some of the equipment was obtained from dental supply houses or from dentists who were closing down their practices. The clinic was open on Monday, Wednesday, and Friday evenings from 7:00 to 10:00, like the medical clinic, it attracted volunteers from all walks of life. Barbara Gundle, a student at Reed College, volunteered at the clinic. Reflecting on her experience, she said, "I thought the work I was doing was important.... I felt like we were building a movement." Dr. Duane Paulson, a pediatric dentist who signed on from the very beginning, said, "I had students from the OHSU waiting in line to volunteer at the clinic.... They were eager to get involved because they wanted the experience and they wanted to feel like they were doing something good.... I took two to three students with me every evening." Dr. Clarence Pruitt, the first black graduate of the University of Oregon Dental School and a part-time instructor at the school, oversaw the clinic. Pruitt's widow, Joy, said, "My husband really enjoyed working with the Panthers.... He was interested in the Panthers' philosophy, especially their emphasis on helping poor people." Before Pruitt came on board, Moscow had approached the dental school about donating equipment, which they did. However, once Pruitt saw the antiquated items that had been donated, he quickly reached out to administrators at the University of Oregon Dental School. Ford notes, "Pruitt went to the dean and other administrators and jumped all over them ... I think he even gave the president an earful ... the next thing we know, we got newer and better equipment."[28]

In addition to the three weekdays that the clinic was open, early on, the Panthers also opened the clinic one Saturday a month. On those days, patrons were introduced to preventive care measures and given tooth-care kits that contained floss and other items. "You'd be surprised," Ford recalls, "at how many people didn't know how to floss or know how long you should keep a toothbrush." As more and more people heard about the clinic, more dentists signed on. Moscow even convinced Dr. Gerry Morrell, a white general practitioner dentist and head of community outreach for the Multnomah County Dental Association, to volunteer his time, expertise, and tools in establishing the clinic. Morrell recalls that his assistant "came down to the clinic and sterilized all of the hand instruments." Morrell volunteered at the clinic for five or six years. "Volunteering at the Panthers' dental clinic was a very rewarding experience," he said. "Many, but not all of the patients were indigent, but they were very appreciative, they were a joy to work with . . . the entire experience was very enjoyable." Moreover, Morrell successfully found other dentists (some of whom were from the dental study club in which he was involved) and students from the University of Oregon Dental School who were willing to work in the clinic. "Among the services that we performed included taking X-rays, doing restorations, performing root canals, extractions, and so forth. . . . What we didn't do was make dentures or fit patients with braces." Describing such crucial volunteer work, Ford said, "All of our volunteer dentists were very supportive, especially Morrell and Pruitt . . . they were a godsend." About Pruitt in particular, Ford said, "He was a pioneer, plus he was also a good crown-and-bridge man."[29]

Kent Ford recalls one of the groups' early meetings in which the cadre, along with Morrell and others, talked about the prospect of launching a clinic. "We met at Paul Knauls's restaurant, Geneva's . . . we all sat in a semicircle in a private area of the restaurant. Some of the leading dentists in the city were there. . . . It was at that meeting I think where we hammered out the preliminary steps." "We started off with more than twenty dentists," said Morrell. "Some moved, some were scared off by the political aspects of the Black Panthers, and some were just all talk and no action." Paulson recalls, "We did lots of prevention that included talking to people about what foods to eat or not eat, the proper way to brush your teeth, how to use floss, and how many times a day one's teeth should be brushed. We were filling a need . . . like putting your thumb in a dike, but at least it was a start." Glamorous work it was not, but it was sorely needed. Morrell also recalls a funny incident that occurred at the Oregon State Dental Association annual convention one year. Weeks earlier Morrell had gotten the bright idea of giving a presentation on the Panthers' dental clinic. He thought it would be a nice way of giving the clinic some publicity and of informing his colleagues and their students about the good work they were doing in the community. After his presentation, Morrell was milling about with several other conference attendees when one of his colleagues approached him and said half-jokingly, "Hey, Gerry, now you're going to be on the attorney general's list for working with the Panthers," to which Morrell, without hesitating, responded, "Well, I'm gonna be on God's list too."[30]

Dwindling funds and a small stable of volunteers required the Panthers to do much of the day-to-day work in both clinics themselves. Sandra Ford, who married Kent Ford in June 1970, was particularly important in this effort. As both clinics grew, she assumed the job of receptionist, did all of the appointment scheduling for both the health and the dental clinic, and ultimately oversaw both clinics' daily finances and operations. Looking back, Moscow said, the community desperately needed the clinic. "We got referrals from the health department, a lot of whites were referred to the health clinic ... our clientele was multiracial. As far as the dental clinic is concerned, there was only one other dental clinic in Portland; it was called Buckman, located in the southeast section of the city; it was in danger of being closed down." Health RAP, however, succeeded in keeping it open. During the 1969–70 calendar year, members of the group held demonstrations, submitted articles to the *Willamette Bridge*, and made presentations to the city council. Robert Spindel remembers, "Jon [Moscow] and I showed up with a bunch of our activist friends who weren't necessarily members of Health RAP; we made signs, we stood outside picketing ... we put signs in the hands of any and everyone who was willing to hold them ... we made it seem like Health RAP was this really big organization." "There was certainly enough demand for two dental clinics," Moscow recalled. Ultimately, by the efforts of leadership and grassroots volunteers, many African Americans in Albina now had access to basic health and dental care who would otherwise have had none.[31]

Although these programs clearly helped fill the previously neglected needs of Albina's black residents by providing spaces of social relief and community empowerment, they required financial and material support from the people and businesses of northeast Portland. The Portland Black Panther Party derived much of its income from selling the Black Panther newspaper at twenty-five cents a copy. The paper was well-received in Portland's radical circles. Percy Hampton, the branch's distribution manager, stated, "When we first started out, the San Francisco office sent us approximately three hundred papers, but after a while the number grew between five hundred and eight hundred. The papers arrived via United Airlines on Wednesdays, and by Thursday morning we were dropping them off all over northeast Portland. Safeway and Fred Meyer were two of the chains that allowed us to leave bundles of the newspaper." Students at Portland State University and at Reed College were particularly receptive to the Panthers' message. Hampton noted, "PSC [Portland State College, later PSU] was a happening place, full of activity . . . the Brown Berets, SDS [Students for a Democratic Society], and communists were all there. . . . White radicals were good customers."[32]

The newspaper's appeal to white radicals was evident at the Vortex I concert in the summer of 1970. Although not billed as such, Vortex I was to Portland what Woodstock was to upstate New York and the Altamont Speedway Free Festival was to San Francisco, but without the inclement weather that saddled the former, or the violence that plagued the latter—or the musical star power of either. Vortex I, which, ironically, was a government-sponsored effort to avoid a possible violent clash between antiwar activists and attendees of the American Legion national convention in Portland, attracted thousands of young people, mostly whites, to the eight-hundred-acre McIver State Park located less than thirty miles southeast of Portland. Not only was the weather beautiful, the mood was festive. Concertgoers were free to express themselves in whatever way they saw fit—from taking hallucinogens to skinny-dipping to indulging in the occasional mud bath. The concert proved to be an excellent venue for selling the Panther paper. Hampton said, "Willie James Brown and I loaded up the car with newspapers and headed out there. . . . There were so many people there, I had to park my car a good ways away from where the actual festival was being held and walk the rest of the way. We had to park so far away that we ended up selling newspapers as we walked . . . we sold half of the papers before we even got there." "Percy was the perfect person to sell the newspaper; he knew how to get out there and hustle," said Ford. Quick to give credit to others, Hampton stated, "I had a nice little crew around me that consisted of a number of dedicated young Brothers and Sisters. They did a really good job of selling the paper."[33]

Newspaper sales reflected the party's local, national, and international appeal, as well as the organizational ability of the local branches. Not only did the newspaper cover matters of national and international interest, but each issue contained a one-page news bulletin put together by Oscar Johnson, the branch's assistant deputy minister of information, that kept readers abreast of the local goings-on. The Panthers viewed their newspaper as the voice of the masses. Many of the other 225 black-oriented national newspapers, as far as the Panthers were concerned, were out of touch with the daily realities of the average citizen, especially young African Americans and black radicals. Most of the papers were owned by elderly men who had not changed their periodicals (in terms of content and format) since launching their publications years earlier. Many of them could no longer be counted on to address racism. Moreover, many were tied to the Democrat and Republican parties, which made it difficult for them to challenge such issues as war, the environment, and poverty. Writing in 1974, Baxter Smith lamented that a few black newspapers contained information on all aspects of racist oppression, but that the majority remained wedded to the past and to the dream of assimilation into the colonial world.[34]

Above all, the Panther newspaper was relevant, timely, and dogged in its protest of injustices toward oppressed peoples of the world. The Panthers used profits from newspaper sales to help defray the costs of some of their community survival programs. Richard's Cigar Store and the campuses of Portland State College and Portland Community College were three locations where the newspaper also sold well. "Friday and Saturday nights were good for newspaper sales," Ford remembered. "We'd stand in front of the liquor stores, and the papers would sell like hotcakes. We had a lot of success selling papers in front of the state liquor store on Union Avenue.... Sometimes brothers from the Nation of Islam would be out there as well selling *Muhammad Speaks*... we would easily outsell them two to one." Not everyone was receptive to the party's paper, however. Percy Hampton said, "Jefferson High School was one of several high schools that wanted to avoid having any material like the Panther paper in their school... I guess administrators there thought it might inflame students or something."[35]

Even at the paper's peak, with a distribution of eight hundred newspapers per week, earnings were nowhere near enough to cover operating costs, especially since half of the proceeds were sent to the Bay Area's national office. As a result, the Panthers were forced to solicit donations from businesses and local residents, all while knowing that their failure to do so might spell the end of their community survival programs. According to Vernell Carter, "The 88 cent store would sometimes give us cash, as would a Chrysler and Plymouth dealership, both of which were located on Union Avenue." There were also times when donations came from unexpected sources. For example, in the early 1970s, the Reed College chapter of Students for a Democratic Society (SDS) came up with an idea to help support the Panthers' free breakfast program. According to historian and former Portland resident Maurice Isserman, members of the chapter agreed to forego a number of meals on their meal plan, and "the college would in turn donate that money to the Panthers free breakfast program." Although the overwhelming majority of donations came from whites, such as the weekly sum of one hundred dollars provided by the owner of a local pizza parlor, there were some African Americans who provided the Panthers with a consistent cash flow. "Don Vann, owner of Vann and Vann Funeral Home, gave us fifty dollars a week," said Ford, "and Dr. Walter Reynolds as well as Paul Knauls, a local business owner, would slip us between one hundred and one hundred and fifty dollars per month . . . without us even asking. . . . Sometimes the money would be delivered to us, but mostly I would send someone to pick it up."[36]

In addition to receiving support from the volunteer doctors and dentists who worked in the clinics, the Portland Panthers, often led by Linda Thornton, visited countless businesses in Albina with the hopes of raising funds and supplies. Thornton, who worked primarily on the breakfast program, usually approached businesses during midday with a group of Panthers in tow to request support from owners and managers. Ford recalls that there was a nearby dairy where "we would get cartons of milk and orange juice; Corno's Vegetable and Fruit Market would on occasion give us cases of apples and oranges, but for the most part local establishments turned us down . . . Redd Meat Market and a chain called Fred Myer were especially hostile." Said Ford, "Redd Meat Market was owned by two brothers who would talk about black people like a dog . . . call you everything but the 'N word,' and Fred Myer wouldn't even hire blacks until a black lawyer with the NAACP initiated a picket of the store. . . . The owner eventually gave in, but he made it clear that he was only interested in light-skinned blacks." Likewise, contrary to an article published in the *Oregon Journal* in 1970, Kienow's grocery store on Union Avenue did not provide the Panthers with any weekly food donations. "Kienow's didn't give us anything; whoever wrote that is lying," said Ford.[37]

This inaccurate account is not altogether surprising, as neither the reporters nor the editors of the *Oregonian* or the *Oregon Journal* felt obliged to adhere to the journalistic standard of objective reporting where the Portland Panthers were concerned. An expansive study of the press coverage of the Portland Panthers between 1969 and 1973 by Jules Boykoff and Martha Gies bears this out. According to Boykoff and Gies, both the *Oregonian* and the *Oregon Journal* failed to recognize or record three important things: the African American community's frustration with what many saw as a systematic pattern of police brutality, a frustration that led directly to the formation of an NCCF office and later a branch of the Black Panther Party; the courage required for young African American men and women to mount a campaign of self-defense; and the idealism that lay behind the party's community survival programs. The *Oregonian* was especially influential in molding public opinion, as it was the city's paper of note. Not only was it the largest-circulating newspaper in the city and the state, it was also the largest-circulating newspaper in the Pacific Northwest, selling more than three hundred thousand copies daily. Janet Goetze, who began working at the paper in 1968, commented that "the *Oregonian* was known as the cash cow of the Newhouse chain." Few newspapers in major metropolitan areas were as right-leaning as the *Oregonian*, which had a history of endorsing Republican candidates for statewide and national office. In fact, until its endorsement of Bill Clinton, the *Oregonian* had never backed a Democrat for the presidency.[38]

Fortunately for the Panthers, writers for the *Willamette Bridge* and, later, the *Scribe* countered the unfavorable framing of the group by the city's two major newspapers. Although the *Willamette Bridge* was an underground leftist paper, its circulation and notoriety in Portland and the surrounding area were not inconsiderable. According to Michael Wells, one of the newspaper's founders, "By the summer of 1969 we were selling fifteen thousand copies a week." The *Portland Observer*, a newspaper that catered to Portland's black residents, was also sympathetic to the Panther cause, as was the *Scribe*, another left-wing paper that emerged in 1972 after the *Bridge* went under. Isserman, who wrote for both the *Bridge* and the *Scribe*, said, "We had a lot of articles about the Panthers during the paper's first year of existence in 1972." Likewise, Dorreen Labby, a graduate of Reed College and writer for the *Scribe*, noted, "The Panthers in Portland were regarded as a movement for positive change." On occasion, editors at some of the local high schools might find reason to cover the Panthers' work in the community and their other activities. A February 27, 1970, article titled "Panther Party Works for People," published in the *Frontiersman*, the official publication of Andrew Jackson High School, is but one example.[39]

The city's mainstream papers' portrayal of the Panthers was far from objective, as they seemingly took their cues from officials who considered the Panthers to be subversive. According to police records and news reports, the tactics used by the Portland Panthers to elicit support for their activities walked a fine line between solicitation and extortion:

> A group of black subjects approach a particular business with a
> female being the spokesman for the group. This group numbers four
> to six persons. While the female is engaged in conversation with the
> management of the business, the males mill around in a generally

disruptive manner. If the demand for funds for the Program are not met, or if the persons soliciting the funds are put off or asked to come back at a later date, they attempt to set a firm time as a deadline for contributions. No direct threats are ever made, and as few names as possible are mentioned with no introductions apparent other than the female solicitor, who usually identifies herself as one LINDA THORNTON.

Later that day, or the next day, an anonymous threatening phone call is then received with words used during the threat being generally to the same effect. "You tell the man, or the manager, you're going to get bombed."

Kent Ford admitted that oftentimes one of the Panther women would take the lead in a solicitation while the men stayed in the background. "Linda was the ideal pitch person, as she was small in stature and could be soft-spoken when she wanted to be," said Ford. Ford, however, emphatically denied the accusation that either he or other members deliberately tried to intimidate merchants into making a food or monetary donation. Ford did admit that there were a few instances when he heard that Tommy Mills, a serious, no-nonsense guy, "might have been a bit too assertive" when inquiring about donations. "On those occasions, I would be sure to ask Tommy to tone it down, but other than those rare instances, the party did not make it its business to menace local business owners." Moreover, according to Ford, "often times we wouldn't even mention that we were Black Panthers, because we knew the image that many people had of Black Panthers because of what they heard or saw on TV about Panthers in Oakland."[40]

Still, if Tommy Mills was abrasive at times, as Ford suggests, he was not alone in employing tactics that may have teetered on harassment. The police kept close records on which businesses were and were not willing to provide support to the Panthers. In the case of those who offered money or food, the police verified that the businesses were not being forcibly coerced. If businesses were giving aid willingly, then the police pressed them to withdraw their support. And if that didn't work, police officers would resort to sending incendiary information in hopes of swaying businesses against the Panthers. For example, police officials made copies of a *New York Times* article charging black nationalists with "anti-Zionism" and sent them anonymously to Portland Jewish leaders. Materials critical of the Black Panther Party's objectives were also sent to establishment black leaders throughout Portland. Moreover, the police worked with the Public Solicitation Commission in late 1970 to prohibit the Panthers from obtaining a solicitation permit over technicalities involving the address of the local headquarters and their submission of paperwork.[41]

In an *Oregonian* article titled "Panthers Fail to Seek Permit to Solicit Funds," the impression is given that city officials went to great lengths to accommodate the Panthers' request for a permit. According to the article, after receiving inquiries from various parties as to whether or not the Panthers had been granted a permit to solicit funds, "the city's Bureau on Revenue and Treasury decided to take the mountain to Mohammed." Among the attempts made to furnish the Panthers with the proper paperwork was sending an official to a North Vancouver address, supposedly the Panthers' headquarters, to place the form in the hand of someone at the address, and later sending a certified letter to explain that if the solicitation ordinance was violated, a $500 fine or six-month jail sentence would be imposed. The letter went unclaimed. Later in the piece, the writer mentioned that "the diligent city bureau discovered a new address for the Panther headquarters and issued an invitation to appear at the Wednesday meeting" to no avail. The Public Solicitation Commission recommended to the city council that the Panthers' application be denied. When several former Panthers were asked about these developments, none could recall any attempts by the Public Solicitation Commission to reach out to them. Ford stated,

> Clearly I remember applying for a permit. I, along with several other Panthers, lined up about a dozen character witnesses to go downtown and vouch for us before the Portland City Council. Testifying on our behalf was a number of well-respected doctors, professionals, and other people, both black and white. The whole thing probably lasted ninety minutes. . . . After everyone finished testifying, a city council person asked if there was anyone who opposed granting the Panthers a permit . . . right then a white detective from the Portland Police Bureau stood up and introduced himself and then sat down. No questions were asked of him, still we were denied. After that, we figured the fix was in . . . we weren't going to waste our time with this. Clearly they didn't want us to have a permit, but they went through this dog-and-pony show pretending to be impartial. We just continued to do our thing and we never got fined and no one was sentenced to jail. Whatever we did or wanted to do, some city officials had a problem with . . . if we picketed someone because we believed they were preying on the black community, some city officials had a problem with that too.[42]

Boycotting and picketing merchants and businesses that the Panthers believed were exploiting the black community was a common occurrence around the country, and Portland was no different. "We would picket in a heartbeat if we determined that there was a business that was exploiting or profiting off the black community but didn't want to help support our free breakfast programs or clinics," said Hampton. "It wouldn't matter if the business was white-owned or black-owned, if it preyed on the black community and then couldn't give a donation to our programs, I was more than likely going to organize a boycott... in fact, I picketed so much that I would sometimes find myself in trouble with certain members of the branch's leadership who thought I was going overboard with the picketing and demonstrating."[43]

The Portland Panthers' most prominent clash with a local business resulted in a boycott of a McDonald's franchise at 3510 N.E. Union Avenue in the summer of 1970. According to Al Laviske, the general manager and treasurer of six McDonald's in Portland, Ford and Thornton approached him in late June and demanded one-hundred-dollar contributions to each of the BPP clinics and to the children's breakfast program, a claim that Ford steadfastly denies. Ford explained,

> Initially we approached him and invited him down to see our health and dental clinics. He accepted and jumped in his car and followed us. When we arrived, Linda and I gave him a tour of the facilities. It was midday, if I remember correctly... and the visit was pleasant... we never mentioned anything about money; we just said that we'd appreciate any support he could give. After the visit, he drove back to work. Linda and I thought the visit went well; it only lasted about thirty minutes or so. The next thing I know, he's on TV telling the world that we tried to extort him. Linda and I were shocked... we felt we had been had, hoodwinked, led astray, like Malcolm X said. What kind of man does this sort of thing, I said to myself? There he is sitting at a table jawing about how we tried to extort him... then after telling all those lies he had the nerve to stick out his chest and rear back in his chair. I couldn't believe it.[44]

The Panthers boycotted McDonald's using a disruption strategy reminiscent of the "Don't Spend Your Money Where You Can't Work" campaigns of the late 1920s and early 1930s. To address the problem of white-owned businesses in black communities that would not hire black employees, in 1933 in Washington, DC, Belford V. Lawson, John A. Davis, Sr., and M. Franklin Thorne founded the New Negro Alliance (NNA). The NNA employed the then-radical "Don't Buy Where You Can't Work" approach. The same tactic had been used earlier by activists in Chicago with slightly different wording: "Don't Spend Your Money Where You Can't Work." This tactic was so successful that the campaign sparked a larger boycott of Woolworth stores in the Windy City. In New York, boycott protests led by the venerable Rev. Adam Clayton Powell, Jr., later a congressman, added ten thousand jobs for blacks in just four years. The Panthers likewise put the boycott to good use. In their book *Poor People's Movements: Why They Succeed, How They Fail*, Francis Fox Piven and Richard Cloward write about the value of disruption by dissident groups and poor people: "Since 'the poor have few resources for regular political influence,' their ability to create social change depends on the disruptive power of tactics such as 'militant boycotts, sit-ins, traffic tie-ups, and rent strikes.'" Protest movements, Piven and Cloward explain, gain real leverage only by causing "commotion among bureaucrats, excitement in the media, dismay among influential segments of the community, and strain for political leaders."[45]

Before launching into a boycott of McDonald's, Ford and his comrades researched the company and say that they uncovered a dearth of blacks in supervisory positions within the McDonald's corporation. In early August a boycott went into effect, for the company's lack of support for the community survival programs and for a supposed national pattern of racially discriminatory hiring practices. At that time, McDonald's was America's most popular fast-food establishment, and the national chain was on the verge of becoming a multinational corporation. It had a store in each of the fifty states, and in more than one thousand locations, including Canada, Puerto Rico, and the Virgin Islands. Also, by 1970, McDonald's had sold its five billionth hamburger. The Panthers believed that Laviske was in a position to proffer support.[46]

For approximately one month, the Panthers picketed the establishment from noon to 8:00 p.m. on weekdays, and from noon to 10:00 p.m. on weekends. Retired police officer Jeff Barker remembers the boycott: "What the Panthers asked for exactly I do not know, but, according to the manager, the Panthers asked for money, and the manager claimed that he would give them food, but not money." On August 14, Judge Phillip J. Roth issued an injunction against the BPP to halt the picketing after reports of damage to personal property and anonymous threats of violence against the business. The

Panthers ignored the injunction and continued to picket. Within the week, a process server showed up at the picket line with subpoenas in hand. In the meantime, Roth had to leave town to deal with a personal matter before he could be informed that his ruling violated a 1968 US Supreme Court edict that provides that restraining orders pertaining to matters of free speech cannot be granted without the benefit a public hearing. The Panthers' attorneys—Nick Chaivoe, Joe Morehead, Ross Brown, and Charley Merton—later appeared before circuit judge Robert E. Jones with Laviske's attorneys and contested the order. After considering eyewitness testimony and hearing an array of charges and countercharges, on Saturday morning, August 15, 1970, Judge Jones granted a twelve-month injunction to Hamburger Union Enterprises, restraining protesters from encroaching on the facility's property and from "harassing, threatening bodily harm, or discouraging" patrons from entering or leaving the premises. However, he ruled that the Panthers could resume their boycott as long as the number of those picketing did not exceed more than ten individuals and as long as they engaged only in "informational picketing." The Panthers were not to physically discourage anyone from entering or leaving the McDonald's restaurant. In addition to carrying boycott signs in the parking lot, the Panthers distributed flyers that criticized McDonald's for their unwillingness to support the breakfast program or the clinics. The flyers also questioned the police's frequent use of the building's parking lot as a meeting point for transferring arrestees, noting, "McDonald's is used as a base area for PIG attacks on the BLACK COMMUNITY!" Consequently, although the Panthers technically complied with the court's orders, their rhetoric remained both accusatory and fiery.[47]

At approximately two o'clock in the morning on August 22, some residents were jolted from their beds when a bomb exploded in front of McDonald's and shattered its front window. Although no Black Panther was ever suspected or charged in the incident, both the *Oregonian* and the *Oregon Journal* tied the incident to the Panthers' picketing. The next day, Laviske announced the temporary closure of the restaurant until the damage could be repaired. The police investigation revealed that the blast appeared to be the result of one stick of dynamite placed alongside the north wall. The outward concussion from the explosion was enough to set off the alarm at a nearby grocery store. The court issued another injunction against the Panthers and their boycott, yet found insufficient evidence to charge the group with the bombing or with the lesser charge of extortion. "There was no reason for us to bomb McDonald's, because the boycott was working," Hampton maintains. While Laviske may have had his suspicions publicly, he had no way of knowing who was responsible for the bombing. He was quoted as saying that "his organization had never refused contributions of commodities and products to charitable organizations in the neighborhood." In other words, Laviske was amenable to donating food supplies to whomever asked, but not money.[48]

In the minds of some, bombing or burning down buildings was striking a blow against the establishment and corporate America. Portland experienced several bombings in 1970, including the March 12 bombing of a police community relations unit office in the northeast section of the city. Two of the more spectacular bombings that made their way onto nationally televised newscasts that year occurred in southern California and in the Midwest. In February 1970, radical elements allegedly burned down the Bank of America in Isla Vista, a student-populated area near the campus of the University of California, Santa Barbara.[49] Then, in August, there was the bombing of Sterling Hall (where the Army Mathematics Research Center was housed) on the campus of the University of Wisconsin–Madison, which caused millions of dollars worth of damage and claimed the life of a young scientist who had been working late. While some dissidents found the use of explosive devices to be an effective way of drawing attention to their cause, it was not without risk. That same year, an accidental explosion devastated a New York townhouse that had been used by the Weathermen, a radicalized splinter group of Students for a Democratic Society, as a bomb factory. Ted Gold, Terry Robbins, and Diana Oughton, all members of the Weathermen, were blown to bits. Cathy Wilkerson and Kathy Boudin barely escaped intact.

A month after the Panthers began picketing McDonald's, Laviske sent word to Kent Ford via Herman Plummer, the head of the Neighborhood Service Center, that he wanted to talk. "I was at a red light when Herman Plummer pulled up alongside me, rolled down his window, and hollered, 'Hey Kent, Laviske told me to tell you that he wants to talk,'" said Ford. One week later, the two men met in the conference room at the Neighborhood Service Center. At the meeting were Laviske and his wife, and across the table sat Kent and Sandra Ford, along with the two-hundred-and-fifty-pound Jeff Fikes. The meeting got off to an inauspicious start, as the first thing out of Laviske's mouth was, "I'm not going to donate any money!" At that point, Kent was preparing to leave until Sandra nudged him and quietly urged him to hear Laviske out. The meeting lasted for about an hour, and Laviske and Ford agreed to put aside their differences. Laviske agreed to provide the Panthers' breakfast program with fifty pounds of meat and five hundred paper cups every week. According to Kent Ford, "There were no more problems after that. . . . I was surprised that things went so smoothly given Laviske's previous position. . . . The meat would come in on Monday like clockwork, and we'd pick it up by 10:00 a.m. that day. . . . A year later I asked Laviske if we could use his parking lot to do sickle cell anemia testing, and he said yes. He even gave me, without me asking, between one thousand and fifteen hundred gift cards . . . we used the gift cards to entice people to get tested for sickle cell anemia."[50]

Not surprisingly, during the negotiations little was made of the dearth of blacks in supervisory positions, suggesting that it was not the Panthers' primary concern. Laviske's unwillingness to contribute to the Panthers is what concerned them most. The lack of blacks in managerial roles was a public-relations issue the Panthers shrewdly used to galvanize support for the boycott. The result was a substantial contribution of foodstuffs and supplies to the breakfast program, but little changed in terms of blacks in supervisory positions. Nevertheless, the most widely publicized conflict between the Portland Panthers and local businesses over the funding of their community survival programs came to an amicable end. Those who benefitted the most from this harmonious ending were the residents of Albina. The Panthers' picketing of McDonald's sent a message to merchants and corporations in the area that their relationship with their patrons was not an asymmetrical one in which the omnipotent establishment provides goods and services to its buyers but has no ethical or moral responsibility to invest in the community from which it profits or, in some cases, pilfers greatly.

The Portland Panthers' campaign against police brutality and its opposition to the white police presence in northeast Portland exemplified another major effort on the part of the Panthers to defend Albina against the intrusions of what they viewed as a racist and undemocratic system of city governance. Like many of the survival programs, this campaign was part of the Black Panther Party's nationwide program. One practical yet unconventional aspect of the Panthers' campaign against police brutality involved the monitoring of cases that they believed were blatant miscarriages of justice. Members of the Portland branch often went to the courthouse and sat in on cases. Many of the cases that the Panthers monitored involved extralegal force against black residents or trumped-up charges. Sitting in on cases not only afforded the Panthers the opportunity to stay abreast of the goings-on

of the police, but also enabled them to evaluate attorneys' levels of compe-
tence and to determine which judges were fair-minded and which were not.
They would then make their findings known to the wider community. One
case of a twenty-year-old man charged with shoplifting is indelibly etched
in Ford's memory. "I remember it so vividly because the guy didn't seem to
be able to write his own name. This young man was what you would call a
functional illiterate. . . . I couldn't believe that someone that young in that
day and age not being able to write his name . . . this wasn't the 1950s, but the
1970s . . . seeing that was sobering."[51]

The party's work around police brutality drew on the seventh point of
their platform, which states, "We want an immediate end to POLICE BRU-
TALITY and MURDER of black people. We believe we can end police brutality
in our black community by organizing black self-defense groups that are
dedicated to defending our black community from racist police oppression
and brutality." As a safeguard against police harassment, the Portland Panthers undertook weapons training. Johnson remembers how "the Panthers
used to have target practice at a ranch owned by an older black couple . . . it
was a pretty big ranch with a creek running through it." Percy Hampton gave
an even more vivid account:

> The ranch was located up in the hills in a place called Scappoose, twelve
> to fifteen miles west of Portland, off Highway 30. It was on an old lumber
> farm. . . . It was an ideal place for target practice . . . there were no houses
> close by. Tommy Mills would take us up there for an hour or two and
> practice shooting. Tommy Mills was a Vietnam War veteran . . . he taught us
> how to use an AK-47, handle a revolver, and shoot a high-powered rifle. He
> also instructed us in firearms safety.[52]

Like their Bay Area brethren, the Portland Panthers initially walked the
streets wearing some variation of the iconic BPP uniform. Percy Hampton
said laughingly, "I always had on my leather jacket, but I almost never wore
a beret. . . . Floyd Cruse, on the other hand, was someone who would not
be caught dead without his beret . . . he also had the nerve to sport an ascot
and smoke a pipe."[53] Cruse was clearly one of the more colorful personalities among the group. His sense of style was not out of character, given his
artistic nature. In addition to being a Panther, Cruse was also a member
of the Echelons, a popular a cappella singing group. When the edict came
down from the national headquarters to discontinue wearing the uniform,

the Portland Panthers complied, donning the uniform only on special occasions. Unlike Panthers in the Bay Area, the Portland Panthers did not walk the streets brandishing weapons at any time during their existence. However, like the Bay Area Panthers the Portland Panthers worked to raise awareness of episodes of police brutality against blacks, and they pushed for the removal of police officers whom they considered racist and for laws that would require officers to live in and patrol their own neighborhoods. By responding to national instances of injustice, such as the imprisonment of Huey P. Newton, and local cases of police brutality, including the trials of Kent Ford and Albert Williams, the Portland Black Panthers undertook a massive public relations campaign to defend Albina's black community and expand its political network.

The Portland Panthers' first major effort to raise awareness of the police's abuse of power centered on the national movement to free Huey P. Newton from prison after he allegedly shot and killed an Oakland police officer in October 1967. During their tenure as a branch of the NCCF and in the early months of their official Black Panther membership, Kent Ford and other leftist Portlanders made the "Free Huey" movement the first element of the Panthers' campaign against police oppression, arguing, albeit presumptively, that Newton had been falsely accused and that the evidence against him was weak. It did not take long before the "Free Huey" campaign took the form of a movement and spread across the country like wildfire. Throughout 1969 and 1970, the Portland NCCF (and later the Panthers) held rallies and distributed flyers about Newton throughout the city, especially in the area around Portland State College—which, to reflect its full university status, was renamed Portland State University (PSU) in late 1969. On May 1, 1969, the NCCF, PSU's Black Student Union, the Portland branch of SDS, and other groups held a rally as a part of a nationwide "Free Huey" day in cities across the United States. Flyers distributed at the demonstration listed the BPP's platform and described Newton as "a political prisoner of the racist power structure of this country . . . [and] the symbol of the movement for liberation." To offset the cost of Newton's defense, the Portland cadre helped with a moderately successful fundraiser that featured a lecture by Charles Garry (the famous Bay Area Black Panther attorney) at Lewis and Clark College. The event was held on a Saturday night to maximize attendance, and faculty and students from the city's various colleges and universities were indeed turned out in high numbers. A reception was also held in Garry's honor that evening at the home of Dr. Morris "Mo" Malbin, a highly regarded radiologist known for his liberal politics. For effect, NCCF members dressed in full Panther regalia, despite the fact that the group had yet to be granted full Black Panther status.[54]

The NCCF's willingness to not only make the Huey Newton trial a priority but also to help drum up support for Newton's defense in Portland speaks to the good working relationship that existed between the Portland cadre and the organization's headquarters. On occasion, the national headquarters would lend its support to the Portland cadre. For example, after the Portland Panthers established their health clinic, Dr. Tolbert Small, national chairman of the Black Panther Party's Sickle Cell Anemia Project, and Doc Satchel, deputy minister of health for the Illinois chapter of the BPP, were dispatched to Portland to start up the branch's sickle cell anemia component. As the distribution manager, Hampton remembered "having a good relationship with Oakland and San Francisco . . . for instance, I was in constant contact with [Bay Area Panther and head of party newspaper distribution] Sam Napier . . . sometimes we would talk two to three times a week." Ford likewise stated, "For a while there, one of us would travel to Oakland pretty regularly for ideological workshops until those visits became cost prohibitive."[55]

When the Portland cadre was not handing out leaflets about the Newton trial, they were distributing a one-page document that listed the names of judges and lawyers to avoid. "We made it a point to inform people of those judges that we and others considered white supremacists," said Ford. "We'd slip the lists inside the Black Panther newspapers, post them on telephone poles, drop them off at barber shops and beauty salons, or just stand on the street corner and hand them out there . . . this was something we did on a regular basis."[56] This was a continuation of the work that Ford, Mills, and others had embarked years earlier, long before the group became a branch of the NCCF, when members of the cadre would monitor cases they believed were blatant miscarriages of justice. Given the frequency with which blacks seemed to encounter the criminal justice system in Portland, the Panthers' evaluation of judges and attorneys seemed to be of practical import. However, while being knowledgeable about the racial philosophy and political leanings of judges is certainly helpful, how one would put such information to good use was not entirely clear, as a client and his lawyer can only do so much to avoid standing before any particular judge.

In 1970, the California appellate court released Newton from prison because of problems with the initial trial, and, following two more mistrials, the state abandoned its efforts to convict him. While NCCF members celebrated the victory, their efforts quickly turned toward concerns about police brutality in their own community. While the "Free Huey" movement increased the Panthers' notoriety in Portland, the simultaneous trial and acquittal of Kent Ford on the charge of "riot" stemming from the chaotic events of June 1969, and his successful lawsuit against the Portland police, put the Panthers and their anti–police brutality campaign in the city's spotlight. Before the trial, Don Hamerquist put Ford in contact with an attorney by the name of Nick Chaivoe, a white leftist who had graduated from the Northwest College of Law and had passed the bar exam in the age of McCarthyism. Originally named Benjamin Meislin, Chaivoe was a native New Yorker but was raised in Los Angeles, where he long aspired to be an actor. "He was really serious about becoming an actor at one point," said his son, Harry Chaivoe. "He even acted in a number of stage productions in Portland." After getting an up-close look at how actors' careers were derailed and their lives ruined by the likes of Joseph McCarthy and his senator cronies, Chaivoe decided on law as his vocation. However, because of his ties to the Communist Party, he was not allowed to practice for nearly ten years. "He was blacklisted, plain and simple," said his daughter, Karen Chaivoe. To support himself and his family, he worked as a law clerk and as an investigator for a local attorney by the name of Nels Peterson. But once allowed to practice law, he became the go-to attorney for activist-minded Portlanders. "There were other attorneys who represented activists, but Nick was the best in Portland," said David Horowitz, a longtime history professor at Portland State University.[57]

Securing Chaivoe's services was one of the best decisions Kent Ford ever made. Chaivoe successfully challenged the police's narrative that Ford had encouraged violence against the officers on the morning of June 13. In early February 1970, following Ford's ten-day trial, a jury acquitted Ford of the trumped-up charge of "riot." A week after the trial, Sandra Ford received a surprise call at the NCCF headquarters. According to Kent Ford, the foreman of the jury called and said to Sandra, "Not all white people hate you all." Because the police had beaten Ford after they arrested and handcuffed him, Chaivoe then filed a civil suit against the Portland Police Bureau. Police retaliated by stepping up their pursuit of Ford and his comrades, including a second arrest of Ford on Sunday June 17, 1970, near N. Williams Avenue and San Rafael Street at 8:18 p.m., when police charged him with "disorderly conduct by abusive language" after he yelled at two police officers, including an African American whom Ford allegedly called a "nigger pig." Tony Newman, the African American officer, and his fellow officer Michael Chase said that Ford had directed obscenities at them as well. Ford claims that he responded to the officers that way only after Newman had insinuated that Ford had a hand in setting the fire that destroyed Grandma's Cookie Co., located on 1806 N. Williams Avenue. "That was a nice job you did on Grandma's Cookies," Newman said, according to Ford. Ford's retort was what Herbert Marcuse called a form of linguistic rebellion, wherein "the methodical use of 'obscenities' in the political language of the radicals is the elemental act of giving a new name to men and things, obliterating the false and hypocritical name which the renamed figures proudly bear in and for the system."[58]

Ford's bail was set at $1,000, an exorbitant amount that caught the attention of the press. Reporters wondered if it was the highest bail ever set for such an offense. A review of Portland Municipal Court records failed to turn up a prior case in which a bail of $1,000 or more was set for a disorderly conduct charge. A "minimum bills" schedule by the court to guide police officers lays out four types of disorderly conduct charges, and specifies bail at $25 for "general" charges, $50 for attempted suicide, $500 for riots, and $500 for "morals." In reality, however, booking slips and court records reveal that police officers set disorderly conduct bail at anywhere from $50 to $250, depending on the circumstances. A $500 bail was rarely levied for the charge. This time, the court handed Ford his first criminal conviction and sentenced him to six months of probation. Still, the ruling did not affect Ford's lawsuit against the police. That September, a federal district court judge awarded Ford $6,000 for "the indignity that [Ford] suffered" and offered a stern warning that "it is time that the community realizes that the police are not authorized to inflict punishment at their own discretion." With Ford's acquittal in February and the successful lawsuit in September, the Portland Panthers had struck their first blow against the brutal behaviors and tactics of some of Portland's police officers.[59]

These two developments helped the Panthers to further their campaign against racist and heavy-handed police officers and to promote their idea of community control of the police. Once again, the Portland Panthers proved willing to work with local whites to spread their message. On February 14, the day after Ford's acquittal, a large group of demonstrators headed by the Portland leadership marched north from the Southwest Park blocks near the PSU campus to the courthouse downtown to support a ballot initiative that would grant "community control" over the policing of neighborhoods. A photograph of that demonstration that appeared in the following day's *Oregonian* above an article titled "Black Panther Claims It's Ballots or Bullets" illustrates the activists' efforts to assert black leadership while engaging white supporters, particularly white leftists from PSU. As the procession moved north past Columbia Street, the photographer captured the power dynamic between Panthers and their white allies: Striding prominently in front of the demonstrators were roughly a dozen African Americans, many of whom were leaders of the Portland Panthers, including Sandra Ford, Percy Hampton, Patty Carter (Hampton), and Linda Thornton. The crowd behind the leaders consisted mostly of white college-aged men and women, some marching with clenched fists held high in the air, a symbol widely recognized as the Black Power salute, in a sign of solidarity with BPP leadership. Both blacks and whites carried signs with slogans such as "Free the Panthers—Jail the Pigs" and "Community Control of Police now." But the sharp racial dichotomy revealed an underlying importance of promoting black leadership in a city where blacks lacked substantial numbers as compared to some other West Coast cities.[60]

Rallying on the steps of the courthouse, Kent Ford called on the mixed audience of whites and blacks to intensify their efforts against the police. "The people are running out of energy for picketing and marching," he proclaimed. "We've got to attack on other levels . . . time is running out. It's got to be power to the people." Likewise, nineteen-year-old Freddy Whitlow, a young supporter and one of the petition's sponsors, went a step further, informing the crowd that they needed twenty-six thousand signatures to get on the ballot. "If we don't get the ballot," the *Oregonian* reported Whitlow as saying, "it has to be the bullet." In other words, without community control of police, the Panthers believed, violent confrontations between blacks and white police officers would undoubtedly continue. Proponents of the petition maintained that the Portland Police Bureau policed blacks more harshly than whites and that they had a separate set of rules when conducting police work in black neighborhoods. Although the ballot initiative fell well short of the necessary number of signatures, the demonstration ultimately helped increase the NCCF's visibility and heightened public awareness of police violence in Albina. Moreover, it let members of the African American community in Albina know that there was an organization willing to meet force with force, if necessary. Blacks did not have to suffer silently the attacks of racist police officers.[61]

While Ford's acquittal and subsequent lawsuit garnered citywide attention, the shooting, arrest, and trial of Albert Williams, a nineteen-year-old black teenager from Albina, became the focal point for the campaign against police brutality in 1970. Just days after the march on the courthouse, Williams, who was not a member of the local NCCF branch, was reportedly standing in front of the groups' headquarters on Union Avenue with Freddy Whitlow when a police car driven by Sgt. Stanley Harmon pulled up next to the two young men. What happened after that depends on one's source of information. According to reports by the *Oregonian*, Officers Harmon and Ralph Larson had a ten-year-old girl in custody, reportedly for shoplifting, when they spotted Williams standing in the doorway of the Panthers' headquarters (rather than outside, in front of the building with Whitlow, as some claim) at 3619 NE Union Avenue. Williams then turned away and walked inside. Under questioning in court, Williams said that he had been afraid of Harmon and had attempted to avoid him. When questioned about his history with Harmon, Williams said, "He jumped on me a couple of times ... beat me up." Other witnesses called to testify painted Harmon as someone undeserving of wearing the badge of the Portland Police Bureau. Gayle Branch and her younger brother, both residents in the community, testified that Harmon had broken into their house in June 1969 following disturbances on Union Avenue. When asked to produce a warrant, Harmon had reportedly told Branch's mother that he did not need one. "Harmon and his fellow officers then tore out light fixtures, pulled out drawers ... beat up one of my little brothers," said Branch.[62]

Upon seeing Williams turn away and walk into the building, officers proceeded to walk toward the entrance. Once there, they called for Williams to come out and give himself up. Officers claimed to have an arrest warrant for Williams; at that point, someone locked the door. Harmon claimed that he returned to the patrol car to verify the warrant via radio. Williams refused to come out, and Harmon kicked open the door, but before doing so radioed for help and two more police officers arrived. Upon entering the premises, Williams ran to a balcony some four to five feet above ground level. As Williams ran, officers say that he grabbed a rifle from some undisclosed location, which was corroborated by Panthers who had been at the scene. According to the Panthers, Williams overpowered Joyce Radford, who was at the front desk, and made his way upstairs, where he gained possession of the weapon. Officers also claim that Williams yelled that he was going to kill them, a claim that the Panthers neither confirmed nor denied. A brief but tense standoff ensued. Harmon maintains that he and Larson holstered their weapons and tried to convince Williams to surrender. Police officials say that Williams discharged the weapon at the officers, with the slug landing in the room's ceiling. Eyewitnesses, primarily NCCF members, claimed that, despite reports to the contrary, the weapon that Williams held was never fired. "Albert never fired the rifle," Joyce Radford maintains. "I know that because I had cleaned the rifle that day, and I still had the bullets in my pocket." Likewise, Willie James Brown, a witness for the defense, testified that "the rifle wasn't fired because I had my hand on it." Others recall Joyce Radford eventually convincing Williams to put down the weapon. Officer Nate Griffin, an African American officer who was on the scene, maintained, "Williams definitely fired the weapon. . . . I was the cover car for Harmon and Larson, meaning that when Harmon called for backup, I was the first car on the scene. Obviously Harmon and Larson were in the primary vehicle. In fact, when Williams fired off a shot, I tore up my pants when I hit the ground." At any rate, for reasons that were unclear, Harmon leapt onto a desk, a report that he verified, drew his firearm, and, according to news reports, fired two shots. One of the shots hit Williams in his right arm, and the other hit him in the lower abdominal area, leaving him in critical condition.[63]

Given the charges and countercharges that are typically associated with police-Panther interactions, even the number of shots fired by Harmon is in dispute. Despite some media reports, the Panthers remember Harmon firing just one shot, not two. Whatever the case, Williams was then transported by patrol car to Oregon Health and Science University, rather than Emanuel Hospital, which was just a few blocks away. Said Griffin, "I radioed the dispatcher and requested permission from the sergeant to take Williams to the hospital rather than wait for an ambulance. . . . I did this for two reasons . . . one, because Williams was losing a lot of blood, and two, because the crowd was becoming hostile." While Williams was in the patrol car, officers were overheard debating the hospital to which Williams should be taken. According to Ford, "Williams said he distinctly heard one of the officers say, 'Let's not take him to Emanuel, because that is the first place those people will go' . . . by 'those people' I assume the officers meant those Panthers or those blacks." Williams was later transferred to Multnomah County Hospital.[64]

Following the shooting, members of the NCCF were inadvertently tipped off that a raid was imminent. According to an article in the *Oregonian*, a reporter at KGW Channel 8 who monitored police calls telephoned the NCCF office and calmly asked "if they had been raided yet, thereby informing the occupants of the impending police action," a warning that, for whatever reason, NCCF members did not heed. The station's news manager blamed the miscue on a young and inexperienced employee. North precinct commander Capt. William Taylor scoffed at the suggestion that the Portland Police Bureau intended to raid the Panthers' headquarters, saying, "That's a bunch of BS. . . . We don't make a raid with a two-man patrol car with a ten-year-old in the car."[65]

On Thursday, February 18, 1970, a day after the shooting, a multiracial group of two hundred protesters stormed city hall and demonstrated inside city council chambers. Williams had been charged with intent to kill because he had allegedly fired at the officer first. Bail was set at $25,000. Spokespersons for the group of protesters called for the suspension of Harmon until a complete investigation could be conducted. Several of the protesters made speeches. Bill Grandby of the Black Berets exclaimed, "Williams should be freed, and Officer Harmon should be suspended from duty and tried for attempted murder!" The crowd cheered, "Right on!" The mayor replied wearily, "The subject has been taken under advisement," which drew catcalls and jeers. Grandby then pulled from his shirt pocket a bullet from a Springfield .36 rifle and spoke into the microphone, "See this, Mr. Mayor, this is exactly how you came to power; why should it be any different for us?"[66] Seemingly embarrassed, some members of the city council bowed their heads while the throng of protesters responded with thunderous applause. Upon learning that reinforcements were on the way, demonstrators, apparently feeling that their point had been made, filed out of the courthouse, chanting, "All Power to the People!" Maurice Isserman, who participated in the demonstration, paints a vivid scene:

> I remember when we left, we walked out between a phalanx of police
> officers, two rows on either side of us, lining and stretched along the hall
> leading out to the street, and it was very tense. We were boisterous and
> defiant, and they were silent and hostile. Violence was in the air. I can't help
> thinking that there was a connection between the mood that day and the
> events a month or so later in May when the Portland Tac Squad attacked
> nonviolent student demonstrations in Park Blocks and sent a number
> of them to the hospital, in the midst of the national student strike that
> followed the killings at Kent State University.

The demonstration lasted approximately forty minutes. In an effort to marshal support for Williams, the Panthers held a pretrial rally at Unthank Park in north Portland a day before the trial. When asked why the Panthers went to such lengths to support someone who seemingly had difficulty staying out of trouble and whose actions brought the Panthers a fair amount of unwanted attention, Ford replied, "We just didn't want to see the young man get railroaded." On that Sunday afternoon, Ford estimates that between five hundred and one thousand people turned out for the two-hour rally that included an abundance of food and was capped with a performance by the Ural Thomas Band. Panther attorney Nick Chaivoe set the tone for the afternoon by imploring the crowd to be careful not to do anything that might adversely affect the outcome of the trial. He insisted that it was important that those who planned to attend the trial behave in an orderly fashion and refrain from engaging in any sort of counterproductive behavior.[67]

Less than two weeks later, a grand jury acquitted Harmon of any wrongdoing. Although the jury absolved Harmon of culpability, it did criticize the officers' behavior prior to the shooting. "It is our opinion that Officers Larson and Harmon did not exercise the best judgment in the placement of the police authority," the jury stated remembering the ten-year-old girl seated in the patrol car. The hearing also resulted in a mistrial for Williams, but a second jury ultimately convicted Williams of assault in October 1970. To say that members within Albina's black community were disappointed is an understatement. Harmon had earned a reputation for his heavy-handed tactics, something that Albina residents obviously did not appreciate. According to one police officer, Harmon was heavy-handed with everyone, regardless of race. What distinguished Larson from Harmon was that Larson was fond of using the "N word." "If he happened to use it and a black officer was nearby, he was quick to say oh, I don't mean you so-and-so, you're not one of them ... he would always assure the black officer that he wasn't referring to him, as if that somehow made it all right," said one officer. This description is not inconsistent with the behavior Robert Landauer experienced as a reporter with the *Oregonian*. Said Landauer, who joined the newspaper in 1966, "I used to do ride-alongs with the police ... the culture was very macho, and their language was very antiblack."[68]

A comparison of the literature distributed by the Portland Panthers with mainstream newspaper coverage of the Williams trial reveals starkly differing perceptions. The flyers and pamphlets that the Panthers distributed in Albina, on the PSU campus, and at courthouse rallies during the trial were unsurprisingly one-sided in favor of acquitting Williams and charging Harmon. On one early flyer, which was distributed in late June prior to the start of the trial, the Panthers drew a crude and graphic image of a chubby white police officer wearing a swastika badge and clutching a riot baton in one hand, and pointing a revolver at the reader with the other. Underneath his boot lay Lady Justice, struggling to hold up her scales. Such political protest art, while not as polished, mirrored that produced by the party's minister of culture, Emory Douglass. The flyer briefly summarized the suspicious shooting and arrest of Williams, specifically noting the police's delay in transporting him to the hospital, and witnesses' reports that Harmon joyously shouted, "I got him! I finally got him!" after he shot Williams. It also provided a short description of the Portland Panthers and their campaign against police brutality, particularly efforts to have Harmon transferred to another precinct and sharp criticisms of the dismal numbers of African American police officers within the Portland Police Bureau.[69]

As the trial gained more attention, the Panthers' flyers and pamphlets became more elaborate. Throughout the October trial, the Panthers held rallies, distributed literature in support of Albert Williams, and encouraged supporters to attend the trial. In a four-page pamphlet distributed in early October titled "Railroad," the Panthers criticized the police's handling of Williams's wounds, Harmon's behavior during the incident, and the persistence of police violence toward the African American community in general. The pamphlet also provided a page of accusations of a systematic attack on the Portland branch of the BPP and throughout the United States, while another page requested donations and outlined the BPP's social programs, addresses, and hours of operation. These flyers and pamphlets served multiple purposes for the Portland Panthers. On the one hand, the Portland branch was able to continue raising public awareness of police behavior in Albina. On the other, the literature helped increase the Panthers' visibility, particularly about their community survival programs and about the city, state, and federal governments' efforts to subvert those efforts.[70]

By contrast, the mainstream media portrayal of the trial tended to be far less favorable toward Williams and the Black Panther Party. Both in their depictions of Williams and in their descriptions of events, newspapers tended to favor the narrative proffered by the police, while subtly attacking the aims of the Portland Panthers and the characters of its members. The *Oregonian*, which provided the most extensive coverage of the trial, consistently reiterated that the shooting had taken place at Panther headquarters but neglected to mention that Williams was not a member of the Portland branch. Moreover, particularly toward the end of the trial, the *Oregonian* emphasized Williams's use of Seconal, a barbiturate, and his history of drug use. The paper tended to lead with police accounts of events given as undisputed fact, while portraying the Panthers' narrative as unsubstantiated claims. For example, when Harmon testified on October 15, Steve Erickson of the *Oregonian* opened his article with, "Albert Williams yelled, 'Harmon, I'm gonna kill you!' before firing a shot at a Portland police patrolman in Black Panther headquarters last February." In contrast, when Williams took the stand the next day, the Erickson article began, "A teen-aged youth charged with trying to kill a Portland patrolman last February testified Thursday that the officer had often threatened him." In both of these articles, Erickson began by framing Williams as the aggressor who had attempted to kill Harmon.[71]

Popular media coverage of the trial, particularly in the *Oregonian*, was overwhelmingly one-sided and tended to favor an anti-Panther narrative that labeled Williams (who the paper conveniently neglected to mention was not a Black Panther) as a cop killer and drug user. It did not help that Williams had a reputation as being in and out of trouble. According to Hampton, "He had served time in prison before the incident at our office, and he was always coming around the office, talking about how we should be out there offing someone." Williams's reputation and prior criminal record were all that were needed to frame him as someone who warranted readers' contempt, not their sympathy or compassion. As a result, for those whose understanding of the Black Panther Party may have been warped from the outset, the Panthers' decision to take up Williams's cause, no matter how commendable, might have only added to their confusion, especially since the media continued to identify Williams as a member of the BPP. With the media continually playing up Williams's past transgressions, it is unlikely that those who knew little about the Panthers before the Williams situation unfolded would have taken the initiative to learn about the BPP's community survival programs and other efforts at empowering Portland's less fortunate residents.[72]

In the first two years of its existence, the Portland Black Panthers' survival programs and antipolice brutality campaign, both of which sought to reclaim spaces for blacks in Albina, provided a more radical vision for Albina neighborhoods than any black organization in Portland had previously. Ron Herndon, a student activist at Reed College and later educator and longtime activist in Portland, maintains,

The Panthers were the only organization in town that not only led a
sustained effort to change things for the better for oppressed people, Black
folk especially, but who also had the support of the community. . . . The
Urban League was here . . . it was good at getting people jobs, but at the
same time you had to understand where it was getting its money from. . . .
The NAACP was also in Portland, but it was weak. The Nation of Islam was
here, too, but black folk didn't take to it like they did the Panthers. No one
from any of those organizations except the Black Panther Party was going
to speak out on any controversial issue or take up the important issues of
the day.

Party member Floyd Cruse offered a harsh critique of the traditional civil
rights organizations in Portland, pointing out that "the party sees the
NAACP, the Urban League, and black people that participate in OEO . . . as
blacks who are working for a neocolonial type program, a program that will
not bring freedom, that will just make them satisfied with being colonized."[73]

The Portland Panthers, rooted in the national "Ten-Point Program and
Platform," localized the national party's goals to fit the needs and circumstances of neighborhood development in northeast Portland. Through the
children's free breakfast program, the Fred Hampton People's Free Health
Clinic, and the Malcolm X Memorial Dental Clinic, the Panthers offered the
poor and working-class residents of Albina's black community places where
they could begin to break the cycle of poverty that had been part of the city's
legacy of discrimination and neglect. Similarly, their campaign to stop police violence and gain local control over neighborhoods in Albina through
highly publicized trials was successful in increasing the Panthers' public
visibility and support. Despite negative attention from the popular media,
the Portland Panthers were widely known throughout Portland by the end
of 1970, and the organization had established a defensive posture against
what they viewed to be an evil and corrupt power structure within city government. These efforts, however, were just the beginning. As the 1970s progressed, the Portland Panthers helped spearhead the fight against one of the
Portland Development Commission's most damaging urban renewal proposals yet: the Emanuel Hospital Urban Renewal Project.

CHAPTER 4

The Emanuel Hospital Expansion, the James Family Saga, and Portland's Dream of a New Urbanism

Portland ran amok with left-wing political activity in 1970, from the anti–Vietnam War demonstration at Portland State University in May that left dozens of students bloodied and bruised at the hands of Portland police officers to the trial of Albert Williams later that fall.[1] Americans responding to a national survey in May 1970 cited campus unrest as the single most important problem facing the country. Many were of the opinion that the protesters, feminists, hippies, yippies, and black militants were keeping decent youth from getting the educational opportunities that their parents had worked so hard to provide. Americans for Constitutional Action, a group that demonstrated a penchant for hyperbole, damned "the terrorists on our campuses" for committing "acts of barbarisms equaled only by the Huns, Vandals, and Goths who wiped out civilization and learning in the last dying days of ancient Rome."[2] In the meantime, Portland's Model Cities program was still searching for a permanent director to replace Rev. Paul Schulze. After poring over scores of resumes, one individual stood out: Charles Jordan. Born in Texas and raised in Palm Springs, California, Jordan was a well-rounded candidate. At six feet seven, the thirty-three-year-old Jordan was an imposing figure. After he graduated from high school in 1956, several schools had offered him basketball scholarships. Ultimately he accepted an offer from Gonzaga University, where he earned bachelor degrees in education, sociology, and philosophy in 1961. After college, Jordan spent two years in the US Army and later completed graduate work at the University of Southern California and at Loma Linda University before working in various administrative capacities in Palm Springs. By all accounts, Jordan was a strong candidate. But there was one thing that his application neglected to mention: he was black.

In response to growing anger and increasing radical resistance among blacks and left-wing whites to the Portland Development Commission (PDC) and the Model Cities program, Mayor Terry Schrunk recruited Jordan to apply for the job. Although the mayor knew who Jordan was, most of the twenty-seven members of the Citizens Planning Board (CPB) in charge of selecting the new director had no idea that he was an African American. When Jordan arrived for his interview, many of the board's older white members were stunned to learn that a black man could possess such impressive credentials. Nevertheless, they were excited at the prospect of having such a highly qualified African American in charge of the project, which they had hoped would please, if not appease, the city's discontented and distrustful black population. The committee was clearly serious about Jordan's candidacy, and flew him to Portland three times before making him a formal offer. Months after Jordan's initial interview, Mayor Schrunk summoned him back to Portland to be interviewed by the citizens' board. Jordan also met with individual members of the CPB and others during his third and final visit to Portland.

Not everyone shared in the CPB and city council's excitement. Some African Americans and white leftists saw things differently. Various sectors of the community, including members of more radical organizations such as the Black Panther Party and the short-lived black militant Black Berets, were not keen on the idea of the city government bringing in an outsider when there were plenty of qualified African Americans already in the city. Some of those who opposed Jordan argued that the job had already been given to Alvin Batiste, an African American resident of Portland and longtime engineer with the Bonneville Power Administration,[3] in 1969, but that arrangement had not panned out, and consequently the committee had widened its search. According to Kent Ford, Batiste shared with him the circumstances that had led to his short-lived tenure as head of Model Cities:

> Batiste told me that the mayor fired him when he discovered that his
> assistant, Vivian L. Barnett, had met with members of the Black Panther

Party to explain to us the various Model Cities resources that were available and how we could access them. After meeting with us, Schrunk then ordered Batiste to terminate Barnett. One week later Schrunk approached Batiste and asked why he had yet to fire Barnett, to which Batiste responded, . . . "I'm not going to fire her . . . she hasn't done anything." Citing insubordination, Schrunk fired Batiste instead. . . . Whether or not Barnett was telling me the truth I can't say, but this is the story he told me.

If the story is true, it also did not help Batiste's cause that Barnett elected to dispense monies to the Panthers so that they could distribute Christmas baskets throughout the neighborhood.[4]

Barnett's meeting with the Panthers suggests that she knew that residents were often not aware of the resources that were available to them. An article published in the *Oregonian* underscores this point. The September 1971 article revealed that more than 80 percent of residents living in the city's target areas for antipoverty funds were unaware of the economic development programs in their neighborhoods, and that the majority of those who were informed believed that such funds were being wasted. Batiste's and Barnett's efforts to reach out to the Panthers was something to which the Panthers were unaccustomed. "None of those blacks involved in those poverty programs or involved in dispensing any of those funds ever reached out to us that I know of," said Raymond Joe. "I can't think of any time," he continued, "where Charles Jordan or anyone from his office reached out to us, but that didn't surprise us, because we never expected them to in the first place."[5]

Just before Jordan's final interview with the CPB, the Black Berets— founded by R. L. Anderson, a large, stern-faced man with a penchant for confrontation—challenged Jordan on his way to the interview and made it clear that locals were not just looking for "a man with a black face" to head the program. Instead, they wanted someone who would defend the interests of their community. Following the interview, after Jordan had left the room and the board had closed the doors to discuss his candidacy, Anderson and his small group kicked in the door, shouted at the board, and expressed their dissatisfaction with the selection process. Anderson demanded that the board hire someone who already lived in Portland. Frightened, several of the board members fled the room. According to a report by the Portland Bureau of Planning, a few of the members were so terrified that they had escaped through windows, and the Black Berets left the building frustrated and angry. Anderson became such an irritant to board members that from then on police officers would, under any flimsy pretext, stop and detain him on the day that Model Cities meetings were scheduled so that business could be conducted uninterrupted. Anderson would respond by holding a press conference at which he would castigate the police bureau for playing dirty pool.[6]

Jordan was ultimately hired as the new director of Portland's Model Cities program. Soon after, in the early morning hours of Saturday, November 21, 1970, a bomb exploded beneath the city hall portico, resulting in $170,000 in damages. Windows were blown out, the council chamber (located above the blast) was wrecked, all of the columns of the portico were damaged, and the Liberty Bell replica was destroyed. Hours after the bombing, two FBI agents showed up at Kent Ford's house. Ford remembers that day well:

> At about 7:30 that morning someone was knocking on the door and I'm thinking to myself, "Who in the hell could that be?" I go to the door and standing there are two white men in suits. They identified themselves as FBI agents and asked to come in. It was cold as I don't know what that morning, but I wouldn't let them in. I said, "No, you stand out here." Then they asked to speak to Sandra, and I said they couldn't speak to Sandra, because she was cooking breakfast for the kids. I said they could speak to her later, after I called my attorney, Nick Chaivoe. Before they turned around to leave, one of them said to me, "Kent, it looked like someone just stuck a whole case of dynamite under the Liberty Bell." I had no idea what he was talking about at the time. Later, I saw the whole thing on the news.[7]

No one ever claimed responsibility for the bombing, and the crime remains unsolved. Given the timing, authorities suspected it was the work of a disgruntled left-wing faction; it is unknown whether the bombing was related to the Jordan hiring.

A month after Jordan settled into his work as director, he received a letter from Housing and Urban Development (HUD), informing him that he had six months to get the Model Cities program in order or its funding would be rescinded. A number of programs were started right away, and during Jordan's tenure, the leadership of Model Cities worked harder to incorporate the black community's voice in city politics and urban planning than had any of the city's previous urban renewal projects. In fact, R. L. Anderson became one of Jordan's biggest supporters and, for a time, was a valuable member of the program. The city's political leadership, however, still refused to compromise on some of their most profitable redevelopment plans. In particular, the PDC kept its most contentious project from the jurisdiction and oversight of the Model Cities program: the renovation and expansion of Emanuel Hospital. This project, which called for the demolition of hundreds of African American homes and businesses in the Eliot neighborhood of Albina without the community's input, became the focal point of the Portland Black Panthers' battle against the city government, the police, and the PDC. Ultimately, the Emanuel Hospital Urban Renewal Project and the concentrated efforts by the Federal Bureau of Investigation (FBI) and local law enforcement to subvert the Portland Panthers began to wear on some of the branch's members throughout the early 1970s.

Constant harassment from authorities, no matter how minor compared to that experienced by other Panther branches around the country, undoubtedly affected the Portland Panthers' effectiveness. "Some of it was just them [the FBI and the police] being an annoyance, constantly approaching us about this, that, or the other . . . you just wanted to say to them 'Hey guys, don't you have something better to do?'" said Oscar Johnson. The objective, of course, was to neutralize the most prominent radical voice in Albina's black community. "They [the police and the FBI] were always coming at us about something . . . if it wasn't one thing, it was another," said Raymond Joe.[8]

While authorities campaigned to undermine the Panthers' vision of community control, the PDC's control over urban renewal projects waned. Out of the decline of these two polar-opposites, a new broad-based and moderate political middle path emerged via the Model Cities program that would thereafter influence citizen participation in city politics and urban planning policies. As Model Cities increasingly gave Portland's African American community a political voice in the city's urban planning process, the city government and the PDC still looked for legal and political loopholes to continue their preexisting projects. Nowhere was this clearer than in the PDC's decision to remove the highly unpopular Emanuel Hospital renovation and expansion project from Model Cities program oversight and bypass the input of northeast Portland's black community.

Since the early 1960s, city planners and hospital executives had wanted to expand the hospital's campus to keep it technologically state-of-the-art and large enough to meet the needs and demands of Portland's growing population. That campus, nestled in the heart of the Eliot neighborhood, was just north of previous displacement and renewal projects in the Albina district. With the creation of the Model Cities program, the proponents of expansion saw a new opportunity to develop the hospital. In 1967, the PDC proposed the Emanuel Hospital Urban Renewal Project as a component of the Model Cities program. Early in the summer of 1968, the CPB approved the project on the condition that Emanuel Hospital and the PDC compensate displaced individuals for their property. Over the next two years, the hospital completed a new medical building and an extended-care facility, and had plans for further expansions, including a large lecture hall, a senior-citizen residence, employee apartments, a laundry facility, and additional parking. By the time Charles Jordan arrived in late 1970, the project was already well underway.[9]

Shortly after becoming director of the Model Cities program, however, Jordan received a letter from HUD officials informing him that they would terminate funding for Model Cities unless the program demonstrated a clear direction with regard to planning and resolved internal conflicts with the PDC, including a dispute over whether or not to continue the Emanuel Hospital expansion. As a result, during his first months as director, Jordan carefully navigated between the PDC and the CPB, its working committees, and northeast Portland's black community. Following numerous public meetings and discussions with the residents of Albina, Jordan and the CPB looked for ways to make Model Cities work better for the community, ultimately drafting a number of specific planning proposals and revisions.[10]

The CPB's Comprehensive Development Plan for the Model Cities District challenged the hospital's continuing expansion and noted that since the early proposals for the Emanuel Hospital expansion in 1966 and 1967, the social and political environment of the Eliot neighborhood had changed sharply in opposition to the hospital. "Many people, particularly the elderly, want to remain," the report stated. "Rehabilitation and rebuilding of the Eliot neighborhood for residential purposes is consistent with a broad community goal of improving the variety and quality of housing opportunities."[11] Consequently, Jordan, the CPB, and residents of the Eliot neighborhood and northeast Portland encouraged the PDC to significantly alter or abandon the hospital renovation.

The PDC, however, had invested too much in the Emanuel Hospital project to abort the initiative. To avoid having the project scrapped altogether, the PDC quietly removed the Emanuel Hospital Urban Renewal Project from the Model Cities program during a sparsely attended and unpublicized session of the CPB, effectively taking the project out of the control of the CPB and the black community. Nonetheless, the CPB, with the cooperation of several organizations, including the Emanuel Displaced Persons Association, managed to pressure the PDC and Emanuel Hospital to work closely with residents of the Eliot neighborhood. In April 1971, the CPB signed an agreement with the PDC, Emanuel Hospital, and other local social organizations to address problems stemming from the displacement of residents, including increased poverty and homelessness. Still, the city of Portland undercompensated or simply denied benefits to save city and federal funds, which further inflamed tensions between the city government and the northeast neighborhoods.[12]

Despite the continuation of the Emanuel Hospital Urban Renewal Project, during Jordan's two-year tenure the Model Cities program was productive and ultimately beneficial for many of Albina's neighborhoods. With the CPB's formation of the Neighborhood Development Plan (NDP) under Jordan's guidance in 1970, the citizens of northeast Portland completed numerous neighborhood improvement projects. Through the use of Model Cities federal loans and grants, city workers and local citizens planted more than six hundred trees, expanded local parks by seven acres, improved five miles of substandard roads, and rehabilitated nearly two thousand housing units—particularly in the area around Emanuel Hospital—in order to accommodate displaced residents. In addition, each of the eight neighborhoods developed their own specific policy plans for community revitalization and planning through the NDP, although the city government and the PDC never adopted any of these plans.[13]

As Jordan and the CPB backed away from the PDC-dominated vision for Model Cities in the early 1970s and increased their focus on community revitalization, some black radicals gradually became more open to the program's community-led efforts. However, these individuals' integration into the fold came neither easily nor with the approval of the city or federal government. R. L. Anderson, one of the city's best-known black radicals, seemed poised to take advantage of these newfound opportunities and effect change from within the system. Anderson surprised everyone when he won a position on the Albina Citizens Together Board, a federally financed community action agency, in 1970, and was elected as the board's representative to the Portland Metropolitan Steering Committee (PMSC) within the year. He also headed the Albina Citizen's Council, a local advocacy group, and founded Vernon Neighborhood Care, a free daycare program. After becoming involved with the Model Cities program as the chair of its law and justice committee, Anderson worked with Portland Police Bureau's community relations program to ensure clearer communication and increased cooperation between Albina residents and the police. The steering committee, recognizing Anderson's willingness to work within the system, considered him as a possible candidate for the office of treasurer. On February 17, 1971, Anderson was elected and had a short and troublesome tenure as treasurer of the PMSC.[14]

The PMSC, which had been established by the Office of Economic Opportunity (OEO) in the late 1960s as a part of President Lyndon B. Johnson's War on Poverty,[15] acted as the OEO's policy formation and implementation body for Portland. In 1964, Congress had passed the Economic Opportunity Act, which authorized a billion dollars to retrain poor residents. This new measure was comprised of a number of different programs. The Job Corps established centers to train residents in basic and advanced skills and established neighborhood programs. The Community Action programs envisioned expanding low-income residents' active participation in the decision-making process and equipping young people with marketable skills. Other programs included rural loans, small business development centers, and Volunteers in Service to America (VISTA). Head Start was created under the direction of R. Sargent Shriver to enhance low-income preschoolers' learning skills so that they could start elementary school on an equal footing with their peers.[16] One of the more controversial components of the new Economic Opportunity Act were Shriver's Community Action programs, which were designed to place greater control in the hands of the residents for whom the programs were intended. The primary objective of the programs was to empower poor neighborhoods and involve them in the policy-making apparatus by giving community residents key administrative and bureaucratic posts.[17]

While some praised the Johnson administration's War on Poverty, not everyone supported it. Bayard Rustin, the behind-the-scenes organizer of the March on Washington and the former director of the civil rights department of the Fellowship of Reconciliation went public with his opposition to Shriver's programs. In a November 15, 1964, *Washington Post* article, Rustin averred, "Shriver is immoral when he claims he can give our youths vocational training in his work camps. All he wants to do is get our boys off the streets. We must not allow our sons to be picked up and hauled off to remote concentration camps." What Rustin was doing, of course, was warning civil rights and community activists against being co-opted by politicians and bureaucrats intent on stifling dissent. But members of the PMSC embraced Shriver's mission. The organization's "Articles of Incorporation" stated that one of the committee's main purposes was to "act as a community action group for the Portland Metropolitan Area through which the local and state organizations and the Office of Economic Opportunity should work." The PMSC, then, was to help in eliminating the paradox of poverty by offering to everyone the opportunities of education and training, decent work, and living with dignity.[18]

Shortly after he joined the PMSC, the irascible R. L. Anderson became a major source of controversy. Anderson had been the leader of the Black Berets (an organization that he conveniently dissolved before becoming PMSC's treasurer), and the local media, in particular the *Oregonian* and the *Oregon Journal*, portrayed him as a "black militant." Some viewed him as an opportunist. Moreover, Anderson's criminal record, which included arrests and convictions for "assault with a deadly weapon" and "illegal possession of a firearm," as well as a long list of other charges, caused problems. Most importantly, the OEO required that all members of the committee secure surety bonding in the amount of $25,000, but their regular bonding company refused to back Anderson because of his criminal exploits. Thomas H. Mercer, regional director of the OEO in Seattle, threatened to withhold $6.2 million of federal funds from the PMSC if Anderson could not secure bonding by April 5, 1971.[19]

Both the *Oregonian* and the *Oregon Journal* covered the story, emphasizing the amount of money involved, and the Portland Police Bureau expanded its investigation of Anderson, keeping surveillance on both his public and private life. Anderson's supporters attempted to counter this negative press by circulating a different narrative. The unsigned document that was disseminated through the community read,

> When R. L. Anderson was elected as a representative for Albina and the poor, all allegations that are now being called to the public's attention were well known by the community and state, and the PMSC board. The community, and the state, and the board had confidence in him then, and his community certainly has confidence in him Now! Could it be possible that the PMSC Board is racist? Could PMSC be practicing racism? Isn't voting a priviledge? [*sic*] After exercising your priviledeg [*sic*] to vote, what or whom gives a few persons the right to crucify the voice of people[?] Did

this man violate any constitutional laws? If so read the charges. This is
Illegal and unconstitutional.

LET THE VOICE OF THE PEOPLE BE HEARD! ALL POWER TO THE
PEOPLE!

Despite the support of Albina's African American community, Anderson was unable to secure the bond, which led him to resign on March 31
(less than two weeks after becoming treasurer) to free up federal funds for
the PMSC.[20] In the weeks and months to come, Anderson received more bad
news. Days after he tendered his resignation, the Supplemental Training
Employment Program withheld $14,000 of federal funds from two organi-
zations with which he was affiliated, Vernon Neighborhood Care and the
Albina Women's League. Five months later, in August 1971, an all-white jury
found Anderson guilty of possession of a firearm, and Judge Phillip J. Roth
sentenced him to a two-and-half-year prison sentence, effectively taking off
the streets one of the African American community's most boisterous advocates of Black Power.[21]

Meanwhile, while some blacks in northeast Portland began to engage
the city's political leadership and urban planning apparatus through the
Model Cities' CPB, other radical elements continued to criticize planning
projects in Albina and to push for neighborhood programs focused on socioeconomic issues. The Black Panthers' public presence served as a constant reminder to the PDC and to the rest of the city government that they
could ignore the voice of the black community at their own risk, especially
in light of the unrest in the summers of 1967 and 1969. Since the organization's emergence as the NCCF in the late 1960s, the Portland Panthers had
continually spoken out against the Model Cities program, which it viewed as
yet another example of the city's costly and devastating urban renewal projects in northeast Portland. Several Panthers had attended early Model Cities meetings and citizens' board sessions, handing out literature that railed
against the behavior of city officials, the police, and the PDC. One flyer proclaimed that the city had once again disregarded the rights and the will of
the people. Likening social, economic, and spatial discrimination in Albina
to a slave plantation, the flyer encouraged blacks to refrain from participating in the program, stating, "The people of Albina have no business showing
up at these meetings, because when you're on a slave plantation there's only
the slaves and the masters and they know who the slaves are."[22] While the
majority of Albina's black residents did not share the Panthers' refusal to en-

gage with Model Cities and eventually moved to follow Jordan's leadership, the persistence of the Panthers revealed continuing feelings of alienation and anger toward the city among some African American residents.

As the weeks and months passed, Jordan began to win over some sectors of the African American community, but the PDC's decision to withhold the Emanuel Hospital Urban Renewal Project from Model Cities gave the Portland Panthers a new high-profile target on which to focus their attacks: the city's undemocratic urban planning process. Shortly after the decision to remove the hospital expansion from the Model Cities program in mid-1971, the Panthers turned their focus toward securing jobs for poor blacks or stopping the project altogether. From their point of view, local blacks should have been among the first hired for any job that was created as a result of the project. In an interview with the *Portland Community College Bridge*, Ford explained, "I would like to see the people downtown stop trying to make a political thing out of everything. I'd like to see them really come down to the community level . . . so that [their projects] are meaningful for the people they should be serving." Ford's comments may have prompted law enforcement officials to increase their surveillance of him. An officer's report from the Portland Police Bureau at that time shows that officers were keeping close tabs on Ford's living arrangements. The report states, "Kent Ford moved to 2407 N. Williams Ave on June 7, 1971. A search of his former house was made by the FBI in which large quanities [*sic*] of ammo was seized. No guns were found." For Ford and other Panthers, the Emanuel Hospital project represented a continuation of the ideology and policies that had ravaged much of their community since the 1950s.[23]

In the midst of the Panthers' campaign to pressure officials at the Emanuel Hospital to hire a representative number of black residents for its expansion project, a local attorney and supporter of the Panthers asked Kent Ford to look into an assault on an FBI agent by a female student at Thomas Jefferson High School. Not one to say no, Ford agreed to do so, but the Panthers' willingness to get involved in this matter forced them to juggle yet another issue with far-reaching consequences. On January 4, 1971, agents with the Federal Bureau of Investigation went to the James residence on Jarrett Street in north Portland intending to arrest Charles James, Jr., a US Navy Vietnam veteran who was AWOL from the Long Beach Naval Base. Charles, who had been raised in a religious family, had reportedly gone AWOL because he wanted to marry his fiancée, who was expecting their first child. According to Charles's sister, Martha James, the James children had been raised in the church, and Charles wanted to do the right thing and get married. While many believed that Charles was genuine in taking leave to marry his child's mother, the fact that Charles chose to remain in Portland suggests that he was in no hurry to return to the navy. His decision to go AWOL would have dire consequences. According to a newspaper article, an FBI agent who spotted Charles inside the house called out, "Come on boy, we're taking you." Charles responded, "Don't call me 'boy.'" When the agents attempted to handcuff Charles, the family dog, which was in the grasp of a younger brother, pounced on them. After freeing themselves from the dog, one agent grabbed the fourteen-year-old boy and, while choking him, angrily asked, "Did you sic that dog on me boy?" Upset at the way the agent was manhandling her younger brother, Charles's seventeen-year-old sister, Cheryl, retrieved a rolling pin from the kitchen and yelled, "Turn my brother loose" before belting the agent over the head.[24]

After the agents subdued Charles James, they took him into custody. Less than a half hour later, the agents returned with backup—this time to arrest Cheryl James. In their haste, they mistakenly grabbed Cheryl's sister, Martha James, and threw her to the ground, smashing her face into the floor. Martha recalls the painful memory:

> It was awful. I had just gotten home from school . . . I hadn't had time to put my books down when the next thing I know there are about a half dozen agents at our door. Immediately their attitude was that of intimidation. King, our family dog, a German Shepherd, could sense we were being violated . . . so he jumped on one or two of the agents. My father wasn't home. . . . They grabbed me and hurt me real bad . . . they handcuffed me, dragged me out of the house, and took me somewhere . . . I guess it was the juvenile detention center, where they charged me with resisting arrest. I was traumatized by the whole thing so much so that I blocked a lot of things out over the years.[25]

A close reading of court records presents a slightly different version from the story told by Martha James. According to court proceedings, four FBI agents went to the James residence in search of Charles James, Jr. Outside they observed a man answering the description of Charles entering the house with others. The FBI agents then entered the house through the front door, which had been left open by the last person to enter the residence. While an agent did admit to calling James "boy," the agents claimed to have been attacked by the James family. According to the prosecuting attorney, one agent was kicked in the groin as he tried to take control of Charles James, Jr. Charles was also said to have kicked the agent who had been floored by the rolling pin in the face.[26]

News of the incident spread quickly. According to Martha James, "Despite the fact that everyone knew about it, there was no wholesale outrage from the African American community." Kent Ford and fellow Panther Jeff Fikes reached out to Cheryl James's parents and recommended that they attend a meeting of the Albina Ministerial Alliance (AMA) at the Vancouver Baptist Church. Ford remembers, "The purpose of the meeting was to marshal support for Cheryl, but it wasn't very productive at all. Too many egos in the room. . . . What was productive, however, was a meeting with Ann Chess Campbell of the Women's International League for Peace and Freedom [WILPF]."

The Portland branch of WILPF—a global organization founded by Jane Addams in 1915 committed to organizing women in local communities for the purpose of understanding and addressing the causes of wars and human rights abuses—was instrumental in the James case. Portland's WILPF was one of the city's leading opponents of the Vietnam War and one of its greatest proponents of civil rights and nuclear disarmament throughout the late 1960s and 1970s. In its Portland branch newsletters and calls for donations to help Cheryl James, WILPF proudly noted that it had previously contributed to Kent Ford's bail and legal defense in 1969, at a time "when many people feared to help a militant black leader."

"Thank God there were some sympathetic ears in the white community," said Ford. "We didn't even have any support from the black churches. . . . I guess I shouldn't have been surprised by that because we [the party] couldn't get any support from them either." Ford's memory in this case may be a bit too dismissive of the AMA and of church leaders such as Revs. John H. Jackson and Gordon Dickey. The AMA, which represented thirty-five local churches, met with the James family and publicly supported both Cheryl James and the eventual Cheryl James Defense Committee and Cheryl James Fund, stating in organizational resolutions and in letters to newspapers that summer, "We encourage individuals and church social action commissions to aid the Cheryl James Defense Committee." In fact, Ann Chess Campbell of Portland's WILPF and Rev. Jackson of the AMA, in coordination with Charles James, Sr., acted as trustees for the Cheryl James Fund and sent signed letters soliciting donations in late 1971. Nevertheless, prior to the summer of 1971, support for Cheryl James was driven by grassroots organizations such as WILPF and the Portland Panthers.[27]

At an early brainstorming session with members of Portland's WILPF branch, which several Panthers attended, it was agreed that a number of things needed to be done. First, a press conference would be held to make people aware of the case. Second, a defense committee would be formed to organize a campaign. Third, Cheryl would be bailed out of jail so that she could finish high school. Fourth, leaflets publicizing the case would be designed and distributed throughout the city. Fifth, a rally was proposed to drum up support. Lastly, though perhaps most importantly, they would need to secure the services of a competent lawyer.

The press conference was held at the James's home and was covered by KATU 2, KGW 8, KOIN 6, and KTPV 12, and by local newspapers, including Portland's alternative press. Within a week of the press conference, the Portland WILPF bailed out Cheryl James, allowing her to return to school. Shortly thereafter, a group of James's supporters formed the Cheryl James Defense Committee, headed by Campbell, with Arthur Spencer serving as secretary. Meanwhile, a trial date was set. With a court-appointed attorney by her side, Cheryl James went to trial in April. During closing arguments, the prosecutor presented as Exhibit 1 the blood-stained white T-shirt of the FBI agent whom James had clubbed over the head. Kent Ford remembers vividly the judge's response: "The prosecutor propped the T-shirt up on Federal Judge Gus Solomon's bench, prompting him to say, 'What is this?' The prosecutor replied, 'This is the agent's T-shirt.' Appearing irritated, Judge Solomon replied, "Ah, get it outta here . . . if he has a thick skull, he won't bleed as much, if he has a thin skull, he'll bleed a lot.'" Before the sentence was handed down, Judge Solomon, according to Ford, crowed, "'You mean to tell me you hit an agent of the Federal Bureau of Investigation over the head. . . . Eighteen months!' he exclaimed as he slammed down the gavel." On April 14, 1971, Cheryl James was convicted of assaulting federal officers and sentenced to eighteen months at the Terminal Island Federal Correctional Institution in Los Angeles County, California, a low-security federal prison for female inmates. In the related James cases, Charles was sentenced to six years in a Colorado federal prison, while Martha received three years of probation.[28]

Although Cheryl James was sentenced to prison, she was allowed to finish out the school year. At some point during the spring term, Judge Solomon was invited to speak to a law enforcement class at Portland State University. Two days before Solomon's visit, Kent Ford received a telephone call from instructor Gary Waller, informing him of Solomon's impending visit. Immediately Ford and Fikes started calling their supporters, urging them to attend the lecture. Thirty supporters, both black and white, showed up. During the question-and-answer period a female African American student confronted the judge about Cheryl James. She asked the judge how he could sentence James to eighteen months in prison when all she was doing was defending her family? Before the judge could answer, Kent Ford chimed in with, "Judge Solomon, I'm surprised at you . . . you used to be a labor activist back in the 1930s, and from what I heard, a darn good one at that." Solomon interjected and ordered the federal marshal who had escorted him to campus that afternoon to arrest Kent Ford. As the students looked on, bewildered, Ford shot back, "On what grounds are you going to arrest me: for passing around a petition, for asking you a few questions about the case, for confronting you on this issue"? Solomon again shouted to the marshal to arrest Ford. Ford responded by sticking both his arms out in front of the marshal in anticipation of being handcuffed. But seeing that the marshal was not going to arrest Ford, a frustrated Solomon turned and walked out of the classroom, with the marshal in tow.[29]

Cheryl James completed her senior year without incident. On the day of her graduation, her sister recalls seeing the horrified looks on people's faces as they watched agents placing Cheryl in handcuffs moments after she had walked across the stage to receive her diploma. Meanwhile, the Cheryl James Defense Committee plotted its next move. After calling an emergency meeting, the committee followed Ford's advice to secure the services of Nick Chaivoe as the attorney on appeal. Committee members also circulated a petition, in hopes of getting enough signatures to sway the judge to commute James's sentence. Days later, leaflets were printed outlining the particulars of the case and including a photo of Cheryl. The leaflets were passed out to people on the street, inserted into the Black Panther newspaper, and circulated on local high school and college campuses. In May, Panthers Willie James Brown, R. V. Poston, and Charles Moore, with the help of several others, disseminated another batch of leaflets at Thomas Jefferson High School. Emblazoned in black on the leaflet was "Come see about Cheryl at UnThank Park." The Panthers had decided to hold a rally at the park to mobilize enough support to keep James from being sent to prison. The Panthers were not successful in this attempt, but they were not alone. In June, just days after Cheryl's imprisonment, Portland's WILPF sent a letter to Judge

Solomon, arguing that "a different perspective regarding the totality of the events surrounding Cheryl's case is now emerging," and asking the judge to "vacate Cheryl's sentence in the interests of equal justice for all segments of the population." Then, in early July, the national WILPF assembled for its annual convention, which was held, coincidentally, at Marylhurst College in Marylhurst, Oregon (a suburb south of Portland). Among the series of resolutions passed by the two-hundred-delegate assembly from around the country, WILPF voted overwhelmingly to investigate the assault and to publicly pressure the Portland courts to reexamine the case.[30]

With strong support from the Portland Panthers and WILPF, over the next several months members of the Cheryl James Defense Committee stepped up their fundraising efforts for the appeal. By September, Cheryl James and her defense committee had the support of numerous organizations, including the AMA, the Methodist Federation of Social Action, the International Longshore and Warehouse Union, the Social Concerns Commission of the Greater Portland Council of Churches, the Portland Federation of Teachers, and many others, from residents of north and northeast Portland to James's schoolmates. By early 1972, according to the *Portland Observer*, even the Multnomah County Democratic Convention had "unanimously adopted a resolution of commendation and support to the Cheryl James Fund Committee." Tragically, however, during her time in prison in early 1972, James was raped by a guard while working in the prison cafeteria. Not long after, it was learned that James was pregnant. Suffice it to say, her supporters intensified their efforts to secure her release. The James family, which was comprised of both parents and more than fifteen children, was devastated. Members of the Cheryl James Defense Committee worked feverishly. Finally, on February 22, 1972, the Ninth Circuit Court of Appeals granted a motion to release James on a bail of $5,000 while her case was on appeal. According to an article in the *Scribe*, "The bail was posted on March 2 and she should be free sometime this week, after being processed through California." However, in late July, Judge Robert Schnacke of the Ninth Circuit Court of Appeals rejected Chaivoe's argument that the Federal Juvenile Delinquency Act (FJDA), which led a seventeen-year-old Cheryl to waive a jury trial, unconstitutionally deprived minors of their right to a jury. Schnacke's judgment consequently affirmed James's prior conviction. However, in a dissenting opinion, Judge Shirley Hufstedler vehemently disagreed with Judge Schnacke and sided with Chaivoe, arguing, "There is not here ... any countervailing legitimate interests of the state which justify chilling the juvenile's right to a jury trial. The jury waiver provisions of FJDA are [there-fore] unconstitutional."[31]

Following additional failed appeals in September 1972 and February 1973 (the latter of which went to the Supreme Court), Cheryl James was ordered to return to prison despite having a four-and-a-half-month-old son. Judge Robert C. Belloni did ultimately grant James an extension until March so that she could finish the term at Portland Community College, where she was a prelaw student. Fortunately, months later, a hearing was held in the federal courthouse in downtown Portland. To the surprise of many, the judge commuted James's sentence to time already served, but not before taking the opportunity to reprove the many supporters who had stood behind the James family during their time of crisis. Arthur Spencer recalls, "I remember the judge feeling it necessary to scold us for, in his words, bringing politics into the case . . . basically suggesting to Mrs. James, who was very religious, that she shouldn't be taken in by us."[32]

The Panthers' involvement in the James case not only spread them thin but detracted from the Emanuel Hospital initiative, a project to which they had been wholly dedicated until they were pulled into the Cheryl James affair. Once the James case was resolved, the Panthers were faced with having to make up for lost time. In response to the PDC's continuation of the Emanuel Hospital renovations, in July 1972 the Panthers organized the Black Community Survival Conference, with some support from PSU's Black Student Union, the NAACP, WILPF, the Eugene Coalition, the White Panther Party, and the Socialist Workers Party. Dr. Bill Davis secured the proper permits to use Irving Park as the location. By all accounts, the conference was a success and much was accomplished. The primary purpose was to hold a large rally in Irving Park to raise public awareness of the hospital project's detrimental impact on northeast Portland and to demonstrate the community's united opposition. Over the course of three days—July 2, 3, and 4—the group held an extended rally in Irving Park complete with live music, guest speakers, free food, and tests for sickle cell anemia. According to Ford, "With the help of several nurse practitioners, we tested more than 3,500 people for sickle cell anemia over those three days." After the conference, the Panthers spent the next several weeks providing at-home counseling to those who tested positive for the trait. "On occasion we would come across an unmarried couple, where we discovered that both the man and woman had the trait," Ford recalls. "We had to be extremely delicate in these instances, especially if the couple had plans to marry and start a family. We had to explain to them the consequences of passing the trait along to their kids . . . that wasn't easy to do."[33]

That same year something happened that can only be described as fortuitous: the Panthers expanded their sickle cell anemia project through a federal grant secured by officials at Emanuel Hospital. Since the Panthers had begun testing residents for the disease as early as 1971, Ford and Jeff Fikes believed that the Panthers had something to offer Emanuel Hospital. Consequently, Ford, Fikes, and Dr. Davis met with Roger Larson, president and chief executive officer of Emanuel Hospital to discuss how the Panthers might access a portion of those grant dollars. At the meeting, the parties agreed that the Panthers would administer tests at all of the elementary, junior high, and high schools in north and northeast Portland. Although the handshake deal did not involve testing college students, the Panthers, via a personal contact, received permission from officials at Concordia College, a small college in northeast Portland, to test students there as well. As compensation, the Panthers received a dollar and fifty cents for each test. This arrangement continued until 1974, when the grant money was exhausted. Both parties benefitted from the arrangement, although Emanuel Hospital probably gained more than the Panthers. Bringing the Panthers in on the grant was a great public relations move on the part of hospital officials, and demonstrated that they were willing to work with the more radical elements of the community. The Panthers' reach into the public schools also benefitted the hospital. It is possible that officials saw teaming up with the Panthers as a way to soften the organization's opposition to the hospital expansion and possibly convince others to follow suit. Said Kent Ford, "I'm sure they thought that, but we were careful to keep the two issues separate. Sure, we were willing to partner on the sickle cell anemia project, but we weren't going to change our position simply because the hospital agreed to put a little money in our pockets . . . they may have believed that at the outset, but they soon found out differently."[34]

A cross-section of Portland's leftist community attended the Black Community Survival Conference. Among the musical acts and speakers on hand was a Seattle-based group named Cold, Bold and Together (originally called Funk Experience), founded by five college students at Western Washington State College. The group's more popular 45s included "Somebody's Gonna Burn Ya" and "Dedication (to Our Wonderful Beautiful Black Sisters)." Pleasure, a horn-driven band that often incorporated jazz overtones into its funk-and-soul foundations, also performed. The band, a group of Portland natives, had formed the same year as the conference. Ford remembers, "When they came on, everyone rushed to the front of the stage, which was really in the form of a flatbed truck ... they brought the house down." Attendees were also treated to the smooth and soulful sounds of the highly popular Billy Larkin and the Delegates. When conferencegoers weren't dancing they were listening to a diverse group of speakers. These included Penny Jackson, the sister of George Jackson; Tom Wilson, who owned an employment agency and was running for state representative (a race he ultimately lost); local minister Rev. Sam Johnson; Ray Eaglin, chair of the Eugene Coalition; and representatives from Lewis and Clark College and Portland State University. When it was Wilson's turn to speak, he sent the crowd into a tizzy when he belted out, "My name is Tom, but I ain't no Uncle Tom." Also on hand were various welfare and health care professionals, university faculty, and local high schools and college students. Maurice Isserman, professor of history at Hamilton College and a graduate of Reed College, attended the conference and distinctly remembers the event being "very festive ... the organizers, especially Kent and Sandra, did a really good job of attracting kids ... it was a nice summer day punctuated with a lot of leftist politics and free food."[35]

According to police reports, by Sunday afternoon, between six hundred and eight hundred people had gathered in the park, leading to concerns within the police department that the event might get out of hand. Remembering the disorder sparked in Irving Park five years earlier, the police closely monitored the progress of the conference in the days and weeks leading up to the rally, and maintained their vigilance during and after the rally as well. In late May, the Portland police began surveilling Tom Wilson and increased their surveillance of Kent Ford and his home, where the rally planners met, as well as the homes of fellow planners Sharon Lieberman and R. L. Anderson. In effect, the police suspected that the rally could serve as a launching point for a movement to elect "radical" politicians or endorse "radical activities" in northeast Portland. According to a report filed by Deputy Chief Robert Steele, the police initially speculated that the event would "attempt to drift away from the BLACK PANTHER PARTY philosophies to a new [ideology] which will be a political power movement." The supposed nature of this "new" political philosophy is unclear from police reports; however, reports from late June reemphasized the police's assumptions, stating, "KENT FORD'S activities will be an attempt to use this meeting to sway feelings against the police and to keep the police out of the black community."

Consequently, patrolling officers were instructed to maintain an active yet covert presence in Irving Park during the rally. However, with no major incidences to report over the two days, and with the crowd reportedly dwindling by late Saturday night to fewer than forty people (most of whom were involved in cleanup), police realized that their fears of violence had been overblown.[36]

A July 3 interoffice memorandum within the Portland Police Bureau shows that city council member Francis Ivancie had gotten so worked up about the festivities on the second evening that he had paid a visit to Portland's east precinct at 11:30 p.m. to urge the police to "go in to the Park and clear it out." The organizers of the rally had only been granted a permit with a 10:00 p.m. deadline. When Ivancie marched into the precinct and demanded to know what the police were going to do about this violation, Lt. H. M. Gowing, the author of the memo, assured him that the matter was under control. Since no one had broken any laws, no action would be taken against those in attendance. Upon being told this, Ivancie left the precinct, "but appeared to be unhappy and said he was going to find a solution to the problem."[37] He also stated that he knew the position the police were in. Lt. Gowing had not succumbed to Ivancie's alarmist disposition because the police were confident that things would not get out of control. A July 2 memo indicated that several FBI informants had been sprinkled throughout the gathering, supplying their handlers with up-to-date information.

Although by the end of the summer in 1972 the Black Community Survival Committee had ceased to exist in name, the loose network of individuals and organizations opposed to the Emanuel Hospital project persisted, this time under the name of The Left Out Ones, Inc.—a reference to the predominately black population displaced by the project. Led by local activist Nate Proby, with the support of Tom Wilson and Ford, the group criticized the Emanuel Hospital project for its unwillingness to hire and train members of the local community for new construction and hospital jobs. In addition, it chastised the hospital and PDC officials for their broken promise to fund the construction of new low-income housing for those who had been displaced. Their supporters, which included Portland Panthers, posted and distributed flyers demanding that Emanuel Hospital develop "in cooperation with various community groups, a plan to recruit minority students for their school for nurses." Likewise, they proclaimed that the hospital needed "to keep the promises it has made to the community it has so drastically changed and to the people it has removed from their homes." Without substantive inclusion of African Americans in the project, the activists argued, the Emanuel Hospital expansion would be nothing more than another destructive urban renewal project with far-reaching social costs.[38]

The following year, the Panthers and other members of the black community stepped up their efforts to block the project by organizing a picket line outside of Emanuel Hospital on the morning of March 21, 1973. Among those who participated in the demonstration were a racially mixed group of people from St. Andrews Church, young people from the Youth Opportunity School, Black Student Union members from Portland State University, and members of the local Students for a Democratic Society chapter. Carrying signs reading, "Emanuel has no respect for Black and Poor People," "STOP the Destruction until You Hire Black People," and "The Clinic Will Continue to Serve the People Body and Soul," the protesters demanded jobs at the hospital and an end to the demolition of their homes and businesses. Intricately connecting job opportunities within their own community to the city's historical legacy of poverty, displacement, and discrimination, the demonstrators made it clear that they saw this project as another element in the perpetual cycle of poverty and discrimination in northeast Portland. Police patrolled the area to ensure that everything remained under control, but if they expected violence, they were disappointed. The crowd in front of Emanuel picketed peacefully for hours and adjourned in the late afternoon.[39] Despite their efforts to gain the public's attention, however, the combined resources and strategies of the Portland Panthers and other black leadership had little to no effect. That year, residents and business owners were required to move to make room for the nineteen-acre expansion. To qualify for a federal grant to complete the hospital expansion project, the hospital had signed an agreement calling for the development of 180 to 300 units of low-income and moderate-income housing. Residents were both shocked and dismayed when they learned that the federal grant for the expansion had fallen through, ultimately leaving vacant lots along Williams and Vancouver Avenues above Russell Street.

In spring 1973, the Portland Development Commission struck its most serious blow to the Portland Panthers' community survival programs with the demolition of the Fred Hampton People's Free Health Clinic. When the National Committee to Combat Fascism had first leased the building on 109 N. Russell Street in 1969, they had been well aware that the city planned to demolish the building to make way for the hospital expansion.[40] Regardless, Ford and the Panthers chose the building for two reasons. First, it was inexpensive, and PDC officials had assured them that they would be given ample time to vacate the premises before the building was to be leveled. Second, and most important, by selecting a location within the expansion zone, the Panthers expressed their defiance of the city's power structure and defended their vision of the black community's use of the space. When, in 1971, Emanuel Hospital and the PDC notified the Black Panther Party that the clinic had to move, the Panthers agreed but demanded the same compensation that everyone else in the area had received.

After a long period of intense negotiations, the brass at Emanuel Hospital and the Panthers came to an agreement. At the designated time, the Panthers would move out of the 109 N. Russell Street location into an office at 2846 N. Williams Avenue. The Panthers signed a five-year rent-free lease with the understanding that, after five years, the Panthers would assume responsibility for the rent. The Portland Development Commission would furnish the Panthers with funds for refurbishing the facility, and Emanuel Hospital officials provided relocation expenses.[41] With that matter settled, the Panthers focused their attention on their impending move. As the days passed, Ford realized that they would be unable to move out by the deadline, so he requested an extension, which was granted. According to Ford, the relocation chief, Benjamin C. Webb, picked him up at the health clinic on Monday, April 30, and the two drove to the Village Inn for coffee. Webb, a man in his late forties, was a World War II veteran and a graduate of the University of Oregon. He was known as a fair man who worked with student groups to end segregation in Portland.

In between sips of coffee, Ford and Webb talked and agreed that the Panthers' move-out date would be rescheduled for the second week of May. Unbeknownst to Ford, shortly thereafter the PDC filed a notice of immediate eviction. The following day, Tuesday May 1, 1973, on an unseasonably warm morning, Ford drove to the clinic. Arriving with a moving truck and boxes, he was shocked to discover that the Multnomah County sheriff, local police, and officials from the Portland Development Commission were already inside the clinic. They had broken in and forcibly removed medical supplies, files, and equipment. In the process, they had ruined more than $1,000 worth of vaccines and other medicines that required refrigeration. Pacific Power had apparently turned off the electricity the night before. Outraged and exhausted after years of struggle in support of Portland's black community, Ford exploded at Webb, who was at the scene. "I read him the riot act," said Ford. When Ford spotted a Channel 2 News van passing by, despite being caught up in the heat of the moment, he had the presence of mind to flag it down. "I wanted to make sure that the people of northeast Portland knew what city officials were doing to their clinic," he said. Ford felt duped and betrayed by the relocation chief, who had promised him that the Panthers would have until the following Monday to vacate the premises. Ford remembers, "The day before we were evicted, the relocation chief and I sat down and had a cup of coffee . . . we had a very cordial and pleasant conversation . . . and at that meeting he agreed to allow us until May 7th, which was the following Monday." The fact that the relocation chief was African American only added to Ford's disappointment and feeling of betrayal.[42]

So, after years of systematic subversion and contests over space in the city's Albina district, Portland had finally evicted the Panthers and continued the expansion of nearby Emanuel Hospital. Ford and other Panthers, for whom the Emanuel Hospital project represented a continuation of the ideologies and policies that had destroyed much of their community and contributed to more than a century of social, economic, and spatial discrimination, felt that someone needed to take responsibility for stopping the city's northward encroachment on black neighborhoods. Each building and each block mattered.[43] To make matters worse, the space into which the Panthers were to move their clinic was inadequate. Repairs were needed, including fixing the leaky roof, installing new plumbing, and replacing faulty wiring. The Panthers quickly realized that, despite PDCs earlier agreement to help cover the costs of renovation, the promise would not be kept. Officials with the PDC claimed that a lack of funding prevented them from making the upgrades. Other city planners claimed that the hospital project had absolutely no money to spare. Feeling that the PDC had lied to them and tricked them, the Panthers posted a notice in the window of the clinic describing the PDC's deception and encouraging the community to protest. "We want Emanuel to live up to its responsibilities in this community," the flyer demanded. "After all, we do aid Emanuel in treating people who are unable to pay for medical attention." The Panthers even sought the assistance of the Albina Legal Aid office, but to no avail. Then, as if things were not bad enough, federal budget cuts eventually forced an abrupt end to the hospital's expansion and left the clinic site vacant.[44]

Undaunted, the Panthers moved what was left of the health clinic into the space occupied by the Malcolm X People's Dental Clinic at 2341 N. Williams Avenue. Although the Panthers were eventually able to get the clinic up and running, the loss of supplies and equipment made it difficult to immediately pick up where they had left off. It was not until October that the clinic began taking appointments again. The Panthers were determined, however, not to let this setback hinder their ability to provide much-needed care to the poor residents of northeast Portland. Weeks before the clinic reopened, Dorreen Labby of the *Scribe* contrasted the atmosphere at the Fred Hampton People's Free Health Clinic with that of a traditional doctor's office. Labby wrote,

> "Everbody's Welcome!" That's Sandra Ford's message to the Albina
> Community and anyone in Portland who needs medical care and can't
> afford to pay for it.... There's a warm, unofficial, friendly atmosphere in the
> tiny clinic waiting room with the staff out talking to visitors, calling regulars
> by name, and making first-timers feel comfortable. Outside through the big
> front window, the blare of a R & B station and the night traffic of cars and
> people on Williams Avenue is reassuring. It's not like the ritual purgatory of
> subdued light, plastic plants, and Ladies Home Journal that prepares you
> for the vision of your family doctor.[45]

Despite working under less-than-ideal circumstances, the Panthers' volunteer physicians continued treating patients, and the Panthers remained committed to raising awareness of specific environmental and hereditary medical conditions affecting African Americans, namely sickle cell anemia and hypertension. According to Kent Ford, the Panthers had tested approximately four thousand people for high blood pressure in one weekend in the autumn of the previous year. Given the seemingly high demand for sickle cell anemia testing, the eviction could not have come at a worse time.

Incidentally, the dismantling of the Panthers' medical clinic coincided with the efforts of the FBI and local police to wipe out the Black Panther Party nationally. Using "any means necessary," the FBI, under Director J. Edgar Hoover and his successor L. Patrick Gray III, sought to eradicate the BPP through a system of surveillance, infiltration, subversion, and co-optation known as the Counter Intelligence Program (COINTELPRO). According to Hoover, the BPP was "the most violence-prone of all the extremist groups" and needed to be eliminated to protect the social and political stability of the United States. Specifically, Hoover was ostensibly concerned that BPP branches and chapters were brainwashing and indoctrinating young African Americans. He described programs like the free children's breakfast and health clinics as the most dangerous and subversive elements of the Panthers.[46] Hoover's declaration was likely not made out of any real fear that the Panthers or their supporters "represented the single greatest threat to the internal security of the United States." Instead, Hoover's pronouncement was a subterfuge to justify law enforcement's grisly efforts to annihilate the group and debilitate its leaders, both nationally and locally. His intention was to influence the media framing of the BPP, and, if that didn't work, to shape the opinions of political figures and the American people via the persistent transmittal of his insidious dogma. By doing so, Hoover hoped to foment a climate that would mitigate any potential outcry stemming from law enforcement's treachery to bring down the BPP. The more successful he was at depicting the Panthers as race-mongering anti-American anarchists, the more likely the American people would find the Panthers deserving of whatever political measures Hoover and other law enforcement agencies took. As director of the FBI, Hoover believed himself (and not the attorney general) to be the nation's top law enforcement officer. As such, he felt entitled to the respect commensurate with such a position. Moreover, like some of his contemporaries, he was of the opinion that blacks were inferior and should stay in their place. Unfortunately the Panthers defied both of these personal convictions, which helps explain why the BPP, more than any other black organization in the latter half of the twentieth century, bore the full brunt of the FBI's counterintelligence program.

Interestingly, the Portland branch of the Black Panther Party was not subjected to the headline-grabbing repressive tactics as branches and chapters in other West Coast cities, such as Los Angeles, San Francisco, Oakland, and Seattle. There were no police raids of the offices in Portland, nor were there any shoot-outs with members of the Portland Police Bureau. Said retired police officer Richard Walker, "The Panthers here were low key . . . they were busy feeding kids and stuff like that . . . so there was no need to raid their offices." Nevertheless, although the Portland branch was small in comparison to some other branches and did not receive the full brunt of the state's wrath, the FBI targeted it just the same. Three tactics on which the bureau relied heavily were constantly arrest Panther leaders, attempting to dissuade potential supporters of the BPP, and contacting businesses or companies that employed Panthers and instigating trouble. For example, in the summer of 1969, Ford was arrested five times in five days. The charges ranged from trespassing to disorderly conduct to resisting arrest. Also, according to Percy Hampton and Oscar Johnson, the Portland branch was under constant surveillance. Said Hampton, "FBI agents would go door to door and ask my neighbors about me and my activities . . . then there were times when I'd look in my rearview mirror and see them following me around town." Johnson recalls an even more bizarre incident:

> One day an FBI agent called me up and asked me to meet him for lunch . . . it was comical to me . . . an FBI agent wanting to have lunch with me. I informed Kent, and he and I went back and forth on the matter. Finally, Kent said, "I'll leave it up to you." I met with the guy at a family restaurant called the Village Inn on 10th Avenue. During lunch, the guy expressed concern about the contents of the Black Panther newspaper, and I'm thinking . . . he invited me to lunch to talk about the Black Panther newspaper? Finally I asked him, "What do you want from me?" Although he did not come out and directly say that he wanted me to be an informant, that was the gist of what he was saying. I played along at lunch, but of course I wasn't going to give him any information about anything or anyone. Also, little did he know that we had him under surveillance the whole time we were eating lunch. Seated at another table were two of our comrades who were there to make sure that this guy didn't pull any funny business. After the lunch, he never contacted me again, but from that point on there always seemed to be two men staked out in front of my house at all hours of the day and night.

Although the agent's invitation was accepted only after deliberation, and although nothing came of it, had Johnson been seen conversing with an FBI agent at a popular restaurant, opponents of the Panthers or even Panther supporters could have easily taken the opportunity to cast doubt not only on Johnson but on the entire Portland branch of the Black Panther Party. It was not uncommon for militant members to take action (sometimes with fatal consequences) against those whom they believed were in cahoots with agents of the state. FBI agents did not lack for creativity when it came to taking down dissident groups.[47]

In a 2008 interview, Kent Ford noted that whenever the leadership of local chapters and branches met, they always had bizarre experiences with the FBI to share. "Each chapter in the United States . . . had one thing in common," Ford recalled, "we all had the same stories about the COINTELPRO operations." Ford remembers that FBI agents would don disguises and show up on his doorstep:

One time a guy wearing a painter's outfit came to my house asking to
do some volunteer painting.... I stepped outside to talk to the guy, and
at some point the guy flipped open his badge and revealed himself.... I
said, "Hey man, I thought you said you were a painter ... you know you're
not supposed to contact me directly ... anything you want to say, you
need to contact my lawyer."…. The guy pointed out that he knew we were
strapped for cash [the branch that is] and offered me money in exchange
for information…. Imagine that, trying to co-opt me, the leader of the
branch. Then, there was this other guy who was constantly snooping around
meetings and leftist circles, a red-headed white guy ... he had become such
a nuisance that a whole bunch of us activists decided to go downtown to the
FBI office at the Crown Plaza Building. We confronted the guy at the office
and demanded that he stop spying on us. We told him we would pursue
legal action if he didn't stop what he was doing.[48]

In the late 1970s, when many FBI documents and memos on COINTEL-
PRO became public, Bill Keller of the *Oregonian* revealed the extent of the
FBI's actions in Portland. According to Keller, in 1970 and 1971, the FBI sent
anonymous letters to Panther volunteers throughout Portland, attempting
to dissuade them from volunteering at or providing medical resources to
the Panthers' clinics, much like Portland police had done in 1969 and 1970
with local businesses that had supported the breakfast program. Among
leftist circles, it was also rumored that the FBI attempted to convince the
Multnomah County Medical Society to set up rival clinics in Albina to turn
people away from the Panthers' health and dental clinics, but these plans
never gained any traction. A May 1970 Portland FBI memo reported that an
unnamed Portland doctor had informed the bureau that he was attempting to encourage the Multnomah County Medical Society to set up its own
free clinic to put the Panthers' Fred Hampton People's Free Health Clinic
out of business. Robert Elsner, who headed the medical society at the time,
said he did not recall anyone at the clinic expressing such an idea. "In all
the time I was there, there was never any discussion of the Multnomah
Medical Society opening its own clinic," said Elsner. "That would have been
a precedent that would have turned off a lot of our members." Elsner noted
that the society actively encouraged its members to volunteer at the free
clinics and that most members considered the Panthers' militant politics
"a side issue" to helping poor people. But, Elsner added, many doctors later
became disenchanted with the clinic as the number of patients dwindled,

and some were concerned that they were being used to generate publicity for the Panthers.[49]

In addition to the FBI's efforts to subvert and co-opt the Panthers' clinics, the FBI and the Portland Police Bureau kept detailed files and maintained close surveillance on the Panthers and their activities. A July 2, 1971, officer's report reveals that officers spoke with Rev. Sam Johnson of the Highland United Church of Christ, with F. F. Runyon of Runyon's 88 Cents Store, and with Al Leviske, general manager of local McDonald's restaurants, about their support of the Panthers' programs. If the officers were hoping to hear complaints, they were disappointed. The officer noted in the report that in July Kent Ford had not accepted the usual seventy-five dollar monthly donation from Runyon, and that Ford had reminded the store owner that the breakfast program did not run during the summer, hence no donation for the breakfast program was necessary.

Whenever police officers tired of hearing supportive merchants sing the Panthers' praises for their community efforts, they could always shift their focus back to the Panthers themselves, most notably Kent Ford and Percy Hampton. FBI agents and investigators not only sat outside Ford's and Hampton's homes but approached and sometimes harassed their friends, families, and employers. On occasion, agents even infiltrated Panther meetings. Even group members with no criminal history were targeted for surveillance. Percy Hampton, who, along with his sister, Patty, was one of the Portland Panthers' earliest, youngest, best-educated, and most involved members, stated that on multiple occasions two white men in suits and ties had come to his mother's home and asked her, "Do you know that your children are involved in the Black Panther Party? You need to protect them from this, because they're headed in the wrong direction." The officers then attempted to get whatever information about the Portland branch that they could gather from his mother.[50]

It is difficult to ascertain the extent to which FBI agents were able to sway members of the black community. As in other cities, there were some who agreed to act as informants, many who kept the Panthers at arm's length, and still more who wanted nothing to do with them. One of the Portland Panthers' strength was the ability to build coalitions and attract both older and younger volunteers to work at the clinics and to help with other community survival programs and activities. Still, few of the Panthers' volunteers were African American. With the exception of Dr. Clarence Pruitt, no African American who held a DDS or an MD degree volunteered at the Panthers' health or dental clinic. Dr. Bill Davis, a PhD in biochemistry, volunteered at the health clinic. But nearly all of the Panthers' volunteers were white. It is possible that black professionals may have believed that volunteering at a Panther facility would adversely affect their businesses or, worse yet, their careers. Sandra Ford explained, "You have to understand . . . a lot of blacks were afraid to get involved with the Black Panther Party. . . . I mean they were afraid to be associated with the Civil Rights Movement, so you know they weren't going to be seen with a militant organization like the Black Panther Party . . . in their minds they believed that doing so would put them at risk somehow, even if what they were doing was something as basic as volunteering at the breakfast program or one of the clinics." Ford's statement is not without merit. In 1957, T. R. M. Howard, a prominent Chicago surgeon (by way of Mississippi) and president of the National Medical Association lamented the fact that many black physicians were not eager to confront Jim Crow. That year, Howard, who was known for being an advocate of civil rights, chided a national meeting of physicians that "too many Negro doctors in this nation have not concerned themselves about this 'all-out fight for first class citizenship for our people,'" adding, "We are spending too much money on Cadillacs, yachts, and mansions in this grave hour." To be fair, while black physicians did not line up at the doors of the Black Panthers' health and dental clinics, it should be noted that black physicians played an important role in the "modern" Civil Rights Movement. The Medical Committee for Human Rights is one such example, although it should be noted that the overwhelming majority of the committee's physicians who joined this group were white, not black.[51]

Given Sandra Ford's remarks, it is possible that the FBI's efforts to dissuade professionals from getting involved with the Panthers succeeded within black professional circles. This is not to say that the Portland Panthers were without black supporters; clearly they were not. There were several black entrepreneurs and other professionals who contributed money or in-kind gifts to the Panthers on a fairly regular basis, but they did so with little fanfare. Dave Dawson, the co-owner of the House of Sounds record store, was a supporter of the Portland branch of the Black Panther Party. Unbeknownst to him at the time, his friendship with Kent Ford was widely known within law enforcement circles. In fact, said Dawson, "The police raided my record store on two separate occasions. . . . I remember one morning in 1970 . . . no sooner than I opened the shop, in walks several police officers with a warrant to search the place. I just sat back and watched them do their thing.... I had surplus ammo that I had purchased legally; they took it but then had to bring it back later ... that was funny."[52] Dawson was one of a dozen of black professionals on whom the Panthers could count for financial, in-kind, and moral support.

However, there were some African Americans whose opposition to the Panthers was a matter of record. Percy Hampton remembers a black administrator at Portland State University making it clear that he did not want any black students getting involved with the BPP. "One day he told me that the Panthers were going to lead to my undoing," said Hampton. It is possible that the administrator's comment had been prompted by recent events in Houston, Texas, and in San Rafael, California. On July 26, 1970, Carl Hampton, the leader of the People's Party II and then of the Houston branch of the BPP, was killed by police officers in Houston. Less than a month later, on August 7, at the Marin County Courthouse, Jonathan Jackson, James McClain, and William Christmas were shot and killed in a botched hostage attempt. While none of the three had been members of the Black Panther Party, Jonathan was the younger brother of George Jackson, who was known for his internationally acclaimed books *Soledad Brother* and *Blood in My Eye*, and who had been given the title "Field Marshall of the Black Panther Party" by Huey P. Newton.[53]

Regardless of the administrator's motive for cautioning Hampton, the Portland Panthers were not without black supporters. "There was still a segment of the African American community that 'thought well of us' ... they supported us ... for example, there were a number of single women with young boys who wanted the male Panthers to serve as mentors to them, and some of us did," said Raymond Joe.[54] While it is nearly impossible to quantify, it is safe to say that the Portland Panthers were supported by various sectors of the greater Portland community. There were individuals who provided face support, those who gave stealth support, and those who supported the party in absentia. "Face support" was given by individuals who were willing to participate in marches, press conferences, and demonstrations. They might post bail, make public statements before television cameras on behalf of the branch's members, or volunteer for one of the party's community survival programs. These supporters were unconcerned about being publicly identified with a Panther effort. While there were some blacks who met this criterion, many of the Portland Panthers would agree that the overwhelming majority of face support came from whites. For example, a cursory look at photographs of rallies and demonstrations show significantly more white than black participants. The overwhelming majority of Panthers volunteers were also white.

"Stealth support" was given by those who believed in what the Panthers were doing but were not interested in advertising or broadcasting their support to the wider public. This is not to say that they went to great lengths to conceal their support; they simply did not feel compelled to make their support known to the general public. Stealth supporters might be inclined to write a check, let the Panthers use their facility for a meeting, or donate food supplies and equipment. Supporters of this ilk may even have been bold enough to sign a petition; however, they would not have been inclined to participate in the public events.

Finally, in absentia supporters contributed to the Panthers or to a Panther-related cause but went to some lengths to avoid being identified as supporters. Support in absentia came in the form of cash donations that would not leave a paper trail, and favorable comments about the Black Panther Party when in the company of like-minded individuals in barber shops, beauty salons, bars, and pool halls. But in absentia supporters would have been unwilling to voice their feelings publicly, to let their sentiments be officially recorded, or to participate in any public community effort that was clearly in direct support of the Panthers. When such individuals spoke to reporters in support of the Panthers, they did so anonymously.

Certainly Portland's white community included supporters in all three categories, but much of the support given by African American residents fell within the categories of stealth support and support in absentia. This may be due to the possibility (real or imagined) of white retribution. At that time, it was not uncommon for whites to exact economic retribution against blacks they perceived to be unsubmissive, let alone radical. One could argue that while the Portland branch of the Black Panther Party did have some support within the African American community, it ironically had no real base there. Its base was among white leftists and progressives. For the most part, black Portlanders responded to the Black Panthers like fans at a sporting event. They were not active participants but spectators watching from a considerable distance. And because they were not heavily involved, it was only a matter of time before the branch withered.

The African American community's reluctance to support the Panthers did not preclude them from publicly seeking the Panthers' assistance in times of need. Indeed, by 1971, the Panthers had firmly established themselves as troubleshooters to whom residents seeking redress could go for help. Some residents took full advantage of the Panthers' willingness to assist. Some who found themselves involved in disputes with various agencies called on the Panthers when they were unable to resolve the matter themselves. It was also not uncommon for residents to ask for help with projects such as house repairs and lawn maintenance. The Panthers following among senior citizens was particularly noteworthy. "They would call on us to do all types of things," Sandra Ford recalls. "Drive them to the store, take them to get their prescriptions filled, take them to the bank . . . you name it, we did it . . . they really liked Kent, he had a way with older people, he really connected with them."[55]

This reputation for community service did not deter the FBI or the local police from conducting surveillance on the Panthers or from trying to mold public opinion against them. In spying on the Panthers and failing to obey a law that ordered police files destroyed, the Portland Police Bureau violated civil liberties, demonstrated poor management, and wasted resources. The folders of intelligence files made up partly of newspaper clippings, photos, interoffice memos, notepads of surveillance activity, and informant testimony that were found covered in cobwebs and dust in a police officer's garage are more reminiscent of the Keystone Cops than of George Orwell's *1984*. However, such comparisons are no consolation when freedoms such as right to privacy are at stake. Oscar Johnson, a former marine who had no police record, recalled two members of the FBI coming to his home to speak with him. Then, one day after returning home from work, he noticed two white men in suits sitting in a car outside of his home. Slightly annoyed, the six-foot-four Johnson approached the vehicle. According to Johnson, "I knocked on the window and said, 'Hey, you guys want anything?' And the guys just drove off. . . . I wasn't doing anything illegal; I just wanted to help my community." Although Panthers were well aware that they were being spied on, in the spring of 1971, a break-in at an FBI office in Media, Pennsylvania, revealed that American citizens of all stripes had been under COINTELPRO surveillance for years. Classified documents were leaked to newspapers throughout the country, particularly the *Washington Post*. The bureau's vast spy network was a startling revelation for many, but for some, it was mere confirmation of what they had always suspected or known. As Ford, Hampton, Johnson, and other members of the organization noted, the daily run-ins with the FBI and the police during the early 1970s interfered with their ability to run the breakfast program, sell newspapers, operate the clinics, go to school, and work at their jobs.[56]

Meanwhile, as the Portland Panthers were fighting the Emanuel Hospital expansion project and the FBI was keeping a close watch on members and supporters, the Panther headquarters in the Bay Area was in a state of flux due to ideological disputes and paranoia brought on by government infiltration, infighting between members and other militant groups, and the murder of several Panthers. On August 21, 1971, Panthers in Portland were stunned upon hearing the news that acclaimed author and political prisoner George Jackson had been gunned down on the grounds of San Quentin State Prison as he was reportedly attempting to escape. News of Jackson's death reverberated across continents. Several Portland Panther women made the eleven-hour trip to Oakland, California, where the funeral services were held. That same year, BPP branches and chapters throughout the country began experiencing a drop in membership due to events such as the feud between Huey P. Newton and Eldridge Cleaver that resulted in the murder of at least two highly valued members of the organization.[57]

The Portland branch of the BPP suffered few defections, but the resultant murders of Robert Webb and Sam Napier, reportedly by loyalists of Newton and Cleaver, respectively, not only had a deleterious effect on morale but left some members scarred. As the distribution manager for the Portland branch, Percy Hampton was in constant contact with Napier. The two talked two to three times a week and had grown close over the years. "I started losing respect for Oakland once Sam was killed," Hampton recalled. Johnson was floored upon hearing the news that Napier had been murdered. "Sam was a good guy, he was one of the hardest-working Panthers I ever knew ... everyone liked Sam, his murder hit everyone like a ton of bricks ... that was the worst day of my life as a Panther." The Portland branch was one of the few branches that elected not to take sides during the fracas. "We weren't going to get involved in that feud stuff, said Hampton. "While I may have agreed with some the things coming out of the East Coast, I wasn't about to take sides. We continued to do in Portland what we had been doing before the feud." Similarly, Ford recalls, "After a while, we even started getting two different newspapers—one from Oakland and one from New York [*Right On!*], but we sold both ... we weren't going to choose one side over the other." The Portland Panthers' decision to stay out of the fray enabled them to avoid many of the pitfalls that hurt some of the other branches. Internal struggles among branch members were not uncommon.[58] Six months after the deaths of Webb and Napier, tragedy struck again. Sandra Lee, Los Angeles Black Panther Elmer (Geronimo) Pratt's significant other, was murdered in Los

Angeles. Her body was found in a sleeping bag in a suburban gutter, shot five times, once in the stomach. Lee had been pregnant at the time. These murders sent shock waves throughout the party.

When the central committee decided to consolidate and move everyone to the Bay Area to work for Bobby Seale's campaign for mayor and Elaine Brown's campaign for city council, most of the organization's prominent branches were shut down, but not the Portland branch. Around that time, the Justice Department estimated that there were only one thousand registered members of the Black Panther Party nationally, a decrease from roughly two thousand to five thousand members in the late 1960s. Some Panthers chose to leave the party rather than move to Oakland, where they would be forced to start a new life in an unfamiliar city. Most of the Portland Panthers did not follow either of those routes. They kept a healthy distance between themselves and the national office. This manifested in the decreased number of visits paid to the Bay Area and in the decreased frequency with which phone calls were placed to the Panthers' headquarters. "I didn't have much to say to anyone in Oakland after all that stuff went down," said Percy Hampton. Likewise, Sandra Ford said, "I never had that close a connection to Oakland anyway, so not being in contact with the headquarters was no big deal to me."[59]

The Portland Panthers continued to operate as they had always done, and their core programs continued to flourish. The health and dental clinics continued to take on volunteers. Indeed, by late 1972, the Panthers were called on to help the St. Andrews Catholic Church establish a clinic of its own. The Health Help Center, as it was called, opened in 1973. Sister Mary Ann Dickey, the clinic's director, worked closely with the Panthers to provide the residents of northeast Portland with quality health care. Dickey said, "We had a very close working relationship. We sat on each other's boards of director . . . we shared supplies. If I had a surplus of supplies, I would send items over to Kent. We also shared volunteer labor. . . . We also coordinated our schedules so that when the Panthers' clinic was closed, we would be open, and vice versa. This worked out well, since both Kent and I were on shoestring budgets."[60]

The Health Help Center relieved the Panthers of some of the burden of caring for Portland's residents, as the Panthers' clinic was in high demand. Unfortunately, the courtesy extended to the Health Help Center by the Model Cities did not apply to the Panthers. According to Ford, "The people at Model Cities were not interested in helping the Panthers. For example, around the same time that we helped Sister Mary Ann Dickey launch her clinic, Dr. Pruitt went before the board of directors for Model Cities to solicit funding for our clinic. After hearing Pruitt's proposal, they gave him a standing ovation.... We just knew we were going to get some money, but we didn't. I guess the idea to fund a Panther clinic was nixed at city hall."[61] In addition to supporting the Health Help Center, the Model Cities board of directors awarded a $170,000 grant to the Albina Health Clinic, which opened in September 1973. Between the three clinics, Portland's north and northeast residents were increasingly well cared for.

The Portland Panthers' visibility began to wane after 1972, as, for reasons that are not entirely clear, local mainstream newspapers abruptly ceased all coverage of the branch. On the surface, it would seem that the efforts of the federal government, along with the city's own power structure, had defeated the Black Panther Party in Portland. Not only had the Portland Panthers been unsuccessful in halting the expansion of Emanuel Hospital in the Eliot neighborhood, but that very same expansion project had destroyed the first Fred Hampton People's Free Health Clinic, thus impeding the Panthers' ability to provide health care services to the indigent residents of northeast Portland. Moreover, intensive efforts by the FBI and the Portland police had subverted the organization. Although the Portland Panthers, unlike their brethren in other parts of the country, did not canvas the city advocating the overthrow of the government, they were certainly anticapitalists. The types of programs they offered and the interviews with them published in the city's mainstream and alternative newspapers all indicate that they advocated a socialist form of government that was consistent with the party line. Although it was never publicly acknowledged, in many ways the brand of socialism espoused by the Panthers resembled that of Tanzania's first president, Julius K. Nyerere, more than that of Karl Marx or Mao Tse-tung. Nyerere saw socialism not as being for the benefit of black men, brown men, white men, or yellow men, but for the service of all men. Nyerere's socialism was in service of human equality for all, regardless of race, creed, gender, or station.[62]

Although the Portland Panthers did not engage in the kind of theatrics that played out on the streets of other cities, the Portland Police Bureau felt compelled to monitor them closely, if for no other reason than their prosocialist stance. While the Portland Panthers may have lost the ground war with the FBI, the police, and the PDC, many of the ideas they stood for persisted. Even as the Black Panther Party's size and influence abated, a more powerful alternative that appealed to many Portlanders was growing in its place. Although the Panthers' influence was no longer at its peak, their vision of a community-led approach to politics, urban development, and social programs filtered into every corner of the city, dismantling the city's old political power structure and ushering in the new form of political leadership that has defined Portland for decades.

Crowd Storms City Hall To Protest Shooting

CITY COUNCIL chambers Thursday afternoon was invaded by more than 200 young people who protested the Wednesday night shooting of 19-year-old Albert Wayne Williams by police. Speakers demanded ouster of several police officers and "community control" of police. Demonstrators stayed about 40 minutes and left peaceably as Police Tactical Squad arrived at City Hall.

See Story on Page One Also

Albert Wayne Williams, 19, remained in serious condition Thursday with bullet wounds inflicted by police Wednesday at the Portland headquarters of the Black Panther party.

Williams underwent surgery at Multnomah Hospital Wednesday night. The wounds were in the lower arm and abdomen, presumably made by one bullet fired by Officer Stan Harmon who with Officer Ralph Larsen was attempting to serve a warrant for Williams' arrest.

Williams had been charged with intent to kill, because he allegedly fired first at the officers. Bail was set at $25,000.

Panther leader Kent Ford said Williams had fired a rifle shot into the office ceiling but had dropped the rifle and had put up his hands when he was shot. Ford was not present at the time. Police denied Williams had dropped the rifle.

The shooting brought more than 200 noisy demonstrators storming into Portland City Hall Thursday afternoon. Protestors staged an impromptu "speech in" before Mayor Terry Schrunk and city commissioners in council chambers.

Councilmen, obviously taken by surprise, listened to several speakers, including Bill Grandby, attorney general of the Portland Brown Berets.

Grandby, with permission from Schrunk, used a microphone to berate the council in language laced with profanity. He said Williams should be freed and that Officer Harmon should be "suspended from duty and tried for attempted murder."

The crowd cheered, "Right on!"

Schrunk replied wearily, "The subject is under complete investigation." That drew catcalls and jeers.

Police Appear

The demonstration lasted more than 30 minutes. Of the five city fathers, only Commission Mark Grayson left the council chambers. Several policemen were in the building and at 2:30 a dozen members of the Police Tactical Squad roared up on motorcycles.

Protestors had apparently had their say by then and they filed out of City Hall chanting, "All power to the people!" There were no clashes between demonstrators and police.

Grayson listened to the speeches in the press room. "I've never heard such language," he said.

Commissioner Frank Ivancie said the confrontation was "unpleasant."

Giving the police version of the shooting, Capt. William Taylor, North Precinct commander, who like Ford, was not present, said Williams had the .303 Enfield rifle in his hands when Harmon shot him.

Taylor said Harmon and Larsen were southbound in Harmon, "I'm going to kill you, Harmon," and fired a shot. The bullet hit the center of the ceiling.

Taylor said Harmon drew his pistol and fired once. Williams fell. No other shots were fired, according to Taylor.

Ford said he was not in the office during the incident. He said witnesses told him Williams was unarmed and had raised his hands to surrender "when Harmon jumped up on a desk and put two shots in him at point-blank range."

Ford said Williams "had a right to defend himself."

He said police had "beefed up patrols" in the neighborhood since Ford was acquitted last week of riot charges stemming from disturbances in Albina last June.

Ford said the Panthers had been "tipped off" that police planned to raid the party headquarters. Taylor termed the charge "a bunch of B.S."

"We don't make a 'raid' with a two-man patrol car with a 10-year-old child in the car," Taylor said.

Taylor said the child made a statement to the district attorney Wednesday night which substantiated the officers' account of the incident.

Ford said the shooting was "a pattern of pig harassment to keep the Black Panthers from serving the community.

"This means no one in the black community is safe from the fascist, racist pigs," Ford said.

FREE ALBERT WILLIAMS

LAST FEBRUARY, SGT. STANLEY HARMON SHOT AND SERIOUSLY WOUNDED ALBERT
WILLIAMS, 19 YEARS OLD, at BLACK PANTHER HEADQUARTERS, 3619 N.E. UNION.
HARMON WAS SEEKING WILLIAMS ON A TWO-MONTH OLD WARRANT FOR PETTY LARCENY.

THESE ARE THE DETAILS:

WHEN WILLIAMS ENTERED BLACK PANTHER HEADQUARTERS, POLICE REINFORCEMENTS
WERE CALLED TO SURROUND THE BUILDING. WILLIAMS WAS INSIDE ON A BALCONY
WITH A RIFLE. HE WAS PERSUADED BY FRIENDS TO PUT IT DOWN. AFTER THAT,
EYEWITNESSES HAVE TESTIFIED THAT SGT. HARMON JUMPED UP ON A DESK AND SHOT
WILLIAMS AS HE WAS PUTTING THE RIFLE DOWN.

WILLIAMS WAS SHOT THROUGH THE ARM AND LIVER. WHEN HE WAS HIT, THE RIFLE
FIRED, AND THE BULLET RICOCHETED OFF THE CEILING. WITNESSES HEARD HARMON
SHOUT, "I GOT HIM! I FINALLY GOT HIM!"

INSTEAD OF BEING TAKEN TO EMANUEL HOSPITAL, A FEW BLOCKS AWAY, WILLIAMS
WAS DRIVEN IN THE BACK SEAT OF THE SQUAD CAR TO PORTLAND ADVENTIST HOSPITAL
ON 60th AND BELMONT, ~~WHERE HE WAS REFUSED~~. HE WAS FINALLY TAKEN TO MULT-
NOMAH COUNTY HOSPITAL. WILLIAMS WAS ON THE CRITICAL LIST FOR FOUR DAYS,
AFTER WHICH HE WAS CHARGED WITH ASSAULT WITH INTENT TO KILL HARMON!

FOR YEARS, THE BLACK COMMUNITY HAS SOUGHT TO HAVE HARMON TRANSFERRED TO
ANOTHER PRECINCT, BECAUSE OF HIS PERSISTENT BRUTALITY TOWARD BLACK PEOPLE.
INSTEAD, HE HAS BEEN PROMOTED TO DETECTIVE DUTY IN THE BLACK COMMUNITY.

THE EVIDENCE INDICATES THAT ALBERT WILLIAMS IS INNOCENT OF THE CHARGE
AGAINST HIM. THIS CHARGE SHOULD BE DROPPED AND PUNITIVE ACTION SHOULD
BE TAKEN AGAINST HARMON.

CONCERNED CITIZENS CAN PROTEST TO CITY, COUNTY AND STATE OFFICIALS ABOUT
THIS INJUSTICE. TELL THEM TO DROP THE CHARGES AGAINST WILLIAMS, WHO IS
GOING ON TRIAL NEXT MONDAY, OCT. 12th, 9:30 AM, MULTNOMAH COUNTY COURT
HOUSE.

JOIN THE PROTEST

ISSUED BY NORTHWEST FEDERATION FOR SOCIAL ACTION

BOX 327, GRESHAM, OREGON   97030

PLEASE SENT FUNDS TO AID IN THIS CASE TO THE ABOVE ADDRESS

LABOR DONATED

COME SEE ABOUT

Multnomah Courthouse

SW 4th & Main

Monday, October 12th

8:30 am

Why did it take 2 hours to get Albert to the hospital?

Why wasn't the 2 month old misdemenor warrant served at

Albert's house?

Why is Harmon still in our community?

Why has Harmon been given a promotion?

Why is Adolf Van Hoomisen trying to make an example of Albert?

FREE ALBERT WILLIAMS!

DEMONSTRATE!

THURSDAY AND FRIDAY, October 8 & 9   11:30 - 1:30

OCTOBER 12 thru 17   from 9 til 5
attend the trial - special civics lesson!

Courthouse · 4th & Main (DOWN TOWN)

Come See About Albert

Albert Williams is Black - a 19 year old man charged with "Assault with Intent to Kill". His trial starts Tuesday, June 30, 1970 at 9:30 a.m. in the Multnomah County Courthouse. Albert Williams' plight and the events leading up to it, are the most recent in the on-going, ever escalating crisis between the Black community and the police force of Portland.

Last Feb. 18, Mr. Williams was standing outside the Black Panther Party headquarters in Albina when a police cruiser pulled up. The police, Stan Harmon and another officer, claim they recognized Mr. Williams and knew that a warrant was out for his arrest on a charge of "petty larceny" (the only warrant ever produced by the police was dated after Feb. 18th.) Mr. Williams went into the office and the police followed. What then happened is unclear. The police claim Mr. Williams fired at them with a rifle. Other witnesses claim his hands were in the air (in a sign of surrender) and he had no weapon when Officer Harmon shot him twice.

Why did this happen? Why does the Black Panther Party exist? Why is there greater and greater hostility between every police force and every Black community in this nation?

In the City of Portland, 5% of the population is Black, while only .8% (6 out of more than 700) of the police are Black. There are even fewer people of other racial origins. Who says racism isn't a problem in Portland?

Flyers and pamphlets such as these, produced and distributed throughout the summer and fall of 1970, illustrate the variety of rhetoric and imagery that the Portland Panthers used in their attempts to combat the local media's framing of the Albert Williams shooting. Courtesy of City of Portland Archives, A2004-005.

As part of their surveillance efforts, undercover police officers covertly took these pictures of Patty (top) and Percy (bottom) Hampton as they and other Panthers conducted informational picketing by carrying signs and distributing literature in front of the McDonald's on August 11, 1970. Courtesy of City of Portland Archives, A2004-005.1810 and A2004-005.1808.

Cheryl James's high school picture was widely distributed throughout her lengthy and protracted defense. Cheryl James, 1972, Cheryl D. James Defense Committee, A307, box 1, folder 1, Special Collections and University Archives, University of Oregon Libraries, Eugene.

In addition to using Cheryl's school picture (which sits atop the bookshelf in this photo), photos such as this one, which emphasized how close-knit the James family was, were distributed as part of the defense committee's efforts. Cheryl's mother (Mary Lee) and father (Charles Sr.) sit with their youngest children on their laps while several of Cheryl's brothers and sisters gather around them. James Family, 1972, Cheryl D. James Defense Committee, A307, box 1, folder 1, Special Collections and University Archives, University of Oregon Libraries, Eugene.

Residents of Albina picketing along the sidewalks in front of Emanuel Hospital. © 1973 *Oregon Journal*. Courtesy of the Oregon Historical Society, digital no. bb002209.

The Portland Panthers' Fred Hampton People's Free Medical Clinic on Russell Street as it appeared in 1972, roughly one year prior to the eviction and removal. Courtesy of City of Portland Archives, A2003-005, 1972.

FRED HAMPTON MEDICAL HEALTH CLINIC

The Peoples' Free Health Clinic has been functioning since 1969 as a community health service center. The service is free and available to anyone.

Since 1971, the Clinic has been told periodically by Emanuel Hospital, that it would have to move from its location at 109 N. Russell St.

We responded by saying that we were agreeable to the move, provided we were given adequate relocation.

After much negotiation, a lease was signed: 5 years rent free, for a building at Williams and Stanton.

It is just a shell, four walls and a roof that leaks. The only thing inside is a wall down the middle.

We were given the impression that because Emanuel had given us the building, the Portland Development Commission would give us the money for renovation. NOT TRUE!! We had been fooled again.

Now, After being served with a notice for immediate eviction, we are told by the president of Emanuel, that Emanuel has no money to complete the expansion project.

So why the rush to remove a clinic that is trying to provide a needed service to the community?

We are aking for adequate money to renovate our "new" building, and a promise that our present building will not be demolished until we can move into the new one.

We want Emanuel to live up to its responsibilities in this community. After all, we do aid Emanuel in treating people who are unable to pay for medical attention.

For more information and how you can help call: 288-7279.

This somewhat unassuming notice,
written by the Portland Panthers and
posted at their clinic, details the relocation

A photographer for the *Oregon Journal*
snapped this photo of Kent Ford
confronting the PDC relocation chief,
Benjamin Webb, as the Portland Panthers
were being forcibly evicted from the Fred
Hampton Health Clinic on the morning
of May 1, 1973. © 1973 *Oregon Journal*.
Courtesy of the Oregon Historical Society,
digital no. bb007179.

CHAPTER 5

Winning the War?

Regime Change, the Triumph of Community Politics,
and the Emergence of Black Leadership in Portland

Nineteen seventy-two marked a critical point in the history of the Black Panther Party. In January, Huey P. Newton announced the BPP's involvement in a massive voter registration drive in Oakland and Berkeley. Four months later, Bobby Seale and Elaine Brown declared their intention to run for mayor and the city council, respectively. To lay the groundwork for this shift in political strategy, the Panthers held two large-scale events: a three-day Black Community Survival Conference in March, and a one-day Anti-War African Liberation Voter Registration Survival Conference in June. Both events reportedly attracted more than ten thousand people.[1] Along with musical acts and well-known speakers, the conferences provided attendees with free bags of groceries and free sickle cell anemia tests. According to some accounts of these two conferences, the Panthers registered thousands of voters, many of them new voters. Over the next sixteen months, the Panthers identified and aggressively campaigned to win several important posts—offices and positions that they believed would enable them to secure for Bay Area residents a more equitable share of the government's bounty.

As a precursor to the 1973 mayoral and city council races, in the summer of 1972 the party fielded a slate of six candidates for the Berkeley Community Development Council Board of Directors, and nine candidates for the eighteen seats on the West Oakland Planning Committee. Four Panthers were elected to the board of directors, and six Panthers were elected to the planning committee, which was responsible for providing citizen's input on how the $4.9 million Model Cities budget was to be used in providing social services and urban renewal financing in a three-square-mile area of West Oakland. With the mayoral race on the horizon, the decision had been made to shut down many of the organization's branches and chapters, and party members were ordered to relocate to Oakland in preparation for what was hoped to be a hotly contested victory in the May general election. The Panthers figured that if Warren Widener, a former US Air Force captain and Berkeley city councilman, had gotten elected as the first African American mayor of Berkeley the previous year, why couldn't the charismatic and photogenic Seale do the same in Oakland?[2]

When Seale and Brown announced their decision to run for mayor and city council in May at a huge rally in DeFremery Park, hovering in the background, figuratively speaking, was a not-so-flattering portrait of the Black Panther Party in the May issue of *Jet*. On the magazine's cover was a photo of the nattily dressed Newton seated in a high-back leather chair. In the piece Newton was referred to as the "Supreme Servant of the People," a title chosen by the party's central committee but one that may have come across as a bit pretentious. Some outsiders viewed the Panthers' move toward electoral politics as a retreat of sorts. Others thought it reformist, failing to understand, as famed Chicago community organizer Saul Alinsky has argued, that revolution cannot be achieved unless it is preceded by reformation. People do not like to step suddenly out of the safe confines of familiar experience. They need a bridge to cross from their own experience into new and foreign territory. A revolutionary must, in short, foment a climate for change. "The American Revolution," John Adams wrote, "was effected before the war commenced. . . . The Revolution was in the hearts and minds of the people. . . . This radical change in the principles, opinions, sentiments and affections of the people was the real American Revolution." Reformation means that the masses have become disenchanted with the status quo. They may not know precisely what action to take, but they know that the system is not working in their best interests, and while they may not act for change, they will not strongly oppose those who do. Then the time is ripe for revolution.[3]

In a speech in November 1972, Elaine Brown explained that her campaign for the sixth district city council seat was "part of a revolutionary process—to build a base of operation in Oakland, New York, Texas, and

Oklahoma, and on through the Midwest and through the East Coast, in fact, throughout the United States." Despite their critics, the party's decision to run Seale for mayor and Brown for city council was, in Newton's mind, a broadening of the revolutionary struggle. Newton saw it as an additional tactic to build the power of the people in Oakland's black communities and elsewhere.[4] Participating in electoral politics, therefore, was a means of bringing the will of the people to bear on the quality of governance to which they were subjected. Newton seemingly came to understand that struggle is of a long-range nature and must pass through different phases and forms before it culminates in the liberation of a people.[5]

Newton's turnabout on the issue of electoral politics seemed abrupt. The previous year, in April 1971, Newton seemed resolute in his opposition to running candidates for office. He wrote, "We will never run for political office, but we will endorse and support those candidates who are acting in the true interest of the people." Newton's public stance on electoral politics was apparently not shared by Panthers in other parts of the country. For example, in the late 1960s, two Philadelphia Panthers, Milton McGriff and Craig Williams, ran for city council seats that had become vacant due to the untimely deaths of the incumbents. On election day, both McGriff and Williams lost by huge margins, but the message was clear that the black community would no longer stand by and allow whites to do all of the political wrangling. Win or lose, the progressive black voice would be heard. Moreover, the Panthers' actions demonstrated to African Americans that there was more to party politics than just Democrats and Republicans. On the other side of the country, Panthers in Seattle also ran for elected office, failing miserably at the ballot box each time.[6]

While there is no direct evidence suggesting that Newton was influenced by the National Black Political Convention (NBPC) that attracted close to ten thousand attendees to Gary, Indiana's Westside High School on March 10–12 in 1972, it is possible that he was. The convention could not have come at a better time. A new movement that critics derisively called the "neoconservative movement" was emerging and had the unintended consequence of moving the country farther to the right. Many white Americans were still oblivious or unsympathetic to the conditions under which many blacks lived. For example, in December 1972, a Harris Poll found that only 25 percent of whites believed that blacks were discriminated against in their interactions with the police, just 29 percent believed that discrimination prevented blacks from quality educations in public schools, and a mere 20 percent believed that discrimination prevented blacks from getting manual labor jobs, while 38 percent believed that discrimination played a role in the way blacks were treated in general. Moreover, there was a sense among some whites that America had done enough for blacks and that it was time to return to the old "morality" and the old verities of free enterprise and rugged individualism. Nearly twenty years after the landmark *Brown v. Board of Education* case, the racial enlightenment that many blacks had hoped whites would experience had seemingly yet to take hold. In this climate, a National Black Political Convention seemed like a good idea. The convention's goal was to adopt a national black political agenda that reflected the interests of African Americans to be used as a tool to run and endorse candidates for elected office. Blacks were encouraged to view themselves as an independent, progressive force for change. The resounding reelection of Nixon over Senator George McGovern would stand in the way of that effort, as the Nixon doctrine sought to repeal those gains made by minorities and women during the revolutionary 1960s.[7]

Seale's run for mayor was emblematic of the NBPC's mission and a recognition of Nixon's goal to turn back the clock. Like Richard Hatcher (of Gary, Indiana) and Carl Stokes (of Cleveland, Ohio), the first two blacks to be elected mayor of major cities several years earlier, Seale could expect little to no assistance in the way of campaign funds from the Democratic Party—or from any other established party, for that matter. The Seale campaign was on its own. Seale's campaign came three years after the historic mayoral victories of Kenneth Gibson in Newark, New Jersey, and James McGee of Dayton, Ohio, and one year after Ted Berry was elected the first black mayor of Cincinnati. These national developments, combined with the election of a black mayor in Berkeley, may very well have prompted Newton to reconsider his seemingly staunch position on running candidates for office.

On the campaign trail, Seale and Brown looked the part of seasoned candidates despite the fact that both were novices at electoral politics. The gregarious Seale shed his Panther garb in favor of a jacket and tie. On any given day, Oakland residents might see Seale and Brown climb aboard a city bus and hold court to the delight and surprise of the passengers. Although a political newcomer, Seale's transition from chairing the Black Panther Party to stumping on the campaign trail was seamless. His folksy ways resonated with Oakland voters. The effervescent and articulate Brown was every bit Seale's equal on the campaign trail, glad-handing potential voters and making public appearances throughout the city. Her personality shone through.

Brown and Seale made a great team, but both ultimately lost their elections. That same year, residents in Los Angeles, Detroit, and Atlanta elected black mayors for the first time in their cities' histories, raising the total number of black mayors in the United States to 153. Included in that number was the first cohort of black women mayors: Ellen Walker Craig-Jones of Urbancrest, Ohio (1972); Doris Davis of Compton, California (1973); and Lelia Smith Foley of Taft, Oklahoma (1973).[8]

Elaine Brown garnered less than a third of the total vote, but Seale mustered enough votes to force incumbent mayor John Reading into a runoff. About their campaigns, Brown later wrote, "When Bobby Seale and I launched our campaign on the streets of West Oakland I could see on our constituents' faces something I had never seen on my mother's face. I saw a resurgence of hope. Whatever the outcome of the campaign, that alone gave it worth."[9] One could argue that Brown's and Seale's campaigns, which registered thousands of new voters, laid the groundwork for Lionel Wilson's victorious mayoral campaign four years later that made him Oakland's first black elected mayor.

Portland Panther Raymond Joe remembers that transformative period. "We met and talked about whether or not to shut everything down. . . . Kent gave comrades the option to go or not to go to Oakland . . . so we all stayed." To some outside the organization, this development appeared to signal a major shift in the Panthers' direction and approach. Many Panthers to whom we have spoken over the years opposed the idea of closing their local offices, believing that doing so would leave a void in black communities throughout the country that would not or could not be readily filled by other groups. The Portland branch of the BPP, however, remained open and conducted business as usual. By this time the Portland Panthers were focusing much of their energy on maintaining the branch's three core programs—the free breakfast program and the health and dental clinics—all of which continued to flourish. Resolving to preserve the branch, Percy Hampton recalled, "None of us had any interest in moving to Oakland; we had important work to finish right here in Portland." This decision was well-founded, given the work the two clinics required. "The way I saw it," said Sandra Ford, "they were asking us to stop our work to do their work . . . we weren't interested in doing that." For the next several years and on into the next decade, the Portland Panthers functioned as they had always done.[10]

By 1972 other social, economic, and electoral developments were unfolding in Portland in particular, and in Oregon in general. Many of these developments suggested that things were changing for the better for blacks. For example, US Department of Commerce statistics indicate that the number of black-owned businesses in the state had increased from 282 in 1969 to 393 by the early 1970s, many of them in Portland. More noteworthy, however, was the election of Commissioner Neil Goldschmidt, a charming thirty-one-year-old white man with a bright, partially gap-toothed smile and a slightly balding head of light curly hair, as mayor on Tuesday, May 23, 1972. With the victory, Goldschmidt became the youngest mayor of a major American city. Said Percy Hampton, "Although we did not come out and publicly endorse Goldschmidt, we were hoping that he'd win . . . he was better than the alternative." Capturing 57 percent of the vote in a field of fifteen candidates in the primary election, Goldschmidt clinched the election, thus avoiding a head-to-head runoff in the fall. Kent Ford remembers seeing Goldschmidt one day standing at the north entrance of the Fred Meyer store on Killingsworth Street passing out campaign literature and talking to potential voters. Ford, along with Jeff Fikes, walked over to Goldschmidt and said, "Hey, let us do this for you, we know you have more pressing things to do today. . . . So Jeff and I started handing out the material . . . we stayed until every piece of literature had been placed in the hands of a potential voter." As Goldschmidt's large coalition of supporters assumed, his tenure as Portland's mayor would ultimately mark one of the most important and transformative periods in the city's history.[11]

Goldschmidt's ascendancy to the mayor's office was meteoric. Attorney Jim McCandlish of the law firm of Griffin and McCandlish characterized Goldschmidt "as a kind of boy wonder politician." After graduating from South Eugene High School in Eugene, Oregon, Goldschmidt traipsed through Europe for a year before returning to enroll at the University of Oregon, where he was elected student body president. Four years later, in 1963, he graduated with a degree in political science and went on to become an intern for Oregon senator Maurine Neuberger in Washington, DC. There, Allard Lowenstein recruited Goldschmidt to do voter registration work during the Freedom Summer campaign in Mississippi. Inspired by Lowenstein's example, Goldschmidt invited Aaron Henry, a Clarksdale pharmacist and the president of the Mississippi chapter of the NAACP, to Eugene, where the two devised a plan to recruit for Freedom Summer by reaching out to students at several neighboring colleges and universities. Not long after, Goldschmidt enrolled at the University of California Berkeley Boalt Hall School of Law, where he earned his degree in 1967. After moving to Portland later that year,

Goldschmidt went on to work as a legal aid attorney in Albina until his election to the Portland City Council at the age of twenty-eight.[12]

Less than a year into his first term on the council, Goldschmidt decided to throw his hat into the mayoral ring. A lifelong advocate of civil rights and community activism, he quickly emerged at the front of a growing generation of new, young political leadership in Portland. During his almost seven-year tenure as mayor, Goldschmidt, a former lawyer, youth program advocate, and head of the Albina Legal Aid office that specialized in employment and housing discrimination cases, restructured the city government (namely in the areas of urban planning, transportation, and policing) as he attempted to resolve the issues of neighborhood disinvestment and unrest that had emerged as a result of Portland's political leadership in the 1950s and 1960s.

Combined with the previous emergence of black community leadership during Model Cities in the late 1960s and early 1970s, Goldschmidt's emphasis on opening avenues for community control over planning and development helped the African American communities in Albina direct the future of their neighborhoods. This period also witnessed the emergence of black electoral power at the state and local level, as African Americans became state senators and city council members for the first time in Portland's history. Although political leaders and community activists in the 1970s attempted to address the same legacies of social, political, economic, and spatial discrimination that organizations such as the Black Panther Party had sought to improve, for many blacks a decade of opportunities and advancements did not easily wash away the stain of the long history of inequity and exclusion. Despite the many successes African Americans achieved under Neil Goldschmidt's tenure, the black communities in northeast Portland continued to be plagued by issues of socioeconomic inequality, education, and misguided planning projects—even those carried out under black leadership.

In the early 1970s, neighborhood activist organizations began to spring up all over Portland to challenge what historian Carl Abbott described as the Portland Development Commission's "ingrained disdain of accountability to the majority of citizens." In many ways, Goldschmidt's political success stemmed from the Model Cities activism of the late 1960s. As a result of Albina residents' success in gaining control over the direction of the Model Cities program, when the Portland Development Commission (PDC) proposed new urban renewal and freeway construction plans in 1969, neighborhood organizations in southeast and northwest Portland quickly emerged. Capitalizing on this rapidly expanding neighborhood movement, Goldschmidt, a former community organizer himself, was able to build a coalition of neighborhood activists throughout the city. As a member of the city council, Goldschmidt pushed for greater influence within Portland's urban planning power structure. Under the leadership of Goldschmidt, first as a city councilman and later as mayor, Portland entered a new era of neighborhood-led urban planning that focused on restructuring the city government's urban planning hierarchy, developing solutions to the city's growing transportation concerns, and reorganizing the city's police bureau.[13]

Goldschmidt was elected to the Portland City Council by an overwhelming majority in 1970, to a seat vacated by Mark "Buck" Grayson. The 1970 city council primary, which had consisted of fourteen candidates, had proved more competitive than the general election. Goldschmidt emerged from the primary having garnered 35,551 votes to Republican Shirley A. Field's 21,437 votes. The general election, however, was a different story: Goldschmidt easily outpaced Field 80,310 votes to 53,615.[14]

Upon joining the council on January 1, 1971, Goldschmidt became the youngest person to serve as a city commissioner, and he boldly told members of the media, "I'm not cut from the same mold as some members of the council 10 years ago." During his short tenure on the council, Goldschmidt became a champion of neighborhood activists and an opponent of the PDC's negligent policies. Between 1971 and 1972, Goldschmidt was the only council member to vote against large community-opposed urban renewal projects south of downtown, in southeast Portland along the Willamette River, and in the Buckman and Lair Hill neighborhoods. With his reputation as the voice of community organizing, Goldschmidt pushed for greater influence within Portland's urban planning power structure. In February 1972, after careful lobbying, he successfully convinced Mayor Terry Schrunk to place the Model Cities program under his jurisdiction of human resources and antipoverty programs to improve coordination, program management, and use of funds.[15]

On March 5, two weeks after gaining control over Model Cities, Goldschmidt announced his candidacy for mayor of Portland in front of a crowd of more than eight hundred supporters at the Westminster Presbyterian Church. Declaring that he was willing to "speak out, to treat no community problem as too small or insignificant to dignify a personal response, to help citizens to help me do the job they want done," Goldschmidt immediately struck a chord with neighborhood activists who had become increasingly disillusioned with city politics and the PDC's urban planning. Shortly thereafter, Mayor Schrunk, perhaps seeing the writing on the wall, announced that, due to declining health, he would retire at the end of the year rather than seek an unprecedented fifth term as Portland's mayor. Portlanders would elect their first new mayor since 1956. Few blacks lamented the loss of Schrunk, who was considered an old-line politician who believed that blacks should stay in their place. Said Kent Ford, "Schrunk didn't know anything about black folk... the only blacks Schrunk came in contact with were probably those who either worked at the Waverly Country Club or the few who were members of the club." Schrunk's reported old-school sentiments about blacks may have trickled down to members of the police bureau, some of whom were not entirely comfortable with the pace at which the Civil Rights Movement was moving. In a survey of Portland police officers in 1966, 86 percent believed that the Civil Rights Movement was "moving too fast," and more than half believed that racial equality was happening "much too fast." Undoubtedly, some police officers across the country felt similarly at that time, but the resistance shown by members of the Portland Police Bureau in the survey is striking.[16]

To many, the election of a new mayor meant the possibility of a new vision for Portland, especially in the area of urban planning. The following month, after fifteen other Portlanders had declared their candidacy, Schrunk endorsed sixty-one-year-old retired industrialist and favorite of Portland's business community R. W. DeWeese to be his successor. DeWeese boasted impressive credentials. He had been the chief fundraiser in Bob Packwood's winning Senate campaign, past president of the Chamber of Commerce, chairman of President Nixon's Committee on State and Local Government Cooperation, and vice president of ESCO Corporation. He was also known for having helped launched Portland Community College in 1961 as a member of the Portland School Board, where he served three terms. Goldschmidt, however, appealed to a rapidly emerging electorate of civic activists. "Aggressive advocates of neighborhood needs must have a stronger voice in central planning, which just isn't responsive to them now," Goldschmidt said. On Sunday, May 7, the *Oregonian*, Portland's foremost news daily, endorsed Goldschmidt for mayor, stating that he was "understanding and empathetic with the problems of youth, the poor, [and] the minorities, among whom he worked for several years." Moreover, the newspapers' editors, joining the growing chorus of civic activists throughout Portland, particularly in Albina, noted Goldschmidt's support among local inner-city communities, stating, "Upgrading the neighborhoods and removal of the barriers between people and their governments have priority in Goldschmidt's plans—and he is a planner, both for his city and his future."[17]

Reporter Howard Waskow of the *Scribe* described the contest between Goldschmidt and DeWeese as "Activist Liberalism against Establishment Conservatism in a tough and well-financed campaign." Despite spending more money than any other candidate, having the support of Portland's business community, and being endorsed by Mayor Schrunk, the right-wing Republican, managed to garner only one-third of the total votes. In contrast, Goldschmidt, who had spent only $219,597 and had campaigned door-to-door throughout the city, carried his community activist coalition to a comfortable electoral victory and the highest political post in the city. With this win, Goldschmidt, like his colleague Wes Ulman, in Seattle, Washington, became part of a new generation of politicians that was capturing mayoral offices around the country at an age when most political aspirants were busy learning the lay of the land and ingratiating themselves with the city fathers in hopes that their opportunity might one day come.[18]

Throughout the mayoral campaign, which lasted nearly a year and a half, Goldschmidt hosted two hundred neighborhood coffees. Portlander Ron Buel notes, "Goldschmidt could do three coffees a night, and his rap changed for everyone. He couldn't say the same thing twice. He talked to ladies in curlers in north Portland . . . he would listen and absorb, learning about the city, its neighborhoods, its government and its problems." In addition to winning 460 of the city's 500 precincts, Goldschmidt won a surprisingly near-unanimous victory in downtown and all of the surrounding neighborhoods, including Albina and greater north and northeast Portland. With this strong mandate from residents, Goldschmidt embarked on an almost decade-long process of revolutionizing Portland's urban planning power structure and city governance.[19]

During his first term as mayor, Goldschmidt focused his attention on a number of issues confronting the city's future, and on three areas in particular. First, and most important, Goldschmidt set about reforming the city's high-minded, though often misguided, urban planning apparatus, which had almost entirely excluded the voices of Portland's residents. In particular, he sought a new urban planning hierarchy that would focus on downtown revitalization and start at the grassroots with neighborhood organizations.

Second, he addressed Portland's infrastructure and transportation needs in an effort to create a city that was centered less on automobiles and suburbs and more on public transportation and its core. These first two goals helped initiate several of the most successful community revolts against proposed freeway construction anywhere in the country. Third, addressing a specific concern among many neighborhoods like Albina, Goldschmidt reformed the Portland Police Bureau to make the organization more accountable to the public and to get it to work more closely with local communities.

A fair amount of Goldschmidt's time during his first term was spent re-configuring the city government's urban planning structure. After Mayor Schrunk's assumption of power in the mid-1950s, the PDC had eclipsed other disparate agencies such as the Housing Authority of Portland (HAP), the planning commission, and the planning bureau. The PDC had dominated the direction and focus of all urban planning in Portland for nearly a decade and a half. Immediately after becoming mayor, however, Gold-schmidt reorganized the council's control over planning bureaus and requested the resignation of the leadership of the PDC, the HAP, and the planning commission. Then, in April 1973, Goldschmidt laid out a working proposal for a new Office of Planning and Development (OPD) to oversee all other branches of urban planning. The OPD consolidated and reapportioned power among all of the city's existing planning and development branches and lessened the PDC's previously unchecked power. All of these agencies had to have their planning and development plans reviewed and approved by the OPD, which was given the task of making sure plans were compatible with local neighborhood organizations and with general city-wide plans. Furthermore, Goldschmidt reorganized the planning commission into a bureau of planning that had the task of creating urban development plans that the PDC would then carry out. He also carefully stacked both the OPD and the planning bureau's leadership with political allies and neighborhood activists that had propelled him into office, thereby effectively limiting the PDC's power from above and from below.[20]

Meanwhile, drawing on concerns over increased traffic, air pollution, suburban sprawl, and neighborhood destruction during freeway construction, Goldschmidt proposed improving and expanding public transportation to preserve neighborhoods while also attracting commerce downtown. In theory, he believed that preventing the expansion of freeways would slow the development of Portland suburbs by inflating housing prices and increasing the necessity of making the city's core more livable. In a June

1973 interview on NBC's *Meet the Press* with mayors attending the United States Conference of Mayors and panelists from national newspapers, Goldschmidt explained his efforts to revive inner-city housing, businesses, and public transportation, and his unwillingness to expand freeways and suburbs. Attacking Goldschmidt's vision for a less automobile-centered future for Portland, conservative columnist Robert Novak of the *Chicago Sun-Times* inquired, "Has there been the experience that if you don't build new freeways, the old freeways just get more and more crowded and you can't force the people off the freeways by not building them?" "Yes," Goldschmidt responded, "they will get crowded, our current freeway system, if we don't build new ones, unless we develop an incentive for people to be on another system and to make it convenient to do so." As incentives, Goldschmidt proposed more affordable public transportation, including a downtown fare-free zone for Portland's Tri-Met bus system and an expansion of service routes. Moreover, he proposed a gas tax as a source of state revenue and as a disincentive for using automobiles.[21]

Though Goldschmidt was frequently challenged by his conservative rivals on the city council, particularly Commissioner Francis Ivancie, his restructuring of the city's urban planning apparatus to include community input and his efforts to take infrastructure and transportation in a radically new direction led to three of the most significant and successful citizen movements in the United States at the time. First, in 1968, Portland created the Southeast Uplift program, which had initially been proposed by local community members of southeastern neighborhoods based on some of the perceived early citizen-led success of the Model Cities program in Albina. After gaining approval from the city council, however, the PDC once again became the lead planning and policy development branch of the program. Following the lead of African American residents in northeast Portland, the predominately white population in the southeast portion of the city quickly organized and applied pressure on the city government and the PDC during the early months of the program to help direct future projects. In particular, in the early 1970s, the planned construction of the Mount Hood Freeway through southeast Portland over the objections of local residents triggered an angry backlash. The proposed five-mile route, for which the state and the PDC initiated plans in 1955, would have destroyed more than seventeen hundred homes and apartments in six neighborhoods. Responding to objections from the southeast neighborhoods, in 1974 Goldschmidt and the city council voted four-to-one to abandon the proposed highway. Instead, the council diverted the $500 million that had been earmarked for the project for public transportation and the installation of a mass transit light rail line, known as MAX, along the preexisting I-84 route. When asked if the Panthers viewed the creation of MAX as a good thing, Ford said, "We were a proponent of MAX ... we thought it was a good thing to connect all of the tri-county area.... Our only gripe was that black drivers did not benefit from this new development ... we thought that black bus drivers with the most seniority should be given first dibs, and that didn't happen."[22]

While citizens in southeast Portland were challenging the Mount Hood Freeway, citizens of northwest Portland were locked in a similar struggle over the construction of a new interstate route, I-505, the second of the three successful citizen movements. Local organizers in the Northwest District Association (NWDA), which was formed by the PDC in May 1969, quickly followed the lead of Model Cities and Southeast Uplift organizers and took control of the organization. They spent much of their first two years attempting to alter the proposed route along lines that best suited local neighborhoods. However, following a suspect and misleading environmental impact study by the state highway department, in 1971 the NWDA and other groups in northwest Portland sued to stop construction of the interstate route. After a drawn-out litigation process, in May 1974 the city council abandoned the proposed I-505 route, much as they had with the Mount Hood Freeway, and similarly shifted the funds toward public transportation.[23]

The third successful citizen movement, also in 1974, was the push to revitalize Portland's core and the creation of a less automobile-centric city, which culminated in the dismantling of Harbor Drive along the west side of the Willamette River near downtown to construct Tom McCall Waterfront Park. Under the leadership of Mayor Goldschmidt and Governor Tom McCall (who shared much of Goldschmidt's vision for downtown revitalization and citizen participation), the state reclaimed the land after more than a century of debate over proper access and ownership. Like the rejection of the Mount Hood Freeway and I-505, the creation of a park in place of a drive emphasized Goldschmidt's commitments to creating a livable inner city, stopping suburban sprawl, and finding new opportunities to expand public transportation. The new green space was appropriately named in honor of Governor McCall (1967–74), as he had helped usher in Oregon's most prominent protection legislation over the preceding years, including public beach ownership, bottle deposits, bicycle path construction, land conservation agencies, and urban growth boundaries.

In 1975, well before the first portion of Tom McCall Waterfront Park was finished in 1978, the Environmental Protection Agency called Portland, perhaps a bit prematurely, the "most livable" city in America. Meanwhile, unemployment in Portland was soaring: 39,000 people (7.8 percent of the population) were out of work. The US Department of Labor had put the city on a national "critical list," along with New Haven, Connecticut; Youngstown, Ohio; and Wheeling, West Virginia. Yet the "most livable" sentiment persisted, and Portland's modern reputation as a city with strong community activism, public transportation, and environmental protection grew.[24] As this reputation evolved the city cultivated an ahistorical origin myth for this new political environment—one that omitted, perhaps deliberately, its black roots.

In addition to addressing issues of urban planning, community development, and transportation, Goldschmidt focused on another significant issue that had long been important to many African Americans, especially the Portland Black Panthers: the Portland Police Bureau. Goldschmidt, recognizing the legacy of confrontation between white police officers and young African Americans in Portland and in other major US cities throughout the late 1960s, placed an emphasis on addressing social conditions in communities with higher crime rates rather than funneling more money into an inefficient centralized police system. After gaining control of Model Cities as commissioner in 1972, Goldschmidt was criticized by HUD for the ineffectiveness of the program's Police Community Relations unit. While Goldschmidt defended the overall work of the Model Cities program, he recognized the shortcomings of the program and of the Portland Police Bureau in general, and announced his intentions to make changes within the department. This was welcome news to blacks, especially members of the Portland branch of the BPP, who had long considered the police department an agent of repression rather than an agency to whom they could turn in time of need. In a letter to Goldschmidt, attorney John Toran spoke to black people's frustration with what many considered a department that comprised of too many trigger-happy gunmen: "It appears that the Police Department is now shooting at people who are interrupted in the commission of a burglary.... We should be reminded that there was a great public outcry when a Clackamas County deputy killed a young man in the course of stealing a turkey. It would be most unfortunate if the Portland Police killed a youth while in the course of stealing a portable TV set."

Days after Toran sent his letter, on June 20, a special police report titled "Informant Information" did little to assuage black people's concerns. The document revealed that the police were using an informant who considered himself a "peaceful militant" to infiltrate the Portland branch of the BPP. The informant told the police that an unnamed group had purchased several boxes of flares that they were going to use at a rally: "the purpose is to cause the public to realize that there is black descent [dissent]. This will also harass the police and fire bureaus." A short time later, in a report dated June 23, the bureau's use of an informant specifically infiltrating the BPP is cited: "The informant has indicated a desire to provide us with information concerning possible upcoming activities of the local Black Panther group headed by Kent Ford." The report further states that Ford took the informant into his house and showed him a large cache of guns. To this day, Ford maintains that no such thing ever happened. "I never did anything like that . . . if I did, I would have no trouble admitting it today."[25]

Whether or not Goldschmidt was aware of the extent to which the police harassed black residents is unknown; however, one of his more decisive moves during his first year as mayor was to request the resignation of Police Chief Donald McNamara. McNamara had been appointed in 1964 and was serving his second stint as police chief. Goldschmidt initiated a major reorganization in 1972, including dissolving the Police Community Relations unit in favor of a decentralized self-investigation system that responded to local residents, in the hope that the newly structured department would reduce crime and work closely with the neighborhoods. While these efforts did not result in the community control of the police bureau that the Panthers had long desired, they were a step in the right direction. Although this approach drew criticism from the police department, Bruce Baker, Goldschmidt's newly appointed chief of police, noted that crime progressively decreased throughout the mid-1970s. Between 1974 and 1975 alone, robbery and burglary rates dipped 4 percent, while automobile theft declined by more than 10 percent.[26]

In the same 1973 interview on NBC's *Meet the Press* in which he challenged Goldschmidt's transportation policy, columnist Robert Novak also testily commented on his stance on police. "You not only don't like freeways," Novak snidely remarked, "you don't like too many policemen either. . . . How do you account for your theory that you are going to fight crime by not adding policemen?" In response, Goldschmidt stated that his platform was not "against policemen," noted that data collected by the city showed that 60 percent of burglaries were committed by individuals under the age of eighteen, and suggested that funds spent on expanding police might be put to better use in education or delinquency prevention programs. Ignoring Goldschmidt's response, Novak bluntly responded, "Mayor Goldschmidt, you have a very, *very* small black population in Portland. Would you perhaps suggest that in cities where there are racial tensions that your ideas about the police not being all that helpful in combating crime might not be as applicable?" Goldschmidt paused momentarily. "I don't think it is a racial issue," Goldschmidt replied coolly. "I feel very strongly that the City of Portland shouldn't be in a position of following the mistakes that other communities have made. I think we can learn some lessons in other communities, and I think we can—by the work we are trying to do now—help some other communities as well." Moderator Bill Monroe, sensing that Novak was about to launch into a lengthy debate with Goldschmidt, turned the focus to another panelist, but the exchange had shown Goldschmidt's firm commitment to creating a social environment and police force that would foster a healthier relationship between city government and local communities.[27]

Years later, when Richard Walker, former chief of police for Portland, was asked about Goldschmidt's relationship with the police bureau, Walker, while not as harsh as Novak, did note,

> Goldschmidt did not trust or have a very good relationship with the bureau. For example, when he came in, he proposed a supplemental retirement system that was designed to encourage many high-ranking officers to leave.... This was Goldschmidt's way of ridding the bureau of officers who had a long history with the department. Also, when it was time to hire a police chief, he made it clear, to me, at least, that he did not want an internal candidate. He ... hired Bruce Baker, who had been the police chief of Berkeley, California. At the end of the day, the police bureau is given a mission to carry out, and you would like to think that the commissioners and the mayor would provide the bureau with the necessary resources to fulfill that mission ... that wasn't necessarily the case under Mayor Goldschmidt.

Walker's contention that Goldschmidt was not wholly supportive of the Portland Police Bureau is not one that Oscar Johnson finds convincing. When told of Walker's comments, Johnson said, "You could have fooled me ... they always seemed to be around spying on us or hovering over us for no apparent reason but to irritate us ... to let us know they were watching us." "I agree with Oscar," Ford added. "We expected to have to deal with the average police officer, but on some occasions members the police bureau's brass would show up on the scene when it involved us."[28]

Ford remembers a particular incident with a plainclothes police officer on January 18, 1974. Ford and others had arrived for a scheduled meeting with a local administrator about whom neighborhood residents had expressed serious concerns. The altercation had started when Gretchen Boynton, director of the Albina Child Development Center (ACDC, one of Portland's Head Start initiatives) had failed to show up for a scheduled meeting with the Panthers. Parents, workers, and community residents had complained about Boynton's dictatorial management style and her inability to connect with the residents of the mostly black Albina community. Other complaints included a failure to adequately fumigate one of the rooms in which lice were present and the requirement that teachers tape-record the goings-on in their classrooms. At least two hundred grievances had been filed against Boynton. One of those was a complaint by an employee, Jean De Master, who claimed that the "four key people in charge of running the ACDC were not meeting the needs of the low-income community." In November, De Master was fired, according to some, for speaking out against Boynton and others. Kent Ford tells the story:

> A lot of parents lodged complaints against this white lady who was the director of this child development center, but nothing was being done about it. Some parents came to us and asked us to look into the matter, so we scheduled an appointment with the lady. The Head Start program was located inside a church. When Sandra, Jeff, Raymond, and I arrived at the church, Vern Summers was standing out front. The door was locked, so he let us in after exchanging pleasantries. I couldn't shake the feeling that something didn't feel right. What was Vern Summers doing here, I asked myself? Anyway, once inside, I see someone I know, and he agrees to show us where the lady's office is. As we're walking down the hallway, I noticed that Raymond is not with us. . . . I learn later that he had been straggling back and wasn't able to catch the door as it was closing, so he got locked out. As we're walking down the hallway, I see Oliver O'Ferrell standing outside an office. The office turned out to be the receptionist area that led to the director's office. When we arrive at the receptionist area, the door is ajar, and, like I said, Oliver O'Ferrell is standing there. Bad blood had been boiling between Oliver and the Panthers for weeks now. I said, "Oliver what are you doing here? . . . This is between us and the director." The guy

who walked us to the office then tells us that the director is not there, and I'm thinking, why didn't you say that in the first place? Something tells me this is a setup, so I decked Oliver, and he spills backwards onto the office floor. Standing near the receptionist desk is a white man who yells out, "I'm a police officer," meanwhile, I pick Oliver up off the floor and start on him again. Again the guy yells, "I'm a police officer" but doesn't bother to produce a badge. Jeff then goes upside his head with the telephone; by that time uniform police officers arrived, including Police Chief Bruce Baker, and hauls me and Jeff down to the police station. To this day, I have never met the director of that daycare center. She never called to apologize for missing the appointment or to reschedule.

Several weeks later, in response to mounting pressure from residents, an extensive investigation was launched into the Head Start program, which ultimately resulted in Boynton's resignation. Forty years later, Ford believes the whole thing was a setup. "Why would the chief of police show up for something like that? The police chief has better things to do . . . my instincts told me it was a setup, and till this day I still believe that," he recalls. Ford's suspicions are not far-fetched given the low-level events described above; however, a police chief showing up at a crime scene where one of the victims happened to be a fellow officer is not unprecedented. If, indeed, the whole thing was a setup, Ford played right into the conspirators' hands by launching into an unprovoked attack of O'Ferrell.[29]

Walker's assertion that Goldschmidt was not a strong ally of the police may be linked to Goldschmidt's dogged efforts to root out corruption within the police force. For example, following a series of thefts by a reservist police officer, James Wesley Liming, in 1975, Goldschmidt criticized the police for lack of supervision, pushed for greater cooperation between officers, and called for less "isolation on the beat." Moreover, when the subsequent investigation revealed that a number of police officers had been receiving gifts from Liming and lying to investigators about it, Goldschmidt personally dismissed them from the police force. Retired Police Officer Donald Conner said, "Actually, Liming was stealing items from an electronics store where he worked as a security guard and selling the merchandise to other officers . . . whether or not the other officers knew that the merchandise were stolen goods I can't say, but they suffered the consequences nonetheless." Ultimately, Goldschmidt was uncompromising in his belief that an effective Portland Police Bureau was useful so far as it was trusted by and honest with the communities it sought to serve and protect.[30]

Goldschmidt's desire to rid to the police bureau of corruption was commendable, but the corruption on which he set his sights were the kind to which his predecessor had turned a blind eye for many years: gambling, prostitution, pay-offs, and other such vices; police use of extralegal force against black residents did not appear to be high on Goldschmidt's list. Said Raymond Joe, "I didn't see much of a difference between Goldschmidt's time as mayor and when Schrunk was mayor where police brutality was concerned, but, honestly, by that time I wasn't too concerned with Goldschmidt . . . we had our own problems to deal with." The problem to which Joe referred was the unwanted media attention from Huey P. Newton's criminal activities in the Bay Area. Although the Watergate scandal had commanded much of the national press's attention, Newton's sadistic exploits still managed to find their way onto the pages of many of the Bay Area's newspapers. In 1974, Newton was charged with pistol-whipping Preston Callins, a fifty-two-year-old tailor who had gone to Newton's penthouse to fit him for a suit, and with the shooting death of seventeen-year-old Kathleen Smith, a reported street-walker who had, according to witnesses, offended Newton by calling him "baby," the same offense of which the tailor was guilty. While these crimes had been committed more than six hundred miles away, the residual effects were evident in Portland. In the minds of some residents, the Portland Panthers were guilty by association. "The media coverage of these events didn't do us any favors here in Portland," said Kent Ford. When the formal charge against Newton came down on November 1, Newton, fearing jail time, jumped bail and fled to Cuba, where he remained for three years.[31]

Despite the bad press stemming from the unspeakable acts committed by Newton, as well as the senseless death of Louis "Tex" Johnson and the mysterious murder of Betty Van Patter, Elaine Brown, by then the party's new chairman, was purportedly steering the BPP toward another, more productive course of action. David Hilliard wrote, "Under Elaine's leadership, and even without the survival programs, the party has become a political power in Oakland. Taking off its berets and leather jackets and putting on three-piece suits, the party has realized Huey's vision of a 'people's political machine,' an organization that exercises influence at both local and state levels, forcing bureaucracies and institutions to address the needs of the black community, attracting accomplished intellectuals to aid in party work, and winning appointments and grants."[32]

The Panthers suffered yet another electoral defeat when Elaine Brown lost a second race for the Oakland city council, but she had a significantly better showing than two years earlier.[33] Locally, Portland residents were surprised by news in March 1975 that Terry Schrunk, whose reign as mayor had spanned four terms, had died suddenly of a heart attack, his second in four years. That same year, the Portland Police Bureau found itself, yet again, at the center of controversy—this time over the shooting death of a young black male. Seventeen-year-old Ricky Charles Johnson was shot in the back of the head by Officer Kenneth Sanford under what could only be described as bizarre circumstances. Ricky's mother was an employee at St. Vincent's hospital, and his father, in addition to working full-time at the Armour meat packing plant, also purchased and refurbished homes in and around Portland. From time to time, without his parents' consent, Ricky and his friends would use one of the dwellings as a hangout. For reasons that are difficult to comprehend, one day, after placing an order for Chinese food at the Pagoda Chinese Restaurant on 39th and Broadway, Ricky and his friends called the Radio Cab Company and gave specific instructions for the order to be picked up and delivered to the house they were using as a hangout spot. When the cab driver arrived, he was told to put the food down and leave the house. With a pistol pointed at him, the cab driver wisely did what he was told. Once the driver was in the clear, he contacted the police and recounted the story, but for reasons that are unclear, the police, perhaps believing it to be a prank, chose not to pursue the matter. Less than a week later, the boys were at it again. This time the Portland Police Bureau decided to follow up. Minutes after the boys called the Radio Cab Company, the Portland Police Bureau sprang into action. The cab driver agreed to let the officer assigned to the call go in his stead. Wearing a Radio Cab Company jacket, the officer made his way to the house. After entering the home, he was told to put the food down and leave, but the officer foiled the boys' plans, identified himself, and ordered Ricky to put down the gun. The boys then took off running in different directions. According to Officer Sanford, as Ricky was running away, he half-turned around and pointed the gun in his direction, whereupon Sanford fired at him, striking Johnson in the back of the head and killing him.

News of the shooting spread quickly. Of the three boys, only one was apprehended and subsequently arrested. Local radio personalities Danny Dark of KGAR AM 1550 and Roy Jay of KQIV FM 107 were among those outraged over the incident. Their radio stations were flooded with calls about the shooting. Concerned members of the black community organized a meeting at the Knott Street Community Center. The auditorium was packed with attendees calling for a full-scale investigation. Using the airwaves, Dark and Roy Jay, a DJ and the general manager of KQIV, helped politicize the issue and rally listeners. At the time, KQIV FM 107, which predominately featured R&B and jazz music, had a large following and was among the top two or three stations in Portland. Said Jay, "We had a journalistic responsibility at KQIV to report what was going on in the community ... if there was someone in the community selling drugs or pimping ... if a furniture store was ripping people off by selling goods at marked-up prices or at exorbitant rates, I would make them a superstar ... I would call them out on the radio ... put them right on front street ... we were the black *60 Minutes* ... we had to hold people accountable." Jay also credits Dark with raising people's consciousness. "I called him the Blue-eyed Soul Brother," said Jay.[34]

Within days of the shooting, a multiracial group of residents were protesting in front of the Portland Police Bureau central headquarters on 2nd and Oak Street. Kent Ford said, "One of the protesters, Herman Stevens, if I remember correctly, came up with the slogan 'Who's next, Chief Baker, who's next?'" For more than an hour, protesters, including several Panthers, marched and belted out this catchy slogan in unison while a small group that included Ricky's father and sister went inside to discuss the matter with the mayor and Police Chief Bruce Baker. In response to the Knott Street meeting held by community residents, police officials held a relatively small and hurried meeting of their own in the Model Cities conference room in the Walnut Park building. The gathering consisted of a few community residents sitting opposite the precinct captain and other police officials. Kent Ford, who was present at this meeting as well, said, "The whole purpose of that meeting was so that the police could tell their side of the story." While residents and police officials were meeting, Ford secured for the family of the boy who was arrested the services of attorney Nick Chaivoe. Ford also reached out to Ann Chess Campbell of the Women's International League for Peace and Freedom about putting up bail for the young man. After consulting with members of the organization, Campbell contacted Ford with the good news that the league had agreed to post bond. Then something happened that turned the tide in favor of the police officer. The trial had barely gotten under way when one day, while being driven to the courthouse, the boy inexplicably jumped out of the car and fled. Authorities later caught up with the boy at his parents' residence. His behavior raised doubt in the minds of those who wanted to believe in his innocence. At the conclusion of the inquest, the six-member jury, consisting of five whites and one black woman, voted 5 to 1 to exonerate Officer Kenneth Sanford, with the lone dissenting vote belonging to the African American juror.[35]

By 1975, Portland Panther branch membership had dwindled to less than a half dozen full-time members: the Fords, Jeff Fikes, Raymond Joe, and Joyce Radford. Percy Hampton, Tom Venters, Oscar Johnson, and Claude Hawkins remained dedicated to the party's ideals but for a variety of personal and professional reasons could no longer serve full-time. A number of things took their toll on the Portland Panthers, the least of which was spreading themselves too thin. When organizations spread themselves too thin, members' stress levels soar, morale decreases, fatigue increases, and enthusiasm wanes, culminating in burnout and attrition. But there were seemingly few high-profile issues with which the Panthers were not involved. So, despite the strain put on them, the Panthers felt that they had no choice but to get involved. "I think the old adage, 'The only thing necessary for the triumph of evil is for good men to do nothing' is appropriate here," said Kent Ford.[36]

Dwindling membership within the branch, however, did not keep the Portland Panthers from serving the people of Albina. That year, Dr. Clarence Pruitt paved the way for the Panthers to move the dental clinic into a more spacious facility at 214 N. Russell, which was grander in every conceivable way. At the time, Dr. Pruitt was a consultant at Kaiser Hospital. After the move, Pruitt encouraged Ford to give Dr. Gerry Morrell more responsibility by making him the clinic's director. Ford did, and the clinic flourished under Morrell's guidance. "We came a long way from those early days. When we first started, I remember using folding chairs, the kind one would put on their lawn or on your porch," remembers Duane Paulson. The Panthers occupied the second floor of the building, which had ten operating stations. Instead of the three-day-a-week schedule, however, the new clinic was open only on Monday and Tuesday evenings. "Even though we were open two days instead of three, we really accomplished much more in that location ... we had the newest and best equipment ... it was state of the art ... the first clinic only had one chair, if memory serves me correctly," said Morrell.[37]

In an effort to provide Albina residents with the best possible service that autumn, the Panthers approached Cleveland Gilcrease, head of the Portland Metropolitan Steering Committee (PMSC), with a written proposal to fund two receptionist positions at their new dental clinic. According to Kent Ford, Gilcrease promised the Panthers an answer within two weeks. Before two weeks had elapsed, Ford received a telephone call from Dr. Pruitt informing him that a rumor had been circulating that someone was trying to start another dental clinic. Several Panthers, including Ford and Fikes, immediately marched down to the Kaiser building and asked to see the on-site administrator. The gentleman informed Ford that another party had indeed inquired about starting a free dental clinic. When Ford asked for the person's name, the administrator pulled out the paperwork and read, "A Mr. Cleveland Gilcrease." Convinced that Albina could use another dental clinic, the administrator had agreed to allow Gilcrease and his small group to set one up in the Kaiser building for one night a week. Furious, Ford hurried over to Gilcrease's office to confront him. Unsatisfied with Gilcrease's explanation, Ford and Fikes took the matter up with other members of the branch and decided that a meeting with members of the Kaiser Hospital board was in order. The Panthers believed that the best way to gain an audience with all of the members was to attend the board's regularly scheduled meeting and ask to be put on the agenda. When it was Ford's turn to speak, he informed the board that the Panthers already had a free dental clinic and that Gilcrease was appropriating their idea to put them out of business. Ford explained that he and others had approached Gilcrease about funding two secretarial positions, something that Gilcrease had seemed opened-minded about. Rather than fund the positions, however, Gilcrease had decided to launch his own clinic. Board members listened and promised to take Ford's claims seriously.[38]

After the board meeting, the Panthers discussed how best to respond to what they believed to be a double-cross on Gilcrease's part. They decided to form a picket line in front of the PMSC building on Russell Street. "We recruited everyone we knew . . . we wanted to disrupt their day-to-day activities," said Ford. To the Panthers' surprise, PMSC employees dug in their heels and were determined not to become unglued as a result of the boisterous picketing outside. "We had a megaphone and everything . . . but they were determined not to let our activities bother them," Ford recalled. After two weeks of picketing, the Panthers raised the stakes by picketing outside of Gilcrease's home in southwest Portland. The climax occurred on Thanksgiving morning. "As we picketed in front of Gilcrease's home, his wife stepped outside and yelled to no one in particular, 'Get that trash from in front of my house!' Now, here we are serving the community in ways that few organizations are ... we're doing what's best for the residents of Albina, and this lady is calling us trash," said Ford.[39]

A few months later, the PMSC was scheduled to have its annual banquet at the Lloyd Center, with tickets going for twenty dollars. Somehow the Panthers were able to identify the business that PMSC had contracted to print the tickets. They learned then that seven hundred tickets had been printed for the event. Believing that twenty dollars per ticket was more than the average resident could afford, the Panthers came up with an idea. They purchased one ticket and took it to a printing shop across town and ordered seven hundred tickets of their own. To their delight, the copied tickets were exact replicas of the originals. The Panthers, in Robin Hood fashion, distributed all seven hundred tickets throughout southeast Portland. On the night of the affair, the organizers and the hotel staff were horrified when they were confronted with hundreds more guests than anticipated. Amused, the Panthers watched as they scrambled to find additional seating. "Staff members could barely catch a breather ... as soon as one staff person finished waiting on one person, another guest would signal for help ... folks kept them hopping ... it was a sight to see," said Ford. Approximately three weeks later, in the Portland Metropolitan Steering Committee newsletter, Gilcrease bragged that despite the unexpected turn of events, the affair had been a success. When Ford was asked if the measures taken by the Panthers in relation to the PMSC's banquet had been unethical, he was willing to offer no more than the following: "That depends on where you stand."[40]

The 1970s was indeed a mixed-bag for the Panthers. Nineteen seventy-five was particularly trying, for, as Ford noted, "By late spring, things really started to get tough, right around the fall of Saigon.... Around that time a lot of our white anti–Vietnam War supporters started falling by the wayside," said Ford. The year also proved to be a difficult one personally for members of the branch, as they lost Claude Hawkins, who was killed in a gruesome automobile accident. "I had known Claude since he was a teenager ... he was part of my crew that helped me sell candy ... he was a great help as a member of my crew because he was really good at math.... At the time of his death, Claude was still developing as a man, still coming into his own," Kent Ford remembered. Although Hawkins's Panther activities had trailed off long before his death, he was still considered a member of the Panther family. He was married to Diane Trigg (Hawkins), Sandra Ford's youngest sister. As Kent Ford fondly recalls, "Our kids loved themselves some Uncle Claude." The loss of human capital, combined with several members' need to secure full-time employment to support themselves and their families, meant that the Panthers were no longer able to maintain the free breakfast program. Moreover, other agencies, including the Portland city school system, taking their cue from the Panthers, began offering the kind of breakfast for which the Panthers were known.[41]

Dwindling manpower also forced the Panthers to discontinue one of their most promising endeavors—the busing to prison program. The program had been inspired by events at San Quentin State Prison in 1971, when George Jackson was felled by a guard's bullet, and the havoc that had erupted the following month at Attica Prison in upstate New York, where scores of inmates were slaughtered by the state police and the National Guard after a protest resulted in inmates taking guards hostage. These events prompted the Panthers, who were concerned that prisoners were living a life of isolation, to establish a prison busing program that would take residents to visit their friends and loved ones at the Oregon State Penitentiary and at the Oregon Correctional Institute for juveniles. Kent Ford said, "We called it the 'busing to prison program,' but we didn't even have a bus ... that's how scarce resources were. Instead of a bus, we had a Volkswagen van that belonged to the party and a Ford Econoline van that we borrowed from Saint Andrews Church." Every Saturday, and sometimes on Sundays, the Panthers made the hour-long trek from Portland to Salem, where the facilities were located. The program did not last very long, however, as the Panthers were stretched beyond their means. "Making the trip every week just proved too costly and too time consuming," said Ford. Unlike the national headquarters, the Portland Panthers did not have access to benefactors with deep pockets and, by all accounts, the Portland branch could not depend on the national office for manpower or financial support. According to Percy Hampton, "Raising funds was always a constant struggle for us. . . . We didn't get anything from Oakland . . . if they had just paid our light bill or phone bill, that would have helped out a lot in terms of easing our financial burden." Interestingly, the minimal assistance that the Portland branch did receive from headquarters remained constant despite compositional changes to the organization's governing body over the years, regardless of who was running the organization. Funds raised through the Oakland office were not routed to Portland, not even when members needed bail money.[42]

In late 1975, Kent Ford took a welcome break from the day-to-day struggles in the Rose City and traveled with a group to China on a three-week fellowship. "The fellowship was through the US China Friendship Association. . . . I applied because I wanted to broaden my horizons. As a member of the party, I had heard so much about China . . . I wanted to see for myself what it was like," said Ford. Ford left Portland bound for San Francisco on November 2. The group of twenty-two spent two days in a downtown hotel getting acquainted before heading off to Tokyo. From Tokyo, the group flew to Beijing. The trip was not exactly what Ford had expected. "I was thinking that the trip would aid in helping me expand my ideology, but what I saw surprised me . . . they we so far behind the US in the area of technology . . . everything was so outdated." On November 28, 1975, Ford returned to Portland refreshed and ready to resume serving the people through the party's community survival programs.[43]

Nineteen seventy-six was the country's bicentennial year; it was also the year that voters ushered Democratic former Georgia governor Jimmy Carter into the White House, making him the first president elected from the Deep South since Zachary Taylor in 1848. With public trust in government at its lowest since the advent of scientific and professional polling, the Democratic Party presented this little-known born-again evangelical Christian and former naval officer as a moral, competent, and highly religious outsider who possessed the skills needed to clean up the mess left behind by the Watergate scandal. This happened to coincide with the end of Goldschmidt's first term as mayor. Goldschmidt continued to enjoy the support of neighborhood activists, and his successful efforts to revitalize downtown housing and commerce had even won him favor among the wealthier, more conservative neighborhoods that had opposed him in 1972. As a result, when Commissioner Francis Ivancie, with the support of the police unions, some local businesses, and former allies of Terry Schrunk, challenged him for mayor in the 1976 election, Goldschmidt easily won the majority of voters in the May primary by a margin of 74,753 to 59,002, despite being outspent by Ivancie $307,742 to $265,311. Avoiding another general election runoff in November, Goldschmidt was elected to a second term with a strong public consensus. Ivancie, the former protégé of Mayor Schrunk and planning commissioner on the city council from 1967 to 1972, had come to power the old-fashioned way. After teaching at Rigler Elementary School, Mayor Schrunk had brought him on as his executive assistant, and he was later appointed to fill the vacancy left by retiring Commissioner Ormond Bean in 1966. With the help of some of Portland's deep-pocket power brokers, such as Portland Meadows owner Paul Ail and attorneys Cliff Alterman and Ray Kell, Ivancie was a fixture on the city council for fourteen years.[44]

In 1976, however, Ivancie had run a confident campaign on a platform that assumed most Portlanders were not pleased with Goldschmidt's radical restructuring of Portland politics. A key issue in the campaign had been the Mount Hood Freeway, which Ivancie had hoped to revive after casting the lone dissenting city council vote to keep the project in 1974. Billboards all over town were plastered with the clever but not so subtle proclamation, "If Ivancie were mayor, you'd be home now." His resounding defeat sent a signal to other critics that Goldschmidt's vision for the city's future had broad public support. With the backing of neighborhood organizations and a strong mandate to pursue his transformative approach to city governance, Goldschmidt continued his community-centered urban planning until his departure in 1979.

During Goldschmidt's tenure in the 1970s, African Americans in Portland made their greatest gains in the field of politics, urban planning, and community development in the twentieth century. A longtime advocate of civil rights, Mayor Goldschmidt was a vocal proponent for addressing the issues of Portland's black community. "We have serious racial problems in Portland," Goldschmidt told Early Deane of the *Oregonian*. "There are people who suffer from discrimination all the time. It's contaminating, contagious. In the city government, we must learn to be the peace-making faction."[45] As a result, Goldschmidt did more to encourage and increase the presence of African Americans in city politics and urban planning than any of Portland's mayors before or since. The ascendance of Charles Jordan, executive director of Model Cities, to the city council marked a significant turning point for black political representation. However, while blacks genuinely found a growing voice within city politics for the first time, a decade of increased representation and community involvement did not and could not erase the legacy of discrimination and spatial exclusion.

Although black leaders were widely supported by neighborhood organizations throughout Portland, including Albina, many were still initially hesitant or resistant to trust Goldschmidt and his proposed plans. Immediately after being given control of Model Cities in 1972, Commissioner Goldschmidt had proposed consolidating organizations such as the Model Cities Citizens Planning Board (CPB) and the PMSC into a single Bureau of Human Resources. Though committed to promoting antipoverty programs and a community-centered focus to urban planning, Goldschmidt had argued for a centralized, streamlined approach under a new bureau to improve efficiency. Cleveland Gilcrease viciously attacked the proposal as an

attempt to strip the PMSC of its power, emasculate the poor, and institution-
alize community action rather than allowing for the development of grassroots movements. Gilcrease said,

> I opposed the idea because I sensed that Goldschmidt had a hidden agenda.
> In exchange for my support, Goldschmidt offered to make me head of the
> Bureau of Human Services . . . but I didn't want to be head of the Bureau
> of Human Services, I wanted to continue on as executive director of the
> PMSC. . . . You see, as head of the PMSC, I answered only to my board, which
> was very supportive of me . . . , if I had accepted Goldschmidt's arrangement,
> not only would I have to answer to him . . . , he could get rid of me any time
> he saw fit. . . . Also, by agreeing to this consolidation idea, all of the twenty-
> six programs that we had would have eventually been wiped out. . . . You see,
> the Portland Metropolitan Steering Committee was making a big impact
> in the lives of Portland residents. . . . I wasn't going to let someone mess up
> what we had going.[46]

While not directly stated, Gilcrease saw Goldschmidt's offer as way of trying to co-opt him. Gilcrease's logic is hard to argue with, but it is likely that
Goldschmidt's efforts were designed to consolidate the mayor's powers in a
city where those powers were no greater than those of his colleagues on the
city council.

Although a portion of the black community in Albina agreed with Gilcrease, others were more receptive to the mayor's proposal. After some initial concerns and discussions with the mayor-elect, by late August Model
Cities director Charles Jordan and the CPB leadership had come out in support of the new bureau and the consolidation. Jordan and the CPB leaders
were still concerned with the allocation of poverty funds and the eventual
execution and leadership of the Bureau of Human Resources, but they believed that the new bureau would give them a permanent voice within the
city's power structure. Likewise, while Portland's neighborhood activists
frequently praised Goldschmidt's policies concerning the police, the black
community in Albina also expressed concerns with the new policies and a
perceived lack of action in some cases. For example, during the 1976 campaign, Goldschmidt proposed easing regulations on shotguns for the police
department, a move that drew sharp criticism both from African Americans
concerned with the long history of police brutality and from police seeking even greater firearm deregulation. Seizing an opportunity to try to steal

some of Goldschmidt's African American supporters in Albina, far-left mayoral candidate Cliff Walker, an African American himself, took advantage of the situation by accusing Goldschmidt of not investigating the deaths of five African Americans during a police altercation months earlier. "Cliff's a nice guy," said Hampton, "but he didn't have a snowball's chance in hell of getting elected . . . he just wanted to get his name on the ballot so that he could say that he ran for mayor." The majority of the black population in Albina voted overwhelmingly to reelect Goldschmidt in the 1976 primary, namely because of his commitment to giving African Americans a voice in Portland's political arena. Walker received a mere 555 votes.[47]

Despite the reservations and concerns of many African Americans, Mayor Goldschmidt took major steps to increase the presence of Portland's black community in politics. In a move that would have been the first opportunity to strengthen the political power of the Albina district, he supported revising the city charter and the makeup of the city council to be more representative of local neighborhoods. Under a plan proposed in 1973, Goldschmidt advocated restructuring the problematic charter that had existed since 1903 by merging Portland and surrounding Multnomah County. Had the consolidation charter passed, it would have significantly strengthened the mayor's power. Moreover, it would have replaced the entirely at-large election of city council members with a new eleven-member council, eight of which would have been elected by local districts, leaving only three at large. For the first time in the history of Portland, African Americans would have had a real chance of gaining a consistent voice on the city council through district elections. However, through the combined opposition of conservative commissioners Ivancie and Mildred Schwab, of businesses and the chamber of commerce, and of police and fire unions—all of whom portrayed the move as a power grab by the new mayor—the Portland–Multnomah County consolidation charter failed in the 1974 primary election by a landslide margin of 71 to 29 percent.[48]

While the defeat of the consolidation charter initially dashed the hopes of blacks in Albina, that election year still proved to be pivotal for the emergence of elected African American leadership in Portland and in Oregon. Earlier in 1974, city council member Lloyd Anderson had announced his resignation. Goldschmidt endorsed Charles Jordan to fill the vacancy. In an interview with a local reporter that April, Jordan was confident that he would retain the appointed seat in the upcoming May primary. "I think I'll be elected," he said. "There aren't enough black votes in Portland to vote me into office, therefore it's got to be an overwhelming majority of white voters to get me in, and I think that once they vote me in, this is going to say to the people of Oregon and say to the people of the world that Portland, Oregon, did it without any pressure . . . so I think that's going to put us in an ideal position to do some other great things." While Jordan's appointment to the council was historic in that it marked the first time that any African American had held that position, the importance that Jordan ascribed to his election may have been overestimated. Goldschmidt thought so well of Jordan that in late 1973, even before selecting him to serve as commissioner, Goldschmidt tapped him to head the city's new Bureau of Human Resources, a move that was widely supported among some neighborhood activists who admired Jordan's work with Model Cities. By 1974, when Goldschmidt, acting on his larger vision for community-led planning, incorporated Model Cities into the new Bureau of Human Resources, Jordan had successfully managed to make the program into a receptive and useful institution for Albina residents. Model Cities' final action plan in 1973–74 noted, "Political consciousness among . . . residents is at a higher level than ever before, as demonstrated by increased voter registration and participation in local public affairs." Moreover, the report emphasized that more than 30 percent of Albina's black population had attended or participated in Model Cities organizational meetings and working committees, or had supported the CPB over the previous years.[49]

Nevertheless, the final report also outlined concerning social and economic trends with regard to Albina's commercial potential and black employment and education. According to the report, the continued destruction and rebuilding of black business centers had left a harsh legacy of economic inequity. The population decline, insufficient purchasing power of local residents, physical decay of the region, lack of off-street parking, poor street layouts, mixed-use industrial and residential areas, and "visual clutter" in the form of trash and worn-out signs all combined, the report suggested, to limit the potential for increased commercial success within Albina neighborhoods. Likewise, the report noted a surprising decline in black education levels and the number of black teachers in public schools. Inversely, residential segregation continued to shift the demographics of local schools toward higher black populations. For example, seven out of eight elementary schools in the region had more than 50 percent black enrollment during the 1972–73 school year, compared to only five schools during the 1966–67 year. Two of those schools, Boise and Humboldt, still had roughly 90 percent black enrollment. Moreover, black teachers represented more than one-fifth of the faculty in only three of these schools, and no school's faculty was more than one-quarter black. Finally, the report noted that unemployment and poverty rates for blacks were two times higher than for whites living in the same area. As a result, it is not surprising that 45.7 percent of residents within the Model Cities boundaries felt that "their problems [were] not understood" by the city council.[50]

Despite continuing problems in education and employment, and the popular opinion that the Portland City Council still did not understand Albina's problems, Jordan remained popular among Albina's residents and other community activists, leading to his ten-year role as a city council commissioner. After receiving approval from the other commissioners early in the spring of 1974, Jordan became the first African American to serve on the city council. A few short months later, Jordan came in first place in the May primary, with 35 percent of the vote, and won the November runoff election to become the first African American ever elected to the city council by the people of Portland. In a surprising move, Goldschmidt quickly transferred two important bureaus to fall under the direction of Commissioner Jordan. First, Goldschmidt appointed Jordan to the position of police commissioner on the council, giving him authority over all of the police departments in the city. For the first time in Portland's history, an African American was in charge of the very organization that had, only a few years prior, helped instigate the Albina disorders of 1967 and 1969. Although instances of racial profiling and discrimination continued in northeast Portland under Jordan's leadership, the appointment of a black commissioner marked an important starting point for a more representative and responsive police force. Early on in Jordan's tenure as commissioner, the Portland police hired more black police officers, including Carmen Sylvester, the city's first African American woman police officer. Sylvester's hiring coincided with a nationwide effort initiated by the White House encouraging both private and public entities not only to promote women's issues but to make available to qualified women opportunities that had previously been closed to them. The founding of the Women's Programs Office by Anne Armstrong, the special assistant on women's issues to President Richard Nixon and then to Gerald Ford, created a liaison between the president and women as a special interest group, encouraged the recruitment of women for top-level government positions, and initiated and assisted in the development of programs, policies, legislation, and regulations supporting women's civil rights.[51]

In addition to his role as police commissioner, Goldschmidt also assigned Jordan to head the newly created Office of Neighborhood Associations (ONA), which opened in 1974 to provide technical support and training to new citizens groups. Within Goldschmidt's OPD-centered planning
structure, the ONA acted as an arm of the planning commission and worked
with neighborhood activists and organizations—such as the CPB in Albina,
the NWDA, and similar groups throughout Portland—to facilitate localized
planning and input. Interestingly, despite the fact that the Panthers had
been on the scene for several years and had preceded the founding of many
of the area's neighborhood associations, neither the ONA nor the planning
commission ever reached out to the Panthers. By stipulating that only new
groups were eligible for technical assistance and training, veteran groups
like the Portland Panthers were left on the outside looking in. Some within
the local branch believe that this was by design. "Why limit the groups that
could benefit from those resources to those that were newly formed, what
about groups like the Panthers who had been around for a while but could
have used some assistance? . . . I can't think of any group that was doing
more in Albina than the Panthers," said Percy Hampton.[52]

At the time of ONA's founding, the Panthers' community survival programs had dwindled down to just the health and dental clinics, which continued to experience heavy foot traffic. As early as 1971, one could hear public service announcements on 101.9 KINK FM about the clinics, and student
and other community groups held benefit dances as a way of raising money
for them. These efforts helped to make Portland residents aware of the resources available to them. According to a June 22, 1972, article in the *Oregon
Journal*, the Panthers had tested thousands of residents for sickle cell anemia. By the end of 1972, the sickle cell anemia project was the health clinic's
most popular component.[53]

Despite throwing their full weight behind the sickle cell anemia effort,
the Panthers still felt the need to assist with other community efforts, most
notably the boycott of grocery stores by the United Farm Workers (UFW)
and their supporters, who wanted to draw attention to the inhumane work
conditions and the fact that they could not get union grapes into stores such
as Safeway and Fred Meyer. Panthers Kent Ford, Jeff Fikes, and Tom Wilson,
a close ally of the Panthers, participated in picket lines in front of the Safeway on Hawthorne Boulevard in southeast Portland. Kate Morosoff, the director of the Portland boycott, said, "The boycott started when growers of
table grapes brought in scabs. . . . The UFW endeavored to boycott around

the entire country.... We would go around to different stores and persuade them not to carry table grapes.... The boycott was a political awakening for me." Don Orange, a longtime friend of Morosoff, added, "In addition to trying to convince stores not to carry table grapes, lettuce, and wine, we also fought against legislation that was designed to prevent farm workers from organizing." One of the boycotters, Elizabeth "Betty" Barton, remembered, "Even though the hub of the boycott was in the Willamette Valley, there was a lot of support from people who lived in Portland." When asked about the makeup of the picket lines, she said, "On the picket lines in which I participated, most of the demonstrators were white, but you'd see people of all ages and professions.... I remember there was at least one demonstration at Kienow's where I had my three year old daughter with me." The result of the boycott, according to Morosoff, was that the sale of table grapes dropped more in Portland than in any other city.[54]

In addition to the drop in table grape sales, Kent Ford is proud of the Panthers' involvement in the boycott of the Fred Meyer in Walnut Park. Ford readily admits that the Safeway boycott did not prove very effective. "People who were on the picket line were frustrated that the boycott wasn't getting the desired results, so I suggested that we boycott Fred Meyer.... We weren't picketing for long before we got management's attention ... next thing you know, management started sending home some of its employees." Over the next few years, he continued, "we would help the farm workers as best we could, but we could only do so much without running ourselves ragged." The boycott of head lettuce, table grapes, and Gallo wines was a long protracted struggle. For instance, in May 1974, Cesar Chavez visited Portland to rally support for the United Farm Workers around two issues: the cavalier position of the Department of Justice in letting growers use illegal immigrants from Mexico to break UFW strikes, and the attempts by the International Brotherhood of Teamsters to use strong arm tactics to break the UFW strikes against the growers. "Chavez and his followers were fighting the good fight, said Ford. "Again, we supported them, but, like I mentioned before, our resources were limited in terms of manpower, time and money."[55]

In the ensuing years, Portland residents witnessed a significant increase in the number of community groups and neighborhood organizations. Raymond Joe remembers thinking that perhaps these new groups might help lighten the Panthers' workload. Between 1974 and the end of 1979, the number of neighborhood associations skyrocketed from thirty (most of which had been formed within the previous five years), to more than sixty. Under

Jordan's guidance and oversight, the ONA worked with all of these organizations throughout the 1970s to help construct, review, and amend projects and polices developed by the planning commission. Although Jordan played an integral role in the creation of Goldschmidt's new urban planning structure and neighborhood outreach, the two did not always see eye to eye, and between 1976 and 1978, Jordan became increasingly frustrated with some of the mayor's decisions. For example, on January 12, 1978, Jordan surprised many when he publicly lambasted the mayor's appointment of Jerry Jones to the PDC's redevelopment and planning agency board. According to Jordan, for nearly three years Goldschmidt had ignored all of his proposed PDC candidates and even placed a resident of northeast Portland on the commission. "There are a lot of people being relocated from that area," Jordan contended, "and we need someone on the Portland Development Commission who is sensitive to that issue." Goldschmidt had retorted that it would have been impossible to have every neighborhood represented on the PDC.[56] Although Goldschmidt had taken steps to increase the political voice of Portland's neighborhoods, except for Jordan, the residents of Albina still lacked representation within the PDC and the higher echelons of urban planning.

Charles Jordan's service on the Portland City Council, which ended in 1984, when he left Portland to administer public parks in Austin, Texas, was not the only major step forward for increasing the black voice in city and state electoral politics. Bill and Gladys McCoy climbed into positions of state and local political leadership in a style reminiscent of the influential and politically active E. D. Cannady and Beatrice Morrow Cannady in the 1920s and 1930s. In 1968, Bill McCoy launched an unsuccessful bid for city council in Portland. That year, Goldschmidt entered the realm of Portland politics as a campaign aide to McCoy, an experience that helped build a logistical foundation and networks for his own run for city council two years later. In 1974, the same year Jordan became commissioner, McCoy became the first African American elected to the Oregon State Senate, representing the legislative seat for north and northeast Portland. McCoy pushed state ratification of the Fourteenth Amendment as his first symbolic legislative act, became a major advocate for senior citizens and individuals with disabilities, and was overwhelmingly reelected to the position for more than twenty years. When he died in 1996, he was the longest-serving member of the state senate. Gladys McCoy became equally prominent within Oregon politics. In 1970, she was elected to serve on the Portland School Board, a position that she held until 1979, when she became the first African American elected to the Multnomah County Board of Commissioners. Seven years later, in 1986, voters elected her to chair the council, where she remained until her death in 1993. Said Percy Hampton, "The one thing I can say about the McCoys that I can't say about a number of other black elected officials is that they always seemed to be genuinely interested in working on behalf of black people.... People like Charles Jordan and Dick Bogle, another city councilman . . . we saw them as tokens . . . they weren't going to rock any boats."[57]

During Goldschmidt's stint as mayor, some felt that opportunities were available like never before. In a 1976 newspaper article, Lucius Hicks, director of the Portland State University Education Center, said he was encouraged by changes that had made blacks more visible in positions of power. "We now have a black state senator, a city councilman, and city of Portland and Multnomah County affirmative action officers are all black. Five or six years ago you couldn't say that," he boasted. A small but emerging visibility in state and local politics, and a growing voice in local planning policies had both positive and negative effects on the black community in Albina. By the mid-1970s, the PDC had abandoned much of its proposed expansion of Emanuel Hospital due to the loss of federal funds, but only after the city had demolished a significant number of homes and businesses to the south and east of the hospital. Eventually, the city replaced the areas with public parks, but for many locals, the razing of the center of black businesses along Russell Street and Union Avenue marked a devastating turning point of the economic future of the African American community in the region. To improve the neighborhood and attract business, during the final year of Model Cities, local residents and the city government created and implemented the Union Avenue Redevelopment Plan. The project, however, resulted in unexpected further damages. Part of the redevelopment involved installing a landscaped meridian strip down the center of Union Avenue to decrease traffic accidents, but the strip's construction removed on-street parking and had the unintended deleterious effect of further discouraging the patronization of local businesses. As a result, even under the guidance of black community leaders, revitalization projects produced unforeseen negative results. Still, at the very least, African Americans could now at least take partial responsibility for both the failures and successes of their attempts to change their urban spaces. Ultimately, while the black freedom struggle in Portland made notable progress during the 1970s, political freedom and inclusion did not necessarily translate into immediate success. While the rise of individuals such as Charles Jordan, Bill McCoy, and Gladys McCoy marked an important turning point, their political successes were not representative of the broader black community in northeast Portland.[58]

Goldschmidt, who was both supported and distrusted by African Americans in Portland, was successful only as far as he was able to bring community movements into the mainstream of city politics. Somewhat unsurprisingly, the Portland branch of the BPP was not among the groups to whom the liberal-minded Goldschmidt extended an olive branch. In fact, even as Goldschmidt ingratiated himself with various neighborhood organizations, the city's regime was seemingly busy concocting schemes designed to undermine Panther outreach efforts. For example, in 1978, the US attorney Sidney Lezak issued a federal investigation into the alleged misuse of federal funds at the Panthers' Fred Hampton People's Free Health Clinic. In a February 27, 1978, *Oregon Journal* article, Lynn Parkinson, who represented the clinic, noted that a recent grand jury had subpoenaed Sandra Ford, the clinic's record custodian, to produce financial records and dental records for certain patients who visited the clinic between 1975 and 1977. Portland's leftist community cried foul, arguing that the investigation was yet another example of a continued pattern of harassment of the Panthers by authorities, and that the FBI was probably behind it. Bill Keller of the *Oregonian* queried Lezak about the matter, who said that he was unaware of past FBI activities against the Black Panther clinics but that the current investigation had no political motive. "As far as we are concerned, this is a straight investigation of allegations of possible misuse of funds supplied by the federal government," Lezak maintained. In a move that left some scratching their heads, Lezak's office eventually dropped the case, but only after a groundswell of support for the Panthers from various sectors of the city called his motives into question. Said Kent Ford,

> I don't know if they had any intention of following through on the case, because the same exact thing happened years earlier ... we get this subpoena informing us that we are required to furnish the medical records of our patients (which of course we could not do without the expressed written consent of our patients) and bring them to a hearing that was scheduled on such and such a date. ... We gather up the documents, then several weeks later our lawyer is contacted and told that Lezak has decided not to pursue the case. ... I guess it was just their way of messing with us, interrupting our daily routine so that we wouldn't be able to get our work done.

In many ways the administration's disposition toward the Panthers was not appreciably different under Goldschmidt than it had been under Schrunk. Goldschmidt did not resolve the legacy of discrimination and exclusion by any means, but his vision for the future of Portland politics opened a brief window for genuine progress toward racial justice.[59]

In 1979, several developments greatly affected both the city of Portland and the Portland branch of the Black Panther Party. Goldschmidt's tenure as mayor came to an end in August when he resigned to serve in President Jimmy Carter's cabinet as secretary of transportation, a position he held until Carter left office in 1981. Goldschmidt's resignation as mayor of Portland came as a surprise to some, especially those who saw the move as risky. After all, Carter's first term was coming to an end, and despite his modest achievements during the first half of his presidency,[60] his prospects of winning a second term against candidates such as Republican Ronald Reagan or fellow Democrat Ted Kennedy were tenuous. Furthermore, Carter's popularity was at a woefully low 30 percent. There were also some who were anything but surprised, as they viewed Goldschmidt as a climber and an opportunist. Kent Ford remembers Father Bert Griffin of Saint Andrews Church telling him years ago that he believed that Goldschmidt wanted to be president. Goldschmidt had publicly supported Carter's presidential bid in 1976, and Carter had certainly remembered that. Impressed by his record on mass transit and perhaps looking to reward his loyalty, Carter tabbed Goldschmidt as his transportation secretary to replace Brock Adams, whom he had fired as part of a major shake-up of his cabinet. Reagan handily defeated Carter in the 1980 election, riding a wave of voter dissatisfaction stemming from soaring inflation and spiraling interest rates that even the most astute Keynesian scholars had difficulty explaining, and compounded by the Iranian Hostage Crisis. Wayne Thompson of the *Oregonian* believed that Goldschmidt's departure was a loss for Portland. He stated, "Neil created the notion of neighborhood organizations... no mayor before him had done anything like that.... He developed urban growth, and he encouraged people to have a voice in community affairs."[61]

The late 1970s were tough years for the Black Panther Party in general, and for the Portland branch in particular. While some viewed Huey P. Newton's return to the United States from Cuba after his three-year self-imposed exile as a cause for celebration, others were justifiably not as pleased. In the summer of 1977, Newton presented himself for trial in the murder of Kathleen Smith. Nine months later, the murder charges pending against Newton received a public airing. Meanwhile, other court battles were sprouting up left and right. In May 1978, Newton went to trial where he faced charges of assault with intent to kill after a barroom fracas in Santa Cruz. Four months later, he was hauled into court on charges of firearms possession. This time Newton was convicted and sentenced to two years in prison. He was released on $50,000 bond, however, pending the outcome of his murder trial. In March 1979, the trial for the murder of Kathleen Smith commenced. After twenty-one hours of deliberation, the jury reported itself deadlocked at 10 to 2 for acquittal. Black Panther attorney Charles Garry's motion for a mistrial was granted, and the case was closed.[62]

Newton's critics (with good reason) pointed to his legal troubles as evidence of someone who was not in possession of his full faculties. In the years leading up to Newton's escape to Cuba, his behavior had become dangerously unpredictable and erratic. He became infatuated with Francis Ford Coppola's *The Godfather*, much the same way later generations were enamored of *Scarface*. Some party members remember Newton watching *The Godfather* repeatedly. At one point, Newton made the original novel by Mario Puzo required reading for members of the Buddha Samurai, a closed inner circle of tried-and-tested comrades whom he authorized to carry out a variety of tasks, some of which were highly sensitive. Newton's leadership style at that time mirrored that of a mob boss. As David Hilliard wrote in his memoir *This Side of Glory*, "Before, we've used Cuba, Algeria, and China as examples of revolutionary struggle . . . now Mario Puzo's novel provides the organizational map, a patriarchal family, divided into military and political wings." In many ways Newton had effectively become the godfather of a small but useful fundraising apparatus that resembled a moderately successful Mafia family, with its shakedowns, extortion, robberies, and protection rackets. His street antics continued to attract the attention of the media. Even before the events that led up to Newton fleeing the country in 1974, many found his behavior unsettling and counterrevolutionary. In many ways it can be directly traced to the departure of many formerly committed Panthers. As Aaron Dixon writes in his memoir *My People Are Rising*: "So many good soldiers had been expelled or run off—dedicated sisters and brothers, people who had been in the trenches from the early days into the peaceful times."[63]

Upon Newton's release from jail in the summer of 1970, his leadership style seemed to draw heavily on Niccolò Machiavelli, whose writings Newton studied closely. In *The Prince*, Machiavelli instructs leaders on how to gain and keep the upper hand; maintains that there's no such thing as justice, honor, or integrity; and proposes that morality has no place in one's dealings—except for feigning morality to gain an advantage. What Newton did not realize was that, while Machiavelli's instructions may help a person obtain power, they guarantee failure in other areas of life, leaving a person with few friends or with followers who are loyal not because they love you, respect you, or believe in your vision but because they fear retribution for disloyalty. Given Newton's regard for the People's Republic of China, it is somewhat surprising that he chose to subscribe to the teachings of Machiavelli rather than follow the path of Confucius, the ancient Chinese philosopher who prescribed wisdom, justice, and moderation, and who counseled leaders to rule not by force but by virtue. In the party's final years, Newton ruled the Black Panther Party like Stalin controlled Russia—with an iron fist. Anyone who questioned his decisions or his authority did so at considerable risk. Newton's return to the United States in 1977 was the death knell of the Black Panther Party.[64]

The Portland Panthers faced more immediate challenges. Friends of the Fords were sent to prison, leaving their only son in the care of Kent and Sandra, who already had four children of their own. This addition to the Ford household brought with it increased parental responsibilities that neither Sandra nor Kent had anticipated. A year later, the boy's mother was released from prison and reconnected with her son, but the father remained behind bars. By 1978, the Fords' marriage was under tremendous strain. Although both Kent and Sandra remained committed to the political struggle, their relationship was deteriorating. After ten years of marriage, they divorced in 1979. Keeping the branch afloat in the wake of the dissolution of the partnership between the cadre's leader and the person responsible for running the community survival programs was a tall task. That same year, tragedy struck as Jeff Fikes, a highly valued member of the party, was killed under mysterious circumstances. Fikes had been found dead behind the wheel of his wife's car not far from Jefferson High School. He had been shot in the head at point-blank range. "It was a horrible shock to us all," said Sandra Ford.[65] Fikes's murder remains unsolved, and theories abound. Kent Ford intimated that it would not surprise him if Fikes's murder was related to an incident that occurred shortly before his death. Three weeks before, police officers had walked into the health clinic and handed Ford four tickets. "I remember like it was yesterday," he said. "After they handed me the tickets, I immediately called Chaivoe, who told me to come down to his office, which

I did . . . the tickets were total bullshit." He related, "Before the case went to trial, Chaivoe assured me that we had a good judge on this one . . . sure enough, the case was dismissed." A police officer had made a number of contradictory statements, irritating the judge, who responded by throwing the case out. Amused by it all, Fikes had chided the officer for his inability to keep his story straight. "Fikes laughed heartedly at the officer as we exited the courtroom," said Kent Ford. Seemingly embarrassed, the police officer shouted out, "We're over there twenty four hours a day; sooner or later we are going to nail one of you guys!"

Fikes's death hit the party hard. It hit Kent Ford particularly hard. Ford said, "It was like a death in the family. He was only twenty-nine years old. I had known him since he was fourteen. He was a smart dude . . . someone you could always count on to do what was needed for the people." Raymond Joe had similar memories of Fikes, saying, "Jeff was a big guy, outgoing, always smiling and laughing. . . . He was really good with kids, liked to have fun, but he could get serious when he needed to . . . he was always there when you needed him. . . . The thing I remember most about him is that he had a lot of connections and he was always out there selling papers, he could sell some papers. . . . In the end, Jeff was a soldier." Like Joe, Sandra Ford recalls Fikes fondly: "He was an amazing guy, very engaging." Fikes was the kind of guy about which everyone seemed to have a kind word. He was well-liked and was considered quite the character. His effervescence apparently spilled over into many areas of his life. Kent Ford remembers Fikes writing a paper for one of his classes at Portland State University titled "Using Bob West's rules for Playing Black Jack with Food Stamps." Bob West, a maintenance worker at Portland Gas and Electric in his fifties, was one of the Panthers' staunchest community supporters. According to Kent Ford, when West and several others settled in for a game of cards one evening, one person pulled out a book of food stamps to the laughter and protestations of others. West interrupted, saying, "No, no, he can play . . . a food stamp is just as good as a greenback. . . . In Bob's mind, a food stamp held the same value as a regular dollar." West's unorthodox take had so inspired Fikes that he made it the subject of his paper. Apparently, said Sandra, "Jeff's professor was so intrigued by the paper that he called Jeff in for a meeting to discuss the paper. The professor must have liked it, because I remember Jeff telling us that he received a good grade on it."[66]

After Fikes's death, the Portland branch of the BPP closed its ranks and did not accept any new members. "Jeff was a worker bee; it would have been hard to replace him even if we wanted to," said Ford. The murder of one of their members, coupled with the branch's shrinking membership, might have hindered other branches, but the Portland Panthers soldiered on. Sandra Ford summed it up best, "Our chapter was very tight. We were friends and comrades, some of us knew one another before joining the party . . . we trusted each other, we supported each other, we were like a family." This affinity obviously served the branch well. The dwindling numbers meant that those who remained were forced to rely on one another even more. However, it was only a matter of time before battle fatigue would finally set in.[67]

Following Goldschmidt's departure from Portland, a month-long power struggle ensued among city council members to elect a new mayor. Francis Ivancie, who had aspired to the office since the departure of his mentor Terry Schrunk, had the backing of fellow conservative council member Mildred Schwab. On the other side, Connie McCready, a liberal Republican who had been a close ally of Goldschmidt's, supported Charles Jordan. Eventually, Ivancie pulled a clever maneuver and chose to resolve the situation by backing McCready, and, with the additional support of Charles Jordan, McCready became the forty-sixth mayor of Portland. Ivancie had pulled this ruse believing that the other candidates might have been more popular and difficult to defeat in 1980, so he had backed McCready so that he could eventually run against her. His scheme paid off. McCready lacked the popularity and charisma of her predecessor. As Portland's decade-long economic boom began to decline in late 1979 and early 1980, Ivancie was able to garner support from local business leaders and working-class whites to defeat McCready by more than thirteen thousand votes in the May 1980 primary.[68]

Nineteen eighty was also the final year of the publication of the *Black Panther*. No more would residents see Panthers on the street hawking the paper as they had done for a decade. Since sales from the organization's newspaper had been a constant source of revenue for the Portland cadre even before they had received an official charter from central headquarters, they would have to find other ways to support the health and dental clinics. This was no short order, given the fiscal conservatism that characterized the Reagan years.

By 1980, Portland's neighborhood movement, in which the Panthers played a large part, was coming to an end. The citywide neighborhood movement that had begun with the CPB wresting control of the Model Cities program from the PDC in the late 1960s had brought together a brief but powerful coalition of neighborhood organizations in the 1970s. During Goldschmidt's seven years as mayor, Portland's city government, urban planning and transportation structures, and police force had changed considerably. While Goldschmidt's reforms had been far from radically transformative (like the reforms the Portland Panthers had envisioned), the political revolution in Portland in the 1970s nevertheless aimed to address the concerns about neighborhood control, community uplift, poverty, discrimination, and spatial restrictions. Goldschmidt, a lifelong civil rights advocate, had been able to draw on the power of neighborhood groups to reform the city's politics and urban planning apparatus. However, while it is true that neither Goldschmidt nor the citizens of Portland created this community activist movement out of thin air, African Americans' participation in Model Cities during the mid-to-late 1960s helped trigger the growing national movement. As a result, by the close of the 1970s, Portland had done much to address the legacy of racial discrimination and of political and spatial exclusion that had plagued it throughout the twentieth century. Still, this brief moment of progress was neither permanent nor universal among Portland's black population, as the decades since the triumph of community activism and the ascendancy of Goldschmidt have continued to reveal the lasting socioeconomic legacy of discrimination and exclusion.

CONCLUSION

Legacies and Life after the Party

The lives of those who served in the Portland branch of the Black Panther Party (BPP) have taken various turns over the years. As one would expect, the transition to civilian life has proven more challenging for some than for others. Of those who held leadership positions within the Portland branch of the BPP, three are deceased. Tommy Mills, the branch's deputy minister of defense and a decorated Vietnam War veteran who for many years struggled with a drug addiction, died on November 2, 2007, at the age of sixty-five. He is buried at Willamette National Cemetery in Portland. Golden "Tom" Venters II, who served as deputy minister of education, died of cancer on January 7, 2011, at the age of seventy-three while living in California. For a number of years Venters worked as a delivery driver and, according to his son, "enjoyed a rich life of extensive travel to such places as Africa and China.... He liked live music, visual and performing arts.... He remained a steadfast human rights activist" until the very end.[1] As a Los Angeles resident, Venters spent some of his free time playing in a Brazilian marching band. He resided in picturesque Santa Monica for more than thirty years and is buried at Riverside National Cemetery. The charismatic Floyd Cruse, who went on to become a dedicated social worker and a popular mainstay on the Portland music and theater scene, passed away on March 17, 2015, at the age of seventy-three. His ashes reside at Willamette National Cemetery.

Also deceased are some of the Panthers' most prominent volunteer supporters. Clarence Pruitt, DDS, the first African American graduate of the University of Oregon Dental School (in 1954) played an integral part in helping the Panthers launch and sustain their dental clinic. After the Portland branch of the BPP closed its doors, Pruitt continued to practice and teach at Oregon Health and Science University (OHSU), where he was an associate professor of dentistry. Pruitt passed away on May 19, 2009, at the age of eighty-two, in Lake Oswego, Oregon. Attorney Nick Chaivoe, another Panther supporter and longtime partner in the Peterson, Chaivoe, and Peterson law firm, eventually left the firm, preferring to maintain his own law office. Chaivoe died in 2000 at the age of eighty-eight.

George Barton, MD, and Gerry Morrell, DDS, both of whom are now retired and in their eighties, were indispensable to the health and dental clinics. A neurologist, Barton continued practicing medicine, while Morrell's private dental practice flourished over the years. Jon Moscow, Reed College graduate and New York transplant, left Portland in the early 1970s and returned to New York City. He married in 1974 and from that union has two sons. Moscow was involved in cofounding the Parents Coalition for Education, and helped found three New York City Public Schools: the Bronx New School, the Twenty-first Century Academy for Community Leadership, and the Global Neighborhood Secondary School. He is a member of the Anti-Islamophobia Working Group of Jews for Racial and Economic Justice and currently lives in Teaneck, New Jersey.

Percy Hampton, Vernell Carter, Oscar Johnson, and Kent Ford continue to live in Portland. In 1975, Hampton joined Local 296 of the Laborers International Union of North America. In the ensuing years, he rose through the ranks, becoming its president twice.[2] He retired in 2009 after thirty-nine years of service. He married in 1984 and has children. Johnson retired from a long career at Pacific Northwest Bell. After his tenure in the party came to an end, Carter enlisted in the US military before eventually returning to Portland.

Former deputy chief of staff Raymond Joe left Portland and moved to Oakland in 1982. For more than a decade, Joe was employed as an optician with the Cole National Corporation. "Much of my time as an optician was spent in the eyewear department at Sears and Montgomery Ward department stores," said Joe. In the mid-1990s Joe joined up with his brother, who was in the real estate business. For nearly twenty-five years, Joe was part of a group that put together the *Commemorator*, a newspaper published by former members of the Black Panther Party.[3]

While Linda Thornton, Joyce Radford, and Sandra Ford never officially held leadership positions, they ran the branch's core community survival programs, which made them an integral part of the operation. After leaving the party, Thornton worked at a local bank. She currently works in the public defender's office in Portland. Joyce Radford (now Williams) attended Portland State University (PSU) after the organization shut down but eventually moved to Houston, where she earned a degree in social science from the University of Houston in 1999. Sandra Ford's post-Panther life included a stint at the University of Washington, where she completed a certificate program in 1981. Since that time, Ford has enjoyed a rather lengthy career in the health care industry and since 2005 has been employed at the Cascadia Behavioral Health Clinic Garlington Center as a physician assistant.

Over the years, Kent Ford has held a variety of jobs, including private contracting and refurbishing homes and businesses. Even after the branch closed, Ford remained politically active. Prior to his decision to work for himself, Ford struggled to make ends meet, largely because of a conscious decision not to pursue a mainstream job. Ford preferred to be his own boss, which came at a cost, as contractors can encounter significant periods of down time. Despite the challenges that Ford encountered while serving as captain of the local branch of the BPP and as a civilian, none was as life-altering as the sequence of events that unfolded in the early 2000s as the United States launched its global War on Terror.

In November 2003, the late Judge Robert E. Jones of the Federal District Court, the same judge Kent Ford had stood before in August 1970, sentenced Patrice Lumumba Ford, Kent's son, to eighteen years in a maximum-security federal prison. Lumumba, a Portland native, had been arrested on October 4, 2002, as a part of a series of raids across the United States in Detroit, Seattle, Portland, and New York, and was charged with sedition for trying unsuccessfully to travel to Afghanistan from China in October 2001, before the US invasion of the country. Following the raids and arrests, Attorney General John Ashcroft appeared before the nation on television, describing the raids as "a defining day in America's war against terrorism." Lumumba, a Muslim convert named after the famous African independence leader and first democratically elected president of the former colony of the Congo, stood accused of planning to travel to Afghanistan with six other men, who were mainly African American Muslims. The group would become known as the "Portland Seven." The attorney who prosecuted the case argued that Ford and the others were going to Afghanistan to fight alongside the Taliban in the war against the American troops. The seven men maintained that they had only intended to help with the relief effort.[4]

Patrice Lumumba Ford was, by many reports, a model citizen. As a youth, he was well-mannered and eager to learn. He attended and graduated from Harriet Tubman Middle School and later Benson High School before transferring to Lincoln High School. While in high school, he became involved in the Model United Nations. Upon graduating, he enrolled at Morehouse College. After spending one year in Atlanta, he transferred to Portland State University where he graduated with a BA in East Asian studies and languages. After PSU, he entered graduate school, earning a master's degree from the Paul H. Nitze School of Advanced International Studies operated by Johns Hopkins University in Nanjing. While in China, Lumumba met Shay, a Chinese journalist. The two wed in 2000, and a year later, in January 2001, their only child, Ibrahim, was born.

Lumumba was originally offered a five-year sentence in a plea bargain, but that offer was withdrawn, reportedly after Ashcroft intervened. Initially, an African American judge, Ancer Haggerty, had been assigned the case, but shortly thereafter, the case was unexpectedly handed off to Judge Jones, thus raising suspicion among some in Portland that certain powers-that-be may have been uncomfortable with an African American judge presiding over a case of this magnitude in which several of the defendants were also African American. The thinking here is that the African American defendants may have stood a better chance at winning an acquittal with a black judge than with a white judge, especially given the political climate at the time. Judge Haggerty made clear that he had not been pressured by Ashcroft or anyone else to relinquish the case. "Ashcroft had nothing to do with it. . . . When I realized that this case would require significantly more time than I was able to give, the case was handed to Judge Jones. . . . My docket was full . . . I simply did not have the kind of time necessary to do a thorough job with this case." The day Kent Ford was informed by his son's attorney that Judge Jones would be presiding over his son's case, he went numb. A conservative judge with a reputation for being fair, Jones had previously served as the eighty-fourth associate justice on the Oregon Supreme Court and as a member of the Oregon House of Representatives. Later, as Ford sat and listened to Judge Jones read the sentence, a myriad of thoughts swirled through his mind. "One of the things I remember thinking was this is a never-ending struggle . . . never in my wildest dreams did I imagine this."[5]

Jones's sentence was the result of an investigation prompted by the United States' rapidly expanding counterterrorism powers under the USA PATRIOT Act of 2001, which expanded both state and federal government agencies' surveillance powers to levels that undoubtedly would have made those who stalked the Panthers in the 1960s and 1970s envious. Lumumba and the six other men denied the charges of aiding enemies of the state and claimed that they had planned to travel to China and then Pakistan only to assist the refugees coming out of Afghanistan. Yet, while never publicly admitting to any wrongdoing, one by one the seven men agreed to deals that gave them prison sentences ranging from eight to eighteen years rather than go to trial and risk getting life sentences. Lumumba, the last to compromise, received the most severe punishment.[6]

Since Lumumba's sentencing, Kent Ford has committed his life to fighting for his son's release. In November 2004, Ford distributed hundreds of "Free Lumumba" leaflets at a major Eid al-Fitr festival, celebrating the end of Ramadan, at Memorial Coliseum. Although not a Muslim, Ford moved among a crowd of more than three thousand members of Portland's Islamic community and attempted to raise awareness about his son's imprisonment. "It's the only thing I know how to do," Ford told freelance reporter Martha Gies. "The struggle's the only thing I ever did know." For his actions, as an overwhelmingly sardonic punishment given that particular place's history, police served Kent Ford with a citation that banned him from the premises for ninety days.[7]

The investigation, arrest, and sentencing of Patrice Lumumba Ford reinforces the legacy of Portland's long and continued history of discrimination, political and socioeconomic inequalities, and distrust between the federal, state, and city governments and what remains of northeast Portland's black community. Since the 1980s, socioeconomic and political opportunities for the African American community in Albina have not improved as much as neighborhood organizers in the late 1960s and 1970s had hoped. In fact, the last three decades have seen a continuation of neglect and disinvestment that further have eroded the community and have left a legacy of bitterness and poverty to a segment of the city's African American community. Although the 1970s brought political advancements and increased home ownership and economic improvement for some blacks, financial disinvestment in the area under the mayoralty of Francis Ivancie brought those gains to a halt. By the 1980s, when the last remnants of the Portland Panthers' community survival programs fizzled out, economic stagnation, declining population and home prices, the introduction of crack cocaine, and gang warfare have combined to wreak havoc on the black community and the Albina district. By 1990, the black population of Albina had dropped from 49 to 38 percent. Following new city-led revitalization efforts in the early 1990s, however, the property values and demographics in Albina began to shift dramatically. Reclamation, revitalization, and gentrification increased white homeownership and led to a gradual and ongoing black exodus from Albina and even from Portland itself. In 2000, less than one-third of the city's total black population lived in Albina, and blacks now represent a smaller proportion of the city's population than whites, Latinos, or Asian Americans. Furthermore, over the past decade, for the first time since the ghettoization of Albina, none of the district's neighborhoods contains a majority of nonwhite residents, yet racially segregated schools in the area remain a major concern.[8] As a result, this modern gentrification and revitalization has come at the expense of the city's black community, much as it did in the 1950s and 1960s.

Percy Hampton, one of the early members of the Portland branch of the BPP, left the organization in the mid 1970s but, like Kent Ford, never left northeast Portland. In 2011, Hampton gave an interview to Anna Griffin of the *Oregonian* to discuss recent acts of vandalism and violence directed at the Portland police by black teenagers. Disenchanted by what he viewed as random acts of violence with no genuine or substantive program for social change, Hampton stated, "These kids ... they're just looking for an excuse to break stuff." Echoing historian Robert Self's analysis of the connection between the history of urban space and political struggles, Hampton continued, "*We* were talking about holding the government accountable for poverty, for the lack of affordable health care, for the way urban renewal was eating away at the black parts of town, and especially for the fact that the cops weren't being held accountable for violence.... We talked about *specific things* that helped people *here*."[9]

The story of the Portland branch of the Black Panther Party inextricably links the long history of black social and political struggles to the city's history of metropolitan planning in the twentieth century. The African American community in northeast Portland, systematically excluded from city politics since the early 1900s, confined to the Albina district, and forced to relocate for urban renewal projects that leveled black homes and businesses, fought back in a variety of ways in the late 1960s and early 1970s. Essentially barred from avenues of political representation and the right to determine the future of their own neighborhoods and communities, blacks in Albina developed alternative forms of protest and resistance. The new and creative sociopolitical movements that emerged in Albina by the 1960s ranged from demanding greater input and consultation with urban planners, as demonstrated by the Model Cities Community Planning Board and the Portland Metropolitan Steering Committee, to openly hostile opposition to city government and a demand for complete control over their own community, like the Black Panther Party and other Black Power groups.

Consequently, the history of the Portland branch of the Black Panther Party represented an important moment of uncertainty and historical contingency for the black freedom struggle and for the future of Portland politics and urban planning. For the residents of Albina, the Portland Panthers could not have appeared at a better time. Indeed, the Portland Panthers' rise and early successes can in part be attributed to the city's poorly managed and ill-conceived Model Cities program, which by 1969 had increasingly alienated many black Portlanders. There was a change in outlook among some black Portlanders after the Panthers arrived on the scene. Henry Stevenson, a former member of the Street Corner Singers, remembers, "Kent was a force to be reckoned with. . . . The Panthers were a lot more organized and political than some others." Dave Dawson said, "I credit Kent with so much of that . . . in terms of getting blacks to think about creating change. . . . A number of the Panthers had grown up here, but not Kent. He was from California . . . we needed that outside influence. . . . He preached that we should stand up for our rights . . . he not only preached it, but he did it." David Morris, who as a youngster ate at the Panthers' breakfast program and was attending Roosevelt High School when the Panthers came to the rescue of students who were being mistreated by their white counterparts, offered this perspective on Kent Ford: "Kent was my Martin Luther King."[10]

Attempting to carve out some control over the social and political space in Albina, the Panthers initiated several different campaigns against police brutality and destructive urban planning. Furthermore, over the next several years, they embarked on several community survival ventures, including a health and dental clinic and a free breakfast program for school children. No branch or chapter of the BPP had as comprehensive a health care apparatus as the Portland branch of the Black Panther Party. Portland had both a general health clinic and a separate dental clinic, a claim that no other branch or chapter can make. The Portland Panthers' dental clinic was one of several things that distinguished them from other Panther outposts. It should also be noted that, while there were other Panther health clinics scattered across the country, to our knowledge no clinic enjoyed the consistent volume of volunteer physicians as did the Portland clinic. Also, no other clinic operated without interruption for as many consecutive years as the Fred Hampton's Free People's Health Clinic in Portland.

As a result, even as the subversion of the local, state, and federal governments thwarted Panther efforts nationally, the Portland Panthers' struggle for neighborhood activism and social uplift emanated outward throughout the city. And although the Panthers' dream of complete community control was ultimately dashed, they played a pivotal role in pressuring the city government and the Portland Development Commission to listen to moderate voices within the African American community and, later, to other Portland neighborhoods and communities demanding urban planning reform. "Even though we didn't accomplish everything we set out to do, we never stopped trying," said Ford. "Never stopped struggling against the politicians and bureaucrats who controlled the lives of Albina residents.... Even when we knew the odds of succeeding were not in our favor and it looked like we were fighting a lost cause, we still fought on even after the party faded away."[11]

For many of the Portland Panthers, involvement with the Black Panther Party was their first political experience. Some of them joined the party with pragmatic utilitarian ideas, expecting their political activity to bring about significant observable changes in their lifetime. Others were fighting to make a better life for their children and for those who were not yet born. The odds being what they were, even if the Panthers did not prevail, the miracle is that they endured and left their important, if historically overlooked, mark on the creation of the city's supposedly new neighborhood-oriented eco-friendly urbanism.

Through this understanding of the significance of the Black Panther Party in the history of civil rights and metropolitan space, a number of historical misconceptions about Portland and about Black Power organizations become clear. This study draws three significant conclusions about the Long Civil Rights Movement in the West and in the Pacific Northwest, the complex and localized nature of the Black Panther Party in the 1960s and 1970s, and the legacy of citizen participation and urban planning in Portland. First, this study helps to paint a more complete picture of the Long Civil Rights

Movement in the United States, particularly in the urban American West, which is frequently ignored because of its relatively small black population. This detailed study of Portland contributes a missing piece to the broader chronological and geographical understanding of the black freedom struggle in the urban West. Portland's unique size, location, and demographics reveal as interesting and distinct a narrative of civil rights in the West as do studies of Los Angeles, Phoenix, San Francisco, Oakland, and Seattle. In particular, the element of consistent yet ever-changing interracial coalitions between blacks and white liberals in Portland since the early 1900s, even among the seemingly most radical Black Power organizations, makes the city's civil rights struggle an interesting and unique case study. Although whites worked with civil rights and radical organizations across America, the sustainable civil rights efforts in Portland were consistently predicated on substantive coalitions with whites.

Second, this distinctive microstudy contributes to a more detailed understanding of the localized efforts of national social and political protest movements such as the Portland branch of the Black Panther Party. Recent studies show that the organization was not as nationally monolithic or as hierarchically rigid as some scholars portrayed it. As Mumia Abu Jamal writes in his book *We Want Freedom: A Life in the Black Panther Party*, "The Black Panther Party was one party; yet it was [also] several parties . . . divided by region and culture."[12] Although the Panthers' national headquarters dictated the organization's platform and ideological basis, the leadership of the branches and chapters formed policies and launched protests responding to local issues. This was particularly true in the late 1960s, when, for a time, key national leaders were successfully neutralized by the state, and in the early to mid-1970s, when the national leadership was imploding from within. In addition to responding to specific urban planning and government policies in Albina, one unique feature of the Portland Panthers, as compared with dominant Black Power movement narratives, was Ford's and other leaders' receptiveness to soliciting and accepting the help of local whites. Again, this support for the Panthers was common nationwide but was crucial in Portland, where the black population was only a fraction of that of other major West Coast cities. For an organization like the BPP to exist and to build viable, successful social programs, the leadership had to work closely with sympathetic white allies, such as local businesses, Oregon Health and Science University doctors and dentists, volunteer medical assistants, Portland State University faculty and students, and others. Although it is possible that Portland represents an outlying or unrepresentative case study, further studies of BPP branches and chapters in cities with smaller black populations or with more racially diverse neighborhood demographics may reveal a continuum of interaction with local white liberals. Consequently, the history of the Portland BPP hints at a more complex and distinctly localized portrait of the Black Panthers nationally.

Finally, and most importantly, this study demonstrates that in recent decades historians, sociologists, political scientists, and urban planners have overly idealized and mythologized popular perceptions of Portland as a model city for urban planning and citizen participation. There is undoubtedly truth to the idea that the roots of Portland's community and neighborhood activism, inner-city and public transportation revitalization, and environmental protection developed and evolved during the conflicts of the 1960s and 1970s addressed in this work. However, professional scholars, urban planners, and Portlanders frequently romanticize the city's commitment to those ideals. The history of Portland's black community in Albina reveals a population of citizens that the city government and white citizens excluded from politics in the early twentieth century, that was confined to a conceptually spatialized ghetto after World War II, and was allowed only a minimal role in the city's political revolution during the 1970s. As a result, what remains of Portland's black community today is a group that did not receive an equal share of the benefits of successful neighborhood activism.

The legacy of political, socioeconomic, and spatialized racial discrimination in the urban West, and in the rest of the United States, remains at the core of questions surrounding problems facing community organizers and urban planners. Only one generation removed from the tumultuous years that gave birth to Portland's new urban politics, those who hold the city up as a model for urban planning and citizen participation would do well to remember its complex, deeply rooted, and destructive historical legacy of exclusion toward Albina's black citizens. While Portland's modern-day reputation is partially justifiable, it is important to see both the successes and shortcomings of our model cities in America. To acknowledge only the successes belies the still unresolved planning problems and historical struggles the city faced in the late 1960s and early 1970s that triggered the new urban politics and planning of Portland.

The belief that local communities had a better understanding of how to develop, regulate, and uplift their neighborhoods than high-minded and misguided urban planners was a crucial part of Albina's struggles in the 1960s and 1970s. More importantly, it was central to the movement that mobilized Portland's political revolution and built the foundation for a city that politicians and urban planners hold in such high regard today. Perhaps the greatest contradiction of that period is that the community that helped trigger the neighborhood activist movement still has the farthest to go to overcome the legacy of racial discrimination, political exclusion, and spatial segregation. For Kent Ford, the imprisonment of his son as an enemy of the state is a daily reminder of that tragic and paradoxical legacy.

Notes

Introduction

1   In 1967, Republican legislator Don Mulford introduced a bill making it illegal to carry a gun within incorporated areas. In response, the Panthers sent a contingent to Sacramento to "lobby" against the bill and read a statement to the media. The statement condemned the American government for its participation in the Vietnam War, and for its history of enslavement and brutality exercised against blacks, Native American peoples, and Japanese Americans. For more detail, see Huey P. Newton, *Revolutionary Suicide* (New York: Ballantine, 1973), 162–68.

2   Judson L. Jeffries, *Huey P. Newton: The Radical Theorist* (Jackson: University Press of Mississippi, 2002), xvii.

3   The terms "black" and "African American" are used interchangeably throughout.

4   See the works of Carl Abbott, notably *Portland: Planning, Politics, and Growth in a Twentieth-Century City* (Lincoln: University of Nebraska Press, 1983), and *Greater Portland: Urban Life and Landscape in the Pacific Northwest* (Philadelphia: University of Pennsylvania Press, 2001); and other scholars' works, including Connie P. Ozawa, *The Portland Edge: Challenges and Successes in Growing Communities* (Washington, DC: Island Press, 2004); Dennis L. West, "A Case Study of the Planning Process in the Portland, Oregon, Model Cities Program" (PhD diss., Portland State University, 1969); and Eliot H. Fackler, "Protesting Portland's Freeways: Highway Engineering and Citizen Activism in the Interstate Era" (master's thesis, University of Oregon, 2009).

5   Karen J. Gibson, "Bleeding Albina: A History of Community Disinvestment, 1940–2000," *Transforming Anthropology* 15, no. 1 (2007): 3–25. For other literature on the black freedom struggle in Portland, see Stuart J. McElderry, "The Problem of the Color Line: Civil Rights and Racial Ideology in Portland, Oregon, 1944–1965" (PhD diss., University of Oregon, 1998); *The History of Portland's African American Community, 1805 to the Present* (Portland, OR: Bureau of Planning, 1993); and *Cornerstones of Community: Buildings of Portland's African American History* (Portland, OR: Bosco-Milligan Foundation, 1995).

6   See Jacqueline Dowd Hall, "The Long Civil Rights Movement and the Political Uses of the Past," *Journal of American History* 91, no. 4 (March 2005): 1233–63; Glenda Elizabeth Gilmore, *Defying Dixie: The Radical Roots of Civil Rights* (New York: W. W. Norton and Co., 2008); Thomas J. Sugrue, *Sweet Land of Liberty: The Forgotten Struggle for Civil Rights in the North* (New York: Random House, 2008).

7   For critiques of the "long movement," see Sundiata Keita Cha-Jua and Clarence Lang, "The Long Movement as Vampire: Temporal and Spatial Fallacies in Recent Black Freedom Studies," *Journal of African American History* 92, no. 2 (Spring 2007): 265–88.

8   A few examples of recent urban West studies include Quintard Taylor, *The Forging of a Black Community: Seattle's Central District from 1870 through the Civil Rights Era* (Seattle: University of Washington Press, 1994), and "The Civil Rights

Movement in the American West: Black Protest in Seattle, 1960–1970," *Journal of Negro History* 80, no. 1 (Winter 1995): 1–14; Matthew C. Whitaker, *Race Work: The Rise of Civil Rights in the Urban West* (Lincoln: University of Nebraska Press, 2007); Scott Kurashige, *The Shifting Grounds of Race: Black and Japanese Americans in the Making of Multiethnic Los Angeles* (Princeton: Princeton University Press, 2008); and Robert O. Self, *American Babylon: Race and the Struggle for Postwar Oakland* (Princeton: Princeton University Press, 2003). McElderry, "Problem of the Color Line," 12–13. Finally, for a comparative example from Oregon, see Glenn Anthony May, *Sonny Montes and Mexican American Activism in Oregon* (Corvallis: Oregon State University Press, 2011).

9   J. F. Rice, *Up on Madison, Down on 75th Street: A History of the Illinois Black Panther Party*, part 1 (Evanston, IL: The Committee, 1983); Orissa Arend, *Showdown in Desire: The Black Panthers Take a Stand in New Orleans* (Fayette: University of Arkansas Press, 2009); Jakobi Williams, *From the Bullet to the Ballot: The History of the Illinois Chapter of the Black Panther Party* (Chapel Hill: University of North Carolina Press, 2013); Omari L. Dyson, *Transformative Pedagogy and the Black Panther Party* (Lexington, MA: Lexington Books, 2014); Andrew Witt, *The Black Panthers in the Midwest: The Community Programs and Services of the Black Panther Party in Milwaukee, 1966–1977* (New York: Routledge, 2007); Curtis Austin, *Up Against the Wall: Violence and the Making of the Black Panther Party* (Fayetteville: University of Arkansas Press, 2006).

The most recent example of a popular Bay Area–centric history of the national BPP is Joshua Bloom and Waldo E. Martin Jr.'s *Black against Empire: The History and Politics of the Black Panther Party* (Berkeley: University of California Press, 2013). With all respect to the authors' work, the praise heaped upon this work as being the first "comprehensive" or "definitive" history of the BPP is somewhat misguided and injurious to the party's history, as well as to interested readers. Indeed, *Black against Empire* is a welcome contribution to the ever-growing literature on the BPP, and in it there is something for both the novice and the serious student of Black Panther Party history. But it is not comprehensive. Such a history of the BPP would require several volumes. Bloom and Martin provide readers with snippets of history and information about several branches and chapters, but, with the exception of Chicago and Los Angeles, no in-depth examination of any of them. What's more, the book commits several of the same old errors of which other authors are guilty: an overemphasis on the group's well-known leaders. Even the book's dust jacket—an image of Huey P. Newton with a bandolier strapped across his chest and a shotgun in his hand—is problematic for its popular but skewed portrayal of the Panther organization. For reasons that are unclear, Bobby Seale, who cofounded the party and appears in the original photograph standing next to Newton, has been cropped out of the shot. Also disconcerting is the use a photo of an armed Black Panther that plays directly into the stereotyped image that many people have of the party as gun toting rabble-rousers eager to do battle with the forces of evil. That image is anything but representative of Black Panther Party history. While we realize that the image that appears on a book's dust jacket is sometimes the work of the publisher and not the author, the result is still the same. Therefore, while there is much to learn from *Black against Empire*, a truly comprehensive and innovative history of the Panthers has yet to be written.

10   Recent works are Omari L. Dyson, *Transformative Pedagogy and the Black Panther Party*; Jakobi Williams, *From the Bullet to the Ballot: The History of the Illinois Chapter of the Black Panther Party*; Judson L. Jeffries, ed., *Comrades: A Local History of the Black Panther Party* (Bloomington: Indiana University Press, 2007), and *On the Ground: The Black Panther Party in Communities across America* (Jackson: University Press of Mississippi, 2010); Jama Lazerow and Yohuru Williams, *In Search of the Black Panther Party: New Perspectives on a Revolutionary Movement* (Durham, NC: Duke University Press, 2006); and Robert O. Self, *American Babylon*. For discussions of Portland's Black Panthers, see Matt Nelson and Bill Nygren, *Radicals in the Rose City: Portland Revolutionaries, 1960–1975* (Tempe, AZ: Northwest History Press, 2013); Polina Olsen, *Portland in the 1960s: Stories from the Counterculture* (Portland, OR: The History Press, 2012); Jules Boykoff and Martha Gies, "We're Going to Defend Ourselves: The Portland Chapter of the Black Panther Party and the Local Media Response," *Oregon Historical Quarterly* 111, no. 3 (Fall 2010): 278–311; and Martha Gies, "Radical Treatment," *Reed Magazine* (Winter 2009), accessed June 22, 2011, http://web.reed.edu/reed_magazine/winter2009/features/radical_treatment/index.html.

11   Ronald Herndon, telephone conversation with Judson L. Jeffries (hereafter referred to as "author"), January 2014.

12   See Henri Lefebvre, *La production de l'espace* (Paris: Anthropos, 1974); Michel Foucault, *Surveiller et punir* (Paris: Gallimard, 1975); Self, *American Babylon*.

13   Bruce C. Berg, *Qualitative Research Methods for the Social Sciences* (New York: Simon and Schuster, 1995); Clarissa Pinkola Estés, *Women Who Run with the Wolves* (New York: Ballantine Books, 1992), 17.

14   *Portland City Club Bulletin*, "Law Enforcement in Portland and Multnomah County," vol. 28, February 20, 1948; *Portland City Club Bulletin*, "Law Enforcement in Portland," vol. 49, August 30, 1968.

15   Ben Jacklet, "The Secret Watchers: How the Police Bureau Spied for Decades on the People of Portland," *Portland Tribune*, September 12, 2002.

1. Making and Remaking Albina

1   *The History of Portland's African American Community, 1805 to the Present* (Portland, OR: Bureau of Planning, 1993), 124.

2   Albina had been a separate incorporated city on the east side of the Willamette River, across from downtown Portland, from the late 1880s until it was consolidated with Portland in 1891.

3   Elizabeth McLagan, *A Peculiar Paradise: A History of Blacks in Oregon, 1788–1940* (Portland, OR: Georgian Press, 1980); Konrad Hamilton, "A Decade of Triumph," unpublished paper at Portland Urban League, 1.

4   Jewel Lansing, *Portland: People, Politics, and Power, 1851–2001* (Corvallis: Oregon State University Press, 2003), 250–51.

5   Portlanders also approved numerous progressive political reforms leading up to the new charter, including more direct election of senators, a process for recalling elected officials, and the passage of women's suffrage. Ibid., 271, 289–91, 303; Carl Abbott, *Greater Portland: Urban Life and Landscape in the Pacific Northwest* (Philadelphia: University of Pennsylvania Press, 2001), 87.

6   McLagan, *Peculiar Paradise*, 172; *Cornerstones of Community: Buildings of Port-*

land's African American History (Portland, OR: Bosco-Milligan Foundation, 1995), 25–26.

7   The *Cascadia Courier* (Seattle, WA), "The Ku Klux Klan and My Grandmother's House in Veronia, September 26, 2013," accessed August 14, 2014, http://www.the-cascadiacourier.com/2013_09_01_archives.html; Kimberly Mangun, "'As Citizens of Portland We Must Protest': Beatrice Morrow Cannady and the African American Response to D. W. Griffith's 'Masterpiece,'" *Oregon Historical Quarterly* 107 (Fall 2006): 393; McLagan, *Peculiar Paradise*, 172; *Cornerstones of Community*, 29; James Loewen, *Sundown Towns* (New York: The New Press, 2005).

8   McLagan, *Peculiar Paradise*, 157.

9   William Toll, "Black Families and Migration to a Multiracial Society: Portland, Oregon, 1900–1924," *Journal of American Ethnic History* 17, no. 3 (Spring 1998): 42, 64. Population demographics in Toll's article compiled from the *Twelfth Census of the United States* (1900) and the *Fourteenth Census of the United States* (1920).

10 Ibid., 45–47.

11 Ibid., 39–47, 64–65. *History of Portland's African American Community*, 50; *Cornerstones of Community*, 32–33.

12 *History of Portland's African American Community*, 29; *Cornerstones of Community*, 47–48; Toll, "Black Families," 51–55.

13 *History of Portland's African American Community*, 34–38.

14 Ibid., 39–44.

15 McLagan, *Peculiar Paradise*, 160–72.

16 *History of Portland's African American Community*, 54–55.

17 Diane Pancoast, "Blacks in Oregon (1940–1950)," in *Blacks in Oregon: An Historical and Statistical Report*, ed. William A. Little and James E. Weiss (Portland, OR: Portland State University Black Studies Center and the Center for Population Research and Census, 1978), 37.

18 Carl Abbott, *Portland: Planning, Politics, and Growth in a Twentieth-Century City* (Lincoln: University of Nebraska Press, 1983), 125; Robert C. Donnelly, *Dark Rose: Organized Crime and Corruption in Portland* (Seattle: University of Washington Press, 2011), 49; Brian T. Meehan, "When Kaiser Launched a Thousand Ships," *Oregonian*, December 3, 1992.

19 Abbott, *Portland*, 126.

20 *History of Portland's African American Community*, 57–58; John Egerton, *Speak Now Against the Day: The Generation before the Civil Rights Movement in the South* (Chapel Hill: University of North Carolina Press, 1994), 347; Abbott, *Portland*, 126; Richard Wright, *Black Boy* (New York: Harper and Row, 1945).

21 Pancoast, "Blacks in Oregon," 40; James A. Geschwender, *Racial Stratification in America* (Dubuque, IA: Wm. C. Brown Co., 1978), 185.

22 *Cornerstones of Community*, 58; *History of Portland's African American Community*, 59; Pancoast, "Blacks in Oregon," 40.

23 Abbott, *Portland*, 121; "New Negro Migrants Worry City," *Oregonian*, September 23, 1942; *History of Portland's African American Community*, 60–63.

24 *History of Portland's African American Community*, 64; William A. Little and James E. Weiss, eds., *Blacks in Oregon: An Historical and Statistical Report* (Portland, OR: Portland State University Black Studies Center and the Center for Population Research and Census, 1978), 57–59.

25 *History of Portland's African American Community*, 69–72; *Looking Back in Or-*

der to Move Forward: An Often Untold History Affecting Oregon's Past, Present and Future, compiled by Elaine Rector as part of Coaching for Educational Equity. For a copy of this document, contact elrector@comcast.net.

26 *Cornerstones of Community*, 53–54; *History of Portland's African American Community*, 62–63; "Negro Crisis Given Airing," *Oregonian*, October 6, 1942.

27 *History of Portland's African American Community*, 74.

28 Anita Palmer, telephone conversation with author, July 3, 2014.

29 Abbott, *Greater Portland*, 70; *Cornerstones of Community*, 63; *History of Portland's African American Community*, 76–79.

30 "Portland Once Bore Reputation as 'Most Racist City' in North," *Oregon Journal*, August 8, 1979; Darrell Millner, *On the Road to Equality: The Urban League of Portland, A 50-Year Retrospective* (Portland, OR: Urban League of Portland, 1995), 12; Pancoast, "Blacks in Oregon," 48; *Cornerstones of Community*, 54–55; *History of Portland's African American Community*, 90–91.

31 Pancoast, "Blacks in Oregon," 47; *History of Portland's African American Community*, 86–87.

32 Pancoast, "Blacks in Oregon," 53–56.

33 Henry Stevenson, telephone conversation with author, November 6, 2014; Stuart J. McElderry, "The Problem of the Color Line: Civil Rights and Racial Ideology in Portland, Oregon, 1944–1965" (PhD diss., University of Oregon, 1998), 1–15.

34 *Cornerstones of Community*, 68–69; *History of Portland's African American Community*, 96–101; Scott Hugh, "Rugged Battler for New Civil Rights Law Credits Friends in Legislative Victory," *Oregonian*, April 19, 1953. For more detailed information on the passage of the Public Accommodations Bill, see chapter 4 of McElderry, "Problem of the Color Line."

35 Michael Harrington, *The Other America: Poverty in the United States* (Baltimore: Penguin Books, 1962), 137; Millner, *On the Road to Equality*, 20; *Cornerstones of Community*, 70–74; *History of Portland's African American Community*, 86–88. For more detailed information on housing and civil rights, see chapters 6 and 9 of McElderry, "Problem of the Color Line."

36 Abbott, *Greater Portland*, 139; Stan L. Burton, Jr., "The Portland Urban League, 1945–1965: Two Decades of Change in the Pacific Northwest," unpublished paper, University of Oregon. *Portland People's Observer*, July 20, 1945; Edwin Berry, "Profiles: Portland," *Journal of Educational Sociology* 19 (Nov. 1945): 164–65; "The Negro in Portland," *Portland City Club Bulletin* 26, 59–61; Ruuttila, "The FEP Law," unpublished notes on Ruuttila Collection, OHS. "Report on the Negro in Portland: A Progress Report, 1945–1957," *Portland City Club Bulletin* 37 (Apr. 1957), 357.

37 Millner, *On the Road to Equality*, 5–13; *History of Portland's African American Community*, 94–100; Sandy Polishuk, *Sticking to the Union: An Oral History of the Life and Times of Julia Ruuttila* (New York: Palgrave Macmillan, 2003), 117.

38 The period we are referring to encompasses *Brown v. Board of Education*, the murder of Emmitt Till, and the Montgomery Bus Boycott.

39 Peter M. Bergman, *The Chronological History of the Negro in America* (New York: Harper and Row, 1969), 568; William Hilliard, telephone conversation with author, August 7, 2014; Martin Luther King, *Strength to Love* (New York: Pocket Books, 1964), 114–18; McElderry, "Problem of the Color Line," 295–300.

40 Virginia C. Mitchell and William A. Little, "Black and White Students Enrollment

in Secondary Education in Oregon," in *Blacks in Oregon: An Historical and Statistical Report*, ed. William A. Little and James E. Weiss (Portland, OR: Portland State University Black Studies Center and the Center for Population Research and Census, 1978), 88; *Cornerstones of Community*, 75– 78. For more detailed information on public education and integration, see chapters 7 and 10 of McElderry, "Problem of the Color Line."

41 Abbott, *Portland*, 186–88.

42 The Minnesota Freeway is the local name for I-5, named for N. Minnesota Avenue, which was mostly removed to build the sunken freeway through North Portland. *Cornerstones of Community*, 86–87; *History of Portland's African American Community*, 104.

43 *History of Portland's African American Community*, 110; Portland Development Commission, "Central Albina Study" (Portland, OR: City of Portland, 1962).

44 *History of Portland's African American Community*, 113–15; Abbott, *Portland*, 189.

45 *Cornerstones of Community*, 91–92; *History of Portland's African American Community*, 117–20.

46 *Cornerstones of Community*, 90; *History of Portland's African American Community*, 109–11.

2. Claiming Albina in the Era of Model Cities

1 Demonstration Cities and Metropolitan Development Act of 1966, Pub. L. No. 89-754 (1966).

2 It should be noted that there were other influences on Newton and Seale, such as the Deacons for Defense and Justice, Karl Marx, and a host of other groups and figures. Drawing heavily from these events and actors (and Marx), an ideology was created that, over time, took the form of four phases: black nationalism, revolutionary socialism, internationalism, and intercommunalism. For more details, see Judson L. Jeffries, *Huey P. Newton: The Radical Theorist* (Jackson: University Press of Mississippi, 2002); Milton Viorst, *Fire in the Streets: America in the '60s* (New York: Simon and Schuster, 1979), 40; Reinhold Niebuhr, *Moral Man and Immoral Society* (Louisville, KY: Westminster John Knox Press, 2013); Robert F. Williams, *Negroes with Guns* (New York: Marzani and Munsell, 1962); Black Panther Party for Self-Defense, "Ten-Point Platform and Program" (Oakland: Black Panther Party for Self-Defense, 1966), accessed January 9, 2012, http://history.hanover.edu/courses/excerpts/111bppp.html.

3 The Model Cities program, an element of President Johnson's War on Poverty, was an ambitious federal urban aid program that fell short of its goals. Passed in 1966, the program ended in 1974. The Model Cities initiative created a new program at the Department of Housing and Urban Development intended to improve coordination of existing urban programs and provide additional funds for local plans. The program's goals emphasized comprehensive planning, and involved not just rebuilding but also rehabilitation, social service delivery, and citizen participation.

4 Carl Abbott, *Portland: Planning, Politics, and Growth in a Twentieth-Century City* (Lincoln: University of Nebraska Press, 1983), 169–71.

5 Ibid., 169–88.

6   Demonstration Cities and Metropolitan Development Act of 1966, Pub. L. No. 89-
     754 (1966).
7   City Auditor's Office, City Planning Commission, and Portland Development
     Commission, "Report and Recommendations on Demonstration Cities Program
     for the City of Portland," 1966, box, folder 3, Stella Maris House Manuscript Col-
     lection, Oregon Historical Society Library, Portland, OR; "Model City Plan Bold in
     Assault on Blight," *Oregonian*, July 3, 1967; "City Seeks Planning Funds for Blight
     Area Job," *Oregonian*, July 4, 1967; "Model Cities Program May Become Perma-
     nent," *Oregonian*, July 5, 1967; Department of Housing and Urban Development,
     "Discussion Paper—Portland, Oregon," 1967, Stella Maris House Collection, folder
     4, box 13, Oregon Historical Society Library, Portland, OR.
8   Stan Federman, "Negroes Break Windows, Set Fires: Police Move to Put Down Dis-
     turbances," *Oregonian*, July 31, 1967.
9   John Guernsey, "Portland Police Put Down Scattered Violence: Rowdies Dispersed
     at Park," *Oregonian*, August 1, 1967; Robert Olmos, "Peace Returns after 2 Nights
     of Disorder," *Oregonian*, August 2, 1967; *The History of Portland's African Ameri-
     can Community, 1805 to the Present* (Portland, OR: Bureau of Planning, 1993),
     125–26.
10   Stan Federman, "Albina Adults Deplore Strife, Help Police Rout Gangs," *Orego-
     nian,* July 31, 1967; Robert Olmos, "Portland Negro Leader Claims 'Outsiders'
     Sparked Albina Youth's Disorder," *Oregonian,* July 31, 1967; Robert Olmos, "Ne-
     gro Leaders Declare Albina Refuses to Accept Black Power Theory," *Oregonian*,
     August 1, 1967; Stan Federman, "Police Fail to Confirm 'Outside Agitator' Rumor,"
     Oregonian, August 2, 1967.
11   William Sanderson, "Negro Youths Fear Mayor Missed the Message of City Hall
     Discussion," *Oregonian*, August 2, 1967; *Portland City Club Bulletin*, "Problems
     of Racial Justice in Portland," Portland City Club Foundation, June 14, 1968,
     vol. 49, 9.
12   William Sanderson, "Negro Youths Fear Mayor Missed the Message of City Hall
     Discussion," *Oregonian*, August 2, 1967.
13   Martin Luther King, Jr., "Showdown for Nonviolence," *Look*, April 16, 1968.
14   "Special Meeting Report: Model Cities Program," November 30, 1967, Stella Maris
     House Manuscript Collection, folder 4, box 13, Oregon Historical Society Library,
     Portland, OR; "'Black Man' to Head Model City Here Focused," *Oregon Journal*,
     December 15, 1967; "Minister Appointed to Coordinate Model Cities Plan," *Orego-
     nian*, December 21, 1967.
15   "The Spirithouse Rap," 1, no. 1 (1967), Stella Maris House Manuscript Collection,
     folder 8, box 5, Oregon Historical Society Library, Portland, OR; anti-PDC flyer,
     Portland New Left Vertical File, OHS Research Library, Portland, OR.
16   "Special Meeting Report: Model Cities Program," January 4, 1968, Stella Maris
     House Manuscript Collection, folder 4, box 13, Oregon Historical Society Library,
     Portland, OR; Abbott, *Portland*, 194; "Model Cities Voter Turnout of 1,781 Picks
     16 Governing Board Members," *Oregonian*, March 3, 1968; Kent Ford, telephone
     conversation with author, September 1, 2014.
17   Joe Feagin and Harlan Hahn, *Ghetto Revolts* (New York: Collier MacMillan, 1973),
     105; Eldridge Cleaver, "Requiem for Nonviolence," in *Eldridge Cleaver: Post-
     Prison Writings and Speeches*, ed. Robert Scheer (New York: Vintage, 1969), 74, 76.
18   "Study Shows Portland Could Explode This Year," *Oregonian*, January 28, 1968;

"About Face," editorial, *Oregon Advance Times*, April 11, 1968; "Jeff Due Extra Policeman," *Oregon Journal*, April 10, 1968; "Close Down Jeff? Demand Discipline?"
Oregonian, April 27, 1969.

19 Konrad Hamilton, *A Decade of Triumph*, unpublished paper in possession of
the Portland Urban League, 1. Ronald Herndon, *Racism in the Portland Public
Schools* (bachelor's thesis, Portland State University, 1970), 11–12, 21; "Interracial
Progress," Urban League newsletter, August 1955, 1, Urban League of Portland
Records, 1945–2010, Oregon Multicultural Archives, Oregon State University Li-
brary, Corvallis, OR.

20 See various CPB "Working Committee" Flyers, and the "Help Keep It Moving!"
flyer, Stella Maris House Manuscript Collection, folder 6, box 13, Oregon Historical Society Library, Portland, OR; "Model Cities Program Chief Claims Negro
Leadership Emerging," *Oregonian*, July 11, 1968.

21 "Schulze Quits Model Cities Post, Cites Lack of 'Technical Skills,'" *Oregonian*, October 29, 1968.

22 Harvard Sitkoff, *The Struggle for Black Equality, 1954–1992* (New York: Hill and
Wang, 1993), 212; Michael Kazin, *The Populist Persuasion: An American History*
(New York: Basic Books, 1995), 221–42; Thomas B. Edsall and Mary Edsall, *Chain
Reaction: The Impact of Race, Rights, and Taxes on American Politics* (New York:
Norton, 1991), 76–82; Eve Edstram, "Agnew Assails 'Spoiled Brats' Who Flout
Law," *Washington Post*, September 29, 1968, 4; E. W. Kenworthy, "Nixon, in Texas,
Sharpens His Attack," *New York Times*, November 3, 1968, 1; Larry Berman, *No
Peace, No Honor: Nixon, Kissinger, and Betrayal in Vietnam* (New York: Free
Press, 2002), 1.

23 "Councilmen Disagree on Model Cities Data," *Oregonian*, December 4, 1968;
"Council Can't Meet Model Cities Deadline, Delays Proposal's Submission," *Oregonian*, January 3, 1969; "Portland Model Cities Program to Run Out of Funds
in Week," *Oregonian*, January 10, 1969; "Model Cities Plan Enters Critical Stage,"
Oregonian, January 12, 1969; Abbott, *Portland*, 194– 95; *History of Portland's African American Community*, 129; Kenneth Gervais, interview with author, January 22, 2015.

24 "Manager Charges Police Used Excessive Force; Officer Denies Claims," *Oregonian*, June 18, 1969, 30; "Albina Violence Erupts," *Oregonian*, June 16, 1969.

25 Kent Ford, telephone conversation with author, August 27, 2014; "Five Blazes Hit
Troubled Albina Area," *Oregonian*, June 18, 1969.

26 Kent Ford, telephone conversations with author, November 25, 2013, and May
8, 2014; Jules Boykoff and Martha Gies, "'We're Going to Defend Ourselves': The
Portland Chapter of the Black Panther Party and the Local Media Response,"
Oregon Historical Quarterly 111, no. 3 (Fall 2010): 286; Clay Williams, "The Port-
land Black Panthers: Building the Local African-American Community from the
Ground Up" (bachelor's thesis, University of Portland, 2008); "Portland Black
Panther Captain Describes Cop Attack on Ghetto," *Militant*, August 1, 1969.

27 Kent Ford, telephone conversation with author, June, 20, 2014; Rance Spruill, telephone conversation with author, April 30, 2014.

28 Kent Ford, telephone conversation with author, June, 20, 2014; "Judge Awards
$6,000 Judgment to Black Panther from Police," *Oregonian*, August 28, 1970.

29 Years later, Officer Vic Traversi was shot while on duty and forced to retire due to
the severity of his wounds. He eventually committed suicide. Officer Clyde Har-

mon was also shot while on duty, resulting in permanent paralysis. He was also forced to retire. "Officer's Report by C. F. Trimble, Re: 'People Court' Meetings," January 26, 1970, Police Historical and Archival Intelligence Records, A2004-005, folder 2, box 5, City of Portland Archives and Records Center (hereafter referred to as PARC), Portland, OR; Kent Ford, telephone conversation with author, June 24, 2014.

30 Harold Hughes, "Mrs. Nixon, Julie Arrive for Projects Tour," *Oregonian*, June 17, 1969; "Officer's Report by J. T. Davis and D. L. Turner to Lt. Reiter, Re: Possible Subversive Subject," December 27, 1967, Police Historical and Archival Intelligence Records, A2004-005, folder 1, box 5, PARC, Portland, OR; Kent Ford, telephone conversation with author, June 26, 2014.

31 Kent Ford, telephone conversation with author, December 4, 2013.

32 Kent Ford, telephone conversation with author, December 4, 2013, and July 23, 2014; Bradford Luckingham, *Phoenix: The History of a Southwestern Metropolis* (Tucson: University of Arizona Press, 1989); Franklin J. James, Betty L. McCummings, and Eileen A. Tynan, *Minorities in the Sunbelt* (New Brunswick, NJ: Rutgers University Press, 1984); and Bureau of the Census, "Census of Population: 1960 (Arizona)," vol. 1, pt. 4 (Washington, DC: Government Printing Office, 1963), 4–31 (table 21).

33 Kent Ford, telephone conversation with author, December 4, 2013.

34 Kent Ford, telephone conversation with author, September 19, 2013, and December 4, 2013.

35 Ibid.

36 The Black Impact Meetings was a group of blacks who were inspired by the Civil Rights Movement and wanted to find ways to enhance black people's influence in Portland's city affairs.

37 Kent Ford, telephone conversation with author, June 19, 2014.

38 Kent Ford, telephone conversation with author, December 6–7, 2013, and June 19, 2014.

39 This story was told to the author by Kent Ford, June 16, 2014; Mao Tse-tung, *Selected Works* (Peking: Foreign Languages Press, 1967), 272; Yvonne Joe, telephone conversation with author, July 21, 2014; Sandra Ford, e-mail correspondence with author, September 17, 2014.

40 Sandra Ford, e-mail correspondence with author, September 17, 2014; Kent Ford, telephone conversation with author, June 16, 2014.

41 Naim Akbar, *The Community of Self* (Tallahassee, FL: Mind Productions and Association, 1985), 50; Kent Ford, telephone conversation with author, June 16, 2014; Aaron Dixon, personal conversation with author, December 6, 2013.

42 Antonio Gramsci, *Selections from the Prison Notebooks* (London: Lawrence and Wishart, 1971), 42–43, 323.

43 Kent Ford, telephone conversation with author, August 29, 2014; Stokley Carmichael [Kwame Ture], *Stokley Speaks: From Black Power to Pan Africanism* (Chicago: Chicago Review Press, 2007), 114.

44 Kent Ford, telephone conversation with author, August 29, 2014.

45 Interestingly, the officer who made this comment preferred that he not be named. US Census Office, "Table H1, Occupancy, Utilization, and Financial Characteristics of Housing Units, Portland, Oregon-Wash SMSA" (Washington, DC: Government Printing Office, 1970); City of Portland, "Portland Police Annual Report,"

1963, in A2004-001, City of Portland Archives and Records Center, Portland, Oregon.

46 Kent Ford, telephone conversation with author, September 18, 2013.

47 Bobby Seale quoted in "Panthers Deny Part in Berkeley Slaying," *San Francisco Examiner*, January 13, 1969, 16.

48 Kent Ford, telephone conversation with author, June 25, 2014; Raymond Joe, telephone conversation with author, December 11, 2013.

49 Kent Ford, telephone conversation with author, December 6, 2013; Percy Hampton, telephone conversation with author, December 6, 2013.

50 Percy Hampton, telephone conversation with author, December 7, 2013, and May 10, 2014.

51 Oscar Johnson, telephone conversation with author, December 6 and 11, 2013; Kent Ford, telephone conversation with author, December 6, 2013; Rita Clinton, telephone conversation with author, August 20, 2014.

52 This account comes from Martha Gies's interview with Kent Ford published in her article "We're Going to Defend Ourselves," 286; David Walker, *Appeal, in Four Articles: Together with a Preamble to the Coloured Citizens of the World, But in Particular, and Very Expressly, to Those of the United States of America*, rev. ed. (New York: Hill and Wang, 1995).

53 Michael Wells, telephone conversation with author, October 31, 2013; C. Wright Mills, "The New Left," *New Left Review* 5 (October 1960): 18–23.

54 Joe Uris, telephone conversation with author, July 21, 2014; Martin Luther King, Jr., *Stride toward Freedom: The Montgomery Story* (New York: Harper and Row, 1958), 102–4; William Chafe, *Civilities and Civil Rights: Greensboro, North Carolina, and the Black Struggle for Freedom* (New York: Oxford University Press, 1980), 119.

55 Maurice Isserman and Michael Kazin, *America Divided: The Civil War of the 1960s* (New York: Oxford University Press, 2000), 33; Louis E. Lomax, *The Negro Revolt* (New York: Harper and Row, 1961), 124; General Joseph McNeil, telephone conversation with author, October 9, 2014; John Hope Franklin, *From Slavery To Freedom: A History of Negro Americans* (New York: Vintage, 1969), 623.

56 Matt Nelson and Bill Nygren, *Radicals in the Rose City: Portland's Revolutionaries, 1960–1975* (Tempe, AZ: Northwest History Press, 2013), 18–19.

57 Michael Kazin, telephone conversation with author, September 17, 2014; John McMillian, *Smoking Typewriters: The Sixties Underground Press and the Rise of Alternative Media in America* (New York: Oxford University Press, 2011), 7; Fred Hoffman, "The Underground and the Establishment," *PROVO*, July 16–31, 1967, 7.

58 William Robert Miller, *Martin Luther King, Jr.: His Life, Martyrdom, and Meaning for the World* (New York: Avon Book, 1968), 236; Richard J. Barnett, *The Economy of Death* (New York: Antheneum), 174.

59 Holly Hart, telephone conversation with author, January 30, 2014; Howard Zinn, *Disobedience and Democracy* (New York: Vintage Books, 1968), 64; Tuli Kupferberg and Robert Bashlow, *1001 Ways to Beat the Draft* (New York: Oliver Layton Press, 1966).

60 Jim Houser, telephone conversation with author, September 17, 2014. SNAP was a group comprised of academics, union workers, clergy, and various laypersons who represented the nonviolent element of Portland's Vietnam War opposition.

61 Todd Schwartz, "A Small Insurrection, a Great Divide," *Reed Magazine*, accessed March 10, 2015, http://www.reed.edu/reed_magazine/nov2003/features/small_insurrection/.

62 While young people were seemingly more assertive than those of years past, it should be noted that the groundwork for these more militant youngsters had been laid by earlier generations that included people such as Ida B. Wells Barnett, Dr. W. E. B. DuBois, E. D. Nixon, Rev. Vernon Johns, and A. Philip Randolph, to name a few. Simply put, this new breed of young person did not appear out of thin air. Hannah Arendt, *On Violence* (Orlando, FL: Harcourt Brace and Company, 1970); Samuel Huntington, in M. J. Crozier, S. P. Huntington, and J. Watanuki, *The Crisis of Democracy* (New York: NYU Press, 1975); Alex Carey, *Taking the Risks out of Democracy* (Champaign: University of Illinois Press, 1997); and Elizabeth Fones-Wolf, *Selling Free Enterprise* (Champaign: University of Illinois Press, 1995); Samuel F. Yette, *The Choice: The Issue of Black Survival in America* (Silver Spring, MD: Cottage Books, 1971), 22.

63 "Black Student Arrests All at UO Graduation," *Oregonian*, June 16, 1969.

64 "Statement to the Committee on Race and Education from the Urban League of Portland," March 9, 1964, box 1, folder 3, OSU Archives; David Morris, telephone conversation with author, April 11, 2014; Kent Ford, telephone conversation with author, June 20, 2014.

65 Kent Ford, telephone conversation with author, June 20, 2014.

66 The case was settled in 1971 by a consent decree that became known as the Probasco Decree, in which the city admitted no wrongdoing but agreed to cease specific activities. The court ordered Portland police to stop using "insulting, degrading or ethnically derogatory terms" toward blacks, to ban the use of shot-filled "sap gloves" and leaded batons, and to instruct all officers that they needed to have a search warrant before entering an Albina resident's home. For more detail, see Julie Tripp, "The Guardians: Effect of 1971 Decree Largely Negligible," *Oregonian*, June 7, 1981, 5; "Fourteen Blacks File Suit on Rights, 38 Policemen, City Officials Cited in Action," *Oregonian*, September 18, 1969, 1; *Portland City Club Bulletin*, "Law Enforcement in the city of Portland," Portland City Club Foundation, August 30, 1968.

67 Berkeley owes its reputation in part to the House Un-American Activities Committee showing of the 1960 film *Operation Abolition*, which depicted rambunctious students protesting a committee hearing in San Francisco. Ron Herndon, telephone conversation with author, November 1, 2013; Penny Harrington, telephone conversation with author, April 22, 2014.

68 Kent Ford, telephone conversation with author, June 16, 2014; Tom DeMichael and Rhonda Markowtiz, *The Groovy side of the '60s* (Lincolnwood, IL: Publications International, 2005), 265.

69 It was not uncommon for the leader of a chapter or branch to take on the title of captain. Aaron Dixon of the Seattle chapter is just one example. The individual who holds the position of deputy minister of defense is typically the leader of that branch or chapter, but that was not the case in Portland. Tommy Mills's full name was Thomas James Mills, Jr. Tom Venters's full name was Golden Thomas Venters II. Oscar Johnson, telephone conversation with author, October 17, 2013, and August 4, 2014; Raymond Joe, telephone conversation with author, August 4,

2014; Kent Ford, telephone conversation with author, June 16, 2014; Bill George, *Authentic Leadership: Rediscovering the Secrets to Creating Lasting Value* (San Francisco, CA: Jossey-Bass, 2003), 19.

70 Kent Ford, telephone conversation with author, September 19, 2013, and June 19, 2014.

71 Kent Ford, telephone conversation with author, June 16, 2014; bell hooks, *Outlaw Culture: Resisting Representations* (New York: Routledge, 1994), 245, 248.

72 Oscar Johnson, telephone conversation with author, October 25, 2013; Percy Hampton, telephone conversation with author, October 25, 2013; Sandra Ford, telephone conversation with author, April 25, 2014; Patty Carter, telephone conversation with author, January 2014; Frances Storrs, telephone conversation with author, February 24, 2014; Frances Beal, "Women in the Black Liberation Movement: Three Views," in *Sisterhood Is Powerful*, ed. Robin Morgan (New York: Vintage, 1970), 385.

73 Cheryl Townsend Gilkes, *If It Wasn't for the Women* (New York: Orbis Books, 2001), 26; Beal, "Women in the Black Liberation Movement," 384.

74 Trayce Matthews, "No One Ever Asks, What a Man's Role in the Revolution Is: Gender and the Politics of The Black Panther Party, 1966–1971," in *The Black Panther Party Reconsidered*, Charles E. Jones (Baltimore: Black Classic Press, 1998), 267–304; Angela D. LeBlanc-Ernest, "'The Most Qualified Person to Handle the Job': Black Panther Party Women, 1966–1982," in Jones, *Black Panther Party Reconsidered*, 305–36; Frantz Fanon, *The Wretched of the Earth* (New York: Grove Press, 1961); Kent Ford, telephone conversation with author, January 2, 2015.

75 Sandra Ford, telephone conversation with author, April 25, 2014, and June 24, 2014.

76 This is not to say that few Panther branches were founded by nonnatives of their branch cities; several were native. However, an examination of what the second author calls "substantive branches and chapters" reveals that many branches were founded by individuals who were reared in that particular city.

77 The Panther who relayed this story did not request anonymity, but we thought it best that his name not appear in print. Robert G. Weisbord, *Genocide? Birth Control and the Black American* (Westport, CT: Greenwood Press, 1975), 52–53.

78 Sandra Ford, telephone conversation with author, April 25, 2014; Elaine Brown, *A Taste of Power: A Black Women's Story* (New York: Pantheon Books, 1993), 108–9, 357; Percy Hampton, telephone conversation with author, July 15, 2014.

79 Sandra Ford, telephone conversation with author, April 25, 2014; Raymond Joe, telephone conversation with author, August 2, 2014; Kent Ford, telephone conversation with author, August 24, 2014.

80 Golden Venters, telephone conversation with author, August 21, 2014.

81 Percy Hampton, telephone conversation with author, August 21, 2014. Julius Lester, *Look Out, Whitey! Black Power's Gon' Get Your Mama!* (New York: Dial Press, 1968), 26.

82 Raymond Joe, telephone conversation with author, January 8, 2014; Percy Hampton, telephone conversation with author, September 9, 2013; Kent Ford, telephone conversation with author, August 24, 2014.

83 Oscar Johnson, telephone conversation with author, October 17, 2013; Percy Hampton, telephone conversation with author, September, 20, 2013.

84 *The History of Portland's African American Community, 1805 to the Present*, 122.

3. Serving Albina and Becoming Panthers

1   A large body of historical literature exists on the in-fighting and leadership frag-
    mentation of the BPP under Bobby Seale, David Hilliard, and Eldridge Cleaver in
    the years following Newton's imprisonment.
2   Hubert Fichte, "Jean Genet Talks to Hubert Fichte," *New Review* 4, 37:9–21.; S.
    Marshall, "On Tour for Panthers and Conspiracy," *Los Angeles Free Press*, March
    27, 1, 5.
3   Kent Ford, telephone conversation with author, May 1, 2014.
4   Barbara Boland, "Community Prosecution: Portland Experience," in *Community
    Justice: An Emerging Field*, ed. David R. Karp (New York: Rowman and Littlefield),
    253–78; Robert Staples, Introduction to *Black Sociology* (New York: McGraw-Hill,
    1976); interview with Kent Ford from "Portland Black Panther Party," KBOO Com-
    munity Radio, Portland, February 24, 2008; Kent Ford, telephone conversation
    with author, July 11, 2014.
5   Kent Ford, telephone conversation with author, July 11, 2014; Chuck Armsbury,
    telephone conversation with author, February 20, 2014; Aaron Dixon, telephone
    conversation with author, July 20, 2014.
6   David Hilliard, *This Side of Glory: The Autobiography of David Hilliard and the
    Story of the Black Panther Party* (Boston: Little, Brown and Company, 1993), 211–
    12.
7   "Chairman Bobby Seale," The Movement, March 1969, reprinted in *Black Panther*,
    March 3, 1969, 11; Hilliard, *This Side of Glory*, 211–12; Paul Alkebulan, *Survival
    Pending Revolution: The History of the Black Panther Party* (Tuscaloosa: Univer-
    sity of Alabama Press, 2007), 29.
8   Huey P. Newton, "'Vanguard of the People's Struggle': August 14, 1970," in Louis G.
    Heath, *Off the Pigs* (New Jersey: Scarecrow Press, 1976), 221; Kent Ford, telephone
    conversation with author, November 16, 2013; Sandra Ford, telephone conversa-
    tion with author, June 1, 2014.
9   Andrew Hacker, *The Study of Politics: The Western Tradition and American Ori-
    gins* (New York: McGraw Hill, 1963), 36; Aristotle, *Politica (Politics)*, book 4, chap-
    ters 2 and 11; book 5, chapter 8; book 6, chapter 5; book 7, chapter 10. Richard
    McKeon, ed., *The Basic Works of Aristotle* (New York: Random House, 1941).
10 Kent Ford, telephone conversation with author, November 16, 2013; Andre Witt,
    "Picking Up the Hammer: The Milwaukee Branch of the Black Panther Party," in
    Judson Jeffries, ed., *Comrades: A Local History of the Black Panther Party* (Bloom-
    ington: Indiana University Press, 2006), 180.
11 Rebecca Koffman, "Ex-Black Panthers Recall Social Activism," *Oregonian*, Febru-
    ary 28, 2008; Patty (Hampton) Carter, telephone conversation with author, Janu-
    ary 28, 2014; Kent Ford, telephone conversation with author, December 2, 2013.
12 Rebecca Koffman, "Ex-Panthers Recall Social Activism," *Oregonian*, February 28,
    2008; Percy Hampton, telephone conversation with author, June 18, 2014; Kent
    Ford, telephone conversation with author, December 10, 2013, and May 8, 2014;
    Sandra Ford, telephone conversation with author, June 17, 2014.
13 Rick Goodfellow, "Log Attends Black Panther Breakfast Program," *Pioneer Log*,
    March 6, 1970; Rick Goodfellow, telephone conversation with author, June 13,
    2014.
14 Bill Keller, "Breakfast, Clinic Programs Belie Militant Panther Image," *Orego-
    nian*, November 12, 1971; Ollie Robertson, telephone conversation with author,

April 28, 2014; Kim Green, telephone conversation with author, April 22, 2014; Nathaniel Cross, telephone conversation with author, March 21, 2014; "Breakfast for School Children Programs—NCCF," Black Panther Party Police Records, Police Historical and Archival Intelligence Records, A2004-005, folder 1, box 5, City of Portland Archives and Records Center, Portland, OR. Hereafter referred to as PARC.

15 Linda Thornton, telephone conversation with author, August 13, 2014; Vernell Carter, telephone conversation with author, November 1, 2013; Darryl Thomas, telephone conversation with author, October 28, 2013; Teddy Sanders, telephone conversation with author, March 21, 2014.

16 Joyce Williams, interview with author, January 18, 2015; Kent Ford, telephone conversation with author, November 16, 2013. Goodfellow, "Log Attends Black Panther Breakfast Program"; Bill Keller, "Breakfast, Clinic Programs Belie Militant Panther Image," *Oregonian*, November 12, 1971, 23.

17 Richard Seymour, *The Haight-Ashbury Free Medical Clinic: Still Free After All These Years, 1967–1989* (San Francisco: Partisan Press, 1987); Martin Luther King, Jr., quoted in Herbert M. Morais, *History of the Negro in Medicine* (Washington, DC: United Publishing Corp., 1970), 6.

18 "Fred Hampton Memorial Clinic Application for Solicitation Permit," Black Panther Party Police Records, Police Historical and Archival Intelligence Records, A2004-005, folder 1, box 5, PARC; Gies, "Radical Treatment," *Reed* magazine (Winter 2009): 4–5, accessed June 22, 2011, http://web.reed.edu/reed_magazine/winter2009/features/radical_treatment/index.html; interview with Percy Hampton from "Portland Black Panther Party," KBOO Community Radio, Portland, February 24, 2008; Yvonne Joe, telephone conversation with author, June 2, 2014; Sandra Ford, telephone conversation with author, April 25, 2014.

19 Dr. George Barton, telephone conversation with author, October 29, 2013; Francis Storrs, telephone conversation with author, February 24, 2014.

20 Vicki Nakashima, interview with author, November 5, 2014.

21 Bill Keller, "Breakfast, Clinic Programs Belie Militant Panther Image," *Oregonian*, November 12, 1971; Raymond Joe, telephone conversation with author, January 8, 2014; Dr. George Barton, telephone conversation with author, October 29, 2013; Kent Ford, telephone conversation with author, December 2, 2013.

22 Mark Brody, "Panthers Map a People's Health Plan," *Daily World*, June 26, 1969; Paul Hull, telephone conversation with author, February 16, 2014; Kent Ford, telephone conversation with author, October 19, 2013; "Reporters Scrutinize Panthers' Health Clinic," *Pioneer Log*, March 10, 1970; Rebecca Koffman, "Ex-Black Panthers Recall Social Activism," *Oregonian*, February 28, 2008.

23 Morris Isserman and Dorreen Labby, "Does Wayne Morse Have a Chance? He Thinks So," *Scribe*, April 27–May 3, 1974, 10; Kent Ford, telephone conversation with author, July 9, 2014.

24 "Fast Facts about Sickle Cell Anemia," Black Community Survival Committee Police Records, Police Historical and Archival Intelligence Records, A2004-005, folder 1, box 5, PARC; Gies, "Radical Treatment," 2. For more information on the BPP and their medical clinics in the United States, see Alondra Nelson, *Body and Soul: The Black Panther Party and the Fight against Medical Discrimination* (Minneapolis: University of Minnesota Press, 2011); Raymond Joe, telephone conversation with author, January 8, 2014; Kent Ford, telephone conversation

with author, October 19, 2013; Robert B. Scott, "Health Care Priority and Sickle Cell Anemia," in *Ethnic Groups of America: Their Morbidity, Mortality, and Behavior Disorders*, vol. 2, *The Blacks*, ed. Ailon Shiloh and Ida Cohen Selavan (Springfield, IL: C. C. Thomas Publishers, 1974), 121–22; US Congress, Senate Committee on Labor and Public Welfare, Subcommittee on Health, National Sickle Cell Anemia Prevention Act, hearings on S. 2676 held November 11–12, 1972, 92nd Congress, 1st sess., 1971, p. 15; idem, "Amendments to the National Sickle Cell Anemia Control Act," unpublished transcript from July 15, 1975, hearings, p. 16 (photocopied).

25 Carl Abbott, *Portland: Planning, Politics, and Growth in a Twentieth-Century City* (Lincoln: University of Nebraska Press, 1983); J. E. Moore, "Community Aspects of Childhood Lead Poisoning," *American Journal of Public Health* 60 (1970): 1430–38.

26 Joanne Zuhl, "Prowling Through History," www.streetroots.org, March 21, 2008, p. 10; Kent Ford, telephone conversation with author, November 6, 2013.

27 Kent Ford, telephone conversation with author, November 6, 2013; Addison Gayle, Jr., *The Black Situation* (New York: A Delta Book, 1970), 133.

28 Sandra Ford, telephone conversation with author, May 24, 2014; Barbara Gundle, telephone conversation with author; Dr. Duane Paulson, telephone conversation with author, June 13, 2014; Joy Pruitt, telephone conversation with author, March 17, 2014; Kent Ford, telephone conversation with author, November 12, 2013.

29 Dr. Gerry Morrell, DDS, telephone conversation with author, October 30, 2013, and November 12, 2013; Kent Ford, telephone conversation with author, October 19, 2013, and March 7, 2014.

30 Kent Ford, telephone conversation with author, June 26, 2014; Keller, "Breakfast"; Duane Paulson, telephone conversation with author, June 13, 2014.

31 Gies, "Radical Treatment," 5; Robert Spindel, telephone conversation with author, December 11, 2013; Jon Moscow, telephone conversation and e-mail correspondence with author, October 28, 2013, and December 10, 2013.

32 Percy Hampton, telephone conversation with author, September 20, 2013.

33 The concert was the governor's way of luring young dissidents away from the American Legion convention that was being held in downtown Portland at the same time. With President Richard Nixon scheduled to appear, local and state officials wanted to ensure that the festivities were not interrupted by a noisy group of Vietnam War protesters that called themselves the People's Army Jamboree. Percy Hampton, telephone conversation with author, July 9, 2014; Kent Ford, telephone conversation with author, November 6, 2013.

34 Alkebulan, *Survival Pending Revolution*, 49; Oscar Johnson, telephone conversation with author, October 17, 2013; Staples, Introduction to *Black Sociology*, 93; Baxter Smith, "Issues Facing the Black Press," *Militant*, February 1, 1974, 14.

35 Kent Ford, telephone conversation with author, October 11, 2013; Percy Hampton, telephone conversation with author, November 27, 2013.

36 Vernell Carter, telephone conversation with author, October 23, 2013; Maurice Isserman, telephone conversation with author, July 26, 2014; Kent Ford, telephone conversation with author, October 8, 2013, and June 18, 2014.

37 "Panther Lauds Grocer Aid," *Oregon Journal*, February 17, 1970; Kent Ford, telephone conversation with author, September 18, 2013.

38 Several former reporters for the *Oregonian* claim that the newspaper was more

moderate-to-liberal than conservative, especially after William Hilliard, an African American, became executive editor (in 1972) and then editor (in the late 1980s) of the newspaper. Jules Boykoff and Martha Gies, "We're Going to Defend Ourselves," *Oregon Historical Quarterly* 111 (Fall 2010): 278–311, 306; Janet Goetze, telephone conversation with author, August 5, 2014.

39 Michael Wells, telephone conversation with author, November 1, 2013; Maurice Isserman, telephone conversation with author, December 10, 2013; Dorreen Labby, interview with author, January 22, 2015.

40 "Officer's Report: RE: Black Panther Breakfast Program," September 11, 1970, Black Panther Party Police Records, Police Historical and Archival Intelligence Records, A2004-005, folder 1, box 5, PARC; Kent Ford, telephone conversation with author, May 4, 2014.

41 "Business Firms Contacted with Negative Results," Black Panther Party Police Records, Police Historical and Archival Intelligence Records, A2004-005, folder 2, box 5, PARC; Bill Keller, "Portland Said 1970 Target of FBI Anti-Panther Effort," *Oregonian*, February 26, 1978; "Panthers Fail to Seek Permit to Solicit Funds," *Oregonian*, October 8, 1970.

42 "Panthers Fail to Seek Permit"; Kent Ford, telephone conversation with author, July 6, 2014.

43 Percy Hampton, telephone conversation with author, June 13, 2014.

44 Kent Ford, telephone conversation with author, June 26, 2014.

45 See, for example, *New Negro Alliance v. Sanitary Grocery Co.*, 303 US 552 (1938), in which the court found that federal labor law protected blacks picketing and urging a boycott against a grocery chain that did not employ black clerks, contrary to state court injunctions; Charles V. Hamilton, Adam Clayton Powell: *The Political Biography of an American Dilemma* (New York: Cooper Square Press, 1991), 95–105. See also Lerone Bennett, *Before the Mayflower: A History of Black America* (Chicago: Johnson Publishing Company, 1987), 360–61; Francis Fox Piven and Richard Cloward, *Poor People's Movements: Why They Succeed, How They Fail* (New York: Vintage Books, 1977).

46 "Officer's Report: Info Trespass/Possible Extortion," August 12, 1970, Black Panther Party Police Records, Police Historical and Archival Intelligence Records, A2004-005, folder 2, box 5, PARC; Boykoff and Gies, "We're Going to Defend Ourselves," 293; Kent Ford, telephone conversation with author, December 2, 2013; Sara Gilbert, *Built for Success: The Story of McDonald's* (Mankato, MN: Creative Education, 2007).

47 Jeff Barker, telephone conversation with author, April 22, 2014; Early Deane, "Judge Requires Mutual Concessions in McDonald Picketing," *Oregonian*, August 16, 1970; "Boycott McDonald's!" flyer, Black Panther Party Police Records, Police Historical and Archival Intelligence Records, A2004-005, folder 2, box 5, PARC.

48 "Picketed Hamburger Stand Here Bombed," *Oregon Journal*, August 22, 1970; "Blast Shatters Glass at McDonald's," *Oregonian*, August 22, 1970; Percy Hampton, telephone conversation with author, October 25, 2013; Early Deane, "Hearing to Examine Panther Picket Ban," *Oregonian*, August 13, 1970, 12.

49 Robert A. Potter and James Sullivan, "The Campus by the Sea Where the Bank Burned Down: A Report on the Disturbances at UCSB and Isla Vista, 1968–1970," (Santa Barbara, CA: 1970).

50 Kent Ford, telephone conversation with author, December 2, 2013, and June 27,

2014; "Firm to Aid Panther Project," *Oregonian*, September 19, 1970; Boykoff and Gies, "We're Going to Defend Ourselves," 294.

51 Kent Ford, telephone conversation with author, December 2, 2013, and July 2, 2014.

52 Oscar Johnson, telephone conversation with author, October 18, 2013; Percy Hampton, telephone conversation with author, October 18, 2013; Black Panther Party for Self-Defense, "Ten-Point Platform and Program" (Oakland: Black Panther Party for Self-Defense, 1966), accessed January 9, 2012, http://history. hanover.edu/courses/excerpts/111bppp.html.

53 Percy Hampton, telephone conversation with author, October 18, 2013.

54 "May Day—Free Huey" flyer, Black Panther Party Police Records, Police Historical and Archival Intelligence Records, A2004-005, folder 5, box 5, PARC; Kent Ford, telephone conversation with author, December 2, 2013.

55 Kent Ford, telephone conversation with author, November 25, 2013, and December 2, 2013; Percy Hampton, telephone conversation with author, October 25, 2013.

56 Kent Ford, telephone conversation with author, November 21, 2013.

57 Harry Chaivoe, telephone conversation with author, September 5, 2014; Karen Chaivoe, telephone conversation with author, August 12, 2014; David Horowitz, telephone conversation with author, October 9, 2014.

58 Kent Ford, telephone conversation with author, February 2, 2014, and November 11, 2013; "Panther Bail Sets Record," *Oregonian*, June 9, 1970; "Panther Leader Found Guilty, Meted 6-Month Probation on Disorderly Conduct Charge," *Oregonian*, September 19, 1970, 9; Hebert Marcuse, *An Essay on Liberation* (Boston: Beacon Press, 1969), 35.

59 "Panther Leader Found Guilty," *Oregonian*, September 19, 1970; "Portland," Berkeley Tribe, September 11, 1970.

60 "Black Panther Claims It's Ballots or Bullets," *Oregonian*, February 15, 1970.

61 Ibid.

62 Janet Goetze, "Panther Claims Gunshot Wound Caused His Rifle to Discharge," *Oregonian*, April 1970.

63 Boykoff and Gies, "We're Going to Defend Ourselves," 297; Joyce Williams, interview with author, January 18, 2015; Janet Goetze, "Defense Attorney Asks Mistrial in Panther HQ Shooting Hearing," *Oregonian*, July 7, 1970; Nate Griffin, telephone conversation with author, July 29, 2014; "Railroad: Free Albert Williams!" Black Panther Party Police Records, pamphlet, Police Historical and Archival Intelligence Records, A2004-005, folder 3, box 5, PARC.

64 Nate Griffin, telephone conversation with author, July 29, 2014; Kent Ford, telephone conversation with author, July 7, 2014.

65 "KGW Radio Criticized for Panther Incident," *Oregonian*, February 28, 1970; "Crowd Storms City Hall to Protest Shooting," *Oregonian*, February 20, 1970.

66 Kent Ford, telephone conversation with author, July 16, 2014.

67 "Crowd Storms City Hall to Protest Shooting," *Oregonian*, February 20, 1970; Maurice Isserman, e-mail correspondence with author, July 14, 2014; Kent Ford, telephone conversation with author, July 14, 2014.

68 This officer requested that his name not be mentioned, telephone conversation with author, August 1, 2014; Robert Landauer, telephone conversation with author, August 13, 2014; Steve Erickson, "Jury Clears Policeman," *Oregonian*, Febru-

ary 28, 1970; "Jury Convicts Williams of Assault in Shooting," *Oregonian*, October 21, 1970.

69   "Come See about Albert" flyer, Black Panther Party Police Records, Police Historical and Archival Intelligence Records, A2004-005, folder 3, box 5, PARC.

70   "Railroad: Free Albert Williams!" Black Panther Party Police Records, pamphlet, Police Historical and Archival Intelligence Records, A2004-005, folder 3, box 5, PARC.

71   Janet Goetze, "Panther Claims Gunshot Wounds Caused His Rifle to Discharge," *Oregonian*, July 4, 1970; Steve Erickson, "Final Williams Trial Witness Tells Barbiturate Effect," *Oregonian*, October 17, 1970; Steve Erickson, "Shooting in Panther Headquarters Described," *Oregonian*, October 15, 1970; Steve Erickson, "Threats by Patrolman Claimed in Williams Shooting Trial," *Oregonian*, October 16, 1970.

72   For a more detailed analysis of media portrayals and framings of the Williams trial, see Boykoff and Gies, "We're Going to Defend Ourselves," 297–300; Percy Hampton, telephone conversation with author, October 25, 2013.

73   Ron Herndon, telephone conversation with author, November 1, 2013; "Portland BPP Minister of Information . . . 'I don't give a damn if the air is polluted, etc.,'" *Pioneer Log*, March 3, 1970.

4. Portland's Dream of a New Urbanism

1   The Portland State University demonstration was part of a nationwide student strike in May 1970. The students were protesting not only the war in Vietnam but also the shipping of nerve gas through Oregon, the imprisonment of Black Panther Bobby Seale, and, most notably, the shooting deaths of students at both Kent State and Jackson State University.

2   Founded in 1968, Americans for Constitutional Action focused on trying to influence public and congressional opinion through publicity and means other than lobbying. Americans for Constitutional Action, "Speech Kit," undated 1970, John N. "Happy" Camp Papers, box 6, Carl Albert Center Archives, Norman, OK. Constituent letters are collected in Camp Papers, box 6 and Page H. Belcher Papers, box 152, Carl Albert Center Archives, Norman, OK.

3   The Bonneville Power Administration (BPA) is a federal nonprofit agency based in the Pacific Northwest. BPA markets wholesale electrical power from thirty-one federal hydro projects in the Columbia River Basin, one nonfederal nuclear plant, and several other small nonfederal power plants. The dams are operated by the US Army Corps of Engineers and the Bureau of Reclamation. About one-third of the electricity used in the Pacific Northwest comes from the BPA, which also operates and maintains about three-fourths of the high-voltage transmission in Idaho, Oregon, Washington, and western Montana, and in small parts of California, Nevada, Utah, Wyoming, and eastern Montana.

4   Kent Ford, telephone conversation with author, June 18, 2014.

5   "Portlanders Appear Unaware of Efforts to Fight Poverty," *Oregonian*, September 2, 1971; Raymond Joe, telephone conversation with author, January 8, 2014.

6   *The History of Portland's African American Community, 1805 to the Present* (Portland, OR: Bureau of Planning, 1993),131; Kent Ford, telephone conversation with author, June 20, 2014.

7   Kent Ford, telephone conversation with author, June 20, 2014.

8   Oscar Johnson, telephone conversation with author, October 27, 2013; Raymond Joe, telephone conversation with author, January 8, 2014.

9   *History of Portland's African American Community*, 138; Portland Development Commission, "Timetable," Emanuel Hospital application, Emanuel Hospital Records, A2010-003, folder 1, box 1, Emanuel Hospital Project Records, A2010-003, City of Portland Archives and Records Center (hereafter referred to as PARC), Portland, OR; Portland Development Commission, *Final Project Report Application for Loan and Grant: Emanuel Hospital Project*, Emanuel Hospital application, Emanuel Hospital Records, A2010-003, box 1, PARC.

10   "Citizen Critics Note Lack of Benefits from Model Cities Program Funds," *Oregonian*, March 28, 1971;' *History of Portland's African American Community*, 131–32.

11   Carl Abbott, *Greater Portland: Urban Landscape in the Pacific Northwest* (Philadelphia: University of Pennsylvania Press, 2001), 195.

12   Abbott, *Portland*, 195–96; "Model Cities Due for 'Second Action Year,'" *Oregonian*, April 6, 1971; *History of Portland's African American Community*, 138–40.

13   *History of Portland's African American Community*, 132–33.

14   Black Community Survival Committee, A2004-005, City of Portland Archives. Vernon Neighborhood Care, "A.W.L. News," March 5, 1971, 1; Robert Olmos, "Model Cities Aid Threatens to Blow Whistle on Police Shift," *Oregonian*, March 31, 1971; "Black Militant Wins OEO Post," *Oregon Journal*, February 18, 1971; "Former 'Black Beret' Leader Takes OEO Treasurer Post," *Oregonian*, March 3, 1971; Board of Directors minutes, A2000-007, 1971, City of Portland Archives.

15   In his 1964 state of the union address, President Lyndon B. Johnson announced, "This administration here and now declared unconditional war on poverty," and shortly thereafter the OEO was created.

16   R. Sargent Shriver was the brother-in-law of John and Robert F. Kennedy and the husband of Eunice Kennedy. He eventually ran for vice president with George McGovern; the two lost to the Richard Nixon–Spiro Agnew ticket.

17   Evelyn Forget, "A Tale of Two Communities: Fighting Poverty in the Great Society, 1964–1968," *History of Political Economy* 43 (2001): 200.

18   Quoted in Samuel F. Yette, *The Choice: The Issue of Black Survival in America* (Silver Spring, MD: Cottage Books, 1971), 59; Portland Metropolitan Steering Committee Incorporation, 1964, 2–3, PARC.

19   Thomas Mercer was appointed director of the West Coast region of the OEO in late 1969. The newly created regional office was in line with President Richard Nixon's plan to establish common regional boundaries for various federal offices. As director of the West Coast regional office, Mercer was in charge of operations in Alaska, Washington, Idaho, and Oregon. See "Mercer Appointed OEO Regional Director Locally," *Trumpet*, November 1969, 1; "Panel Officer Found Guilty," *Oregonian*, February 27, 1971; "Bonding Key to Job for Black Militant," *Oregon Journal*, March 22, 1971; "Steering Panel Hits Snag on Surety Bond," *Oregonian*, March 21, 1971; "Anderson Resignation Frees City's Anti-poverty Money," *Oregonian*, April 1, 1971.

20   "Anderson Resigns as Committee Treasurer," *Oregonian*, March 31, 1971; "Anderson Resignation Frees City's Anti-poverty Money," *Oregonian*, April 1, 1971.

21   Judge Phillip Roth served as a circuit court judge of Multnomah County, Oregon, for more than twenty-five years. Prior to that, he served as an Oregon State rep-

resentative and the Portland deputy city attorney. Judge Roth is also father of the acclaimed author of the same name. After Anderson was found guilty, one of the twelve jurors, who was reportedly the last to side with the unanimous verdict, told Judge Roth that during deliberations a juror had brought up allegations of Anderson that were not presented as evidence during the court proceedings. The defense appealed for a mistrial, and after deliberating for more than a month, the judge denied the appeal and convicted Anderson. "Juror Says Irregularities Swayed Vote," *Oregonian*, July 14, 1971; "Albina Activist Sentenced," *Oregon Journal*, August 19, 1971; "Anderson Ouster Bogged," *Oregon Journal*, March 20, 1971.

22 Black Panther Party anti–Model Cities flyer, National Association for the Advancement of Colored People, Portland Branch Records, box 16, folder 16, University of Oregon Library, Eugene, OR.

23 Bill Hedlund, "Panther Leader Tells of Group Goals," *Portland Community College Bridge*, December 9, 1971; officer's report, "Kent Ford," Department of Public Safety, Bureau of Police, City of Portland, Oregon.

24 Martha James, telephone conversation with author, September 3, 2014; "Cheryl James Bail Set," *Scribe*, March 7–13, 1972; Arthur C. Spencer, telephone conversation with author, August 26, 2014.

25 Martha James, telephone conversation with author, August 28, 2014.

26 United States v. James, 464 F.2d 1288 (9th Cir. 1972).

27 Martha James, telephone conversation with author, August 28, 2014; Kent Ford, telephone conversation with author, August 25, 2014; "Cheryl James Fund," *Catholic Sentinel*, August 20, 1971; "Cheryl James Fund" solicitation letter; "Request for Donations to WILPF Revolving Bail Fund," Women's International League for Peace and Freedom, Portland Branch, 1972, notes on the Cheryl D. James legal case, 1971–1973, collected by Arthur C. Spencer, September 1971, A307, file 1, Cheryl D. James Defense Committee Records, University of Oregon Special Collections and Archives, Eugene, OR.

28 The Cheryl James Defense Committee goes by several names, including the Cheryl James Fund, the Cheryl James Defense Fund, and the Cheryl James Fund Committee. To avoid confusion, we will refer to it only as the Cheryl James Defense Committee. Judge Gus J. Solomon was appointed by President Harry Truman to the US District Court of Oregon in 1950 and served as chief judge from 1958 to 1971. He continued to hear cases as a senior judge until his death in 1987. "Women Plan Probe of Trial," *Oregonian*, July 6, 1971; Kent Ford, telephone conversation with author, August 25, 2014; Ralph Friedman, "Man, Storms, and Islands," *Clarke Press*, August 18, 1971.

29 Kent Ford, telephone conversation with author, October 6, 2014.

30 Martha James, telephone conversation with author, August 27, 2014; "Women Plan Probe of Trial," *Oregonian*, July 6, 1971; "Minorities Need Adair, Women Say," *Oregon Journal*, July 6, 1971; Helen Grossman and Ann C. Campbell to Judge Gus J. Solomon, June 9, 1971, notes on the Cheryl D. James legal case, 1971–1973, collected by Arthur C. Spencer, A307, file 1, Cheryl D. James Defense Committee Records, University of Oregon Special Collections and Archives, Eugene, OR.

31 Judge Schnacke was a federal judge on the United States District Court, Northern District of California. He was nominated by President Richard Nixon in September 1970 to a seat vacated by George Harris; he was confirmed by the Senate in October 1970 and received commission on October 15, 1970. Schnacke assumed

senior status in December 1983 and served the Northern District of California until his death in 1994. Judge Hufstedler was appointed judge of the US Court of Appeals for the Ninth Circuit in 1968. Shuck Walbaum, "Hope Runs High in James' Case," *Jeffersonian*, September 17, 1971; Julia Ruuttila, "Cheryl James Released on Bail," *Portland Observer*, March 2, 1972; Oz Hopkins, "Girl Convicted in FBI Assault Claims Prison Rape," *Oregon Journal*, September 1, 1972; "Cheryl James Bail Set," *Scribe*, March 7–13, 1972; United States v. James, 464 F.2d 1288 (9th Cir. 1972).

32 Judge Belloni was appointed to the district court by President Lyndon B. Johnson in 1967. He served as chief judge of the US District Court, District of Oregon, from 1971 to 1976, and assumed senior status in April 1984. "Court Orders Cheryl James Back to Prison," *Portland Observer*, September 14, 1972; Ken Jumper, "Portland Girl Must Go Back to Prison," *Oregon Journal*, February 27, 1973; Oz Hopkins, "Prison-bound Girl Vows to Fight On," *Oregon Journal*, February 28, 1973; Arthur Spencer, telephone conversation with author, August 26, 2014.

33 Kent Ford, telephone conversation with author, November 21, 2013.

34 Kent Ford, telephone conversation with author, July 13, 2014.

35 "Black Community Survival Conference Program," Black Community Survival Committee Police Records, Police Historical and Archival Intelligence Records, A2004-005, folder 1, box 5, PARC; Kent Ford, telephone conversation with author, June 28, 2014; Maurice Isserman, telephone conversation with author, December 10, 2013.

36 "Black Community Survival Conference Intelligence Report," May 25, June 29, and July 2, 1972, Black Community Survival Committee Police Records, Police Historical and Archival Intelligence Records, A2004-005, folder 1, box 5, PARC.

37 "Inter-Office Memorandum: Black Community Survival Conference," July 3, 1972, Black Panther Party Police Records, Police Historical and Archival Intelligence Records, A-2004-005, PARC.

38 Nate Proby ran for the city council (commissioner, position no. 3) in 1970, finishing last in a seven-man race. "Emanuel Breaks Promises," Black Panther Party Police Records, Police Historical and Archival Intelligence Records, A2004-005, folder 4, box 5, PARC.

39 "Inter-Office Memorandum: Demonstrations—Picketing, Emanuel Hospital," March 21, 1973, Black Panther Party Police Records, Police Historical and Archival Intelligence Records, A2004-005, folder 5, box 5, PARC.

40 "Parcel No. RS-4-7," Emanuel Hospital property identifications, Emanuel Hospital Records, A2010-003, folder 5, box 2, PARC.

41 "Fred Hampton Medical Health Clinic," Black Panther Party Police Records, Police Historical and Archival Intelligence Records, A2004-005, folder 5, box 5, PARC.

42 Kent Ford, telephone conversation with author, December 1 and 6, 2014.

43 Kent Ford, telephone conversation with author, December 6, 2014.

44 "Fred Hampton Medical Health Clinic," Black Panther Party Police Records, Police Historical and Archival Intelligence Records, A2004-005, folder 5, box 5, PARC; *Cornerstones of Community: Buildings of Portland's African American History* (Portland, OR: Bosco-Milligan Foundation, 1995), 90; *History of Portland's African American Community*, 111.

45 Dorreen Labby, "Hampton Clinic," *Scribe*, September 15–21, 1973.

46 Dolores Barclay, "Black Panthers Prowl the Streets No More," *Oregonian*, October 11, 1983.

47 Richard Walker, telephone conversation with author, June 28, 2014; Percy Hampton, telephone conversation with author, November 27, 2013; Oscar Johnson, telephone conversation with author, November 27, 2013.
48 Interview with Kent Ford from "Portland Black Panther Party," KBOO Community Radio, Portland, February 24, 2008; Kent Ford, telephone conversation with author, December 2–3, 2013.
49 Bill Keller, "Portland Said 1970 Target of FBI Anti-Panther Effort," *Oregonian*, February 26, 1978.
50 Interview with Kent Ford, Percy Hampton, Oscar Johnson, and Gary Clay from "Portland Black Panther Party," KBOO Community Radio, Portland, February 24, 2008.
51 Sandra Ford, telephone conversation with author, June 20, 2014. In 1958, Howard ran for Congress as a Republican against incumbent William Dawson, losing to him by a margin of 72.2 percent to 27.8 percent. In 1972, Howard founded the Friendship Medical Center', the largest privately owned black clinic in Chicago, on the city's South Side. David Barton Smith, *Health Care Divided: Race and Healing a Nation* (Ann Arbor: University of Michigan Press, 1999), 15; John Dittmer, *The Good Doctors: The Medical Committee for Human Rights and the Struggle for Social Justice in Health Care* (New York: Bloomsbury Press, 2009). In a personal correspondence with Dittmer, he estimated that no more than 10 percent of the organization was comprised of black physicians.
52 Dave Dawson, telephone conversation with author, July 24, 2014.
53 Percy Hampton, telephone conversation with author, November 27, 2013; Charles E. Jones "Arm Yourself or Harm Yourself: People's Party II and the Black Panther Party in Houston, Texas," in Judson Jeffries, *On the Ground: The Black Panther Party in Communities across America* (Jackson: University Press of Mississippi, 2010), 3–40. There is some dispute as to whether the People's Party II ever secured official BPP charter status. Young Jackson went to the courthouse with the intention of taking hostages in exchange for the freedom of his brother, George Jackson, and for Fleeta Drumgo and John Clutchette, who were known as the Soledad Brothers. Jackson went to Judge Harold Haley's courtroom armed to the teeth. San Quentin prisoner James McClain was there, defending himself against charges of assaulting a guard following the beating death of another black inmate by prison officials. Inmates Ruchell Magee and William Christmas were also in the courtroom, serving as witnesses for McClain. Judge Haley, assistant prosecutor Gary Thomas, and three jurors were taken as hostages. To ensure a safe getaway, Jackson tied the end of a shotgun barrel to the neck of Judge Haley. What Jackson and the others failed to consider was the state's willingness to sacrifice their own to foil the escape. The men made their way to a van, into which they loaded the hostages; however, as they attempted to drive out of the parking lot, San Quentin guards quickly arrived on the scene and fired round after round into the van, killing Jackson, Christmas, McCain, and Haley. Thomas and Magee were seriously wounded, and one juror suffered minor injuries.
54 Raymond Joe, telephone conversation with author, January 8, 2014.
55 Sandra Ford, telephone conversation with author, June 20, 2014.
56 Oscar Johnson, telephone conversation with author, November 27, 2014; interview with Kent Ford, Percy Hampton, Oscar Johnson, and Gary Clay from "Portland Black Panther Party," KBOO Community Radio, Portland, February 24, 2008.

57 Robert Webb was gunned down in New York City in March 1971, and Sam Napier was tortured, shot to death, and incinerated in a building fire in April 1971.

58 Percy Hampton, telephone conversation with author, October 18, 2013; Oscar Johnson, telephone conversation with author, October 17, 2013; Percy Hampton, telephone conversation with author, October 18, 2013; Kent Ford, telephone conversation with author, October 19, 2013.

59 Jack Olsen, *Last Man Standing: The Tragedy and Triumph of Geronimo Pratt* (New York: Random House, 2000), 93. Pratt initially believed that Lee's death was connected to the Newton-Cleaver feud but later came to believe that her connections to the New York underworld is what got her killed, but there is no way to know for sure. Her murder remains unsolved. "Serious Ideological Disputes Threaten Future of Black Panther Party," *Oregonian*, March 1, 1971; Percy Hampton, telephone conversation with author, October 19, 2013; Sandra Ford, telephone conversation with author, June 20, 2014.

60 Mary Ann Dickey, telephone conversation with author, November 23, 2013.

61 Kent Ford, telephone conversation with author, December 6, 2014.

62 Jules Boykoff and Martha Gies, "We're Going to Defend Ourselves: The Portland Chapter of the Black Panther Party and the Local Media Response," *Oregon Historical Quarterly* 111, no. 3 (Fall 2010): 291. Julius Nyerere was elected Tanzania's first president in 1962, and retired in 1985; Julius K. Nyerere, *Ujamaa: Essays on Socialism* (London: Oxford University Press, 1968), 38–39.

5. Winning the War?

1 Hugh Pearson, *The Shadow of the Panther: Huey Newton and the Price of Black Power in America* (New York: Addison-Wesley, 1994).

2 The four Panthers elected to the board of directors were Ericka Huggins, Audrea Jones, Herman Smith, and William Roberts. The six Panthers elected to the planning committee were Mariah Hilliard, Millicent Nelson, Ruth Jones, Steve McCutchen, Sam Castle, and John Seale. Pearson, *Shadow of the Panther*, 248.

3 Saul Alinsky, *Rules for Radicals* (New York, Random House, 1971), xxii.

4 Rod Bush, *We Are Not What We Seem: Black Nationalism and Class Struggle in the American Century* (New York: New York University Press, 1999).

5 Bush, *We Are Not What We Seem*; Huey P. Newton, *To Die for the People* (New York: Random House, 1972), 50.

6 Newton, *To Die for The People*, 50; Omari L. Dyson, Kevin L. Brooks, and Judson L. Jeffries, "'Brotherly Love Can Kill You': The Philadelphia Branch of the Black Panther Party," in *Comrades: A Local History of the Black Panther Party*, ed. Judson L. Jeffries (Bloomington: Indiana University Press, 2007), 214–54; Reggie Schell, personal communication, January 27, 2006, and April 2006.

7 Nixon defeated McGovern by a landslide, winning forty-nine of fifty states. McGovern's campaign was weakened when his running mate, Senator Thomas F. Eagleton of Missouri, withdrew from the Democratic ticket after his medical history had been made an issue in the campaign. Specifically, Eagleton had revealed that he had undergone electric shock treatment for mental fatigue in the 1960s. Eagleton was replaced by Sargent Shriver. Lerone Bennett, Jr., *Before the Mayflower: A History of Black America* (Chicago: Johnson Publishing Company, 1987), 436–437.

8   Minion K. C. Morris and Richard Middleton IV, "African Americans in Office," in
     African Americans and Political Participation: A Reference Handbook, ed. Min-
     ion K. C. Morrison (Santa Barbara, CA: ABC-CLIO, 2003), 282.
9   Elaine Brown, *A Taste of Power* (New York: Pantheon Books, 1993), 322.
10   To this day, the Portland Panthers maintain that no one from central headquar-
     ters followed up with a directive to shut down the chapter and move to Oakland.
     When Aaron Dixon, captain of the Seattle chapter, was asked why the Portland
     office was allowed to remain open, he was at a loss for words. Dixon then posed
     the same question to Elaine Brown, who was also unable to shed any light on
     the subject. Raymond Joe, telephone conversation with author, January 8, 2014;
     Percy Hampton, telephone conversation with author, June 13, 2014; Sandra Ford,
     telephone conversation with author, June 24, 2014.
11   Percy Hampton, telephone conversation with author, June 13, 2014; Kent Ford,
     telephone conversation with author, August 5, 2014; Robert Olmos, "Albina:
     'American Dream' Replaces Black Militancy," *Oregonian*, December 12, 1976; John
     Painter, Jr., "Goldschmidt Takes Top City Post: New Mayor Tallies 57% of Total
     Vote," *Oregonian*, May 24, 1972.
12   Allard Lowenstein wore many hats in the world of politics, from foreign policy as-
     sistant to Senator Hubert H. Humphrey to a delegate to the Democratic National
     Conventions in 1960, 1964, and 1968. From 1969 to 1971 he served in the House
     of Representatives for the state of New York. Lowenstein's steadfast commitment
     to fighting injustice and racism began with his opposition to apartheid in South
     Africa. He wrote *Brutal Mandate: A Journey to South West Africa* in 1962, mak-
     ing him one of the first Americans to publicly voice his protest of South Africa's
     inhumane government. In 1963 and 1964, Lowenstein mobilized white college
     students at Yale and Stanford to volunteer for "Freedom Summer" in Mississippi,
     where they joined African Americans fighting for the right to vote. Jim McClan-
     dish, telephone conversation with author, January 14, 2013; Jewell Lansing, *Port-
     land: People, Politics, and Power, 1851–2001* (Corvallis: Oregon State University
     Press, 2003), 397.
13   Carl Abbott, *Portland: Planning, Politics, and Growth in a Twentieth-Century
     City* (Lincoln: University of Nebraska Press, 1983), 176, 196–97.
14   Mark "Buck" Grayson was a popular figure in Portland history. He was a three-
     sport start at Jefferson High School and a second-team All-American basketball
     player at Oregon State University in the 1930s. In 1958, Grayson won a primary
     election of eighteen candidates and the general election to become Portland's
     commissioner for Position 2. He served until 1970; Shirley Field was a Republican
     legislator in the House of Representatives, serving in 1956–60 and 1962–66.
15   Steve Erickson, "Neil Goldschmidt: I'm Not Cut from the Same Mold as Some
     Members of the Council," *Oregonian*, January 3, 1971; "Model Cities Authority
     Goes to Goldschmidt," *Oregonian*, February 15, 1972; Abbott, *Portland*, 176.
16   "Goldschmidt Enters Mayor's Race," *Oregonian*, March 6, 1972; Kent Ford, tele-
     phone conversation with author, June 16, 2014.
17   ESCO develops and manufactures wear and replacement products used in re-
     source mining, infrastructure, and oil and gas industries. Accessed April 18, 2015,
     http://www.escocorp.com/EN/company/about/Pages/mission.aspx. Abbott,
     Portland, 175; *Sarasota Herald*, May 26, 1972; "Neil Goldschmidt for Portland's
     Mayor," *Oregonian*, May 7, 1972.

18 Howard Waskow, "The Big One: Mayoral Race," *Scribe*, March 7–14, 1972; John Painter, Jr., "Goldschmidt Takes Top City Post: New Mayor Tallies 57% of Total Vote," *Oregonian*, May 24, 1972.

19 Ron Buel, "The Goldschmidt Era," *Willamette Week*, 1976, accessed July 1, 2014, http://wweek.com/_AH_OLD_HTML/25-1976.html; Abbott, *Portland*, 175.

20 "Development Commission Member Quits," *Oregonian*, January 5, 1973; Abbott, *Portland*, 167–69, 177–79; Lansing, *Portland*, 400.

21 Abbott, *Portland*, 180; interview with Neil Goldschmidt by Robert Novak, "Meet the Press," National Broadcasting Company, San Francisco, June 17, 1973; "Goldschmidt Lists Priorities for Solving Portland's Problems," *Oregonian*, January 28, 1973; Huntly Collins, "Goldschmidt and Ivancie: 'Poles Apart' May Be Too Narrow a Distinction," *Oregonian*, April 12, 1976.

22 Abbott, *Portland*, 196–97; Carl Abbott, *Greater Portland: Urban Life and Landscape in the Pacific Northwest* (Philadelphia: University of Pennsylvania Press, 2001), 89; Lansing, *Portland*, 405–6; Kent Ford, telephone conversation with author, June 16, 2014.

23 Abbott, *Portland*, 197–98.

24 Lansing, *Portland*, 406–7. For more detailed information on neighborhood organizations and the Mount Hood Freeway in southeast Portland, I-505 in Northwest Portland, and the dismantling of Harbor Drive, see chapters 3 and 4 of Eliot Fackler, "Protesting Portland's Freeways: Highway Engineering and Citizen Activism in the Interstate Era" (master's thesis, University of Oregon, 2009).

25 "Goldschmidt Defends Model Cities Work," *Oregonian*, August 31, 1972; letter from John Toran, Jr., to Mayor Neil Goldschmidt, cc'd to Police Chief Donald McNamara, June 13, 1972, Police Historical and Archival Intelligence Records, A2004-005, folder 1, box 5, PARC, Portland, OR; special report, unnamed author and recipient, June 20, 1972, Police Historical and Archival Intelligence Records, A2004-005, folder 1, box 5, PARC, Portland, OR; officer's report from to Lt. Smith, "Subject: Special Duty Report," June 23, 1970, Police Historical and Archival Intelligence Records, A2004-005, folder 1, box 5, PARC, Portland, OR; Kent Ford, telephone conversation with author, June 25, 2014.

26 Donald McNamara first served as police chief from May 1, 1951, to January 1, 1953. "Mayor-Elect to Take Over Police," *Oregonian*, December 21, 1972; "Mayor Outlines Future of Police Bureau," *Oregonian*, February 25, 1973; "Goldschmidt Plans to Appoint New Police Chief by Fall," *Oregonian*, August 3, 1973; Huntly Collins, "Change Has Been Goldschmidt's Forte," *Oregonian*, April 19, 1976.

27 Interview with Neil Goldschmidt by Robert Novak, "Meet the Press," National Broadcasting Company, San Francisco, June 17, 1973.

28 Richard Walker, telephone conversation with author, July 14, 2014; Oscar Johnson, telephone conversation with author, August 15, 2014; Kent Ford, telephone conversation with author, July 18, 2014.

29 Charlene Myers, "PMSC," *Scribe*, March 2–15, 1974; Kent Ford, telephone conversation with author, July 18, 2014.

30 "Mayor Criticizes Police Supervision," *Oregonian*, May 20, 1975; "Board Backs Goldschmidt Police Firing," *Oregonian*, July 22, 1975; Donald Connor, telephone conversation with author, June 16, 2014.

31 Raymond Joe, telephone conversation with author, January 4, 2014; Kent Ford, telephone conversation with author, August 19, 2014.

32 Betty Van Patter was an accountant hired on by the BPP in December of 1974. Her badly beaten body was discovered in San Francisco Bay in January 1975. Rumor has it that in going over the Panthers' books, she found some irregularities that she then brought to the attention of Panther leadership, who supposedly had her killed. No one was ever charged with the crime, nor was any evidence presented that linked the Panthers to her murder. Despite the lack of evidence, many believe that there was a correlation between her murder and her work with the Panthers. David Hilliard and Lewis Cole, *This Side of Glory: The Autobiography of David Hilliard and the Story of the Black Panther Party* (Boston, Little, Brown and Company, 1993), 384.

33 Elaine Brown lost the 1975 city council race but was able to garner 44 percent of the vote.

34 Roy Jay, telephone conversation with author, August 20, 2014.

35 Kent Ford, telephone conversation with author, August 15, 2014.

36 Ibid.

37 Duane Paulson, telephone conversation with author, June 13, 2014; Gerry Morrell, telephone conversation with author, November 12, 2013.

38 Kent Ford, telephone conversation with author, December 2, 2013.

39 Ibid.

40 Ibid.

41 Kent Ford, telephone conversation with author, December 2, 2013, and June 25, 2014.

42 Kent Ford, telephone conversation with author, December 2, 2013, June 25, 2014, and July 9, 2014; Percy Hampton, telephone conversation with author, July 9, 2014.

43 Kent Ford, telephone conversation with author, January 11, 2015.

44 Ormond Bean was first elected to the city council in 1932, serving until 1939, when he was appointed Oregon Public Utility commissioner. After World War II, Bean was elected once more to the city council, serving from 1949 to 1967. "Mayor Warns Police of Hazards in Political Arena," *Oregonian*, February 10, 1976; Huntly Collins, "Goldschmidt, Ivancie Clash from Freeways to Finance," *Oregonian*, April 12, 1976; Huntly Collins, "Goldschmidt Stays in Mayor's Job," *Oregonian*, May 27, 1976; Abbott, *Portland*, 180–81; Steve Forrester, "Ivancie the Terrible," *Willamette Week*, accessed July 1, 2014, http://week.com/_All_OLD_html/25-1974.html.

45 Early Deane, "Goldschmidt Committed to Bettering City," *Oregonian*, September 25, 1977.

46 Cleveland Gilcrease, telephone conversation with author, July 25, 2014.

47 Bill Keller, "Metropolitan Steering Committee Leery of Goldschmidt Plan," *Oregonian*, May 7, 1972; Peter Morgan, "PMSC Charges Goldschmidt Plan Emasculates Poor," *Oregonian*, August 24, 1972; "Portland Police Shotgun Rule Eased: 'Appropriate Tool Needed,'" *Oregonian*, January 3, 1976; Huntly Collins, "Change Has Been Goldschmidt's Forte," April 19, 1976; Huntly Collins, "Seven Mayoral Candidates Cover All Points," *Oregonian*, April 22, 1976; Percy Hampton, telephone conversation with author, June 13, 2014.

48 Mildred Schwab, a lawyer by trade, served as a city commissioner from 1973 to 1986. She was appointed to fill the vacancy created when Goldschmidt was elected mayor. "Goldschmidt Speaks in Favor of Consolidation," *Oregonian*, February 22, 1973; Lansing, *Portland*, 402–3.

49 "Charles Jordan Talks about Portland," *Scribe*, April 6–12, 1974, 4; Office of the Mayor, City of Portland, *Portland Model Cities Third Year Action Plan Extension—FY 73/74* (Portland, OR: City of Portland, April 13, 1973).

50 Ibid.

51 Lansing, *Portland*, 402–3.

52 Percy Hampton, telephone conversation with author, July 15, 2014.

53 "People's Clinic Put on 'Probation,'" *Willamette Bridge*, March 25–31, 1971; "Sickle Test Bares Poisoning," *Oregon Journal*, June 22, 1972.

54 Kent Ford, telephone conversation with author, January 30, 2014; Elizabeth "Betty" Barton, telephone conversation with author, February 7, 2014; Kate Morosoff, telephone conversation with author, February 7, 2014; Don Orange, telephone conversation with author, March 4, 2014.

55 Kent Ford, telephone conversation with author, January 30, 2014; Jeff Moscow, "Chavez," *Scribe*, May 25–31 1974.

56 Raymond Joe, telephone conversation with author, January 4, 2014; Abbott, *Portland*, 200–201; Lansing, *Portland*, 404; "Jordan Blasts Mayor on Commission Choices," *Oregonian*, January 12, 1978.

57 Steve Erickson, "Neil Goldschmidt: I'm Not Cut from the Same Mold as Some Members of the Council," *Oregonian*, January 3, 1971; Nancie P. Fadeley, "Bill McCoy Quietly Made a Difference," *Register-Guard*, April 30, 1996; *Cornerstones of Community: Buildings of Portland's African American History* (Portland, OR: Bosco-Milligan Foundation, 1995), 81; Percy Hampton, telephone conversation with author, June 13, 2014.

58 Robert Olmos, "Albina: 'American Dream' Replaces Black Militancy," *Oregonian*, December 12, 1976; *Cornerstones of Community*, 90; *The History of Portland's African American Community, 1805 to the Present* (Portland, OR: Bureau of Planning, 1993), 133.

59 Peter Grant, "FBI Harassment of Panthers Clinic Here Alleged," *Oregon Journal*, February 27, 1978; Bill Keller, "Portland Said 1970 Target of FBI Anti-Panther Effort," *Oregonian*, February 26, 1978; Kent Ford, telephone conversation with author, July 8, 2014.

60 In Carter's first two years, he established the Department of Energy and legislation that kept Social Security solvent. He also brokered the Camp David Accords, which provided for Israeli withdrawal from Egyptian territory captured in the 1967 war, established diplomatic relations between Egypt and Israel, and opened negotiations on Palestinian rights. Carter also presided over an improved economy that followed the mid-decade recession and suffered only modest midterm losses of eleven House seats, three Senate seats, and six governorships in 1978. Democrats continued to control both houses of Congress. However, Carter's final two years in office were troubled. They began with the return of stagflation; economic growth slowed, and inflation and unemployment rose. After rising for decades, average real wages began a fifteen-year decline. Unions faced new challenges from hard-pressed employers, and the chasm between the haves and the have-nots began to widen for the first time since the 1920s. Debt to foreign corporations and major banks began piling up, and federal budget deficits soared to peace-time record levels. Once the planet's mightiest creditor, the United States was on its way to becoming its most burdened debtor.

61 Brock Adams was elected to the House of Representatives as a Democrat in 1965

and served six terms. On January 22, 1977, he resigned his seat to accept the position of secretary of transportation under President Jimmy Carter. He was later elected to the Senate in 1986 in the state of Washington; Kent Ford, telephone conversation with author, August 5, 2014; Wayne Thompson, telephone conversation with author, August 7, 2014.

62 Michael Newton, *Bitter Grain: Huey Newton and the Black Panther Party* (Los Angeles, CA: Holloway House, 1991), 213.

63 In his book *Will You Die With Me?*, Flores Forbes writes, "I LEARNED THE REAL REASON WE WERE READING THE NOVEL *The Godfather*, by Mario Puzo. Huey thought it was important that he have an operational for the Buddha Samurai that would protect the chain of command if we were infiltrated or an operation got botched. He didn't want the trail leading back to 1200 Lakeshore." See Flores Forbes, *Will You Die With Me?* (New York: Atria Books, 2006), 93; David Hilliard and Lewis Cole, *This Side of Glory*, 93; Aaron Dixon, *My People Are Rising* (Chicago: Haymarket Press, 2012), 246.

64 Niccolò Machiavelli, *The Prince, with Selections from the Discourses*, ed. and trans. Daniel Donno (New York: Bantam Books, 1985); Confucius, *Confucius Analects, with Selections from Traditional Commentaries*, trans. Edward Slingerland (Indianapolis, IN: Hackett Publishing Company, 2003).

65 Sandra Ford, telephone conversation with author, June 17, 2014.

66 Bob West, a husband and father, moved to Portland from Texas. He was introduced to the Panthers by his friend Bob Frost, who often cooked for the Panthers' breakfast program. As a PGE employee, Frost had access to resources that he passed along to the Panthers. Kent Ford, telephone conversation with author, November 13, 2013, June 16, 2014, and October 25, 2014; Raymond Joe, telephone conversation with author, June 13, 2014; Sandra Ford, telephone conversation with author, June 17, 2014.

67 Kent Ford, telephone conversation with author, November 13, 2013; Sandra Ford, telephone conversation with author, April 25, 2014.

68 Connie McCready served in the Oregon House of Representatives from 1967 to 1969 and was appointed to the city council in 1970. Abbott, *Portland*, 181; Lansing, *Portland*, 410–14.

Conclusion

1 Golden Thomas Venters III, e-mail correspondence with author, September 29, 2014.

2 According to Hampton, he served as president of the union for three years in the early 1990s, and again from 2000 to 2010.

3 Raymond Joe, telephone conversation with author, December 27, 2014.

4 Martha Gies, "A Father's Story," *Portland Monthly*, March 2005, 148.

5 Ancer Haggerty, telephone conversation with author, July 29, 2014; Kent Ford, telephone conversation with author, July 16, 2014.

6 Gies, "Father's Story," 147–51.

7 Ibid., 191.

8 Karen J. Gibson, "Bleeding Albina: A History of Community Disinvestment, 1940–2000," *Transforming Anthropology* 15, no. 1 (2007): 17–20.

9 Italics added for emphasis; Anna Griffin, "Onetime Portland Black Panther Percy

Hampton Reflects on the Movement, Issues that Remain Today," *Oregonian*, February 19, 2011, accessed June 22, 2011, http://www.oregonlive.com/O/index. ssf/2011/02/onetime_portland_black_panther.html.

10 Henry Stevenson, personal conversation with author, November 6, 2014; Dave Dawson, telephone conversation with author, July 24, 2014; David Morris, telephone conversation with author, April 11, 2014.

11 Kent Ford, personal conversation with author, July 16, 2014.

12 Mumia Abu Jamal, *We Want Freedom: A Life in the Black Panther Party* (Boston: South End Press, 2008), 47.

Selected Bibliography

Manuscripts, Archives, and Special Collections

Cheryl D. James Defense Committee Records, 1967–1975. University of Oregon Library, Eugene, OR.

Emanuel Hospital Project Records, A2010-003. City of Portland Archives and Records Center, Portland, OR.

Portland National Association for the Advancement of Colored People (NAACP) Archive Collection, Branch Records: 1938–1981. University of Oregon Library, Eugene, OR.

Portland Police Investigative Files, Black Community Survival Committee Police Records. Police Historical and Archival Intelligence Records, A-2004-005. City of Portland Archives and Records Center (PARC), Portland, OR.

Portland Police Investigative Files, Black Panther Party Police Records. Police Historical and Archival Intelligence Records, A-2004-005. City of Portland Archives and Records Center, Portland, OR.

Stella Maris House Manuscript Collection, 1940–1973. The Oregon Historical Society Library, Portland, OR.

Urban League of Portland Records, 1945–2010. Oregon State University Library, Corvallis, OR.

Newspapers and Periodicals

Berkeley Tribe (Berkeley, CA)
The Black Panther (San Francisco, CA)
Cascadia Courier (Seattle, WA)
Eugene (OR) Register-Guard
Frontiersman (Portland, OR)
Jeffersonian (Portland, OR)
Look
Los Angeles Free Press
Movement (San Francisco, CA)
New Left Review
New York Times
Oregonian
Oregon Journal
Pioneer Log (Portland, OR)
Portland City Club Bulletin
Portland Community College Bridge
Portland Observer
Portland People's Observer
Portland Tribune
PROVO

Reed Magazine (Portland, OR)
San Francisco Examiner
Scribe (Portland, OR)
Spirithouse Rap (Portland, OR)
Washington Post
Willamette Bridge (Portland, OR)
Willamette Week (Portland, OR)

Books and Articles

Abbott, Carl. *Greater Portland: Urban Landscape in the Pacific Northwest.* Philadelphia: University of Pennsylvania Press, 2001.
——. *Portland: Planning, Politics, and Growth in a Twentieth-Century City.* Lincoln: University of Nebraska Press, 1983.
Abu-Jamal, Mumia. *We Want Freedom: A Life in the Black Panther Party.* Boston: South End Press, 2008.
Akbar, Naim. *The Community of Self.* Tallahassee, FL: Mind Productions and Association, 1985.
Alinsky, Saul. *Rules for Radicals.* New York, Random House, 1971.
Alkebulan, Paul. *Survival Pending Revolution: The History of the Black Panther Party.* Tuscaloosa: University of Alabama Press, 2007.
Arend, Orissa. *Showdown in Desire: The Black Panthers Take a Stand in New Orleans.* Fayette: University of Arkansas Press, 2009.
Arendt, Hannah. *On Violence.* Orlando, FL: Harcourt Brace and Company, 1970.
Austin, Curtis. *Up Against the Wall: Violence in the Making and Unmaking of the Black Panther Party.* Fayetteville: University of Arkansas Press, 2006.
Beal, Frances. "Women in the Black Liberation Movement: Three Views." In *Sisterhood Is Powerful,* ed. Robin Morgan. New York: Vintage, 1970.
Bennett, Lerone, Jr. *Before the Mayflower: A History of Black America.* Chicago: Johnson Publishing Company, 1987.
Berg, Bruce C. *Qualitative Research Methods for the Social Sciences.* New York: Simon and Schuster, 1995.
Bergman, Peter M. *The Chronological History of the Negro in America.* New York: Harper and Row, 1969.
Berman, Larry. *No Peace, No Honor: Nixon, Kissinger, and Betrayal in Vietnam.* New York: Free Press, 2002.
Bloom, Joshua, and Waldo E. Martin, Jr. *Black against Empire: The History and Politics of the Black Panther Party.* Berkeley: University of California Press, 2012.
Boykoff, Jules, and Martha Gies. "'We're Going to Defend Ourselves': The Portland Chapter of the Black Panther Party and the Local Media Response." *Oregon Historical Quarterly* 111, no. 3 (Fall 2010): 278–311.
Brown, Elaine. *A Taste of Power: A Black Women's Story.* New York: Pantheon Books, 1993.
Burton, Stan L., Jr. "The Portland Urban League, 1945–1965: Two Decades of Change in the Pacific Northwest." Unpublished paper, University of Oregon, n.d.
Bush, Rod. *We Are Not What We Seem: Black Nationalism and Class Struggle in the American Century.* New York: New York University Press, 1999.

Camus, Albert. *The Rebel: An Essay on Man in Revolt.* New York: Vintage Books, 1951.

Carmichael, Stokley [Kwame Ture]. *Stokley Speaks: From Black Power to Pan African-ism.* Chicago: Chicago Review Press, 2007.

Chafe, William. *Civilities and Civil Rights: Greensboro, North Carolina, and the Black Struggle for Freedom.* New York: Oxford University Press, 1980.

Cha-Jua, Sundiata, and Clarence Lang. "The Long Movement as Vampire: Temporal and Spatial Fallacies in Recent Black Freedom Studies." *Journal of African American History* 92, no. 2 (Spring 2007): 265–88.

Cornerstones of Community: Buildings of Portland's African American History. Portland, OR: Bosco-Milligan Foundation, 1995.

Cruse, Harold. *Rebellion or Revolution.* New York: William Morrow and Company, 1968.

DeMichael, Tom, and Rhonda Markowtiz. *The Groovy Side of the '60s.* Lincolnwood, IL: Publications International, 2005.

Dittmer, John. *The Good Doctors: The Medical Committee for Human Rights and the Struggle for Social Justice in Health Care.* New York: Bloomsbury Press, 2009.

Dixon, Aaron. *My People Are Rising.* Chicago: Haymarket Press, 2012.

Donnelly, Robert C. *Dark Rose: Organized Crime and Corruption in Portland.* Seattle: University of Washington Press, 2011.

Dyson, Omari L. *Transformative Pedagogy and the Black Panther Party.* Lexington: Lexington Books, 2014.

Edsall, Thomas B., and Mary Edsall. *Chain Reaction: The Impact of Race, Rights, and Taxes on American Politics.* New York: Norton, 1991.

Egerton, John. *Speak Now Against the Day: The Generation before the Civil Rights Movement in the South.* Chapel Hill: University of North Carolina Press, 1994.

Estés, Clarissa Pinkola. *Women Who Run with the Wolves.* New York: Ballantine Books, 1992.

Fackler, Eliot H. "Protesting Portland's Freeways: Highway Engineering and Citizen Activism in the Interstate Era." Master's thesis, University of Oregon, 2009.

Fanon, Frantz. *The Wretched of the Earth.* New York: Grove Press, 1961.

Feagin, Joe, and Harlan Hahn. *Ghetto Revolts.* New York: Collier MacMillan, 1973.

Forget, Evelyn. "A Tale of Two Communities: Fighting Poverty in the Great Society, 1964–1968." *History of Political Economy* 43 (2001): 199–223.

Foucault, Michel. *Surveiller et punir.* Paris: Gallimard, 1975.

Franklin, John Hope. *From Slavery to Freedom: A History of Negro Americans.* New York: Vintage, 1969.

Gayle, Addison, Jr. *The Black Situation.* New York: A Delta Book, 1970.

George, Bill. *Authentic Leadership: Rediscovering the Secrets to Creating Lasting Value.* San Francisco, CA: Jossey-Bass, 2003.

Geschwender, James A. *Racial Stratification in America.* Dubuque, IA: Wm. C. Brown Co., 1978.

Gibson, Karen J. "Bleeding Albina: A History of Community Disinvestment, 1940–2000." *Transforming Anthropology* 15, no. 1 (2007): 3–25.

Gies, Martha. "A Father's Story." *Portland Monthly,* March 2005.

———. "Radical Treatment." *Reed Magazine* (Winter 2009): 1–5. Accessed June 22, 2011, http://web.reed.edu/reed_magazine/winter2009/features/radical_treatment/index.html.

Gilkes, Cheryl Townsend. *If It Wasn't for the Women*. New York: Orbis Books, 2001.

Gilmore, Glenda Elizabeth. *Defying Dixie: The Radical Roots of Civil Rights*. New York: W. W. Norton and Co., 2008.

Gramsci, Antonio. *Selections from the Prison Notebooks*. London: Lawrence and Wishart, 1971.

Griffin, Anna. "Onetime Portland Black Panther Percy Hampton Reflects on the Movement, Issues That Remain Today." *OregonLive*, February 19, 2011. Accessed June 22, 2011, http://www.oregonlive.com/O/index.ssf/2011/02/onetime_portland_black_panther.html.

Hacker, Andrew. *The Study of Politics: The Western Tradition and American Origins*. New York: McGraw Hill, 1963.

Hall, Jacquelyn Dowd. "The Long Civil Rights Movement and the Political Uses of the Past." *Journal of American History* 91, no. 4 (March 2005): 1233–63.

Harrington, Michael. *The Other America: Poverty in the United States*. Baltimore: Penguin Books, 1962.

Hilliard, David, and Lewis Cole. *This Side of Glory: The Autobiography of David Hilliard and the Story of the Black Panther Party*. Boston: Little, Brown and Company, 1993.

The History of Portland's African American Community, 1805 to the Present. Portland, OR: Bureau of Planning, 1993.

hooks, bell. *Outlaw Culture: Resisting Representations*. New York: Routledge, 1994.

Isserman, Maurice, and Michael Kazin. *America Divided: The Civil War of the 1960s*. New York: Oxford University Press, 2000.

James, Franklin J., Betty L. McCummings, and Eileen A. Tynan. *Minorities in the Sunbelt*. New Brunswick, NJ: Rutgers University Press, 1984.

Jeffries, Judson, ed. *Comrades: A Local History of the Black Panther Party*. Bloomington: Indiana University Press, 2007.

———. *Huey P. Newton: The Radical Theorist*. Jackson: University Press of Mississippi, 2002.

———, ed. *On the Ground: The Black Panther Party in Communities across America*. Jackson: University Press of Mississippi, 2010.

Jones, Charles E., ed. *The Black Panther Party Reconsidered*. Baltimore: Black Classic Press, 1998.

Joseph, Peniel E. *Waiting 'til the Midnight Hour: A Narrative History of Black Power in America*. New York: Henry Holt and Co., 2006.

Kazin, Michael. *The Populist Persuasion: An American History*. New York: Basic Books, 1995.

Kim, Claire Jean. "The Racial Triangulation of Asian Americans." *Politics and Society* 27, no. 1 (March 1999): 105–38.

King, Martin Luther, Jr. *Strength to Love*. New York: Pocket Books, 1964.

———. *Stride toward Freedom: The Montgomery Story*. New York: Harper and Row, 1958.

Kurashige, Scott. *The Shifting Grounds of Race: Black and Japanese Americans in the Making of Multiethnic Los Angeles*. Princeton: Princeton University Press, 2008.

Lansing, Jewel. *Portland: People, Politics, and Power, 1851–2001*. Corvallis: Oregon State University Press, 2003.

Lazerow, Jama, and Yohuru Williams. *In Search of the Black Panther Party: New Per-

spectives on a Revolutionary Movement. Durham, NC: Duke University Press, 2006.

Lefebvre, Henri. *La production de l'espace*. Paris: Anthropos, 1974.

Lester, Julius. *Look Out, Whitey! Black Power's Gon' Get Your Mama!* New York: Dial Press, 1968.

Loewen, James. *Sundown Towns: A Hidden Dimension of American Racism*. New York: The New Press, 2005.

Lomax, Louis E. *The Negro Revolt*. New York: Harper and Row, 1961.

Luckingham, Bradford. *Phoenix: The History of a Southwestern Metropolis*. Tucson: University of Arizona Press, 1989.

Mangun, Kimberly. "'As Citizens of Portland We Must Protest': Beatrice Morrow Cannady and the African American Response to D. W. Griffith's 'Masterpiece.'" *Oregon Historical Quarterly* 107 (Fall 2006): 382–409.

Marable, Manning. *Blackwater*. Dayton, OH: Black Praxis Press, 1981.

Marcuse, Hebert. *An Essay on Liberation*. Boston: Beacon Press, 1969.

May, Glenn Anthony. *Sonny Montes and Mexican American Activism in Oregon*. Corvallis: Oregon State University Press, 2011.

McElderry, Stuart J. "The Problem of the Color Line: Civil Rights and Racial Ideology in Portland, Oregon, 1944–1965." PhD diss., University of Oregon, 1998.

McLagan, Elizabeth. *A Peculiar Paradise: A History of Blacks in Oregon, 1788–1940*. Portland, OR: Georgian Press, 1980.

McMillian, John. *Smoking Typewriters: The Sixties Underground Press and the Rise of Alternative Media in America*. New York: Oxford University Press, 2011.

Miller, William Robert. *Martin Luther King, Jr.: His Life, Martyrdom, and Meaning for the World*. New York: Avon Book, 1968.

Millner, Darrell. *On the Road to Equality: The Urban League of Portland, A 50-Year Retrospective*. Portland, OR: Urban League of Portland, 1995.

Mills, C. Wright. "The New Left." *New Left Review* no. 5 (October 1960).

Moore, J. E. "Community Aspects of Childhood Lead Poisoning." *American Journal of Public Health* 60 (1970): 1430–38.

Nelson, Alondra. *Body and Soul: The Black Panther Party and the Fight against Medical Discrimination*. Minneapolis: University of Minnesota Press, 2011.

Nelson, Matt, and Bill Nygren. *Radicals in the Rose City: Portland Revolutionaries, 1960–1975*. Tempe, AZ: Northwest History Press, 2013.

Newton, Huey P. *To Die for the People*. New York: Random House, 1972.——. *Revolutionary Suicide*. New York: Ballantine, 1973.

Niebuhr, Reinhold. *Moral Man and Immoral Society*. Louisville, KY: Westminster John Knox Press, 2013.

Nyerere, Julius K. *Ujamaa: Essays on Socialism*. London: Oxford University Press, 1968.

Olsen, Jack. *Last Man Standing: The Tragedy and Triumph of Geronimo Pratt*. New York: Random House, 2000.

Olsen, Polina. *Portland in the 1960s: Stories from the Counterculture*. Portland, OR: The History Press, 2012.

Ozawa, Connie P. *The Portland Edge: Challenges and Successes in Growing Communities*. Washington, DC: Island Press, 2004.

Pancoast, Diane. "Blacks in Oregon (1940–1950)." In *Blacks in Oregon: An Historical and Statistical Report*, ed. William A. Little and James E. Weiss (Portland, OR: Portland State University Black Studies Center and the Center for Population Research and Census, 1978.

Pearson, Hugh. *The Shadow of the Panther: Huey Newton and the Price of Black Power in America*. New York: Addison-Wesley, 1994.

Piven, Francis Fox, and Richard Cloward. *Poor People's Movements: Why They Succeed, How They Fail*. New York: Vintage Books, 1977.

Polishuk, Sandy. *Sticking to the Union: An Oral History of the Life and Times of Julia Ruuttila*. New York: Palgrave Macmillan, 2003.

Rice, J. F. *Up on Madison, Down on 75th Street: A History of the Illinois Black Panther Party*. Part 1. Evanston: The Committee, 1983.

Self, Robert O. *American Babylon: Race and the Struggle for Postwar Oakland*. Princeton: Princeton University Press, 2003.

Seymour, Richard. *The Haight-Ashbury Free Medical Clinic: Still Free after All These Years, 1967–1989*. San Francisco: Partisan Press, 1987.

Sitkoff, Harvard. *The Struggle for Black Equality, 1954–1992*. New York: Hill and Wang, 1993.

Smith, David Barton. *Health Care Divided: Race and Healing a Nation*. Ann Arbor: University of Michigan Press, 1999.

Staples, Robert. *Introduction to Black Sociology*. New York: McGraw Hill, 1976.

Steinem, Gloria. *Revolution from Within*. Boston: Little Brown and Company, 1993.

Sugrue, Thomas J. *Sweet Land of Liberty: The Forgotten Struggle for Civil Rights in the North* (New York: Random House, 2008).

Taylor, Quintard. "The Civil Rights Movement in the American West: Black Protest in Seattle, 1960–1970." *Journal of Negro History* 80, no. 1 (Winter 1995): 1–14.

——. *The Forging of a Black Community: Seattle's Central District from 1870 through the Civil Rights Era*. Seattle: University of Washington Press, 1994.

Toll, William. "Black Families and Migration to a Multiracial Society: Portland, Oregon, 1900–1924." *Journal of American Ethnic History* 17, no. 3 (Spring 1998): 38–70.

Tse-tung, Mao. *Selected Works*. Peking: Foreign Languages Press, 1967.

Viorst, Milton. *Fire in the Streets: America in the '60s*. New York: Simon and Schuster, 1979.

Weisbord, Robert G. *Genocide? Birth Control and the Black American*. Westport, CT: Greenwood Press, 1975.

West, Dennis L. "A Case Study of the Planning Process in the Portland, Oregon, Model Cities Program." PhD diss., Portland State University, 1969.

Whitaker, Matthew C. *Race Work: The Rise of Civil Rights in the Urban West*. Lincoln: University of Nebraska Press, 2007.

Williams, Clay. "The Portland Black Panthers: Building the Local African-American Community from the Ground Up." Bachelor's thesis, University of Portland, 2008.

Williams, Jakobi. *From the Bullet to the Ballot: The History of the Illinois Chapter of the Black Panther Party*. Chapel Hill: University of North Carolina Press, 2013.

Williams, Robert F. *Negroes with Guns*. New York: Marzani and Munsell, 1962.

Witt, Andrew. *The Black Panthers in the Midwest: The Community Programs and Services of the Black Panther Party in Milwaukee, 1966–1977*. New York: Routledge, 2007.

Yette, Samuel F. *The Choice: The Issue of Black Survival in America.* Silver Spring, MD: Cottage Books, 1971.

Zinn, Howard. *Disobedience and Democracy.* New York: Vintage Books, 1968.

Institutional Publications, Government Documents, and Published Interviews

Black Panther Party for Self-Defense. "Ten-Point Platform and Program." Oakland: Black Panther Party for Self-Defense, 1966. Accessed January 9, 2012. http://history.hanover.edu/courses/excerpts/111bppp.html.

Demonstration Cities and Metropolitan Development Act of 1966. Pub. L. No. 89-754 (1966).

Ford, Kent, Percy Hampton, et al. "Portland Black Panther Party." KBOO Community Radio. Portland, February 24, 2008.

Goldschmidt, Neil, interviewed by Robert Novak. *Meet the Press.* National Broadcasting Company, San Francisco. June 17, 1973.

Little, William A., and James E. Weiss, eds. *Blacks in Oregon: A Statistical and Historical Report.* Portland State University Black Studies Center and Center for Population Research and Census. Portland, OR: Portland State University Black Studies Center and the Center for Population Research and Census, 1978.

Office of the Mayor, City of Portland. *Portland Model Cities Third Year Action Plan Extension—FY 73/74.* Portland, OR: City of Portland, April 13, 1973.

Portland Development Commission. "Central Albina Study." Portland, OR: City of Portland, 1962.

Interviews (Conducted by Judson L. Jeffries)

Chuck Armsbury
Will Atchison
Jeff Barker
Elizabeth "Betty" Barton
Dr. George Barton
Patty (Hampton) Carter
Vernell Carter
Harry Chaivoe
Karen Chaivoe
Rita Clinton
Donald Connor
Nathaniel Cross
Floyd Cruse
Dave Dawson
Mary Ann Dickey
Aaron Dixon
James Fleming
Kent Ford
Sandra Ford
Kenneth Gervais
Cleveland Gilcrease

Janet Goetze
Rick Goodfellow
Kim Green
Nate Griffin
Barbara Gundle
Ancer Haggerty
Percy Hampton
Penny Harrington
Holly Hart
Jim Hauser
Ronald Herndon
William Hilliard
David Horowitz
Jim Houser
Paul Hull
Maurice Isserman
Martha James
Roy Jay
Raymond Joe
Yvonne Joe
Oscar Johnson

Michael Kazin
Dorreen Labby
Robert Landauer
Jim McClandish
Gen. Joseph McNeil
Kate Morosoff
Dr. Gerry Morrell
David Morris
Jon Moscow
Vicki Nakashima
Don Orange
Anita Palmer
Dr. Duane Paulson
Joy Pruitt
Ollie Robertson
Teddy Sanders
Reggie Schell

David Simpson
Arthur C. Spencer
Robert Spindel
Rance Spruill
Henry Stevenson
Frances Storrs
Willie Sutton
Darryl Thomas
Wayne Thompson
Linda Thornton
Joe Uris
Golden Venters
Richard Walker
Michael Wells
Joyce (Radford) Williams
Nelson Wolfe

Index